D1478288

An
ENEMY
of the
STATE

An

ENEMY

of the

STATE

The Life of **Murray N. Rothbard**

Justin Raimondo

Prometheus Books
59 John Glenn Drive
Amherst, New York 14228-2197

Published 2000 by Prometheus Books

Inquiries should be addressed to
Prometheus Books
59 John Glenn Drive
Amherst, New York 14228–2197
VOICE: 716–691–0133, ext. 207
FAX: 716–564–2711
WWW.PROMETHEUSBOOKS.COM

04 03 02 01 00   5 4 3 2 1

Library of Congress Cataloging-in-Publication Data

Raimondo, Justin.
    An enemy of the state : the life of Murray N. Rothbard / by Justin
Raimondo.
        p.   cm.
    Includes bibliographical references and index.
    ISBN 1–57392–809–7 (alk. paper)
    1. Rothbard, Murray Newton, 1926– 2. Social scientists—United
States—Biography. 3. Libertarians—United States—Biography.

H23.R67 R35 2000
330.15′7—dc21
[B]   00—024195
                                                              CIP

Printed in the United States of America on acid-free paper

To Yoshinori Abe

CONTENTS

ACKNOWLEDGMENTS

Of the many people who rendered their invaluable assistance in completing this work, first and foremost is JoAnn Rothbard, Murray's wife, whose cooperation was essential to the conception and writing of this book. By subjecting herself to a marathon four-day interview, she gave me the outline of this book—and the inspiration and moral support to finish it.

I am indebted to Llewellyn H. Rockwell Jr., president of the Ludwig von Mises Institute, not only for permission to quote from Rothbard's letters and unpublished papers, but also for his invaluable assistance during the research phase of this project. I also want to thank the entire staff of the Ludwig von Mises Institute, particularly Jeff Tucker and Judy Thommesen, who rendered invaluable assistance with the photographs. I will also never forget Mardie's extraordinary kindness.

I owe a big debt to Robert Kephart, who gave me access to a great cache of Rothbard's unpublished letters and manuscripts, as well as other items of interest. He was a great friend to Rothbard, and he is a great friend of liberty.

I want to especially thank Ralph Raico for reading the manuscript and for his insightful suggestions.

I am very grateful to Williamson Evers, who gave me access to his collection of letters from Rothbard and other relevant documents.

Thanks also go to Anita Anderson, for putting up with me, and to Jeffrey Rogers Hummel, for access to part of his collection of libertarian periodicals.

I especially want to thank Steven L. Mitchell, Editor-in-Chief of Prometheus Books, who believed in this book.

Those cited above contributed greatly to the completion of this project. However, the one who did the most is named on the dedication page of this book.

As much as they helped to make this book possible, not one of the individuals or organizations listed above can be held in any way responsible for its contents. That responsibility is mine alone.

INTRODUCTION

The life and work of an ordinary man is not easily summarized in a phrase, or a book. It is difficult, even in a fairly detailed biography, to capture the complexity of the most prosaic character. How, then, to sum up the life and work of Murray N. Rothbard, author of twenty-eight books, thousands of articles—and a body of ideas that, taken together, constitutes an intellectual system encompassing not only economics and political economy, but also philosophy, ethics, history, and indeed a wide range of social thought?

The problem faced by the biographer is that human beings are creatures of such intricacy and mystery, wearing layer upon layer of personality and motivation, that their essence is rarely visible or obvious. A very few, however, are creatures of a single style, the possessors of a coherent and seemingly inherent quality of mind that imbues them with a clear sense of purpose and sets them apart, almost from the beginning, from the rest of us. This stylization is the hallmark of the creative mind, of the thinker, the artist, the theoretician, the innovator in any field who does not merely rebel against the established order but counterposes his own vision of the ideal order; who, in short, embodies what Lord Acton described as the animating spirit of the classical liberal, who "wishes for what ought to be, irrespective of what is."[1]

If anything describes the Rothbardian mindset in a phrase, then this is it. This youthful spirit is the key to understanding the development of his character, as well as his ideas. It is the leitmotif of his life and work, implicit in his style and his approach to ideas, and made explicit at the end of one of his most politically influential essays, "Left and Right: The Prospects for Liberty," which he concludes by quoting a long selection from the great Randolph Bourne, a turn-of-the-twentieth-century journalist and the conscience of American liberalism:

> Youth puts the remorseless questions to everything that is old and established—Why? What is this thing good for? and when it gets the mumbled, evasive answers of the defenders, it applies its own fresh, clean spirit of reason to institutions and ideas and finding them stupid, inane, or poisonous, turns instinctively to overthrow them.[2]

The fresh clean spirit of rational inquiry, of testing and retesting ideas in light of new evidence, and challenging the most fundamental assumptions, was his own method, one which never failed to yield controversial results. He dared ask the unaskable: The state—what is it good for? His answer: absolutely nothing.

"Youth is the leaven that keeps all these questioning, testing attitudes fermenting in the world," wrote Bourne. "Fermenting" precisely describes Rothbard's effect on a new generation of the freedom movement in the sense that, for many years, much of this activity was beneath the surface, a subterranean heat generated almost single-handedly by Rothbard. "If it were not for this troublesome activity of youth," Bourne continues, "with its hatred of sophisms and glosses, its insistence on things as they are, society would die from sheer decay."[3]

The course of Rothbard's intellectual odyssey, from the Old Right to the New Left and back again, is captured in this image of "troublesome activity." Certainly Rothbard's activities were "troublesome," and not only to statists of every hue but often to his closest allies. Leaving aside the personal aspects of these often turbulent relations, the reason was that Rothbard was constantly testing his logically derived theories in the light of experience, honing and perfecting his evolving theory of liberty, and shifting his tactics as circumstances changed. Rothbard was that rare individual, a theoretician who was also a successful intellectual entrepreneur. In a book-length memo on strategy written in the mid-seventies, meant only for the inner circle of the libertarian Cato Institute and never published, Rothbard describes the importance of "entrepreneurial flexibility of tactics" and points out the key role of what he called the "intellectual entrepreneur." "Just as entrepreneurship is ultimately an art and not a science that can be learned by rote, so ideological tactics, the finding of the right path at the right time, is an entrepreneurial art which some people will be better at than others," wrote Rothbard in "Toward a Theory of Libertarian Social Change." "[Ludwig von] Mises's insight that timing is the essence of entrepreneurship" applies to "ideological as well as economic entrepreneurship."[4]

Rothbard's future biographers are blessed with a wealth of material; not only did he write books on a wide variety of subjects, he also left behind a voluminous correspondence. Fortunately for those who wish to trace the evolution of his thought, and especially his political thought, there is an additional treasure trove of Rothbardiana in the back issues of *Left and Right*, the *Libertarian Forum*, and the *Rothbard–Rockwell Report*. One has only to look over his prolific output of personal journalism to see how he successfully put the principles of intellectual entrepreneurship into practice. At every crucial moment, at every point where the intellectual bodyguards of State power lost their grip on the populace and cracks in the system began to appear, Rothbard was there with his analysis and a strategy to widen the influence of libertarian ideas. As the conservative movement found itself under assault from the "New Right" acolytes of the sail-boating publicist William F. Buckley Jr. and the ex-Trotskyist theoretician James Burnham with their frankly imperial credo, Rothbard defended the legacy of a conservative movement that had once honored Old Right "isolationists" like John T. Flynn, Garet Garrett, and Colonel Robert McCormick, who opposed the New Deal and FDR's drive to war. Just as the United States began to get bogged down in an unwinnable and immoral war in Vietnam and the first stirrings of the student rebellion of the sixties hit the nation's college campuses, Rothbard founded *Left and Right*, a quarterly journal of opinion and analysis. He addressed the rising tide of youthful discontent not by pandering to their prejudices but by carefully and colorfully explaining the roots of their angst—in the tyranny of a centralized national security state apparatus, which had embedded itself in the universities and slowly taken them into its orbit. Long before the New Left burnt itself out, Rothbard turned his sights on the task of consolidating the gains of the sixties into a cohesive and doctrinally independent movement, with its own organizations and institutions. As the Cold War ended, and the predictions of Mises and the Austrian School* that socialism must

---

*It was Mises, in his 1921 paper "Economic Calculation in the Socialist Commonwealth," who was to show that, as Yuri Maltsev puts in in the foreword to the 1991 edition, socialism is "a utopian scheme that is illogical, uneconomic, and unworkable at its core" because "it provides no means for any objective basis of economic calculation and thus no way to assign resources to their most productive uses" (http://www.mises.org/Econcalc/FOREWORD.asp).

collapse came true, Rothbard made yet another turn—a home-coming, in a sense, back to the Old Right of his youth.

With the impatience of youth, which, Bourne writes, "drags skeletons out of closets, and insists that they be explained," Rothbard persisted in challenging the conventional wisdom no matter *whose* ox was gored. He loved nothing more than dragging skeletons out of the deepest, darkest closets, revising the official version of historical events with new facts and a fresh perspective on the machinations of power. He found the myths surrounding the great wars of the twentieth century, including the two world wars, particularly vexing. Opposition to war, as the apotheosis of state coercion, was central to Rothbard's philosophy and always at the top of his ideological-political agenda. As a champion of Harry Elmer Barnes, the dean of world-war revisionism, he contributed a notable essay to the memorial volume published in honor of Professor Barnes, in which he noted that "there have been, after all, but two mutually exclusive roles that the intellectual can play and has played throughout history: either independent truthseeker, or kept favorite of the Court." Barnes coined the term "Court Historian," and Rothbard broadened the concept into the "Court Intellectual" who "spins the apologia" for the state and its agents as they loot, repress, and murder "in return for wealth, power, and prestige"—courtesy of "the State and its allied 'Establishment.' "[5]

If ever the antipode of the Court Intellectual existed, then surely his name was Murray Newton Rothbard. The author of the magisterial two-volume *History of Economic Thought*—a work that raises the question: *how could one man know so much?*—was for thirty-five years a teacher at a school for engineers who were not in the least interested in economics.[6] A true polymath, and a writer of unusual speed and facility, his income from his academic work and his literary output combined was sometimes barely enough to make ends meet.

Bourne made another important point strongly reminiscent of Rothbard's psychology: "Our elders," he wrote, "are always optimistic in their views of the present, pessimistic in their views of the future; youth is pessimistic toward the present and gloriously hopeful for the future. And it is this hope which is the lever of progress—one might say, the only lever of progress." While this latter sentiment expresses Rothbard's views exactly, he also pointed out that this sort of optimism "may be very long range." While he clearly believed that the liberal revolutions of the eighteenth century are irreversible, in his essay *Left and Right* Rothbard warns that, since man is endowed with free will, it is not enough to have truth and right on one's side, nor is it sufficient that the crisis of statism is upon us. What is needed is full exposure of the state as a murderous parasite, and this requires the right leadership: intellectual entrepreneurs with a nuanced sense of timing, a deep intellectual commitment to libertarian principle, and, most importantly, an even rarer quality: what Rothbard called "a passion for justice."

In his unpublished strategy memo to the Cato Institute leadership—in which he gave free rein to his real hopes and aspirations, as well as venting his major frustrations with the libertarian movement—Rothbard emphasized the importance of making the victory of liberty the goal. "This may seem axiomatic," he writes, with a sigh of exasperated wonder, "for if victory is not the goal, then why even bother joining a movement whose goals can never be met?" And yet, he noted that some "prefer the libertarian ideal as an intellectual game," while others are infected with "a profound pessimism" that precludes the possibility of victory. "Holding the victory of liberty as one's primary goal is only likely in those persons whose libertarianism is motivated and moulded by a *passion for justice*: by a realization that statism is unjust, and by a desire to eliminate such a glaring injustice as swiftly as possible."[7]

This is what motivated Rothbard. Not just as an abstract concept, but as a deeply felt personal credo. His passion inspired many, but especially the youth, who crowded around him at seminars and conferences, eagerly imbibing knowledge that seemed to overflow from the man in a veritable torrent. Many a time he had to be literally pulled away from an intense conversation with a gangly twenty-year-old student who was privileged to hear one of the best minds of the century explain the Austrian theory of the business cycle at 4:30 in the morning. At academic conferences and political conventions, Rothbard was always the last to call it quits, holding court in the hotel bar, and then trooping over to whatever greasy-spoon diner was open at that late hour to continue the discussion until the wee hours of the morning.

Young people were drawn to Rothbard, and he received them gladly, generously ladling out great dollops of his time and hospitality while still managing a rate of high-quality literary output that would be hard to beat. The reason for this magnetism was, first of all, his passion, and not only for justice but for good conversation, good laughs, good food, and a good time. Exuberant, vociferous, his laughter easily heard above the din, Rothbard was welcomed by the young because he was, in at least one important sense, one of them. Like Lord Acton, Rothbard grew more radical as he grew older, and this, combined with his intractably bourgeois tastes and mode of living, so distinctly old culture, charmed the young. He appealed to the best in them: to their idealism, their fearlessness, and their sense of life's unlimited possibilities. Rothbard was a man who knew what Bourne touted as "the secret of life," which is

> that this fine youthful spirit shall never be lost. Out of the turbulence of youth should come this fine precipitate—a sane, strong, aggressive spirit of daring and doing. It must be a flexible, growing spirit, with a hospitality to new ideas and a keen insight into experience. To keep one's reactions warm and true

is to have found the secret of perpetual youth, and perpetual youth is salvation.[8]

In the context of this essay, this part of the Bourne quote is clearly meant as a portrait of Rothbard's ideal libertarian. In retrospect, he more than lived up to his ideal.

Rothbard's spirit, far from dimming with age, burned ever brighter. In the last decade of his life, Communism, the great bogeyman whose looming presence had cast its long shadow over the domestic political scene, caught all the experts by surprise and imploded with stunning rapidity. A wave of what is today referred to as an "antigovernment" populism swept the nation, culminating in the great Republican Revolution of 1994. The resulting realignment on the Right, with a whole section abandoning the Buckleyite devotion to global interventionism, gave him an opening to do what (I would argue) he was aching to do all along: return to his Old Right roots. Breaking with many of his followers, and adopting a new strategic outlook, Rothbard, having reached his mid-sixties, moved into a new social and political milieu. Devoted to principle, but devoid of dogmatism, he kept his reactions warm right up until the last day of his life.

At a time when all the wrong people are whining about the alleged lack of "role models," the phrase itself has become odious. In the original sense, however, it is a concept worth reclaiming: For budding young individualists, Rothbard is the perfect role model in the old-fashioned sense: the story of his life is not only fascinating but also instructive, and this is frankly my intent in this book.

Here it is necessary to confess my own bias: for many years I was associated with Rothbard, in one way or another, through our mutual activity in and devotion to the libertarian movement. We met in 1978, and, for a good part of my life since that time—except for one long interregnum during which we had almost no personal contact—we were friends and political allies. While we didn't always agree, Rothbard and I were aligned closely and consistently enough to qualify me as a Rothbardian, a description accurate to this day. However, like Bourne's archetypal youth, and Rothbard himself, I hate "glosses," and so will put none on my subject. Here is a portrait of Rothbard in all his brilliance and eccentricity: hopeful, yet sometimes despairing, heroic if often quixotic. This book is hardly meant to be the full-scale biography its subject deserves: my purpose is neither to appraise Rothbard's thought (a task for which I am hardly qualified) nor to weave the events of his life and work into a pattern made obvious somewhere near the end of the third volume. I hope, instead, in what is little more than an extended biographical sketch, to capture the essential Rothbard, not only his ideas but also his personality and some sense of his historical significance. To those readers unfamiliar with the man and his works, this book is meant as a doorway to discovering the most important and interesting development in the modern history of ideas: the Rothbardian system or paradigm of pure liberty.

The complexity of even the most ordinary individual makes the art of biography a difficult form to master. In reconstructing both the subject and the context in which he operated, the writer is faced with an overabundance of material. In building a narrative, the problem becomes one of what to include and what to omit. To err in favor of inclusion is to risk boring the reader with a shapeless and rambling tome of outsized proportions: the danger of omitting too much is that important facts will be lost in the interest of the story, which has somehow become divorced from its ostensible subject.

This problem of complexity is even more pronounced in Rothbard's case. Here was a man of so many dimensions that it would be virtually impossible, in a conventional biography, to cover all of them in any depth. The writer's job is to tell a story, but Rothbard's biographers are faced with the question of which story to tell.

There is the story of Rothbard the theorist of the Austrian School, who not only systematized and perfected the insights of Ludwig von Mises and his school of pure free-market economics, but also fought to establish an American beachhead for the Misesian school—and did it almost single-handedly.

There is the story of Rothbard the political philosopher: while others have defended private property in the name of justice and prosperity, he was the first to identify the *centrality* of private property to the concept of human society. He showed that it was not only necessary to the free and prosperous commonwealth, but also that the principle—if it has any meaning—must be consistently applied to *all* spheres of human activity. The state, as the primal plunderer, is by its nature the main violator of property rights, and therefore, Rothbard concluded, the main enemy of liberty.

He reached this conclusion not solely by means of armchair speculation, but also through his extensive researches into history, and here is another story: that of Rothbard the historian. His *History* of economic thought is in a class by itself, and the series of books on the origins of the American Revolution alone would put him in the first rank of historians. Whether it was the history of the Federal Reserve system, or the origins of the New Deal in Herbert Hoover's policy of economic interventionism, he saw through the propaganda of well-paid mouthpieces and fearlessly debunked the modern concept of history as a chronicle of the alleged glories of our rulers.

Yet another tale that needs telling is the story of Rothbard the observer of the political and cultural scene, the scholar of liberty on a par with Mises and Hayek* who was nevertheless very much engaged in the battle of ideas on a day-to-day basis. The remarkable record of his prolific political journalism, dating from the early fifties and continuing throughout his life, charts the rise over

---

*Friedrich von Hayek was a student of Mises and author of *The Road to Serfdom* (1944) and *The Constitution of Liberty* (1959).

four decades of a libertarian movement that challenges the conventional orthodoxies of the Left and the Right.

His role as a publicist and political commentator merges effortlessly into yet another major aspect of his story: Rothbard the organizer and intellectual fountainhead of an ideological movement. From his days as an embattled Old Rightist, to his New Left period, through the years with the Cato Institute and the Libertarian Party, and his rapprochement with the Right in the post–Cold War era, a clear pattern emerges: wherever the enemies of war and collectivism rallied to fight the good fight, he was at their side. Rothbard was an idealist, but no utopian: he saw his vision of liberty as fully realizable, and acted accordingly, allying himself with whatever popular movement against state power was in the field at the moment. His strategic perspective changed with the circumstances, but his principles and their application remained constant almost from the very beginning.

To merge all these stories into a single, seamlessly integrated portrait of the man and his thought is the task awaiting Rothbard's biographers. It is a job that even the most ambitious writer would find daunting. Two factors are key in motivating anyone to take on such a project: hubris and an overwhelming interest in the subject. In my case, it is both.

Scholars will long discuss his contributions to economic thought and political philosophy, and I will leave to them the definitive word as to his place in the history of ideas. Given the limitations of space, and my own inclinations, what is peresented here is an overview of his life, not only as a scholar and prolific writer, but as a man. For my purpose is as much to inspire as to instruct.

Somewhere a student is wandering through the library stacks, in search of he knows not what: perhaps some small clue to the mystery and meaning of human freedom. It could be that he wonders at the lack of it, especially when everyone professes their great love of it. If he or she should come upon this book, in a sense the search is ended—and, in another sense, it has just begun. The rising generation of libertarians has much to learn from Rothbard. If this modest volume does its part to make his social and political thought more accessible and readily available to a wider audience, it will have accomplished its purpose.

NOTES

1. Murray N. Rothbard, "Left and Right: The Prospects for Liberty," *Left and Right: A Journal of Libertarian Thought* 1, no. 1 (spring 1965): 8. Reprinted by the Cato Institute in 1979 as a pamphlet; the notes refer to this edition.

2. Ibid.

3. Ibid.

4. Murray N. Rothbard, "Toward A Theory of Libertarian Social Change," unpublished ms. in possession of author, April 1978, pp. 22–24. The reference is to Ludwig von Mises, the leading figure of the "Austrian" or pure free-market theory of economics, Rothbard's teacher and mentor.

5. Murray N. Rothbard, "Harry Elmer Barnes as Revisionist of the Cold War," in *Harry Elmer Barnes, Learned Crusader,* ed. Arthur Goddard (Colorado Springs: Ralph Myles, Publisher, Inc., 1968), p. 314.

6. Murray N. Rothbard, *An Austrian Perspective on the History of Economic Thought,* 2 vols. (London: Edward Elgar, 1995).

7. Rothbard, "Toward a Theory of Libertarian Social Change," p. 4. Rothbard's emphasis.

8. Rothbard, *Left and Right,* p. 31.

1

THE YOUNG ROTHBARD

Describing the political atmosphere in which he was nurtured, Murray Rothbard was characteristically blunt: "I grew up in a Communist culture. The middle-class Jews in New York whom I lived among, whether family, friends, or neighbors, were either Communists or fellow-travelers in the Communist orbit. I had two sets of Communist Party uncles and aunts, on both sides of my family."[1]

On March 2, 1926, the man who would become the antithesis to Marx was born in the Bronx, into a milieu of left-wing Jewish immigrants. There is in this fact the kind of irony that the modern "psychological" school of biography would no doubt make much of. Yet there is an alternative explanation for Rothbard's evolution into the foremost libertarian thinker of his era, other than to ascribe his radical antistatism to murky motives and unknowable psychological processes, one that is simpler and also has the advantage of fitting the facts: the quality of Rothbard's mind. He was remarkably articulate from a very early age—he once recalled debating the capital gains tax, which was just coming in, "in the eighth grade"—and this manifested a level of intelligence that far surpassed his peers.[2] That such a youth should rebel against the socialist orthodoxy that prevailed in New York City left-wing circles during the "Red Decade" of the thirties is not surprising. Intellectuals and writers are inherently averse to what George Orwell called the "smelly little orthodoxies" of political parties and ideological movements. Orthodoxy of any sort is the bane of reason and critical intelligence, and so it became Rothbard's lifelong *bete noir*.

In the late thirties, young Rothbard was not only old enough to have political opinions, he was also bold enough to express them with unusual verve. At one family gathering, when the adults in solemn conclave were pledging devotion to Spain's "Loyalist" (i.e., Communist) government, he piped up to ask: "What's wrong with Franco, anyway?" He described the incident in a short memoir published in 1994: "It didn't seem to me that Franco's sins, however statist, were any worse, to put it mildly, than those of the [Spanish] Republicans. My query was a conversation-stopper, all right, but I never received an answer."[3]

A FAMILY OF INDIVIDUALISTS

In looking for antecedents, personal as well as intellectual roots, his father—whom he describes as "the one exception to this communist milieu"—was a major source of inspiration. A bourgeois petroleum chemist who differed in politics and general disposition from his leftist relations, David Rothbard was born near Warsaw and had emigrated from Poland in 1910, intent not only on quickly learning English, but also "abandoning Yiddish papers and culture and purging himself of any foreign accent."[4]

David Rothbard had been born into the insulated world of the ghetto, or, as his son put it, raised "in an environment of orthodox and often fanatical Jews who isolated themselves from the Poles around them, and steeped themselves and their children in Hebrew lore." In a remarkable memoir entitled "My Autobiography" written in his last year of high school, young Murray reveals that his grandmother, on his father's side, was an exemplar of the family spirit, who rebelled against the prevalent insularity of the closed community in which they lived. Rothbard attributed this seemingly congenital individualism to the "lower middle-class" status of the family, which impelled them "to better their lot and acquire culture and Western civilization. One example was my grandmother, whose ambition was confined primarily to her children, whom she imbued with her own unfulfilled cravings."

When David Rothbard set foot in the New World, the narrow mindset of the Polish ghetto was quickly shed, albeit not without a certain amount of struggle. His son tells us that young David "had a great handicap in that he did not know any established language, since he had spoken only Jewish [Yiddish] in Poland. The isolation of the Jews precluded any possibility of their learning the Polish tongue."[5] This remarkable essay was obviously written as a school assignment, for on the back of the last page there is his grade, A-plus, and the following annotation by his teacher: "A splendid piece of work—carefully organized, clearly and interestingly presented. This gives indication of thought, observation, evaluation. College should offer no insoluble problems for you."

Overlooking this notation, the casual archivist will be forgiven if he mistakes Rothbard's youthful analysis as the work of an adult near fully formed. Its clarity and tone of authority, the easy narrative rhythm, as well as the style and sophistication of this autobiographical essay clearly marks its author as a prodigy. He shows a remarkable grasp of the psychological subtleties of human motivation, for a seventeen-year-old, in his insight into his mother's character and development. Murray's mother, Raya Babushkin, was born in a tiny Jewish village near the Russian–Polish border and came to America with her mother and sister in 1916. She "had been brought up without any necessity of facing the realities of life," writes her young son, "and consequently she shut herself up in a dream world of books and literature, much as Keats had escaped to a dream world of beauty."[6]

The Rothbard family's determined effort to integrate themselves into American life meant political as well as cultural assimilation; or, as Rothbard put it, "devotion to the basic American way: minimal government, belief in and respect for free enterprise and private property." Noting that "Russian and Polish Jews before World War I were swept with communist, socialist, and Zionist ideologies and movements, or blends of the three," Rothbard was obviously proud of the fact that "my father never fell for any of them." Far from being the archetypal rebellious adolescent who rejects his family on general principles, Rothbard was very close to both his parents throughout their lives.[7] According to his own testimony, the moments in his young life that had thus far afforded him "the greatest enjoyment and instruction are the long discussions which I frequently have with my parents. The mutual understanding is so strong," he writes, "as to be ever silently present, a mute god seen appreciatively by us all."[8]

His father was a major source of political and ideological as well as psychological influence and support. While Rothbard blames the baleful influence of Russian literature and its "negative idealism" on his mother's inability to completely free herself from the stultifying hand of the old country and its dangerously inbred traditions, his father embraced America wholeheartedly. Murray took pride in his father's quest for freedom: despite many obstacles, David Rothbard "broke away from old nationalistic ties, and through sheer will and force of character, he has obtained an extensive knowledge of the English language, has no trace of an accent, and displays a vocabulary that would shame many native Americans. Furthermore, he has, by dint of ability and perseverance, risen from an impoverished immigrant to a citizen of value and responsibility."[9]

His father was a strong believer in science and rationalism, and named him Murray Newton. The Rothbards nurtured their son's precocious intellect: family discussions ranged from literature to philosophy and current events, and included "character analyses and self-analysis." When the conversation came to politics, father and son were simpatico: "My father was a radical at twenty, but he was quick to profit by his folly. Strange as it seems, I always attempt to gauge my beliefs and actions by his experience." The youthful Murray reveals that "my father taught me the intricacies of politics without prejudice." Having become "mature enough to form my own conclusions," he says, "I was not too much surprised to find that I agreed with my father on basic political principles"— although, he adds, with endearing bluntness, "sometimes, in my opinion, my father becomes a little imperialistic."[10]

In spite of this shortcoming in his father's political outlook, "our attitude toward socialism is a common one. A belief in free enterprise is basic with my father, and has remained with me ever since I have formed a political philosophy." Socialism, he averred, destroys incentive and "inevitably leads to a great concentration of power in the government, which leads irretrievably to totalitarianism." The intellectual stance projected here—a love of liberty, a hatred of collectivism, and a refusal to be absorbed by the "religious fanaticism" of the Old World Jews—was to remain constant throughout his life.[11]

The resemblance between father and son extended from the psychological to the physical plane: pictures of the young Rothbard replicate to an amazing degree the type represented by his father: an open face, clean-shaven, with eyes that seem both absorbed by and delighted with the sight of the world around him. The high forehead, the nose prominent but finely formed, the half-smile exuding an earnest intelligence. In Murray, the features were sharper, finer, the chin more decisive: the overwhelming impression aside from a luminous intelligence was of a fearless honesty.

ROTHBARD VERSUS THE PUBLIC SCHOOLS

Murray Newton Rothbard was a bright, vivacious child, whose intelligence and independence of mind showed itself early on. He reports that, from infancy, "if I saw anything which puzzled me, I didn't rest until I had received a satisfactory answer"—a mental habit that stayed with him all his life. He learned to read by the age of five, and was soon using the dictionary and the *Encyclopedia Brittanica* to navigate his search for knowledge.[12]

Although he received consistently good grades, he was neither a "grind" nor the intellectual loner type: Murray was always gregarious, and, if he could not be a star player on the athletic field, he found his niche as a topnotch scorekeeper and calculator-of-odds. He showed a penchant for drama and music during grade school, yet he confesses that "I was not much of a social success. I was always cowed and bullied by my playmates, until I finally took recourse in books. Each succeeding year this situation became more acute." The Rothbards moved to Staten Island, a locale at that time "abounding in race prejudice," i.e., anti-Semitism, and this added to Murray's troubles: "My social maladjustment persisted through public school," he reports. His collision with "the evils of a public school system" marked "the unhappiest period in my life." Rothbard's opposition to egalitarianism was forged through his bitter experience of the "leveling" effects of the public school system, which

wreaks havoc on a child of superior ability. The entire method of teaching, the poor quality of the courses, the prevalent regimentation and narrow-mindedness, all contrived to hamper me greatly. I felt myself imprisoned in a steel cage. My mind, which wanted to soar onwards, was chained to the earth by an endless repetition of things that I knew, as well as by trifling but amazing public school restrictions. . . . The individual was completely forgotten in this system. . . . He was swallowed up in a mass of fifty other souls. How well I remember how I chaffed at the multiplication cards which the teacher held up before the class. Two times two equals four, three times two equals six; to me it all seemed a futile waste of time.[13]

Another great problem for Rothbard was that his intellectual precocity meant that he skipped grades "with disconcerting rapidity." Suddenly he was in the midst of an older crowd, and, "in my case the result was disastrous. Instead of overcoming my preschool shyness, I was more bullied and beaten, this time by boys much older than I was. Consequently, the unhappiness which I felt in early childhood was nothing compared with the misery which I bore in public school."[14]

Rothbard's personal crisis apparently reached a climax in the fourth grade: "The need for immediate action was apparent," he writes, but it took a while for his parents to come up with a realistic solution. Their first reaction was to hire on a boxing instructor for their beleaguered and battered son: "I believe he was a trainer of some lightweight champion. But it soon became apparent to all concerned that my career was not along pugilistic lines."[15]

The notes of his public school teachers on Rothbard's development reveal as much about the authors as they do about young Murray. A teacher's report notes that young Murray "has developed a combative spirit which frequently has to be checked. While this attitude in itself is bad, still it is encouraging to see that his courage is increasing. Although this pugnacity has been developed largely in protecting a smaller child in a game against a larger group, it should be watched very carefully for it might very well lead to an antagonism toward the larger group."[16]

His parents soon realized that the problem was "more emotional than physical," and soon related their concerns to the school authorities, who were markedly unsympathetic: "The reason I was unhappy, they said, was that I persisted in thinking and playing differently from the rest of the group. If I would only conform to the rest of the class, my adjustment would naturally follow." The extent of his dissatisfaction was perhaps exaggerated for its dramatic effect in his essay, or else did not manifest itself outwardly, for a report from his fourth-grade teachers declares that "Murray seems so exceedingly happy that it is sometimes difficult to control his activities in the class." One teacher wrote that "His reading is understanding, deeply appreciative and dramatic. His conversation is amusing, informative, wise!" Rebuffed by administrators who "concluded that the fault was all mine, and that I exaggerated my troubles," Rothbard's parents embarked on a systematic attempt to resolve the crisis of their son's education. They consulted "psychologists, friends, journalists acquainted with the subject, and student and parent associations." Finally they consulted Dr. John Levy, eminent psychologist in the field of child guidance. "I clearly recall the actual contour of the room where I sat alone and the unintelligible murmur of voices emanating from the next room. The most momentous decision that has yet affected my life was being reached. Dr. Levy recommended unequivocally that I be transferred to a private school."[17]

LIBERATION

Levy recognzed in young Rothbard a precocious and unique intelligence that required a lot more individual attention than any public school could or would provide. To his parents, the Riverside School, in Staten Island, with its small classes—there were seven students in its fourth grade class—and emphasis on individual attention to students' academic and emotional needs, seemed like the ideal choice. Rothbard's reaction was unrestrained joy: "My mind was at last free from all worthless intellectual and physical restrictions. I was free to think!"[18]

It was the height of the Great Depression and, although David Rothbard had a good job that he managed to hold on to, even with Murray's partial scholarship, private school was an expense the family could ill afford. Yet where the welfare of their son was concerned, there was not question that the sacrifice was worth it.

The two years spent at Riverside were liberating both intellectually and emotionally. In class, he felt free to utilize and develop his powers of expression "without the psychological intimidation which oppressed" him "in public school." Here he could enjoy the company of his intellectual equals, and be appreciated in turn: "I discovered," he writes, "with gratified wonder, that the other children liked me." Rothbard's radical alienation from his peers was over, and the reason for this new spirit of cooperation is clearly stated: "In them I found equals in intelligence, and consequently, similar interests. Thus, it was easy for me to cooperate and become an indissoluble unit of the class, without, however, losing my individual identity."[19]

In this new atmosphere of expansive openness, he joined the glee club, and began to pursue an interest in politics and, inevitably, economics. His grades were excellent, his intellectual interests were expanding, and as a social being he was beginning to develop his own mischievious charm. At the end of the sixth grade, however, he began to discover the limitations of his new-found freedom: Riverside "had served well as a reaction to public school, but its scope was becoming too narrow." He was more crit-ical of the teachers, but the main problem seemed to be that the classes were *too* small. Spreading his wings, he found himself con-fined in such a small space and yearned for wider horizons.

A systematic investigation of a suitable high school for Murray was undertaken by his parents with characteristic thoroughness. His mother was particularly impressed with the Birch-Wathen School, in midtown Manhattan, which he entered in the seventh grade. "I remember my first day there vividly," he writes. "At the foot of the stairs in the hall, I was introduced to Russell Bliss, also a new student." Bliss would become one of his best friends, a rela-tionship that would last through his high school and college years. "We walked up the stairs solemnly, led by a sympathizing teacher." He was entering a different world.[20]

In those days, boys of the wealthier classes were usually sent away to boarding school, but girls went to nearby day schools. Birch-Wathen had threatened to go nearly all-girl, until they began offering scholarships to deserving male students: "The result," writes Rothbard, "was socially anomalous: the girls were all wealthy, driven to and from school in chauffeured limousines, whereas at least half the boys were scholarship lads such as myself." Whatever class distinctions may have existed among the student body, most of them shared a common ethnicity—Russian and Polish Jews—but also a common political outlook. "They were all left-liberals," he later lamented, "what came to be called in New York 'Park Avenue' or 'limousine' liberals—all too literally in their case. I soon became established as the school conservative, arguing strongly in the eighth grade against Roosevelt's introduction of the capital-gains tax in 1938 and later against Mayor Fiorello LaGuardia's left-wing policy of coddling criminals."[21]

THE YOUNG DISSENTER

Rothbard's evolving political views were taking a consciously rightward tilt. This definitely put him in a minority, especially in the New York Jewish milieu of which he and his family were a part. A strong impetus in the development of his views was the far left-wing stance taken by his relatives, on both sides of the family. After covering his home life, school, and some unfortunate experiences at summer camp, young Rothbard writes that "my relatives come under a special category." This was undoubtedly the case. He grew up in an intensely political atmosphere, in which his various aunts and uncles were "definitely Communist sympathizers, or pinkish radicals," if not actual Communist Party members. One older uncle was an engineer who helped build the famous Moscow subway, a showcase of Soviet efficiency and modernity. A younger uncle was an editor of the newspaper of the Drug Workers Union, a working adjunct of the Communist Party. In a family of Stalinists, David Rothbard was the individualist exception; his vigorous dissent was controversial and not infrequently a cause of friction: "Consequently," Murray recounts, "my father frequently becomes involved in heated political debates. When they cannot help but see the logic of his arguments, they just call him a reactionary, a Republican (an abhorred word, for some reason) and hide behind the shield of those generously distributed labels. I usually take part in these discussions with vehemence and a certain amount of relish."[22]

Rothbard's commitment to human freedom came early; it was formed in his childhood struggle with the lowest-common denom-

inator egalitarianism of the public school system and crystallized
in these familial debates; his father was his first ideological soul-
mate and political ally. To even question the moral and practical
superiority of socialism to capitalism, in those days, was a distinctly unfashionable opinion held by a tiny and fast-dwindling
minority. And nowhere was that minority quite so tiny as it was in
New York City in the thirties, known as the "Red decade" of American intellectual history for good reason. To speak up in such circumstances was risky, even dangerous, and bound to make plenty
of enemies. David Rothbard was undeterred, and his son learned
from his example.

By the time he graduated from Birch Wathen, Murray Rothbard was a self-described conservative whose overriding passions
were opposition to New Deal socialism, Communism, and all
forms of egalitarianism. In an unpublished memoir written in the
late seventies, Rothbard writes that "exclusive contact with liberals
and leftists in high school and college only served to intensify this
commitment."[23] While he had yet to formulate a positive and consistent alternative, the intellectual and emotional setting out of
which his libertarianism developed was fully formed by 1940 at
the latest. He was an avid reader of John T. Flynn's newspaper
columns, and regularly tuned in to Flynn's radio commentaries; he
enjoyed the Hearst press and "the marvelous *New York Sun*."[24] A
little later, after the war, he subscribed to his favorite newspaper,
the *Chicago Tribune*, that old warhorse of the anti-Prohibitionist
anti-imperialist Midwestern Republicans. As he prepared to leave
the protected bastion of Birch-Wathen, war clouds loomed on the
horizon: yet there is no mention in his juvenilia of the great debate
between interventionists and "isolationists." In his youthful
"Autobiography" he avers that "I do not believe that the advent of
war has changed my outlook. War has only brought it into sharper
focus and crystallization. I am even more determined now to do

my utmost to serve this nation." Looking forward to college, he exhorts the reader to consider that "college becomes increasingly important in wartime" because "the need for a comprehensive education for youth becomes greater."[25]

The formative period of Rothbard's life, America in wartime, was just ahead, as was his transformation from an unreconstructed Old Rightist into a consistent libertarian. The basic ingredients were there, and were about to be superheated in the crucible of war.

His family had planned a future for him in business. There had even been an abortive experiment, one summer, when he was sent down to the Manhattan office of his father's petroleum company to do some sort of clerical work. But this arrangement did not last very long, for young Murray was utterly miserable at the prospect of working in an office, *any* office, especially if he had to be there at nine in the morning. Clearly, he was meant for other things. He decided to enter Columbia University and major in—but let him tell it: "As improbable as this may seem now," he writes, "I was at one time in college a statistics major. After taking all the undergraduate courses, I enrolled in a graduate course in mathematical statistics at Columbia with the eminent Harold Hotelling, one of the founders of modern mathematical economics. After listening to several lectures of Hotelling, I experienced an epiphany: the sudden realization that the entire 'science' of statistical inference rests on one crucial assumption, and that that assumption is utterly groundless. I walked out of the Hotelling course, and out of the world of statistics."[26]

One of his fourth grade teachers once commented on her precocious young charge's "inquiring mind," his "desire really to *know* reasons, origins, exceptions. He never seems to be satisfied with facts acceptable to most people."[27] By the time he entered college, this quality had only intensified, and because of it Rothbard managed to avoid more than one intellectual pitfall. In the case of statistics, he was skeptical of the premise that truth can be inferred from a statistical sampling based on the alleged infallibility of the normal curve, or "bell curve." The idea is that statisticians can measure everything from unemployment to political opinions, claiming absolute knowledge within a certain "confidence level," because all such characteristics are invariably distributed in the population according to the so-called normal curve, which is represented in textbooks as perfectly symmetrical and bell-shaped. "Well," asked Rothbard,

> what is the evidence for this vital assumption of distribution around a normal curve? None whatever. It is a purely mystical act of faith. In my old statistics text, the only "evidence" for the universal truth of the normal curve was the statement that if good riflemen shoot to hit a bullseye, the shots will tend to be distributed around the target in something like a normal curve. On this incredibly flimsy basis rests an assumption vital to the validity of all statistical inference.[28]

IN WARTIME AMERICA: A YOUNG MAN OF THE OLD RIGHT

Rothbard had been an excellent student in grade school and high school, and he continued in this mode throughout his college years. While his first-year marks are mostly As and B-pluses, by the summer of 1945 he was scoring virtually all As (and a few A-pluses and only an occasional B-plus). He achieved honors-level grades in probability theory, economic analysis, and his courses in economic theory and history—except for the one subject in which he consistently received a C, and sometimes even a C-minus: Physical Education.

Rothbard was draft age when he entered Columbia in September 1942, and the only way he managed to stay out of the slaughter was his poor eyesight, which gave him a 4-F status. Everybody at Columbia during the years 1942–45 was similarly classified—but that didn't mean that the militarization process was completely avoided. The government set up a physical training and military preparedness program on campus; the idea was to get these flabby slackers into shape so they could be drafted. Attendance was mandatory. One day, Rothbard faced a network of ropes stretched between two poles, and was told to go up one side of it and down the other. Rothbard approached this contraption, looked up, and said: "You have got to be kidding!" He walked around it.

In the hopped-up atmosphere of wartime America, this might have qualified as an indictable offense. But neither could Murray pull off any of the *other* feats of physical strength and endurance required to pass the course, and so the authorities simply wrote him off as a hopeless case.

The political and emotional atmosphere of America at war, in the midst of the relentless barrage of wartime propaganda, made a vivid and permanent impression on young Rothbard. It was a time when his uncle on his mother's side, whom Rothbard describes as "a longtime member of the Communist Party," could magnanimously declare to David Rothbard that he would be safe in the postwar world "provided that he kept quiet about politics."[29]

From that time forward, Rothbard's opposition to militarism was confirmed and solidified into a firm conviction. His determined opposition to globalism and imperialism, forged in the furnace of FDR's quasi-authoritarian wartime regime, is the consistent theme that explains his political enthusiasms, from the Old Right to the New Left, down through the years.

The one beacon of Americanism and editorial independence left standing at the war's end was the *Chicago Tribune*, to which Rothbard subscribed for a time, eagerly devouring such articles as a series entitled "Rhodes' Goal: Return U.S. to British Empire," by William Fulton and others that traced the history and influence of the Rhodes Scholars program on American foreign policy. In his later writings, this early influence would be reflected not only in his absolutely consistent "isolationism" but also in the muckraking style and flavor of the old *Tribune* that runs through such works as *Wall Street, Banks, and American Foreign Policy,*[30] *The Case Against the Fed,*[31] and indeed the whole of his political journalism. Always he asked: Who benefits? Like Colonel Robert R. McCormick, the polemical publisher of the *Tribune*, Rothbard was not afraid to name names: Rockefeller, Morgan, Kuhn-Loeb, the plutocracy of the statist order. Both the Colonel and the young Rothbard were agreed on the nature and motives of "the Wall Street–Anglophile Establishment that ran and still runs this country," as Rothbard put it later.[32]

Rothbard was, in short, a man of the Old Right—the "America First" generation of conservatives and classical liberals who were defined by their opposition to war abroad and collectivism on the home front. The problem, though, was that he was a young man, and the Old Right was already on its last legs. Not only that, but the country was lurching uncontrollably to the left under the impact of the war. The United States and the Soviet Union were marching side by side, hand-in-hand, allies against a common foe, and the idea of the free market was not even part of the discussion. As Rothbard puts it in his memoir of that time, the Right on campus was represented by the Social Democrats, with "the Communists and their allies on the left, and these factions set the parameters of political debate."[33]

It was in what Rothbard called "this stifling atmosphere" that he first became aware that he was not alone, that a movement dedicated to fighting collectivism and promoting freedom existed. "By the time I got to graduate school," he recalled, in the fall of 1945, "I was a sort of a Chamber of Commerce, NAM [National Association of Manufacturers]-type free marketeer. I didn't argue purely as a laissez-faire theorist, but I was getting there."[34]

The Republican sweep of the 1946 congressional elections was the occasion of a Rothbardian "Hallelujah" letter to the *New York World Telegram*, one of his earliest published writings, celebrating the "glorious victory." He exulted: "Once again there is a bright flame of hope for the cause of true liberalism. In 1948, it is my fervent hope and expectation that the American people shall complete their mandate by turning out Lame Duck Truman, so that the Republican Party can turn us off the road to socialist serfdom and on the road to individual liberty and political and economic freedom."[35] True liberalism, in Rothbard's sense, meant the classical liberalism of the nineteenth century which, unlike that of the twentieth, stood for economic liberty and the minimalist state.

Rothbard joined the Young Republican Club of New York as the war ended. In 1948 he wrote a campaign report attacking the Office of Price Administration and participated in internal debates over the issue of price controls—the wartime "emergency" regulations that had yet to be dropped. In his paper attacking Truman's program, Rothbard asked: What can the science of economics tell us about price controls? His answer was sharp and to the point:

Let us imagine that the government passes a law that gasoline cannot be legally sold at more than two cents a gallon. Absurd? No more absurd in principle than any price control. What would happen?

1. At first, buyers are happy; their cost of living has been magically cut by simple government order.

2. They soon find that no gasoline is being produced and sold.

3. Black markets form where people can get gasoline at prices that sellers are willing to accept. But now they are criminals, and prices go even higher on the black market than before to compensate the sellers for the risk of being arrested.

4. Honest people who obey laws find they can't get any gasoline.

5. The government then sets up hordes of detectives to enforce the law and crush the black markets.

6. Left-wingers proclaim that the control is a failure because gasoline producers are producing kerosene instead, and because their prices are uncontrolled. The solution is to drive *all* prices down to near-zero.

7. The result again is a gigantic system of black markets, a general choice between law-breaking and starving. Morals and orderly life disintegrates.

The ultimate result is a state of war between the government and the people: "If the people win out, the result is a network of black markets approximating the old free markets, though with great distortions. If the snoopers win out, people starve and must be forcibly put to work."[36]

Rothbard and his fellow antiprice control Young Republicans were definitely in the minority; the typical New York Young Republican was an underemployed young lawyer on his way to job security in Gov. Thomas E. Dewey's machine. Yet even in that less than fruitful milieu, Rothbard tirelessly promoted free-market ideas and became an outspoken proponent of the Right in New York City Republican politics. At a series of forums with the general theme of

"Which way for the Republican Party?" Rothbard represented the Right in debate with spokesmen for the Left and Center.[37]

When George J. Stigler, a young economics professor from Brown University, began to teach at Columbia in the fall of 1946, he caused a sensation. His first couple of lectures consisted of an attack on the concept of rent control—an idea very dear to the hearts of many New Yorkers to this day—and a refutation of the idea that a minimum wage does anything other than lock low-wage workers out of the market. The assembled leftist students were taken aback, and surrounded Stigler after class, arguing furiously with this heresy. Rothbard was delighted. Stigler had coauthored with Milton Friedman a pamphlet on the subject of rent control, *Roofs or Ceilings?* published by the Foundation for Economic Education (FEE). Rothbard wrote to the FEE for a copy of the pamphlet and more information about the organization. This was his first contact with the organized libertarian movement. As a Ph.D. candidate in the graduate economics department at Columbia University, he had occasion to experience and be "appalled at the attitude of the great majority of intellectuals," especially exhibited by his fellow students in the social sciences, "of passionate hatred of the capitalist and private enterprise system, admiration of ... ruthless power groups ... (e.g., organized labor, the Soviet Union), and a shocking ignorance of the whole tradition of Western liberalism." Bitterly noting that "anyone who dares support the principles of the Rule of Law, of political and economic freedom, is immediately accused of being a 'Fascist,' a 'black reactionary,' a 'paid agent of the NAM [National Association of Manufacturers],' and is forthwith ostracized from 'intellectual' society," Rothbard is heartened by the existence of the foundation, for "it is imperative that organizations exist which disseminate the principles of economic liberalism."[38]

Founded by Leonard E. Read in 1946, and ensconced in a large house on the banks of the Hudson River in upstate New York, FEE was staffed by a corps of free-market agricultural economists, such as F. A. "Baldy" Harper, of Cornell, and Orval Watts, formerly chief economist of the Los Angeles Chamber of Commerce, of which Read had been the president. The organization was a beacon light to the still-tiny but growing libertarian movement, and employed a whole generation of young libertarian economists and activists, including Dr. Paul Poirot, Richard Cornuelle, William Marshall Curtis, Ivan Bierly, and Ellis Lamborn.

A LIBERTARIAN IN ACADEME

On the academic front, Rothbard had entered Colombia Graduate School, received his M.A. degree in 1946, graduating with honors in economics and mathematics, and became a Ph.D. candidate in economics that same year. He was also looking for work, and in some unlikely places. In March 1945, he wrote the Personnel Department of the Sperry Gyroscope Company, in Brooklyn, inquiring about a position with the firm. With one course to complete for his masters, and that taken at night, he was "therefore available for work immediately."[39]

Luckily for the cause of liberty, the Personnel Department of the Sperry Gyroscope Company was not impressed enough to make him an offer; at least, no record of any such job offer survives.

He passed his oral examination in April 1948, and was busily working on his dissertation, "National Public Opinion on the Panic of 1819." He had also met the woman who would become the emotional framework of his life, Virginia-born JoAnn Schumacher, who, in her words, was "just hanging around" Columbia at the time. They met through mutual friends, and eventually developed a deep friendship that would blossom into romance. They would talk for hours in the library, and soon became inseparable; he called her Joey. While isolated politically, on a more personal level Rothbard was forging an alliance that would endure through all the days of his life. "To Joey, the indispensable framework," reads the dedication page of his 1963 book, *America's Great Depression*, an inscription that defines the centrality of their relationship.

Rothbard's letters to Joey during their courtship are passionate and funny, filled with anecdotes of New York City social and intellectual life in the postwar years interspersed with expressions of his undying devotion. An intellect in her own right, JoAnn Rothbard was a cultured and highly intelligent young woman who was the perfect complement to her husband. Throughout their lives together she had a calming effect on his natural volatility. Whenever he showed signs of taking one of his enthusiasms too far, she gently pulled him back on track. He would have found this intolerable in anyone else, but Joey was an exceptional woman. After earning her bachelor's degree in history at Columbia, she went on to get her masters at New York University. Joey had an abiding interest in music, particularly opera: she was an expert on Richard Wagner. She could have had her own career; instead, she devoted herself to the care and nurturing of Murray Rothbard.

One day, she came home to find Rothbard sitting on her stoop, practically in tears: he had submitted his doctoral dissertation to his academic advisor, Professor Joseph Dorfman, who, though inclined to approve it, had been restrained by a comment from Arthur Burns, head of the department—and a future head of the Federal Reserve—that, while this was acceptable work from anybody else, more was expected of Murray Rothbard. The problem was not that of the young libertarian up against his socialist professors, as would not be hard to imagine, but "was really more personal . . . intraprofessional rather than ideological," as he put it later. He had known Burns most of his life, and they had lived in the same apartment building since high school: "And so in graduate school," he remembered, "we got along very well. I thought he was a brilliant theorist, by the way, his . . . critique of orthodox theory and so forth, was excellent. . . . But he didn't really use it, I mean he didn't publish in that area. What happened was that he had a different view of what my thesis should be like than my professor. . . . [Between] the two of them—it was impossible for me to do anything since both of them ended up contradicting the other."[40]

Murray was devastated at the prospect of having to rewrite major sections of his work. He thought he would never be able to do it, and was therefore finished in the world of academia. When Burns heeded the call to go to Washington, however, in 1953, the main obstacle to his progress was eliminated: he resubmitted his thesis. With Burns safely ensconced in Washington as a member of the Council of Economic Advisors, he finished his dissertation, "The Panic of 1819: Reactions and Policies," and was awarded a doctorate in economics in 1956.[41]

While Rothbard describes the campus political spectrum that ran from Social Democrats on the "right" to Stalinists on the left, he apparently had an easier time of it than libertarians in academia have today. In those days, colleges were not political indoctrination centers but were genuinely committed to scholarship as the pursuit of truth, an idea that American academics nowadays knowingly sneer at. The all-pervasive thought-control of political correctness now strangling the nation's schools was entirely lacking. There was also a kind of distance between the professoriat and the student body that would today be considered "elitist" and archaic. "I didn't argue much with my professors," Rothbard recalled, although he did not often agree with them, because "there was not much give and take." Asked for his advice to young free-market advocates working toward their doctorates, Rothbard said, "I really sympathize with the kids nowadays who have become Austrians first and then try to combat the current orthodoxy. I wasn't an Austrian" as yet. "I was . . . increasingly libertarian, but as far as economics went all I knew was I was skeptical of what was going on, that was number one. So I was much better off in a sense than someone who starts in as a Misesian and tries to confront the Friedmanism and math and everything else. Second of all, there was much less math in those days. Economics was a sort of pleasure. I really don't know if I'd go into economics now if I were a young graduate student because I mean there wasn't all that math." Not that Rothbard found the math intimidating: far from it. Math was one of his best subjects from a very early age. What he means to say here is that while "econometrics had math," economics had not yet degenerated into an incomprehensible set of obscurantist equations, endless graphs, charts, and jargon. The journals were written "in good English. They had [prominent free-market economist] Frank Knight and had philosophical articles and . . . it wasn't like today, it wasn't monolithic in that sense."[42]

In that intellectual atmosphere, dominated by a relatively relaxed leftism, he was able to find his way to libertarianism. In what Rothbard described as "a true—and infinitely exhilarating—culture shock," one day in the Columbia bookstore, amid the usual debris of Trotskyite and Stalinist tracts, one pamphlet stood out from the others, the title emblazoned on the cover in bold letters and even bolder language: *Taxation Is Robbery*, by Frank Chodorov.[43] A more succinct statement of the central premise and policy of libertarianism is hard to imagine: "This," said Murray, "was *it*; once seeing those shining and irrefutable words, my ideological outlook would never be the same again."[44] He had found the political lodestar that would set him on his course.[45]

A disciple of the literary critic and writer Albert J. Nock, Chodorov had been kicked out of the Georgist Single Tax movement, where he had edited their magazine, for opposing U.S. entry

into World War II. He had been publishing his valiant little periodical, *Analysis,* out of a loft in Lower Manhattan, since November
of 1944, barely eking out a living. Rothbard met Chodorov at an
FEE cocktail party, thought he was "a delightful fellow," and
started reading *Analysis,* "which influenced me a great deal."[46] In
its pages, Chodorov blasted away in issue after issue with such
broadsides against statism as "Washington: A Psychosis" and
"Don't Buy Bonds!" In comparing the British Empire to Imperial
Rome, Chodorov detected the rise of "A Byzantine Empire of the
West" in America's postwar hegemony.[47] Rothbard contributed a
review of H. L. Mencken's *Crestomathy;* it was his first published
article.[48] Other articles followed, and they started corresponding
regularly in the summer of 1947.

Rothbard's libertarian education included the works of Nock,
Garet Garrett, Isabel Paterson, "and all the greats," and he describes
himself, at this point, as "not yet an anarchist yet just on the brink
of anarchy." A 1949 letter to Chodorov finds Rothbard ordering
books from Chodorov's book service, including Albert Jay Nock's
Memoirs of a Superfluous Man and *Journal of Forgotten Days,* Herbert
Spencer's *Man versus the State,* Sir Ernest Benn's *Confessions of a Capitalist,* Henry George's *Science of Political Economy,* as well as books
by Mises and Mencken. In reading *Analysis* and corresponding
with Chodorov and others, Rothbard was coming in contact with
the rich tradition of libertarian thought: he discovered Nock the lit-
erateur whose elegant prose style enlivened the *Freeman* and such
magazines as the *Atlantic* in the earlier part of the century. He was
particularly struck with Garrett, an editor at the *Saturday Evening
Post,* whose bitter chronicle of the decline of the old American
republic, *The Revolution Was,* he often found occasion to quote over
the years. Although busy with his dissertation, Rothbard embarked
on a project seeking out libertarian voices of the past, and in his
research came "across some items of interest. I've 'discovered' the

American Mercury of the 1920s—there are many fascinating articles on the interventionist 'crusade' of World War I and great editorials and book reviews by H. L. Mencken." He was puzzled, however, upon reading back issues of the old *Freeman* of the early twenties (edited by Nock and Francis Neilson), that these self-avowed libertarians could possibly have published paeans to labor unions and the Bolshevik Revolution.[49]

With teachers like these, Rothbard "arrived at a libertarian position much more from a moral-political point of view than from a strictly economic point of view." As he put it, "I didn't arrive at a libertarian position from some sort of analysis of externalities or transaction costs or anything of that sort. It was a question of justice versus criminality."[50]

Chodorov's thoroughgoing antistatism led logically to anarchism—or more precisely, as we shall see, to anarchocapitalism—but Rothbard had yet to realize the full implications of the ideas he had accepted until, one day, after "engaging in the nth, umpteenth [debate with] friends of mine in graduate school about conservatism versus liberalism and so forth," he remembered, "after they had left I realized that something very important had taken place." His friends had argued that if society can make and enforce a "social contract" agreeing on the necessity of a police force, then "why can't society also agree to have a government build steel mills and have price controls and whatever? At that point I realized that the laissez-faire position is terribly inconsistent, and I either had to go on to anarchism or become a statist. Of course for me there was only one choice there: that's to go on to anarchism."[51]

As his ideological outlook evolved in a more radical direction, Rothbard's contacts with the growing libertarian movement increased. Way out in Kansas City, the legendary Loren "Red" Miller, one of the earliest libertarian activists, was the source of a much-needed infusion of energy and scarce funds; Miller supplied the energy, and his friend and associate, Harold W. Luhnow, a prominent businessman, supplied much of the funding. Luhnow had been a supporter of the anti-interventionist America First Committee before the war, was now a big supporter of FEE, and was enthusiastically committed to expanding the scope of libertarian scholarship. As head of the William Volker Company—a nationwide wholesale distributor of household goods—and the accompanying Volker Fund, Luhnow was in a position to build a libertarian movement from the ground up, and that is precisely what he and his lieutenants proceeded to do—with fortunate consequences indeed for Rothbard the budding young scholar.

LUDWIG VON MISES, TEACHER AND MENTOR

It was the Volker Fund that arranged for Ludwig von Mises, who had fled Nazi-occupied Austria and arrived in New York with no academic position, to teach as a Visiting Professor at New York University, where he conducted his famous seminar—an eventuality that would, in many respects, become the central axis of Rothbard's intellectual development. For here was the second great discovery of his youth: the existence of the "Austrian" or pure free-market school of economics.

Mises was a part-time staffer at FEE, and when Rothbard first went up there "all I knew about Mises was that he had written . . . *Socialism* . . . I didn't even know that Mises was still alive. I didn't know that he had contributed to anything in economics except that." In the spring of 1949, Rothbard learned from someone at FEE that Mises was coming out with a book: "I said what's in the book? What's the book about? He said the book's about *everything*. So sure enough that was it."[52] *Human Action*, by Ludwig von Mises, was published by Yale University Press in the winter of 1949. Rothbard heralded Mises's achievements in a review of *Human Action* for *Analysis*:

> The integration of the theory of money into the general framework of individualist "utility" economics; the demonstration that free banking leads to "hard" money rather than "cheap" money; a complete portrayal of the evils of inflationism and credit expansion; the superb analysis of the causes of the business cycle (the result of credit expansion; the demonstration that world socialism is economically unfeasible; the demonstration that interest is an eternal category of human action and not the wicked device of usurers; a demonstration of the possibilities of capital consumption and forced savings; and a thoroughgoing portrayal of the vicious effects of every type of governmental intervention in economic life.[53]

All this was wrapped up in the basic Misesian insight that, as Rothbard put it, economics is a category of *individual* human action and not the interaction and conflict of classes, masses, and other collectivistic constructs. Although Mises never used the term "natural law," for Rothbard the discovery of Mises was the bridge between his passion for justice and his equal passion for truth scientifically arrived at:

> Economics as it emerges from his direction, is a series of "praxeological laws," laws which are eternally part of the nature of human action. Praxeological law, like physical laws, are always with us, and are disregarded by human beings only to their own peril. Men have learned that they cannot afford to ignore the law of gravitation, but they persist in ignoring the praxeological laws of economics.[54]

In a letter to Mises, Rothbard writes of his eagerness to attend Mises's seminar on Marxism at New York University. He reports being in the midst of reading *Human Action* for the first time, and imparts a sense of his own excitement: "The impact is especially vivid for someone like myself who has spent all of his intellectual life at Columbia University. Although the differences of opinion among the professors there are vivid and provocative (particularly between the mathematico-Keynesians and the Veblen-Mitchell institutionalists) they all join in presenting the following view of the history of economic thought: classical theory, taught by Ricardo, advanced to neoclassical theory, represented by Alfred Marshall [and] had now proceeded onward to modern theory, consisting of Hicks, Samuelson, and their followers. . . . As a result, a Columbia graduate gets a thorough training in Marshall, Hicks, Veblen, and Mitchell, but is only dimly aware of the existence of the 'Austrians.' " Mises had clarified Rothbard's critique of the institutionalists as naive worshipers of statistics and of the mathematicians as outright fantasists who had completely lost touch with the real world of thinking, acting human beings: "*Human Action*," he wrote,

> has shown me the value of both these criticisms and has presented an entirely new approach to economic theory that avoids the pitfalls of the others.

Mises's masterful analysis had

> for the first time established a firm methodological base for economic theory in praxeology [the study of human action] and has also brought out with great clarity the difference between theory and history, and the functions each performs.[55]

In this letter he also reveals his early interest in a project that would be the capstone of his career: a history of economic thought from the Austrian or Misesian perspective. "It would be splendid," he wrote, "if you should now undertake the task of providing us with a *Dogmengeschicte* that would properly evaluate all the contributions to economic thought. As far as I know, no good history of economic thought exists. Certainly the intellectual world needs one desperately."[56]

Rothbard became a regular participant in the Mises seminar. It was an experience that shaped his thought, and the course of his career, leading as well to many long-standing friendships, including that of Mises. The exiled giant, whose prestigious Viennese seminars had been the center of a flourishing Austrian school, was reduced to teaching what Rothbard called "uncomprehending business students" who took the course for an easy credit. About one-half to one-third of Mises's audience consisted of libertarians and what would become the first generation of Austrian economists in America. At the end of the formal session of the seminar, Mises and his favorite students would repair to Child's Restaurant and continue the discussion in roundtable format. As Rothbard would later recall, the great Mises would address the humblest beginning student with the following friendly admonition: "Don't be afraid to speak up. Remember, whatever you say about the subject and however wrong it might be, the same thing has already been said by some eminent economist."[57]

Through all his years at Columbia, in the course of his studies at graduate school, Rothbard had never come across any discussion of or reference to the subject of Austrian economics. Now he was on his way to becoming an expert on the topic. Rothbard knew—had always known—what he was against: the New Deal, the Fair Deal, the herd mentality of the Columbia University graduate class in those days. "It was just after the war," he recalled, and "there was a big influx of veterans," and the class was quite large: "Instead of being maybe twenty people in it or forty, it has about one-hundred and fifty. And all these people were extreme leftists and very politically oriented."[58] For Rothbard, *Human Action* was "an enormous revelation." The twenty-three-year-old Rothbard "had a definite, instinctive feeling or insight or whatever that there was something wrong with all the schools of economics. I was very unhappy with all the [schools of] economic theory. I thought that . . . when the institutionalists were criticizing the orthodox, Anglo-American economics that they were right; and, when the orthodox people were criticizing the institutionalists, *they* were right. The criticisms were right, and I believed that the simple supply and demand stuff was correct, but I didn't really have a good theoretical base. I wasn't happy with any theories offered. And when I read *Human Action*, the whole thing just slipped into place, because everything made sense."[59]

"Every once in a while the human race pauses in the job of botching its affairs and redeems itself by producing a noble work of the intellect," he opined in the September 1950 *Analysis*. "Throughout the history of mankind, a handful of individuals have significantly enriched the thought of man. Both creators and systematizers, they have carved out new paths in the search for truth and have integrated the truths they have found into a great edifice. It is no exaggeration to assert that *Human Action* is such an edifice. . . . A work of monumental grandeur, . . . [the book] demands and deserves a lifetime of study." Mises is praised as "a mind of rare power and creative ability" who "belongs in the economist's Valhalla," along with Smith, David Ricardo, Carl Menger, Eugen von Bohm-Bawerk, and Léon Walras. "The first half of the twentieth century has produced only a Mises to rank with the greats of the eighteenth and nineteenth centuries."[60]

Rothbard sent a copy of the piece to Mises, who responded by thanking him for "the fine review," agreeing with him on the need for the seminar to investigate the epistemological problems of economics, and ending with the hope that Rothbard would soon finish his thesis and "have time enough to begin to write a great book on the problems you refer to in your letter. But please remember that an adequate treatment of these matters requires a reading knowledge both of German and of French."[61]

Rothbard wrote that he deeply appreciated his newfound mentor's "kind and encouraging words" and "I only hope that I may prove worthy of them." He promised to acquire "a reading knowledge of German" and soon followed up by taking lessons.[62]

In the world at large, the collectivist consensus was solid, dissent was inaudible, and Left and Right seemed to have merged into a single party of the Welfare-Warfare State. In the economics profession, the welfare statist Keynesians had won the day; their critics, such as Mises, were forgotten, and everywhere they were in power: in the universities, and in the councils of state.

Beneath the surface, however, in the free-market intellectual underground that had grown up after the war, things were stirring. The Volker Fund, dedicated to finding and funding libertarian scholars of promise, hired Rothbard's friend Herbert Cornuelle as liaison officer. Cornuelle was an administrative genius who would later go on to become CEO of Dole Pineapple and a very successful businessman in his own right; in the meantime, he directed his considerable talents to the task of nurturing libertarian scholars wherever they might be found. It was he who suggested that Rothbard write a primer for students of Austrian economics, in which the ideas of Mises would be simplified and presented in a format appropriate for a textbook. "At that time," Rothbard reminisced, "I was just going to Mises' seminar for a few months, and he didn't know me from Adam."[63] Rothbard wrote a sample chapter that met with Mises's approval. A multiyear grant from the fund enabled him to complete his work. The result, published a decade later, was far from a textbook: this project soon became the monumental *Man, Economy, and State*, a comprehensive treatise on Austrian economics.

When Rothbard began working on the book in 1952, he also began working for the Volker Fund—at first part-time, then full-time—in its never-ending quest for libertarian talent of note. Along with his friend Frank S. Meyer, who was the only other "senior analyst" at the Volker Fund at that time, Rothbard reviewed books, journals, manuscripts, and other material, busily scouring the world of ideas for intellectual allies or *some* sign of intelligent libertarian life. For a decade he worked for the Volker Fund in his capacity as an intellectual entrepreneur—an occupation that was always full-time with him, wherever he was employed, and a role that suited him well. "That was a great deal," he said, years later. "They subscribed to all the journals for me. They'd say your task is to see whether there are any good people. Seek out . . . good articles, good people and write about it. That was a really fun job."[64]

And Rothbard was very good at it, not only because of his enthusiasm but due to his ability to read (and comprehend what he was reading) very quickly: he was a fast study, as they say, and he sent off reams of reviews, letters, reports, and memoranda to Volker in a fairly constant stream.

"Murray had a happy life," says JoAnn Rothbard. "He never had to get up and go to an office, and he never did anything he didn't want to do." Although the pay was low, he enjoyed his job at the Volker Fund as nurturer of the flame of liberty. With a fairly consolidated and systematic if not yet fully matured view of economics and politics, the young Rothbard was now embarked, fully armed, on a remarkable career as a thinker, philosopher, economist, historian, and all-around champion controversialist.

Murray Rothbard was, over the years, involved in all of the

most vigorous disputes of his day: the effect of reading his collected writings in chronological order would be to read the history of virtually every significant controversy in American politics and economics since World War II. It would be the history of modern times as seen through the lens of an astonishingly well-read and unashamedly partisan lover of liberty, written in a combative and colorful style. And coursing through that vivid narrative, shining through the story of liberty versus power in virtually all the social sciences, would be the indomitably joyous spirit of the author, gleefully demolishing the myths of the court intellectuals and pointing the way to the final victory of the free society. For only an indomitable spirit such as his could possibly hope to survive the decade with his principles intact.

NOTES

1. Murray N. Rothbard, "Life in the Old Right," *Chronicles* (August 1994).

2. Interview with Walter Block and Walter Grinder, "Rothbard Tells All," p. 1, unpublished transcript in possession of author.

3. Rothbard, "Life in the Old Right."

4. Ibid.

5. Murray N. Rothbard, "My Autobiography," unpublished manuscript, no date [probably 1943].

6. Ibid.

7. Ibid., p. 2

8. Ibid., p. 4

9. Ibid., p. 3.

10. Ibid., p. 5.

11. Ibid., p. 6.

12. Ibid., p. 8.

13. Ibid., p. 10.

14. Ibid., p. 9.

15. Ibid., p. 10.

16. Mary Elizabeth Nells and Leah Sibley, "Report of Murray Rothbard," 21 December 1934.

17. Ibid., p. 11.

18. Ibid., p. 12

19. Ibid.

20. Ibid., p. 13.

21. Rothbard, "Life in the Old Right."

22. Rothbard, "My Autobiography," p. 19.

23. Murray N. Rothbard, "The Betrayal of the American Right," unpublished manuscript, p. 59

24. Rothbard, "Life in the Old Right," p. 18

25. Rothbard, "My Autobiography," pp. 22, 23.

26. Murray N. Rothbard, "Statistics: Destroyed From Within?" *The Free Market* (February 1989). Reprinted in Murray N. Rothbard, *Making Economic Sense* (Auburn, Ala.: Ludwig von Mises Institute, 1995), pp. 38–39.

27. Margaret Elizabeth Nells and Leah Sibley, "Report of Murray Rothbard," 21 December 1934, emphasis in original.

28. Rothbard, "Statistics."

29. Rothbard, "The Betrayal of the American Right," p. 60.

30. Murray N. Rothbard, *Wall Street, Banks, and American Foreign Policy* (Burlingame, Calif.: Center for Libertarian Studies, 1995).

31. Murray N. Rothbard, *The Case Against the Fed* (Auburn, Ala.: Ludwig von Mises Institute, 1994).

32. McCormick's editorial insight that Herbert Hoover was "the greatest state socialist in history" perhaps sowed the seeds of Rothbard's research into this question.

33. Rothbard, "The Betrayal of the American Right," p. 69.

34. Block and Grinder, "Rothbard Tells All," p. 1.

35. Rothbard to *New York World-Telegram*, 6 November 1946.

36. Murray N. Rothbard, "Price Controls," *Campaign Research Bulletin* no. 4 (New York: Young Republican Club, fall 1948): 5.

37. A postcard meeting announcement issued by the Junior Group of the Women's National Republican Club in midtown Manhattan advertises their January [1950] debate on "Which Way Should the Republican Party Go—Left, Right, or to the Center?" with Rothbard representing the Right. Another meeting notice put out by the Hamilton Republican Club of the 7th Assembly District asked "What Sort of Republican Are You?" As the point man of the conservative Republicans, Rothbard was pitted against a "Middle of the Road Republican" as well as a spokesman for Liberal Republicans. Copy in possession of author.

38. Rothbard to Foundation for Economic Education, 22 November 1946.

39. Rothbard to Personnel Dept., Sperry Gyroscope Co., 31 March 1945.

40. Block and Grinder, "Rothbard Tells All," pp. 12–13.

41. Rothbard's doctoral dissertation was published in 1962 as *The Panic of 1819* (New York: Columbia University Press; Columbia University Studies in the Social Sciences, No. 605).

42. Block and Grinder, "Rothbard Tells All," pp. 11–12.

43. Frank Chodorov, *Taxation is Robbery* (Chicago: Human Events Associates, 1947).

44. Rothbard, "The Betrayal of the American Right," p. 73.

45. See especially Murray N. Rothbard, "Frank Chodorov, RIP," *Left and Right* 3, no. 1 (winter 1967): 3–8.

46. Block and Grinder, "Rothbard Tells All," p. 3.

47. See Charles Hamilton, ed., *Fugitive Essays: Selected Writings of Frank Chodorov* (Indianopolis, Ind.: Liberty Press, 1980).

48. *Analysis* (August 1949).

49. Rothbard to Frank Chodorov, 30 January 1949.

50. Block and Grinder, "Rothbard Tells All," p. 3.

51. Ibid.

52. Ibid., pp. 5–6.

53. Murray N. Rothbard, review of *Human Action*, by Ludwig von Mises, *Analysis* (May 1950): 4.

54. Ibid.

55. Rothbard to Ludwig von Mises, 22 September 1949, p. 1.

56. Ibid., p. 2.

57. Cited in Murray N. Rothbard, *Ludwig von Mises: Scholar, Creator, Hero* (Auburn, Ala.: Ludwig von Mises Institute, 1988), p. 63.

58. Block and Grinder, "Rothbard Tells All," p. 2.

59. Ibid., p. 6.

60. Murray N. Rothbard, review of *Human Action*, *Analysis* (September 1950).

61. Ludwig von Mises to Rothbard, 29 May 1950.

62. Rothbard to Ludwig von Mises, 13 June 1950. He learned to read French passably.

63. Block and Grinder, "Rothbard Tells All," p. 8.

64. Ibid., p. 9.

2

THE OLD RIGHT'S LAST STAND

David Rothbard was instrumental in shaping his gifted son's ideas, particularly his political ideas, not only by means of his words, but also by his example and experience. As a manager at the Bayonne, New Jersey, Tide Water Oil refinery, David Rothbard had had dealings with union thugs for some thirty years: it was the great Bayonne oil workers strike during the winter of 1951–52 that gave real direction and immediacy to young Murray's nascent political consciousness. In answer to a letter from his old friend from Birch-Wathen, Russel Bliss, in which unions are praised, Rothbard relates:

> It might interest you to know that my father, for the last six weeks, has been marooned, beleaguered, and virtually imprisoned in his Bayonne plant. No letup is in sight. As a result, neither my mother nor myself has seen hide or ha'r of my father, since he has been there twenty-four hours a day since the Friday after New Years. All this, and much more, as a direct result of

gangster-unionism (and believe me, these two words deserve a perpetual connection).[1]

Union power rests "exclusively on violence and the threat of violence" and the union shop means "tyranny unlimited" for the worker, who is forced to subsidize his own serfdom by paying union dues. Unions, he wrote, are fast evolving into a regime of "private industrial dictatorships" whose thuggery was vividly dramatized in Rothbard's account of the Bayonne strike:

> The climax is now on at Bayonne. . . . The issue is that the union, having badgered and tyrannized over management for decades, now wants to take over management and decide how to operate the plant. The management, such as my father, have to stay at the plant in order to prevent an explosion or fire—it's an oil refinery—and to keep the machinery warm; otherwise it would take many months to start the machinery up again. They have to stay there all the time *because the union gangster goons will not permit them to reenter.* Freedom is a mockery in this country when people cannot come and go as they will. Yet, as in all other cases, the police do nothing—they remain, as they put it, "neutral." Therefore, *food* has to be shopped in to my father and the others by water, and that has to be smuggled in late at night.[2]

"Unfortunately," he remarked to another friend, "no attempt has been made to import 'strikebreakers.' "[3] The union thugs were the bullies of public high school come back to threaten not only him but his whole family. In a letter to his father, held hostage in Bayonne, the son hails "the forces of Rothbard reaction" that will cause the "Red unioneers to wither on the vine." He continues:

> Remember, O small beleaguered garrison of mighty warriors, that you are, each one of you, carrying on the good fight against

the forces of Red unionism run rampant. (All unions are Red by definition.) "Red" is a term defined by expert pink-baiter Joseph P. Kamp as including communists and Socialists, and of course, unions are by their very acts, socialistic.) Shall we organize a network of Bundles for Bayonne?[4]

The failure of the police to do anything but proclaim their vaunted "neutrality" provoked young Rothbard to score points on the anarchist front: "Here, in the failure of the police force, is another living example of the necessity of Right-Wing An– . . . (oops, I mean) . . . Voluntaryism."[5]

In another missive to the elder Rothbard, written in the mock-serious tone of a war bulletin, young Murray enthuses over his new-found cause, but not without a touch of irony: "The slogan now is: 'out of the trenches by Lincoln's birthday!' " Like a guerrilla leader reporting to his commander, Rothbard relates the story of how he put a sympathetic reporter for the *New York Herald Tribune* on the story of the siege of Bayonne. Since this is supposed to be a morale-building letter, to perk up his father's spirits during the siege, he also sprinkles his missive with generous dollops of commentary on various other subjects: the shocking news that "a little college in New Jersey named Bloomfield College, which has officially declared that they will fire and refuse to hire any professors who are Commies or Socialists" has been "refused donations by all the top New Jersey millionaires." He also mentions that John T. Flynn "commentates daily over WMGM . . . at 7:30 as part of the magnificent nationwide Liberty Network" and is "now far and away the best commentator on the air. . . . Spread the Flynn gospel. Maw is trying to high-pressure Evelyn to listen in nightly."[6]

Rothbard's relationship with his family was unusually close; there was a mutual protectiveness that was often fierce. Rothbard's mother called him every day, at least once, until well after he had been married, and there is some indication that Raya Rothbard, especially, was none too thrilled when he decided to go ahead and marry Joey. In spite of initial opposition from his mother, and from her side of the family—how, they asked, could he even think of marrying a *goy*?—Murray and Joey were married on January 16, 1953. It was the beginning of an adventure for the both of them, and a love that never flagged.

THE POLEMICIST

This expansion of his personal life took place in the context of a more general expansiveness, both intellectually and politically. Rothbard's increasing interest in politics had little outlet, except for his occasional forays into local Republican party activities; but this only stimulated his real appetite for political expression. He was already engaged in an energetic correspondence with a wide variety of people, fellow Austrian economists such as Ludwig Lachmann, the eminent sociologist and revisionist historian Harry Elmer Barnes, the staff of the Foundation of Economic Education, and many others, and decided to supplement these wide-ranging contacts with an informal (typed) newsletter, variously titled the *Individualist Newsletter* and *The Vigil*. The May 1952 issue of *The Vigil* lauds Milton Friedman, "hitherto not distinguished for a sound approach on the subject of money," for coming out for the abolition of the Federal Reserve System and a 100 percent reserve requirement for bank demand deposits. *The Vigil* was filled with book reviews, "movement news," gossip, quotable quotes, essays, and polemics, such as "Buckley Revealed," a devastating review of the utter phoniness of William F. Buckley Jr.'s claim to be a "libertarian follower of Frank Chodorov."[7] These newsletters were written with great gusto, and it is clear that he found this sort of writing enjoyable; for Rothbard, it was the beginning of a lifelong habit of political journalism. Aside from the sheer pleasure it afforded him, however, his intent was to fill a niche that had been empty for too long: with the demise of Chodorov's *Analysis*, the "purist" libertarianism espoused by Rothbard had no voice, no magazine, no independent presence of its own, and while he was willing (for the moment) to consider himself part of a broad movement of the Right, he was not the sort to mute his own views in the name of unity. In "Enemies and Friends of the Public Schools," Rothbard denounces fellow rightists Mrs. Lucille Crain and Allen A. Zoll, who "assure the public that they are not really enemies of the public schools, but merely critics of the socialism taught there." Rothbard would have none of this: "*Vigil* proudly takes its stand as a convinced enemy of the public schools," he wrote, because they "are socialism in action, by their very nature." While others may waffle, "it is on issues such as this that the 'radicalism' of *Vigil* contrasts to the other 'conservative' publications."[8]

In the pages of *The Vigil*, Rothbard elaborated the distinctively libertarian position on the issues of the day, carefully separating it out from the program and methods of his conservative allies. In response to the announcement that the House of Representatives would be investigating "subversive activities," and specifically the left-wing activities of the Carnegie Endowment, the Rockefeller Foundation, and the Guggenheim Foundation, among others, Rothbard maintained that "much as we can rejoice in the possible discomfiture of the Carnegie, Rockefeller, etc. outfits, we are not too happy about such Congressional investigations" on the grounds that "if Congress can pillory Red textbooks today, they can pillory 'White' textbooks tomorrow." Having survived the blatant repression of the war years, when conservative isolationists were silenced and some of them hauled into court on charges of "sedition," the Right ought to be all too well-acquainted with the dangers of such investigations: "Logically," he wrote," those gallant fighters who stood up against the Buchanan witch-hunt should be equally as critical of the Cox expedition, even though it will hit people whom we don't like." The Buchanan committee had recently dragged a bevy of right-wing organizations in for interrogation as to their activities and sources of funding: Joseph P. Kamp, of the Constitutional Educational League, a leading "Red-baiter," had gone to jail for refusing to divulge the names of his contributors, and even the Foundation for Economic Education had been hauled before investigators. The only way to "eliminate the problem posed by special governmental privilege to foundations via income tax exemption is to remove this privilege—by abolishing income taxation!" Unlike the leftist "civil libertarians," however, Rothbard was all in favor of red-baiting: "the following types are perfectly all right and often praiseworthy: (a) voluntary exposures by private organizations, such as 'Red Channels,' etc., and (b) charges against government officials, who as bureaucrats should be considered fair game—such as the charges by Senator McCarthy." On the other hand, "the following types of Red-baiting are bad because they involve persecution of dissenting opinion by government officials: (a) persecuting acts such as the Smith Act and the McCarran Act, and (b) subpoena-armed Congressional investigations."[9]

Another sharp contrast to his conservative allies was the muckraking style of *The Vigil*, which, in speaking truth to power, did not hesitate to name names. In "The International Bankers Versus the Taxpayers," Rothbard warns against the "relatively obscure 28-nation conference" that had recently convened to consider the question of what to do about Germany's burgeoning external debt. Having loaned West Germany $3.2 billion since the end of the war, the United States had agreed to settle for 37 cents on the dollar, or $1.2 billion, payable over 35 years at an interest rate of 2.5 percent. Not only have the American taxpayers been bilked out of two-thirds of their "investment," but as Rothbard points out, certain large investment banking institutions have somehow managed to profit from the debacle: "In exchange for this boon to West Germany, *the Bonn government will agree to pay off prewar German debts to U.S. banks and private investors in full and including accrued interest.*"[10]

Rothbard was far from being an economic determinist, but often found that the exhortation to "follow the money" produced a whole new perspective on current events. In tracing the links between policy and personalities, he combined his extensive knowledge and prodigious memory with an incisive analytical style to produce some first-rate investigative journalism:

> Now, let us consider the U.S. officials who have decided upon this solution so helpful to our bankers. Top official is U.S. High Commissioner in Germany, John J. McCloy. McCloy is a member of the swank Wall St. law firm of Cravath, Swaine, and Wood. CSW, associated with the Morgan interests, handled much of the legal work for the international bankers who floated the extensive American loans to the German government in the 1920s. Partners in the Cravath firm were S. Parker Gilbert and Russell C. Leffingwell who kept alternating between their work for the firm and government service related to German reparations and finance. Gilbert served as Assistant Secretary of War and Agent General for Reparations in Germany. Leffingwell was Assistant Secretary of the Treasury. Both were later rewarded with posts as J. P. Morgan, Co. partners. Another top Wall Streeter in our officialdom is William H. Draper, now top U.S. civilian in NATO, and formerly director of the economic division of the U.S. occupation in Germany. Draper was recruited for government service from the Wall Street firm of Dillon, Read, & Co. investment bankers, which made many of the loans now to be repaid.[11]

The intersection of corporate interests and government power had long been a theme of right-wing populist movements in America, but by the mid-fifties it was considerably muted if not forgotten. This was one Old Right tradition that was kept very much alive in the pages of *The Vigil*.

As early as January of 1952, however, the future of Rothbard's journalistic foray was in doubt. Rothbard considered either scrapping it, or else continuing it on an informal basis with a limited circulation, and there was some talk of duplicating it inexpensively: Richard Cornuelle, who had just started working for the Volker Fund, wrote that he enjoyed reading *The Vigil* "very much" and hoped Rothbard would decide to continue it. A few months later, however, it appears to have expired: at least, there are no surviving copies beyond mid-1952, and no evidence that it was reproduced by any method other than making carbon copies.[12]

Another reason for the demise of *The Vigil* may have been that its audience was shrinking. The death of Senator Robert A. Taft, in 1954, followed the next year by *Chicago Tribune* publisher Robert R. McCormick, meant the end of the Old Right as an effective national political force. The America First generation was passing into history, with most of the survivors (Flynn, Nock, Chodorov, Garet Garrett), sidelined, retired, or dead. The second generation, which counted Rothbard in its ranks, was far less numerous and influential. Rothbard says he "began to notice isolationist sentiment starting to fade away, even among old libertarian and isolationist compatriots who should have known better." The new generation of Cold Warrior conservatives knew nothing of the Old Right and had "never even heard of the isolationist alternative."[13]

Determined that they *would* hear of it, Rothbard helped put together an all-peace issue of the magazine *Faith and Freedom*. This was the journal put out by Spiritual Mobilization, a libertarian organization founded in 1935 by the Reverend James W. Fifield, pastor of the 4,500-member First Congregational Church of Los Angeles. Combining opposition to the "social gospel" of left-wing clergymen with radical antistatism, Spiritual Mobilization sought to instill libertarian principles among the (primarily Protestant) clergy and their congregations. Ralph Lord Roy's 1953 book, *Apostles of Discord*, in the chapter titled "God and the 'Libertarians' "— the earliest known attack on the modern libertarian movement— accused the group of embracing "an anarchistic 'libertarianism,' " a charge that many of its leaders were happy to plead guilty to. In spite of the antireligious dogmatism that grips the libertarian movement of today, the largest and most effective libertarian organization of the postwar period was explicitly organized by Christian fundamentalists; Ralph Lord Roy could hardly contain his horror as he detailed the movement's belief in "unregulated laissez-faire capitalism," its opposition to the United Nations and the welfare state, and its characterization of "social gospelers" as advocating "socialized covetousness, stealing, and the bearing of false witness." Worst of all, "all viewpoints that diverge in any particular from the narrow 'libertarianism' of Spiritual Mobilization are sharply condemned as 'anti-God,' 'contrary to the Moral Law,' and 'conducive to statism.' "[14]

In his high school "Autobiography," Rothbard noted that "I was brought up with only rare entrances to temples or synagogues and with no adherence to orthodox customs." The orthodoxy of his mother's parents did not impress him: "my frequent first-hand observations of their adherence to religious traditions does not cause me to change my nonreligious views. Consequently, in my religious beliefs, I am a mixture of an agnostic and a reform Jew."[15]

By this time, the agnosticism was predominant, and Rothbard's secularism was if anything more pronounced. Yet this did not stop him from associating himself with *Faith and Freedom*, a magazine whose writers routinely referred to themselves as libertarians. That one of those writers was Murray Rothbard, writing under the pseudonym "Aubrey Herbert,"[16] was inevitable. In the struggle for liberty—always a lonely one—Rothbard was willing to ally with anyone who agreed on the essential justice of a system based on the sanctity of private property. Whether the source of that sanctity is God, or Natural Law, or some other concept or deity, he thought this ought to be a matter of friendly debate, and that it was possible to disagree about such matters without provoking a split in the coalition. This was always his policy, as part of a conscious strategy to gain as wide an audience for libertarian ideas as possible.

As he explained some years later, he wrote under a pseudonym for two major reasons: "One was . . . not wanting to foul up my Ph.D., etc., until I got it, and two" was the view of Herbert Cornuelle, of the Volker Fund and a chief backer of *Faith and Freedom*, who "also felt that somehow this conflicted with scholarship." In Cornuelle's view, Rothbard's political writing amounted to "pamphleteering." This squeamish attitude when it came to venturing outside the ivory tower and confronting real-world issues was definitely not shared by Rothbard, who nonetheless cloaked his foray into the ideological arena in the guise of a pseudonym. Another reason for "Aubrey Herbert" may have been that, as Rothbard explained some years later, he was named Washington correspondent of *Faith and Freedom* "even though I had never been in Washington and wasn't in Washington during the whole time I was a Washington correspondent." Since he rarely traveled outside Manhattan and environs—for reasons, as we shall see, that were compelling—anybody who really knew him would have seen through the ruse.[17]

ROTHBARD VERSUS THE COLD WARRIORS

As Aubrey Herbert, Rothbard had what he had long wanted: an outlet for his views in a regular column, "Along Pennsylvania Avenue." He took an avid interest in the direction and future of the magazine, and his correspondence with the editor of *Faith and Freedom*, Bill Johnson, a friend of Herbert Cornuelle's from the army, is full of suggestions for articles and a running commentary on national and world events, as well as the goings on inside their own little movement. At Rothbard's suggestion and with his enthusiastic assistance, Johnson put out an issue entirely devoted to pushing isolationism: in "The Suicidal Impulse," Garet Garrett attacked the idea of "imposing universal peace on the world by force" as "a barbarian fantasy." The millionaire industrialist Ernest T. Weir, of the National Steel Corporation, weighed in with an admonition against "charging about the world to free it from bad nations and bad systems of government." "Aubrey Herbert" pointed a finger at "The Real Aggressor": not Commie bogeymen on another continent, but collectivists in power right here at home.[18]

From the tone of this article, it is clear that Rothbard is venting his long-suppressed outrage at recent developments on the Right. Not that he had voluntarily suppressed his views or muted his feelings in fear of alienating his conservative allies; it was only that, up until this point, he had never had an outlet for the expression of his political views. Unleashed by the editors of *Faith and Freedom*, Rothbard gave voice to his frustration and indignation in a lengthy article that for the first time set forth his views—specifically his foreign policy views—in systematic fashion. The piece was aimed at conservatives' "schizophrenic pursuit of both liberty and collectivism." While calling for free trade and free enterprise, Rothbard pointed out that this conflicted with their stance in favor

of a complete embargo on Communist countries: "Have they forgotten that both parties benefit from trade?" The rightist support
for lower taxes and less government is fatally subverted because
"on the other hand they are calling for a virtual holy war against
Russia and China, with all the costliness, death and statism that
such a war would necessarily entail." Once champions of peace
and "isolationism," the conservatives of 1954 "have in truth
become outright internationalists." In their rapid evolution from
America First isolationists to "anti-Communist" internationalists,
American conservatives were caught in their own contradictions:
"The notion—very widespread—that we should not have entered
the Korean War, but once in it should have launched a total war
against China, flouts rules of logic. The best preventive of war is to
refrain from warring—period." In the case of the Korean War, a
cease-fire or (better yet) complete withdrawal "would have saved
thousands of American and Korean lives."[19]

In framing the terms of the debate between the old America
Firsters and the up-and-coming internationalists of the Right,
Rothbard did not spare the delicate sensibilities of his conservative
audience, made up largely of Protestant ministers and their fervently anti-Communist flocks: "Here I think one point should be
made and made bluntly. Some people may prefer death to communism; and this is perfectly legitimate for them—although death
may not often be a solution to any problem. But suppose they also
try to impose their will on other people who might prefer life
under communism to death in a 'free world' cemetery. Is not
forcing them into mortal combat a pure and simple case of
murder? And is not anti-Communist murder as evil as murder
committed by Communists?"[20]

The sudden and inexplicable conservative faith in the perni-
cious doctrine of "collective security" organizations such as NATO
and even the United Nations was a capitulation to the "interna-

tional collectivism [that] has already dragged us into one disastrous war after another during the present century." The right-wing crusade to make the world safe from Communism was little different from the liberal internationalism of the previous century which had promised to make the world safe for democracy. Both implied

> [a] faith in world government, supposedly restricted to the enforcement of so-called world law. This is a fantasy in which the various world states are seen as resembling a family of policemen taking it upon themselves to enforce a preservation of the status quo.[21]

The conservatives of yesteryear foresaw the coming of the New World Order and contemplated the imperial ambitions of its architects with plain horror. Garet Garrett had grimly noted that we are "passing the boundary between Republic and Empire," and John T. Flynn had warned against the rise of a permanent war economy, a militarist machine fueled by inflation and endless wars.[22] Colonel Robert McCormick's *Chicago Tribune*, the voice of midwestern "isolationist" nationalism, had thundered away against the Anglophiles, Russia-Firsters, and miscellaneous world-savers who would submerge America into some supranational entity. In 1954, the battle for the heart and soul of the American Right was going badly for the old isolationists, who were mostly out of action—but it had not yet been completely lost. There was still a chance to turn the tide, and in the tone of Rothbard's piece, with its slashing rhetoric and merciless logic, there is a sense that he knew that this was the final struggle. In making the argument that internationalism even of the ostensibly conservative sort implied a "faith in world government," Rothbard succeeded in simultaneously playing on the strongly nationalist sympathies of his audience and making a crucial point about his theory of the state.

Rothbard made the case against the new interventionism on

two levels. In the realm of empirical fact, he pointed out that the strategy of the Russian Communists was clearly subversion from within rather than military conquest from without. Revolution rather than outright invasion accounted for Communist successes since the end of World War II. He characterized the Korean War as a "civil war, and there is even considerable evidence that it was begun by the South." As for the Chinese, they "intervened not only after the United States did, but only when our troops reached her borders." As a short-term threat, "the Russian military menace is for the most part a bogey" and strictly defensive: in the long term the "Commies," as he calls them, are even less threatening. "We should have no fear of conquest by the Russians, or by the Chinese either," who are backward to begin with and hobbled by "a relatively inefficient economic system." Conservatives were "sinking ever deeper into a war psychosis," fighting the wrong sort of war against an enemy too narrowly defined. "What we really have to combat is all statism, and not just the Communist brand. Taking up arms against one set of Socialists is not the way to stop socialism—indeed it is bound to increase socialism as all modern wars have done." Why are all too many conservatives failing to recognize that "the enemy is statism, rather than simply communism"? "The fundamental reason," writes Rothbard, moving on to the next level of his analysis as easily as a bird takes to flight, "is that there is still an inadequate understanding of the very nature of a state."[23]

While agreeing with conservatives that force is justified in self-defense, Rothbard dissented from the conclusion that this defense can be justly provided by a state. If it is a crime for racketeers to band together and extort money from hapless victims under the threat of coercion, then this activity is not sanctified if the racketeers call their syndicate "the state." The state robs Peter to pay Paul, redistributing its ill-gotten plunder to its sycophants, and "what is worse," complains Rothbard, "the state gang does not even leave

the scene of [the] crime after collecting, as any self-respecting rack-
eteer would do. Instead it hangs around to harass Peter and his
kind, insisting on continually higher sums of money in tribute."
Peter, the prototypical good guy, is "a peaceful citizen, devoted to
productive work and minding his own affairs." The gangsters who
run that protection racket called the state live to exploit and dupe
poor Peter, who persists in aiding and abetting his own enslavement. Robbing him under the rubric of "taxation," "pressing the
Peters into the state army when competing robber bands attack,"
and coercing poor Peter "to regard the decrees of the state as valid
laws to be obeyed by all righteous persons," the racketeers of state
power finally expropriate their subjects' spirit as well as their
worldly possessions. And let's not have any of this nonsense about
"democracy": what a system based on universal suffrage and representative form of government does "is simply . . . increase the
number of state groups: Are we much better off now, having several groups (or parties) of would-be plunderers, each desiring the
control of a good thing? I think the answer must be No."[24]

Having established the essential criminality of all states everywhere, Rothbard outlines the libertarian alternative, a society where
"it is the individual, and not the state, which has the primary choice
as to where and how his defenses shall be maintained." In the midst
of this polemic against warmongering on the Right, Rothbard
sketched in a capsulized portrait of fully free society, in which even
the state's monopoly on defensive force has been completely priva-
tized. In such a society, he points out, an individual "has the right to
fight in his own or another's defense; or, if he adjudges it foolhardy
or disbelieves in fighting altogether, he has the right not to fight at
all. And similarly he has the right to subscribe voluntarily to police
forces and courts which offer defense, but also the right not to subscribe." Citing Nock, he defines the state as "a monopoly (or
attempted monopoly) of crime." Applied to the realm of interna-

tional relations, this theory of the state as an engine of oppression and pillage means that "instead of having a group of policemen, we have in actuality a group of gangster states aggressing against their subject-citizens" and against each other. Recognizing the existence of states as a reality, however evil, with no "likely prospect of their imminent disappearance," libertarian conservatives must face the question of what view to take of these conflicts. Rothbard cites the well-known example of police who "look the other way during a gang war. If one set of gangsters 'aggresses' against another set, the police do not participate. Why waste the taxpayers' money protecting one gangster against another?" Some version of this principle "ought to be applied to foreign affairs."[25]

The libertarian position on war, therefore, is to always minimize the depredations of state terror, to localize the damage done, and to put limits and rules on the conduct of war, outlawing "as many weapons of destruction as possible—starting with the worst." The subjects of warring states have a common interest in peace.

But peace will not be achieved by the United Nations, "for it is the seedling of a *world* state, a master imperialistic power," and committed to the idea of collective security, "and is therefore a warmongering organization in its very essence." In the age of nuclear weapons, the moral imperative of negotiations with the Communist "enemy" was obvious to Rothbard. Without endorsing the selling of peoples into subjection such as at Yalta, Rothbard called for joint disarmament. The United States should get out of the U.N., out of NATO, and, indeed, out of its overseas protectorates in Europe and across Asia. Furthermore, wrote Rothbard, it is high time for the U.S. government to recognize "Red" China. Recognition did not mean moral approval; it merely acknowledged that a state exists, and, as such, "is an act of sanity, not an act of praise." Economic sanctions against Communist states must end: international free trade would do more to break down the iron curtain than any military assault—in addition to benefiting the West.[26]

What is particularly instructive about "The Real Aggressor" is that it shows how Rothbard had basically worked out the essential structure of his philosophical system in the early fifties, from its ethical base (the nonaggression axiom) to his theory of the state and even a theory of international relations. Naturally, this elaboration of a unique position—anarchocapitalism—did not attract the attention of his critics so much as the inflammatory call to recognize "Red" China. This raising of the old isolationist flag, even if for the last time, did not go unnoticed—or unpunished. It aroused the ire of William Henry Chamberlin, the ex-Communist fellow-traveler and ex-isolationist turned rabid Cold Warrior, who wrote a red-baiting attack singling out Rothbard and Weir in the Social Democratic organ, *The New Leader*. Rothbard's piece, charged Chamberlin, "laid down a blueprint for American policy tailor-made to the specifications of the Kremlin."[27]

Replying in a letter to the *New Leader*, Rothbard made the trenchant point that, only a few years earlier—when the alleged enemy was Nazi Germany—Chamberlin had been urging nonintervention, peaceful coexistence, and free trade: and he had been right the first time. The hooliganish rhetoric and tactics characteristic of the ex-Communists in the conservative movement found its full expression in Chamberlin's distortion of Rothbard's foreign policy views, which omitted all mention of the libertarian view of the Yalta agreement. Furthermore, this smear job was nothing new: "From time immemorial, isolationists and pacifists have been smeared by warmongers as being either willing partisans or misguided dupes of the raging subhuman enemy posed for the attack. Mr. Chamberlin's arguments are redolently reminiscent of the World War II war-cry that anyone critical of the Roosevelt foreign policy was 'parroting the Goebbels line.' It is ironic that Mr. Chamberlin . . . was undoubtedly a recipient of these blows himself." As "the author of *America's Second Crusade*,[28] a work challenging the wisdom of U.S. intervention in World War II, as well as a contributor to *Perpetual War for Perpetual Peace*,[29] a book edited by one of our leading 'wrongheaded appeasers' [Professor Harry Elmer Barnes]," Chamberlin was in no position to denounce all peace efforts as "another Munich." "But perhaps," remarked Rothbard, "this is all we can expect from a man with the ideological elasticity to be a regular contributor both to the *New Leader* and to the *Wall Street Journal*."[30]

Chamberlin lashed back, noting that Weir had recently been lauded in *Trybuna Ludu*, the Warsaw Communist Party newspaper, and that no doubt Rothbard would "soon receive his appropriate recognition from the same or a similar source."[31]

The experience of being red-baited was certainly a novel one for Rothbard. However, the novelty would wear off all too soon. He had always considered himself to be on the far right side of the political spectrum, and now he found himself under attack from a growing legion of ex-Communists turned "conservative," whose program was unadulterated militarism and whose methods never rose above character assassination.

Embarked on a one-man crusade to restore the Old Right tradition of peace, nonintervention, and America First, Rothbard took up the cudgels with both hands. Month after month in *Faith and Freedom* he hammered away at the interventionist conservatives: recognize "Red" China, start meaningful disarmament talks with the Soviet Union, get out of the U.N., free the captive nations of the American Empire, Hawaii, Alaska, and Puerto Rico. Before the Cold Warrior consensus on the Right had time to harden into a dogma, Rothbard made the case against imperialism in libertarian terms: citing Randolph Bourne's dictum that "war is the health of the state," Rothbard made the vital point that, for libertarians, the enemy is right here at home: it is our own State, and not any foreign government, that taxes us into poverty, plunders the economy, and regulates us within an inch of our lives. Not content with having subjugated the United States to a tyrannical federal power, America's ruling elite now sought to extend that power over the rest of the world—a monstrous possibility that had to be stopped.

In a few years, such a column could not appear in any conservative periodical; but for a while, Rothbard let them have it. It wasn't until 1955, when he scored another hit on the powerful China lobby, that the ax came down. In his March column, Rothbard confronted the China lobby head on and dared to ask: Why fight for Formosa? How would *we* feel, he asked, if the Chinese had a military base bristling with weaponry a few miles off our shoreline? He pointed out that no less a figure than General Douglas MacArthur, the hero of the hard right, had urged a peaceful resolution of the Formosa crisis, and praised Rep. Eugene R. Stiler (R-Ky.), who had voted "nay" on the blank-check resolution of January 29 because he had promised the voters he would never "engage their boys in war on foreign soil."[32]

This article, printed at a time when the China lobby was pressing for war with Beijing over Formosa, led to a contretemps with Willi Schlamm, also a columnist for *Faith and Freedom*. Schlamm was yet another ex-Commie turned "conservative" whose sole preoccupation was conducting a holy war of retribution against his former comrades. Once the editor of *Rote Fahne* (Red Flag), the official newspaper of the German Communist Party, Schlamm was typical of the ex-Communist breed that was flocking into the conservative movement at the time: as Rothbard put it, "I could never—and still cannot—detect one iota of devotion to freedom in Schlamm's world view."[33]

In a series of two debates, Rothbard accused Schlamm of calling for a preventive war, while pointing out that the United States had not been attacked by either Russia or China. He also pointed out that war would mean the total destruction of human civilization, and asked: is Formosa worth it? He asked again a question repeated often in his *Faith and Freedom* columns: "why do the prowar conservatives, supposedly dedicated to the superiority of capitalism over Communism, by thirsting for an immediate showdown, implicitly grant that time is on the side of the Communist system?"[34]

Rothbard, of course, knew otherwise: as a Misesian, the economic impossibility of Communism was, for him, a given: Mises had long ago proved that prices could not be calculated under socialism, and that the whole structure of socialist society must inevitably collapse. It was only a matter of time.[35]

To Schlamm, of course—who had no interest in economics, free market or otherwise—none of this mattered. All that he was interested in was purging the Right of the isolationist remnants and clearing the way for World War III. Disdainfully citing Rothbard's contention that since communism is inefficient, "therefore time is on the side of a free economy," Schlamm writes: "I should like to call this 'therefore' the suicidal particle in the libertarian grammar. That freedom stimulates productivity is a meaningful statement only in a society which puts productivity above any other social goal. If you want the lurid but quite real satisfactions of herd existence, you can do beautifully without freedom, and its corollary, unfettered productivity; so long, that is, as you produce the commodities of military strength. . . . The trouble with libertarian economists," he sneered, "is that they presume everybody else to be guided by their own genteel value system (in which productivity excels). They are right as economists, but fatally wrong as theologians: they do not perceive that the Devil is real and that he can generously satisfy powerful human cravings."[36]

As it turned out, the Devil, in the form of the Communist rulers, could not begin to satisfy the powerful cravings of the people for the ordinary comforts of a free and prosperous society. Rothbard and his "genteel value system" were right, and the theologians of Schlamm's stripe were wrong, but this was far from obvious at the time. The Cold War was in full swing and the image of a mighty Soviet Union—partly the result of official U.S. propaganda during the war, when "Uncle" Joe Stalin was our staunch ally—dominated the popular consciousness. The isolationist remnant of the Old Right was fighting an uphill battle.

Rothbard was not Schlamm's only target: Chodorov, Rothbard's predecessor as Washington correspondent of *Faith and Freedom*, also came under vicious attack from this early ancestor of today's "neo"-conservatives.

In March 1951, the ideological independence of the libertarian movement had been seriously compromised by Chodorov's unfortunate decision to merge *Analysis*, which never had more than four thousand subscribers, with *Human Events*, then a modest newsletter run out of Washington, D.C., by Frank Hanighen, Felix Morley, and Henry Regnery. The only voice of the pure libertarian creed had been submerged in the conservative movement. As an associate editor of *Human Events*, Chodorov's monthly articles were more topical than had been his custom in the old *Analysis*. However, in the fall of 1954, he took over the editorship of *The Freeman*, then the premier magazine for conservative intellectuals. As a measure of the decline of intellect in general on the Right, *The Freeman*, previously a weekly, was at this point coming out every month under the auspices of the Foundation for Economic Education.

It wasn't too long before Schlamm and his warhawks, including William F. Buckley Jr. swooped down on Chodorov; in the November 1954 *Freeman*, Chodorov and Schlamm had it out. We must abandon freedom for this generation, argued Schlamm, in order to preserve it for future generations. In reply, the man who had stood up to war hysteria when it came from the Left warned of another dark age about to descend, this one authored by the Right. The last war had deprived us of our liberties, economic and civil, and ushered in the postwar national security-welfare state:

> All this the "isolationists" of 1940 foresaw. Not because they were endowed with any gift of prevision, but because they knew history and would not deny its lesson: that during war the state acquires power at the expense of freedom, and that because of its insatiable lust for power the state is incapable of giving up any of it. The state never abdicates.[37]

As if to underscore Chodorov's point, which today seems prescient, Buckley joined the fray, declaring that yes, indeed, big government—"even with Truman at the helm of it all"—was inevitable and desirable until the final victory over the Kremlin.[38]

Chodorov was shortly afterward ousted as editor of *The Freeman* by the Trustees of the Board of FEE who took the Schlamm line. Fifteen years earlier, he had been the victim of a similar purge, fired as editor of another periodical called *The Freeman* (in this case, the official organ of the Georgist Single Tax group), and for the very same reason: his refusal to jump on the prowar bandwagon.[39]

At *Faith and Freedom*, Rothbard hung on a bit longer—but not much longer. The final defeat of the Taft forces in the Republican party in 1952 by the Eastern establishment had effectively driven Rothbard out of the GOP, and he had been agitating for a third party for years. The takeover of the Republican party by the Eastern Eisenhower wing finally drove him into the waiting arms of . . . Adlai Stevenson! While giving formal support in 1956 to the third-party ticket of T. Coleman Andrews (Eisenhower's former IRS commissioner who came out for repealing the income tax), and, for vice president, former congressman Thomas Werdel (R-CA), Rothbard told his *Faith and Freedom* readers that, in any contest between the two major candidates, Stevenson was infinitely preferable to Eisenhower.

To the purely economic libertarians of the present-day, and their equivalents in 1956, such a position seemed incomprehensible: how could a laissez-faire libertarian and self-described right-winger like Rothbard support a liberal Democrat for the highest office in the land? On domestic issues, there was little difference between the major candidates: both called for a continuation of the postwar New Deal–Fair Deal policy of welfare statism. On the vital foreign policy front, however, there were significant areas of divergence. Ike, the personification of Republican internationalism, was committed to fighting the Cold War. Stevenson called for a ban on nuclear arms tests and vigorously opposed the draft. As far as Rothbard was concerned, there was absolutely no contest: it was Stevenson all the way. Though its fabric was tattered and its symbols went unrecognized in this age of ignorance, the banner of the Old Right was yet held high by Rothbard.

After the election, Bill Johnson, the editor of *Faith and Freedom*, flew East to inform Rothbard that his column was being dropped. While Johnson himself had always approved and supported Rothbard's writings for the magazine, the readership, which consisted mostly of Protestant ministers of a highly conservative coloration, "had come to the conclusion that I was a 'Communist.' " Rothbard's protestation that he "had consistently attacked government, and defended the individual," month in and month out, "and how could this possibly be Communist" went unheard and unheeded.[40]

THE CIRCLE BASTIAT

Most of the up-and-coming libertarians and conservatives of that period were obsessed with the "Communist conspiracy" and knew nothing of their Old Right heritage. But a few had a different perspective, one they in large part acquired through Rothbard. A group of young people he had met at the New York University Mises seminar came to know, love, and be profoundly influenced by the man they invariably referred to as Murray. Most were then high school seniors, and one, Leonard Liggio, was a sophomore at Georgetown University. Some of this group had formed a Cobden Club at the Bronx High School of Science. They went citywide during the 1952 GOP primary, coalescing around the Youth for Taft organization in New York City, and constituted a very informal group known as the Circle Bastiat, named after the nineteenth-century French theorist of laissez-faire.

In addition to Rothbard and his wife, Joey, the Circle Bastiat consisted of Leonard Liggio, Ralph Raico, George Reisman, Robert Hessen, Ronald Hamowy, and Fred Preisinger. Virtually all were destined for distinction in the world of academia and libertarian scholarship, although some would eventually choose divergent paths. But for the moment, they were a happy—even rollicking—group of friends who held endless discussions, went to the movies, sang and composed songs, played board games, and, according to Rothbard, "joked about how we would be treated by 'future historians.' "[41]

For Rothbard, the songs were an important part of the mix. He loved music, from Gregorian chants to the popular tunes of the twenties and thirties, and was wont to burst into song with minimal provocation. Both the libertarian politics and radical spirit of the Circle Bastiat were audible in the lyrics, exuberantly sung by this merry band of anarchists. The "Circle Theme," sung to the tune of "America the Beautiful," set the tone:

> It's ours to right the great wrong done, ten thousand
>   years ago.
> The State, conceived in blood and hate, remains

our only foe.
O, Circle Brothers, Circle brothers,
    victory is nigh.
Come meet your fate, destroy the State,
    and raise the banner high.[42]

Rothbard tried his hand at songwriting, but Ralph Raico "was unquestionably our Major Poet." In the last years of his life, Rothbard remembered the words to these "fight songs," every stanza and verse: "Several themes can be noted," he remarked: "megalomania, black banners, and references to 'Circle brothers,' since there were almost no females in the group, with Joey being the only core woman."[43] "The Battle Hymn of Freedom," sung to the tune of "The Battle Hymn of the Republic," serves up libertarian ideology with a flourish of black banners waving in the breeze, and one can almost hear it echoing down through the years, defiantly, joyously subversive:

Look up there, Circle brothers, see the black banners unfurled,
How they wave in expectation of a new and better world.
The lines are drawn, the ranks are firm, the challenge has
    Been hurled.
The Circle marches on.
Vict'ry, vict'ry lies before us (repeat twice)
The Circle marches on.

In this prophetic hymn, Raico radiates the sunny optimism that infused this tiny group of radical free-marketeers, celebrating the downfall of Communism and statism-in-retreat forty years early:

One by one the States are dying, see the age-old monsters fall,
As the world resounds in answer to the Circle's trumpet call.
We'll not rest until all States are gone and men are freemen all,

Onward, onward Circle brothers (repeat twice)
For that day lies at hand.

These "fight songs," as Rothbard referred to them, were sung in
the midst of a real political fight. As the Old Right faded away, and
the New Right of William F. Buckley Jr. and *National Review* moved
in to fill the vacuum, the populist spirit and militant antistatism of
the older creed had one last burst of defiance, one final gesture of
contempt for their conquerors. The charismatic if flawed personality of Senator Joseph McCarthy attracted the same following as
the old America First movement, with the *Chicago Tribune* and all
the previously vilified opponents of Roosevelt's war in the front
lines of a spirited defense of McCarthy against the liberal-estab-
lishment counterattack. In his later writings, Rothbard is a bit hard
on himself and his fellow libertarians of the time for underesti-
mating the transformative effects of domestic red-baiting on the
foreign policy of the country. In retrospect, it seemed to him
obvious that a campaign directed at Commies on the home front
would have to mean, eventually, an armed crusade against their
foreign paymasters. But there were other, more compelling reasons
for Rothbard and his circle to take up the cause of Tail-Gunner Joe
and his embattled comrades-in-arms, Roy Cohn and David Schine.

The occasion for this defense was noted in an essay by the
phony "conservative" Peter Viereck, who held the unofficial post,
during the fifties, of the Left's favorite rightist, on account of his
thoroughly statist and fanatically Anglophilic views. Viereck's "The
Revolt Against the Elite," published in 1955, was included in an
anthology, *The Radical Right*, edited by Daniel Bell, in which the
assembled intellectual giants of the New York Left diagnosed the
growing movement against big government as symptomatic of
"status resentment," paranoia, and a predilection for the psy-
chopolitical pathology of fascism and Nazism.[44]

McCarthyism, according to Viereck, was "the same old isolationist, Anglophobe, Germanophile revolt of radical Populist lunatic-fringers against the Eastern, educated, Anglicized elite." But, says Viereck, "Bigotry's New Look" was exemplified by

> a McCarthy mass meeting in the North at which racial discrimination was denounced as un-American and in which anyone defending civil liberties against McCarthy was called Communistic. At the same meeting, a rabbi accused the opposition to Roy Cohn of anti-Semitic intolerance. Next, Cohn's was called "the American Dreyfus Case" by a representative of the student McCarthyite organization, Students for America.[45]

The occasion was a rally at the Hotel Astor, in New York, on July 28, 1954, where such right-wing notables as Godfrey P. Schmidt, Colonel Archibald Roosevelt, George Sokolsky, Alfred Kohlberg, William F. Buckley Jr., and Rabbi Benjamin Schultz spoke out in defense of McCarthy, Cohn, and Schine. The speech quoted above was delivered by George Reisman, and written by Rothbard; its original flavor was somewhat lost in Viereck's translation. The haughty Viereck, who hated all populism, worshipped England, and made a career for a while out of being the favored domesticated "rightist" in the leftists' academic harem, naturally was shocked by the radical populism emanating from that podium. What, asked Reisman, was the *real* reason for the intensity of the hatred against McCarthy, Cohn, et al.? The Rothbardian answer: an assault on domestic Reds in the American government directly threatened the "Socialists and New Dealers, who have been running our political life for the last twenty-one years, and are *still* running it!" This brought the crowd of 1,500 to its feet: "As the *Chicago Tribune* aptly put it," continued Reisman, "the Case of Roy Cohn is the American Dreyfus Case. As Dreyfus was redeemed, so will Roy

Cohn when the American people have taken back their government from the criminal alliance of Communists, Socialists, New
Dealers, and Eisenhower–Dewey Republicans."[46]

While the liberal intellectuals of the mid-fifties were proclaiming "the End of Ideology," and predicting that no extreme
currents of left or right would ever again disturb the stagnant
waters of the centrist swamp, Rothbard took great pleasure in
thumbing his nose at this fatuous conceit. The Reisman speech was
meant to horrify Viereck and his crowd, and indeed one can practically hear Rothbard cackling delightedly as he composed and
read the text to his coconspirators in the Circle Bastiat. In any
event, Viereck *was* horrified by what he called "this outburst of
direct democracy" which "comes straight from the leftist rhetoric
of the old Populists and Progressives, a rhetoric forever urging the
People to take back 'their' government from the conspiring
Powers That Be."[47]

The Reisman speech stole the show, and all the New York
papers[48] carried the story about the seventeen-year-old who wowed
the McCarthyites, with the *New York Journal American* remarking
that he received "the loudest acclaim" and the *New York World
Telegram* giving a breathlessly admiring account of the incident,
which was dolefully but dutifully reported in *Time* magazine.[49]
Rothbard was genuinely moved by the experience: "You should
have heard the cheers for almost every line of that speech—people
leaped to their feet, shouted for more, in a terrific demonstration. I
never expected that this would happen: I thought surely that the
bitter denunciations—and I wrote the speech in a fine lather—of
socialism, of the Eisenhower administration, etc.—would shock the
masses there. But they didn't. On the contrary, the masses loved it!
Those who were shocked were the self-anointed leaders."[50]

Rothbard believed that the corporate liberal elite of the
postwar period—drawn from big business, big labor, and liberal

Ivy League intellectuals—"could only be overthrown by educating a new generation of intellectuals." But that was a long-term strategy; in the short run, however, "the only hope to dislodge this new ruling elite was a populist short-circuit."

> There was a vital need to appeal directly to the masses, emotionally, even demagogically, *over the heads* of the Establishment: of the Ivy League, the mass media, the liberal intellectuals, of the Republican-Democrat political party structure.[51]

McCarthy filled that need. Rothbard's quip to the Circle Bastiat at the time was that, unlike the anti-Communist liberals, who approved McCarthy's ends but not his "radical and demagogic" means, libertarians could enthusiastically endorse his means (a "radical assault on the nation's power structure") if not his ends.[52]

In the darkest days of the libertarian movement, when virtually all traces of organized opposition to the welfare-warfare state had been wiped out, with the Old Right decimated by death and defection, it is little short of amazing that Rothbard could maintain this kind of optimism. For that was the operative factor in his support for the McCarthyite crusade to "take back America"—a familiar phrase that rings down through the years, uttered by various voices. Each time, Rothbard embraced this new antigovernment populism, whether of the right or the left, as it developed; the "reactionary" rage at the liberal elites of the fifties, a "leftist" rebellion against this same elite during the Vietnam era, and, later still, the "rightist" revolutionary upsurge against the federal Leviathan. Each time, hope seized him, buoyed him up and reinforced his natural optimism, his belief that liberty would *have* to triumph in the end simply because it is *right*.

Rothbard's political enthusiasms were born of his eternal optimism: they sprouted over the years as fast as they wilted. While his basic stance and loyalties remained largely unchanged since 1950, toward the end of the decade and the beginning of the next the old categories of Left and Right began to blur and dissolve. Rothbard, the Old Rightist, found himself adrift, a stranger in a strange land, a political and ideological orphan in search of his long-lost home.

NOTES

1. Murray N. Rothbard to Russell Bliss, 14 February 1952, p. 1.

2. Ibid., p. 2. Emphasis in original.

3. Rothbard to Richard Cornuelle, 5 February 1952, p. 2.

4. Rothbard to David Rothbard, 23 January 1952, p. 1.

5. Ibid.

6. Rothbard to David Rothbard, 6 February 1952.

7. Murray N. Rothbard, "Buckley Revealed: Review of William F. Buckley Jr.'s 'A Young Republicans' View,' " [*The Commonweal*, January 25, 1952] *The Vigil* no. 3 (May 1952).

8. Murray N. Rothbard, "Enemies and Friends of the Public Schools," *The Vigil* no. 3 (May 1952).

9. Murray N. Rothbard, "Quizzing Foundations," *The Vigil* no. 3 (May 1952).

10. Murray N. Rothbard, "The International Bankers Versus the Taxpayer," *The Vigil* no. 3 (May 1952). Emphasis in original.

11. Ibid.

12. Richard Cornuelle to Rothbard, January 9, 1952.

13. Murray N. Rothbard, "The Betrayal of the American Right," unpublished manuscript, p. 134.

14. Ralph Lord Roy, *Apostles of Discord* (Boston: Beacon Press, 1953), pp. 285–307.

15. Rothbard, "My Autobiography," unpublished manuscript, p. 6.

16. The reference is to Auberon Herbert, the nineteenth-century British libertarian, which Rothbard felt certain was obscure enough to escape detection.

17. Interview with Walter Block and Walter Grinder, "Rothbard Tells All," unpublished transcript in possession of author, p. 8.

18. "Aubrey Herbert" [Murray N. Rothbard], "The Real Aggressor," *Faith and Freedom* (April 1954).

19. Ibid., p. 23.

20. Ibid.

21. Ibid., p.24.

22. See Garet Garrett, *The People's Pottage* (Caldwell, Idaho: Caxton Printers, 1953). See also John T. Flynn, *As We Go Marching* (New York: Doubleday, 1944).

23. Ibid.

24. Rothbard, "The Real Aggressor," p. 24.

25. Ibid., p. 25.

26. Ibid., p. 27.

27. William Henry Chamberlin, "Appeasement on the Right," *The New Leader* (May 15, 1954).

28. William Henry Chamberlin, *America's Second Crusade* (Chicago: Henry Regnery Company, 1950)

29. Harry Elmer Barnes, ed., *Perpetual War for Perpetual Peace* (Caldwell, Idaho: The Caxton Printers, 1953), pp. 483–554.

30. Rothbard to *The New Leader*, 31 May 1954.

31. *The New Leader* (June 25, 1954).

32. Aubrey Herbert [Murray N. Rothbard], "Fight for Formosa or Not?" *Faith and Freedom* (May and June 1955).

33. Rothbard, "The Betrayal of the American Right," p. 141.

34. Ibid., pp. 141–42.

35. As it turned out, far less time than even the most optimistic libertarians imagined, Rothbard included.

36. William Schlamm, "Fight for Formosa," *Faith and Freedom* (June 1955): 18.

37. Frank Chodorov, "The Return of 1940?" *The Freeman* (September 1954).

38. William F. Buckley Jr., "A Young Republican's View," *Commonweal* (January 25, 1952).

39. Chodorov's always precarious financial condition was made worse by the illness that practically debilitated him in the last years of his life.

40. Rothbard, "The Betrayal of the American Right," p. 150.

41. Ibid., p. 151.

42. Rothbard to Kate Dalton, undated letter (mid-90s).

43. Ibid.

44. Daniel Bell, ed., *The New American Right* (New York: Criterion Books, 1955); revised edition, *The Radical Right* (New York: Anchor Books, 1964).

45. Ibid., p. 166.

46. Rothbard, "The Betrayal of the American Right," p. 164.

47. Bell, *The Radical Right*, p. 167.

48. "McCarthy Says He'll Keep Cohn As Advisor," *New York Herald Tribune*, 29 July 1954; "2,000 Honor Cohn at Dinner in Astor. Pay Homage Also to Sen. McCarthy," *World Telegram and Sun*, 29 July 1954; "Cohn Pledged to Continue As McCarthy Consultant," *New York Journal-American*, 29 July 1954, all played up the Reisman speech.

49. "One Enchanted Evening," *Time*, 9 August 1954, p. 15.

50. Rothbard to Richard C. Cornuelle, 11 August 1954, p. 6.

51. Rothbard, "The Betrayal of the American Right," pp. 161–62. Emphasis in original.

52. Ibid.

3

THREE ENCOUNTERS

Mises, Buckley, and Rand

Rothbard's overriding conviction that the apparent gloom of the present only concealed the coming dawn of a new day motivated him in another sense. While the give-and-take of current political events continued to fascinate and engage him throughout his life, these concerns only reflected an ideological commitment on a deeper level. For while he was attacking the depredations of the China Lobby, dueling with Schlamm, and fighting a valiant (if rearguard) action against the ex-Communist takeover of the Right, he was also writing *Man, Economy, and State*, the book that established him as the leading American economist of the "Austrian" School.

THE MISES SEMINAR

Rothbard, the happy warrior, carried on the struggle on many levels at once, devoting the morning to an article debunking the lies of the China Lobby, and in the evening demolishing the methodology of the mathematical economists, making mincemeat of "econometrics." While doing battle with Schlamm and Buckley in the pages of *Faith and Freedom* and defending the foreign policy (and the honor) of the Old Right, he was also taking on the critics of Mises in the professional journals.[1]

During these years the axis of Rothbard's intellectual and personal life really was the Mises seminar, the focus of much of his energy, and he regularly detailed its progress in his correspondence: "Recently," he confided to Richard Cornuelle, "the Mises seminar had a very good attendance. We've been discussing history, capitalism, revolution, and allied topics. We have quite a bloc now of people who are considerably to the right of Mises, and when Mises has a particularly fertile insight, we tend to pick it up, discuss, and develop its right-wing implications. For example, when Mises criticized the sort of approach of Beard's *Economic Interpretation of the Constitution*, we started questioning Mises closely. George Koether forced Mises to admit that Beard's foreign policy researches were good; I brought out that it is certainly a plausible hypothesis that state bondholders would favor a Constitution on the expectation of Federal assumption of these depreciated bonds, etc. In general, there is a strong 'extreme right-wing' tone to the assembly, far more than in earlier years. Last session, for example, we had in attendance [Percy] Greaves, [George Koether], Bettina [Greaves], myself, [George] Reisman, [Ralph] Raico, . . . and Bill Peterson with Felix Wittmer. . . . Plus this there were the standard perennials: the Lawyer, the Mongolian Idiot, etc. I think there was only one guy who is an 'outsider,' and he must be bewildered indeed at the goings-on. Last week, we were talking about falsifying history, and Percy led the attack on FDR and Pearl Harbor; the outsider muttered something about the people supporting Lend-Lease, and a half-dozen of us squelched him. Afterwards, good old George Koether wanted to know: 'Who is that Marxist plant?' "[2]

The Mises seminar, in stark contrast to the rest of the world during the grim fifties, was a libertarian refuge where serious thought and discussion flourished—and where a young Ralph Raico could joke about how Mises is "the extreme left-wing" of the libertarian movement. While the exact identity of "The Lawyer" and "The Mongolian Idiot" is lost in the mists of time, the increasing renown of Mises and his circle was reflected in the growth of the seminar and the high quality of the students. "The Court of St. Ludwig is proceeding very well, thank you," wrote Rothbard to Ludwig Lachmann in 1957:

> Mises never fails to amaze me. He gets more alert and sprightly and incisive every year, and this is the seventh or eighth year I've attended. My fondest hope is to be as alert as he is at his age, but since he has twice as much energy as I have now the hope is rather dim. Since I love Mises dearly, I am happy to say that part of his good spirits comes from the growth in the number of his disciples since he began. Most of them are very young. . . . Another thing is that, for the first time, Mises is surrounded by a group of disciples *further to the right than he is*!! Whereas formerly Mises' disciples were always straining leftward, now Mises suddenly finds himself being "pushed to the Right," and I can assure you that he is not chagrined. Whereas when Mises first came to America he had to battle groups of Leftist students, he now finds himself surrounded by a group of fractious and determined followers, eager to spear to the wall any stray Leftist who happens to wander into the precincts.[3]

In 1956, Rothbard's famous "In Defense of Extreme Apriorism" raised the banner of the pure Misesian "praxeological" approach, defending the radical proposition that all economics can be deduced from a single axiom, the concept of human action, and a few empirical postulates that are hardly "empirical" in that they are self-evident.[4] In a previous series of polemics between Fritz Machlup and Terence Hutchison, the latter had accused the former of being a secret advocate of the Misesian "extreme apriorist" position in the methodological debate. To which Rothbard replied: if you want the *real* "extreme apriorism," then here it is! In a trenchant and elegant article, Rothbard not only took on the two varieties of empiricism represented by Machlup and Hutchison, but also set out his own slightly modified version of the Misesian-praxeologic method, starting with the Fundamental Axiom (Action), and its twin postulates (diversity of resources and leisure as a consumer good). In elucidating the issue of whether or not firms are always attempting to maximize their profits, Rothbard makes the important point that "from our Axiom is derived this absolute truth: that every firm aims always at maximizing its *psychic* profit." This is not necessarily a money-profit, and "when an entrepreneur deliberately accepts lower money profits in order to give a good job to a ne'er-do-well nephew, the praxeologist is not confounded." Hutchison had charged that the founder of the neo-Austrian school had slipped "wholesale political conclusions" into the body of an allegedly "value-free" science. Rothbard retorted that economic science can only establish the existence of "if-then" propositions or "existential laws." *If* this action is taken, *then* certain results will follow. Economics is concerned exclusively with the fact that men must employ certain means to achieve certain ends. While making no valuation of the particular ends, the praxeologist confines himself to analyzing the means utilized to achieve a particular goal. In studying economics, the goals of most human beings are abundance and harmony, but "perhaps Mises is overly sanguine in judging the extent of such unity," retorts Rothbard. "Those who choose contrasting goals . . . who, through envy, judge social equality as more worthwhile than general abundance or liberty would certainly not accept liberalism, and Mises would certainly never say that economic science proves them wrong." The role of the economist is merely to apprise the citizenry "of the consequences of various political actions." It is "the citizen's province, knowing these consequences, to choose his political course."[5]

On the theoretical front, Rothbard was at this time very much concerned with waging the war against the methodological absurdities of modern economics, especially training his fire on its scientistic conceits. In 1960, Rothbard's "The Mantle of Science" was published.[6] In this major essay, the author not only attacks the importation of the methods of the physical sciences into the study of man (and economics), but outlines—succinctly and elegantly—the praxeologic alternative, its axioms and postulates, as well as its social, economic, and political implications. What this wholesale transfer ignores, says Rothbard, is that human beings, unlike electrons, photons, the weather, and the stars in the sky, possess consciousness and free will. Rothbard shows that all attempts to deny free will necessarily assume its existence. Scientism denies the existence of individual consciousness by borrowing analogies from biology and physics: man is either part of an organic whole, or a photon set on its predetermined orbit around another will-less subatomic particle. In both cases, the result is the obliteration of the acting, thinking, individual consciousness. In language clear as a freshly washed windowpane, Rothbard condenses complex concepts without losing clarity or color—and certainly without losing his sense of humor. Rothbard's rogues' gallery of false mechanical analogies is the author at his polemical best. The idea of man as some kind of servomechanism "reverses reality by attributing determinism to men and free will to physical particles." If human beings are just machines, then "who created man and for what purpose?—a rather embarrassing question for materialists to answer." On the concept of "social engineering," a conceit which is, today, in disrepute, but was once a popular leftist analogy, Rothbard quotes FDR advisor Rex Tugwell's "The Dreamer," an infamous ode to the New Deal:

> I have gathered my tools and my charts
> My plans are finished and practical.
> I shall roll up my sleeves—make America over.[7]

"One wonders," adds Rothbard, "whether his admiring readers thought themselves to be among the directing engineers or among the raw material that would be 'made over.' "[8]

The tools that the planners would use to "make America over"—"model-building" and econometrics, calculus and colorful charts—are allegedly the products of value-free "science." But these instruments measure nothing but the prejudices of their creators. In the intellectual atmosphere of 1960, the scientistic conceit was riding high (if not higher than today), and social scientists were eagerly denying the meaningful existence of individuals:

> The psychologists deny consciousness, the economists deny economics, and the political theorists deny political philosophy. What they affirm is the existence and primacy of social wholes: "society," the "collective," the "group," the "nation." The individual, they assert, must be value-free himself, but must take his values from "society."

The social and political implications of scientism are clear: "It is hardly sheer coincidence," concluded Rothbard, "that the political views of the two opposing camps tend to be individualist and collectivist, respectively."[9]

Rothbard's discussion of the "organismic analogies of scientism" is illuminating, particularly his example of the case of international trade. He points out that, during the era of the gold standard, "how often did the cry go up that 'England' or 'France' or some other country was in mortal danger because 'it' was 'losing gold'?" In reality, individuals were "voluntarily shipping gold overseas and thus threatening the banks in those countries with the necessity of meeting obligations (to pay in gold) which they could not possibly fulfill. But the use of the organismic metaphor converted a grave problem of banking into a vague national crisis for which every citizen was somehow responsible."

In a footnote to this vital point, Rothbard goes on to argue that a similar metaphor is put to the same propagandistic uses in foreign policy matters, masking bloody and self-interested policies behind an organismic facade. He illustrates this point with a long quote from Parker Thomas Moon's classic book, *Imperialism and World Politics*: Moon saw the organismic fallacy as an attempt to "conceal the facts and make international relations a glamorous drama in which personalized nations are the actors," forgetting "the flesh-and-blood men and women who are the true actors"—and the true victims who perish in anonymity.[10]

Another foray onto the battlefield of methodology was "The Politics of Political Economists," in which Rothbard defends Mises against Professor George J. Stigler, who challenged the Misesian claim that quantitative economics and socialism are necessarily linked. Rothbard's article is a masterly theoretical and historical analysis of the role of statistics as an adjunct of government policy and central planning.[11]

Mises admired his student's polemical skill, and, in his review of *Man, Economy, and State*, remarks that "in every chapter of his treatise," Rothbard "adopt[s] the best of the teachings of his predecessors, and adds to them highly important observations."[12] One such observation, as Misesian scholar David Gordon points out, is Rothbard's debunking of the idea that "monopolistic" firms will inevitably dominate a free market, broadening the Misesian economic calculation argument against socialism to define the natural limits on the size of private firms. On the related subject of so-called monopoly prices, Rothbard points out that, since there is no objective price somehow inherent in a product, there is "therefore no way of distinguishing, even conceptually, any given price as a 'monopoly price.' "[13]

It is interesting to note, in *Man, Economy, and State*, the *style* of the author's personality at work: Gordon observes that Rothbard's critique of conventional welfare economics rejects hypothetical "preference scales, refusing to budge from the firm ground of the way people in fact behave. The case is quite similar for monopoly prices: he wants to be shown an *actual* monopoly price, not some hypothetical construct. . . . More generally, we can see the same personality trait [operating] through Rothbard's work in economic theory. The constant insistence on 'apodictic' truth (another favorite phrase of his) manifests the personality of a man who demands ironclad standards of rigor in argument."[14]

Rothbard's book raised the question, as Mises put it, "for whom are essays of this consequence written?" Is economics a realm of interest only to a few specialists, like the study of electricity, or is it "for all of the people"? Mises recognized in Rothbard the fusion of the scholar and the intellectual entrepreneur, the one who could bridge the distance between the rarefied circles of Austrian economists and the masses. At the end of his review of what he calls Rothbard's "epochal contribution to the general science of human action," Mises launches into a stirring call to "avoid the destruction of Western civilization and the relapse into primitive wretchedness [by] chang[ing] the mentality of our fellow citizens."[15]

Mises himself did not appear to have much hope for what he called "the masses of semibarbarians led by the self-styled intellectuals, [who] entirely ignore everything that economics has brought forward." Their ignorance "is the main political problem of our age. There is no use in deceiving ourselves."[16] Perhaps contrasting his own somewhat saturnine temperament with Rothbard's eternal optimism, Mises clearly saw in his student an intellectual catalyst, capable not only of enduring the intellectual and political isolation he himself had experienced, but of breaking out of it. Hope was in short supply, for libertarians in those days, but Rothbard managed to find it, to seek out and take full advantage of any opening to make the case for liberty.

NATIONAL REVIEW AND THE BUCKLEY CIRCLE

With the Old Right an increasingly dim memory—which had in any case been relegated to the Orwellian Memory Hole by the arbiters of official history—*National Review*, a magazine started by William F. Buckley Jr. and staffed by a coven of ex-Communists such as James Burnham and the omnipresent Willi Schlamm, increasingly came to dominate the Right. For the first five years of its existence, Rothbard moved in *National Review* circles, writing a dozen or so book reviews, attending various events, and generally keeping in touch with Buckley and his associates. Rothbard had worked with *National Review* editor Frank S. Meyer at the Volker Fund, and they had been great friends ever since. According to Rothbard, there was talk, at one point, of his becoming the magazine's economic columnist. But this association, always tenuous, turned out to be fleeting. For how long could a man who put opposition to war at the top of his political agenda mingle in circles where it was possible for one *National Review* editor to argue with his wife over whether or not we should "drop the H-bomb on Moscow and destroy the Soviet Union *immediately*, or should we give the Soviet regime twenty-four hours with which to comply with an ultimatum to resign"?[17]

Rothbard's assigned role in the *National Review*-dominated Right was, as he put it, "that of a lovable though Utopian libertarian purist" whose views on matters other than economics were not to be seriously entertained. As long as he stuck to economic policy matters, the Buckley crowd thought of him as charmingly eccentric; but as the Cold War heated up and the Buckleyized Right agitated for a military showdown with the Soviet Union, Rothbard "was increasingly unwilling to play that kind of a castrate role."[18]

However, it appears from the correspondence between the two that Rothbard never did play "a castrate role," and was critical of Buckley's foreign interventionism from the start. "As you are no doubt aware," wrote Rothbard to the editor of the newly founded *National Review* magazine in the summer of 1956,

> I have never been happy with the foreign policy position of *National Review* . . . since I believed it to be inconsistent with the Right's supposed libertarian philosophy. However, as I understand it, you are willing to "keep two sets of books" and violate liberty where the Communist issue arises. Although disagreeing, I have come to take this schism on the Right for granted. I cannot, however, let your position on the Suez question go by without registering a protest.[19]

Buckley's response to a three-page defense of anticolonialist movements in the Arab world was to invite Rothbard over to one of *National Review*'s editorial lunches. Although he did attend some parties given by the Buckley crowd, Rothbard's reaction to Buckley's overtures was somewhat cool. Over the course of a year or so, commencing in the summer of 1956, their correspondence registers more such protests on Rothbard's part. In answer to

Frank S. Meyer arguing in *National Review* for an aggressively anti-Soviet foreign policy, Rothbard writes that Meyer had failed "to distinguish between Communism as a revolutionary movement *out of power*, and as a bureaucratic regime *in power*."[20] Out of power, the Communists are certainly dedicated to revolution and Marxism-Leninism. Once the Communists take power, "the situation inevitably changes." Under the new regime "from that point on there is only one way a man can rise above the slave level and make any sort of career for himself: to join the Communist Party." The Reds were inevitably sowing the seeds of their own destruction, he knew, and "we may confidently expect that as time goes on, and the old revolutionary generation dies out, their successors will more and more be simple careerists, and not dedicated Communists at all. The fact that the new opportunists may pay lip-service to Communist ideals then becomes far less important." Communist rhetoric would eventually become nothing but routinized invocations, semantic rituals devoid of real meaning, relics retained only because "they must keep some ideals around, to dupe everyone into believing that they are not simply brigands." This ideological weakening of the Communist system would be, he predicted, the key factor in its demise: "the point is that the new opportunists do not care anymore," and are unlikely to pursue their ostensible goal of promoting world revolution abroad—especially since they will be more and more concerned with staving off revolt at home. In a passage that Buckley would have done well to underline and reread at every opportunity over the years, Rothbard made this stunning prediction:

> I am not expert enough to say how far this process has already gone in the Soviet Union. But the point is that it must, in the nature of things, be underway already, and its importance will grow as time goes on. If we realize this, and remember also that revolu-

tionary inspiration has always, historically, died out after a time, we will see that Time is on our side, and we will realize that we need not dig in for a long and bloody battle to the death with an enemy that is even now withering from within.[21]

It was the winter of 1957, and the howling blizzard of the Cold War had the whole country, indeed the whole world, in its icy grip. The abolition of Soviet power by its downtrodden subjects was not even imagined by conservatives and other "liberationists": the quick suppression of the Hungarian Revolution in the previous year had seemingly ruled out that option entirely. In the United States, both the extreme Right and the extreme Left exaggerated the military prowess and ideological solidity of the Communist bloc, each for their own reasons. Only Rothbard, and a very few libertarians, cut through the Left-Right Cold War "consensus" and saw the underlying reality.

A few years later, what was to become the Gorbachev wing of the Soviet Communist Party temporarily took power in the Soviet Union. The leader of this palace revolution, that premature reformer Nikita Khrushchev, caused a furor when he announced his decision to visit the United States. While the hardliners in the Kremlin looked askance at this dalliance with the bourgeois West and kept their silence, the hardline Cold Warriors on the American Right were more voluble in their opposition to the prospect of superpower rapprochement.

Bill Buckley launched a ridiculous campaign protesting the visit, in alliance with the John Birch Society, and with *National Review* leading the charge. This was too much for Rothbard, who wrote that Buckley's brand of humor, however unintentional, had surely reached new heights of hilarity:

National Review has always prided itself, and properly so, on its wit.

Never has its faculty for wit and satire reached a higher peak than in the last few weeks. We find, for example, the amusing ad of the "Committee for Freedom of All Peoples," amusing particularly because one of its prominent members is none other than Senator Paul Douglas, who has spent the last few decades in a determined attempt to undermine the freedom of the *American* people.[22]

The idea that Senator Douglas—the archetypal big government liberal—was now to be considered a champion of liberty and the "American Way" struck Rothbard (and, no doubt, many conservatives) as more than slightly ironic.

As if this were not enough, the Buckley campaign atttempted to frame the debate with a central image: "Shall an American President Shake Hands with the Bloody Butcher?" The hypocrisy of Buckley & Co. was breathtaking in view of the fact that *National Review* and its allies in the "Committee Against Summit Entanglements," agitating against the Khrushchev visit,

> are always eager to extend their hands to any other Bloody Butcher in the world: including Franco, Chiang-kai-Chek, [South Korean dictator] Synghman Rhee, and General de Gaulle. . . . I pass over in silence the willingness to shake hands with Winston Churchill, Bloody Butcher of the refugees of Dresden, and countless others.

What stuck in Rothbard's craw was the outrageous idea that the Buckleyite warmongers were posing as the stewards of morality and justice when what they really wanted was a military confrontation with the Soviets that could only mean the destruction of the human race. In justifying any and all measures against the Kremlin, *National Review* had often made use of a "moral calculus of suffering" in which it did not matter whether one man was killed or many millions—"in which case Mr. K. is no more of a bloody butcher than any other head of state." To top it all off, the *National Review Bulletin*, a newsletter supplement to *National Review*, had complained that "Mr. K. might be sleeping in the sainted Lincoln's bed," continued Rothbard, "but this surely would be more than apt, considering that Mr. K.'s deeds in Hungary were precisely equivalent to Mr. Lincoln's butchery of the South."[23]

But Buckley and the *National Review* crowd had no time for what they regarded as niggling arguments, so busy were they preparing themselves for their ascension to power. It was Rothbard's worst nightmare. Internationalists had not only succeeded in taking over the Republican party but had also hijacked the conservative movement. As Rothbard puts it in his memoir of that time, "it was time to act."[24]

The trouble was, there was virtually no one to interact *with*. The entire libertarian movement in New York City had been reduced, through a process of attrition, to exactly two: Rothbard and Leonard Liggio, the sole member of the Circle Bastiat who had not either moved out of town to attend graduate school or "surrendered to the blandishments of the New Right."[25]

Politically and emotionally, Rothbard's break with the Right came with the 1960 Stevenson for President campaign. Rothbard, the renegade rightist, had supported Stevenson in 1956 partially on the grounds that he represented a propeace position, but primarily to exact a full measure of revenge against the Republican "left" and, perhaps, recapture the party for liberty and a noninterventionist foreign policy. "Emotionally," writes Rothbard, "I was still a right-winger who yearned for a rightist third party."[26]

But the right-wing third-party efforts of the late fifties, several of which had interested Rothbard, all came to naught. Now he abandoned the Right as hopeless, and followed what he called his "antiwar and isolationist star" into an alliance with what was then considered to be the far-left wing of the Democratic party. This is how Rothbard became actively involved in the New York City chapter of the League of Stevensonian Democrats.

Stevenson had been outraged by Eisenhower's refusal to apologize for the infamous U-2 incident, in which an American spy plane was shot down over Soviet territory, thus wrecking the upcoming summit before it ever began. Rothbard shared his outrage. After Kennedy overwhelmed the Stevensonians at the Democratic convention, Rothbard saw an ad in the *New York Post* for a Stevenson Pledge movement: the League of Stevensonian Democrats was "an attempt by particularly embittered Stevensonians" to shame or otherwise force Kennedy into making Stevenson Secretary of State.[27]

As head of the League's National and International Affairs Committee, Rothbard made a consistently libertarian contribution to the organization's platform, but his role was not limited to theoretician. He rolled up his sleeves and went to work for the Stevenson Pledge organization in New York City: for three days a week, sometimes four, he worked in the League office in Manhattan, answering phones, coordinating volunteers, dealing with visitors, engaging in animated discussion, and generally having a good old time. It was a genuine coalition effort—with Rothbard and his few libertarian confreres in alliance with liberals, leftists, and a few stray Trotskyists. In view of the direction his politics took in the sixties, it was a harbinger of things to come.

THE BETRAYAL OF THE AMERICAN RIGHT

Isolated and for all intents and purposes "underground," the libertarian movement consisted of a small network of individuals who all had one connection in common: Murray Rothbard. The seeds planted by this patient gardener broke through to the surface first in Chicago, where two former members of the Circle Bastiat, Ronald Hamowy and Ralph Raico, were instrumental in founding a student libertarian periodical, the *New Individualist Review*. It wasn't long before the simmering conflict between libertarians and conservatives came out into the open; in the second issue, a debate called "Conservatives or Individualists: Which Are We?" was featured. The libertarians, represented by William Volker Fund fellow Edward Facey, pointed to the conservative attack on civil liberties in this country in the name of the war against Communism—and invoked Garet Garrett's mournful philippics to note that "we have crossed the boundary that lies between Republic and Empire." Facey excoriated Young Americans for Freedom, the recently organized conservative youth group whose founding convention was held on William F. Buckley Jr.'s estate in Sharon, Connecticut: "Instead of committing battle against federal aid to education they ask that the aid be distributed to persons who have taken loyalty oaths."[28] *New Individualist Review* Associate Editor John Weichner's weak reply reiterated the by-now standard Buckleyite line that fear of a Soviet Communist military victory over the West justified the rise of the welfare-warfare state.

In the next issue of *New Individualist Review*, it was Ronald Hamowy's turn to take aim at Buckley. Hamowy's withering critique of the treacherous role played by *National Review* as the great betrayer of the American Right provoked a reply by Buckley, to which Hamowy added a final rejoinder.[29]

Noting the rise of Buckley as the spokesperson for intellectual conservatism, Hamowy charged that the man and his magazine were "leading true believers in freedom and individual liberty down a disastrous path and that in so doing they are causing the Right increasingly to betray its own traditions and principles." Harking back to the forgotten legacy of the Old Right, he recalled the movement's heroes—Frank Chodorov, Garet Garrett, Isabel

Paterson, Rose Wilder Lane, and Albert Jay Nock—deploring their overthrow and replacement by new idols such as Supreme Court Justice Felix Frankfurter, long the *bete-noir* of the Old Right, who had recently been hailed by *National Review* for "trampling upon the civil liberties of Leftists."[30] Both *National Review* and Frankfurter were also agreed in their right and *duty* to trample on the rights not only of leftists, but all draft-age males, whatever their political coloration, in their support of conscription. With his own characteristic rhetorical flair, Hamowy recounted the history of the Right as he had learned it during the heyday of the Circle Bastiat: "Before and after World War II [the Old Right] fought the draft as unconstitutional, as slavery, and as the ultimate aggrandizement by the State. To the current conservative, anyone who dares to raise a principled voice against conscription is labeled a Communist. . . . The same libertarians who during the Second World War were accused by the Left of being 'mouthpieces of the Goebbels line,' are now accused, this time by the Right, of 'doing the work of the Communists.' "[31]

In an ornately facetious reply, Buckley rolled out his libertarian credentials—such as his magazine's "renewed support for editor William F. Rickenbacker's refusal to sign the Census Department's prurient questionnaire"—and then got to the real point of the dispute. Citing the alleged immediacy of a military threat from the Soviet Union—which was even then showing the first cracks and signs of disintegration and decline—he wrote:

> There is room in any society for those whose only concern is for tablet-keeping; but let them realize that it is only because of the conservatives' disposition to sacrifice in order to withstand the enemy, that they are able to enjoy their monasticism, and pursue their busy little seminars on whether or not to demunicipalize the garbage collectors.[32]

Far from keeping the tablets, Buckley and his crew wanted to wipe the slate clean, erase the memory of the Old Right, and replace it with its exact opposite: a movement of warmongering statists whose Anglophilic outlook was well captured by Hamowy when he described the foreign policy position of the New Right as being "that of Colonel Blimp and Rudyard Kipling, the pseudoaristocratic outlook of 'cane the bloody wogs.' "[33] The two-fisted American populism of Colonel McCormick had been displaced, on the Right, by the pretentious faux-British intellectualism of the Buckleyites. As for the legitimacy and necessity of Buckley's self-appointed role as the Shield of the West, Hamowy's rejoinder fairly bristled with scorn:

> It might appear ungrateful of me, but I must decline to thank Mr. Buckley for saving my life. It is, further, my belief that if his viewpoint prevails and that if he persists in his unsolicited aid the result will almost certainly be either my death (and that of tens of millions of others) in nuclear war or my imminent imprisonment as an "un-American."[34]

In a crude attempt to smear Hamowy by associating him with organizations of the Left, Buckley accused his opponent of having recently joined the Committee for a Sane Nuclear Policy, and one Buckleyite wrote, "I hear that Ron Hamowy is IN-SANE."[35] In fact, Hamowy was not a member of SANE. Rothbard had attended one meeting, and no doubt reported back to his coconspirators that working with this collection of Cold War liberals and right-wing Social Democrats would be impossible due to their dogged moderation and complete prostration before the exigencies of the Cold War.

The Hamowy-Buckley brouhaha led to the political neutralization of the *New Individualist Review*: the result of the debate was an agreement among the editors on a policy of never even mentioning foreign policy issues, and keeping its pages focused on the domestic front. Much to Rothbard's chagrin, the Old Right was still without a voice.

RUNNING INTO AYN RAND

During this period one interlude stands out, and that is Rothbard's run-in with Ayn Rand, author of *The Fountainhead* (1943) and *Atlas Shrugged* (1957), her best-selling paean to capitalism, individualism, and reason. Rothbard was well acquainted with Rand in the years before she gave up her career as a novelist and veered off on a tangent to become the avatar of a philosophical movement she dubbed "Objectivism." He had gone to see her with Herbert Cornuelle after the publication of *The Fountainhead*, but the chemistry on that occasion was not right. They did not become friendly at first, but in the minuscule subworld of the libertarian movement, in the days before she had walled herself up within the confines of her own cult, the voluble Rand was still accessible. Yet it wasn't until 1954 that Rothbard really began to see her with any regularity, and then, as he relates in a letter to Richard Cornuelle, it was not an uplifting experience.

The past few weeks had been "particularly depressing and particularly exciting," he wrote, and "I may as well tackle the depressing one first." Against his own inclination and better judgment, Rothbard had allowed himself to be persuaded by his young friends "to go back and see Ayn Rand." She was by this time a legend in Manhattan libertarian circles, the best-selling author and champion of militant individualism, and rumors of her next book were already causing a stir. When the boys of the Circle Bastiat found out that he knew Rand, they jumped at the chance to meet her. Rand's disciples held a regular Saturday night salon in her living room, where they read the latest pages of Rand's new novel fresh from the typewriter, and Rothbard went up there with George Reisman and Ralph Raico. This resulted in a subsequent meeting involving the entire Circle Bastiat. It was not, as Rothbard relates, a very pleasant evening, but certainly it was revealing:

> I thought that with so many people there and with me wiser and a couple of years older, she would not have such a depressing effect, but the effect was depressing enough. I had to laugh when she told me not to bring up a kid who was an esthetic follower of Ezra Pound, because he is an "irrationalist" (what else?) and "I grow intolerant with age." I sort of had a real nostalgia at the affairs, because the thing evolved mainly into a discussion (a mild term) between her and George Reisman, who stoutly upheld the good old Utilitarian faith of our youth. I found that while I agreed (or thought I agreed) mainly with her position, I found myself rooting like hell for George, who found himself under a typical vitriolic Randian barrage, according to which anyone who is not now or soon will be a one-hundred percent Randian Rationalist is an "enemy" and an "objective believer in death and destruction" as well as crazy.[36]

In her biography of Rand, Barbara Branden blames her mentor's increasingly bad humor and growing intolerance on her disastrous affair with Nathaniel Branden, combined with the near universal hiss that went up from the critics and intellectuals in general when her magnum opus was published. But Rothbard reveals that the less attractive features of the Randian persona were in full bloom and even dominant years before the publication of *Atlas Shrugged*. Rothbard's "nostalgia" implies that his previous experience with Rand might have led him to anticipate just such a scene, and he was not at all surprised when it unfolded. "The interesting thing," he writes in a 1954 letter to Richard Cornuelle, "is that

George's emotional reaction after the sessions was the same as mine had been, while the other kids didn't realize the power and horror of her position—and personality."[37]

This was the crux of the matter: a personality conflict of major proportions. These two people, who had so much in common—both had rejected the strictures of a narrow ethnicity and the ideological fashion of the day, and embraced radical individualism—could not have been more different in their approach to ideas and to life. While they appeared to agree in many key areas, Rothbard's emotional reaction to his latest run-in with Rand drove him "to think further about the situation," and as he put in his letter to Cornuelle, "I've come to the conclusion that my position—and yours too, I bet—is not really the same as hers at all."[38]

Rothbard thought that Rand's great attraction was that she offered an alternative to the intellectual poverty of utilitarianism, positivism, and pragmatism. "For us, of course, it is utilitarianism that constitutes the problem." Modern philosophy is dominated by schools of thought that deny the reality or utility of ethics, ontology, esthetics, and so on, and "for us the important gap is in ethics." While the three major philosophic schools of thought "simply deny that such disciplines can exist," the dissenter from this consensus of know-nothings "who stumbles on Ayn finds that there are great truths that we have literally never heard in the classroom." Yet "the good stuff in Ayn's system is not Ayn's original contribution at all. . . . There is an underlying, but as I've written you, growing philosophic position beginning with Aristotle where it is set forth—the idea of a rational ethics based on the nature of man and found by reason, reason determining ends, etc. Aristotle and Spencer were fine on this."[39]

Rand's claim of originality was not something that Rothbard could take seriously. He knew full well that the idea of a rational ethics started with Aristotle, was continued by the Thomists, and comes down to us through Herbert Spencer: "Once one begins to read this material, he finds that Ayn is not the sole source and owner of the rational tradition, nor even the sole heir to Aristotle." Her brand of Aristotleianism, however, is a bizarre variant, "a horrible perversion" of a sound system "with the most unpleasant— and unlibertarian—implications. "For Rand," he averred, "denies against all evidence the existence of even the most primary instincts in man." Her error, he thought, was rooted in her method:

> You notice that she attempts to deduce the nature of man, which is certainly in large part an empirical question and so recognized by Aristotle, purely by armchair speculation. Armchair speculation is the proper method of praxeology, but obviously not for a largely inductive science."[40]

Convinced that she could spin valid theories out of her own head without bothering to investigate facts, Rand denied "that emotions can ever be primary—which loses any independent basis for love, friendship, laughter, pleasure, etc. as values in themselves out the window." He was suspicious of "Ayn's almost fanatically Puritan view that the only development of man's powers that is worth anything is working at developing mental powers." What about such values as "love, friendship, joy, etc., did not they count for anything in the Randian hierarchy of values?"[41]

In theory, they did count: Rand's novels teem with these emotions. In practice, the philosophy she and her followers derived from the novels produced just such a "fanatically Puritan" and joyless group of Randians as Rothbard predicted.[42]

"The implications of this grow more horrifying as you think about it," Rothbard wrote, for in effect Rand "actually denies all individuality whatsoever!" For if there are no primary emotions, and genetics count for nothing, according to the Randian rationalist dogma, then "there is no basis for different interests—only for different complexities of interest. Thus, she maintains that I could be just as good in music as in economics if I applied myself, whereas I know damn well I'd be a flop." While not quite denying that there are differences in IQs, Rand argued that anyone could learn anything, given enough time and effort. Her ignorance of basic economic principles was nearly complete: she had no inkling of the concept of marginal utility—"of more units becoming less values, and of each individual's balancing different ends harmoniously"— which is "one of the key bases of true individualism, since each individual can learn what ends are rational, [and] choose only among these rational ends," leaving room for individual tastes within a broader framework of rationality. "But by ignoring marginalism and denying any sort of degrees in life," he writes, "Ayn is driven to a position that is monomaniacal in its monolithic quality."[43]

The logical consequence of this kind of rationalistic egalitarianism—"and unfortunately I am not exaggerating in the slightest—is that there is no such thing as a unique individual." For if all men, with no inherent differences due to genes or some other factor, are equally endowed with the capacity to reason, and "are only bundles of premises," then everyone would have the same bundle if they chose to be rational. "Therefore, according to Randianism, utopia would be a place where all men are identical, in their souls if not in their personal appearance." The implications of this in the realm of interpersonal relations were extrapolated by Rothbard with some pretty accurate results: "The logical conclusion is, for example, that there is no reason whatever why Ayn, for example, shouldn't sleep with Nathaniel Branden [her chief disciple]," or any of her disciples with any other, "since they all have the same premises, they are all the same people, or rather interchangeable parts of a machine." A few months after those words were written, Rand and Branden did indeed begin an affair, with the knowledge and consent of their respective spouses, based on just such wacky ideas about the relationship between romantic love and philosophical values.[44]

Although the group that Rand had gathered around her was already beginning to take on the characteristics of a cult, it seems her philosophy, which she later called "Objectivism," was still "under construction" regarding some fundamental issues. In detailing the case against Randianism, circa 1954, Rothbard goes on to write that she is afflicted not only with a monomaniacal view of reason, but

> she herself is involved in a contradiction. On the one hand, *she charges that anyone who believes in free will—which is basic to any sort of individualism—is insane, because he is postulating an uncaused element.* Yet she reduced everything back to "thinking" vs. "not thinking," and it is clear that on her own grounds this decision to "think or not to think" is "free" and therefore "uncaused" and therefore, she is as insane as anyone. And if she allows this little grain of free will, why not all of it?[45]

This passage explodes the neo-Randian mythology that Rand had not only abandoned the Nietzschean spirit of her youth—contained in several passages in *We the Living*, her first novel, and expunged from later editions—but also pretty much formulated the essentials of her philosophy before the writing of *Atlas Shrugged*. The exact date of her total enlightenment is never given, but the tendency of her latter-day admirers is to push it back as far as possible. Like Mao as a young man, or a young Joe Stalin, stories of Rand's exploits depict a young Ayn destined for greatness, eerily adult even as a child, solemnly declaring to her philosophy professor that "my ideas are not yet part of the history of philosophy—but they will be." Rand encouraged this image of herself as a genius-in-embryo in the biographical note to *Atlas Shrugged*: "I have held the same philosophy I now hold, for as far back as I can remember. I have learned a great deal through the years and expanded my knowledge of details" and "of specific issues," she wrote, "but I have never had to change any of my fundamentals."

But surely the issue of free will versus determinism is a "fundamental" point. The evidence shows that Rand was not only a determinist up until at least 1954, but also held that anyone who believed in free will was "insane"—"a favorite charge of hers," as Rothbard puts it.[46]

It is instructive to note that the issue of free will versus determinism is brought up nowhere in Rand's earlier works, including *The Fountainhead*; furthermore, the heroes and heroines of her early fiction seem not to have acquired their view of life so much as uncovered it by means of introspection. In their manner and appearance, these characters, a natural aristocracy of egoists, even share certain physical characteristics: all of them have high cheekbones, and their angular gauntness seems emblematic, almost an ethnic or racial trait. In *We the Living* there is a reference to one of the heroes, Leo Kovalensky, as being "born with a whip in his hand," and in spite of the second edition editing job Rand did on the book in the sixties, the spirit of Zarathustra still pervades this work.[47] The same Wagnerian music permeates the emotional and esthetic atmosphere of *The Fountainhead*. It is hardly surprising that Rand had originally planned to put a quote from Nietzsche on the epigraph page: "The noblest soul has reverence for itself." *Atlas Shrugged*, with its operatic structure—complete with arias in the form of long speeches—has the complexity and grand-scale drama of the Ring Cycle, with its cast of gods, heroes, and villains.

In the summer of 1954, Rand had not yet written the major philosophical speech of her main character, John Galt. This character was her vision of the ideal man, a blonde Zarathustra who would assert the death of God and proclaim "a philosophy for living on earth," as Rand liked to put it. The published version of Galt's speech, which today's Objectivists consider nothing short of holy writ, is quite clear on the subject of free will versus determinism. In declaring that "man is a being of volitional consciousness," and basing the Objectivist ethics on the concept of free will, on the choice to think or not to think, Galt was contradicting the received Randian wisdom of the past several years.

When and under what circumstances did Rand change her position on free will? Under ordinary circumstances, this question would be of marginal interest. In the case of the libertarian movement, however, such a seemingly nit-picking question looms large. This is due to their bias in favor of the "genius" theory of history, which asserts that all of human civilization rests on the achievements of a Few Great Men, and if not for them we would all be squatting around a campfire. Combined with the modal libertarian's ignorance of history, and tendency to oversimplify in any case, this idea took shape in the Randian conviction that Ayn Rand had been the first to formulate a philosophy of rational individualism. Not only that, but Rand, they asserted, had done it virtually *alone*. While libertarians have generally disdained the more pretentious claims of Rand's latter-day disciples, they have usually fallen for the central precept of the Randian mythos: her outlandish claim that she owed an intellectual debt only to Aristotle. In an article purporting to chart the rise of a "new" "nonmoralistic" libertarianism by means of statistical analysis, R. W. Bradford reflects the general consensus on this point in libertarian circles: "Formulated by best-selling novelist Ayn Rand and appropriated and expanded by Murray Rothbard, moralistic libertarianism was largely responsible for the modern resurgence of libertarian thinking that began in the 1960s."[48]

The intellectual history of modern libertarianism has been so distorted by cultists and others with ideological axes to grind that it no longer bears any resemblance to reality. The Randian school of falsification has been working overtime to instill the myth of Ayn's immaculate conception in the minds of the credulous. It is high time for some revisionism in this area, and there is no better place for it than in a biography of Murray Rothbard.

According to Barbara Branden, Rand began writing Galt's speech sometime around the fall of 1954, the beginning of a torturously long and drawn out process. Sometime during the next three years, Rand completely reversed her position on free will. While it is clear that Rothbard and Rand had an extended and long-standing argument on the matter, with the former championing free will and the latter upholding determinism—or at least the idea that free will involved an insoluble contradiction—the particular circumstances surrounding Rand's reversal remain unknown.

Rothbard noted that "George Reisman commented, and I think most astutely, that Ayn's system is a perfect engine of complete totalitarianism, but that Ayn herself is a libertarian out of an irrational prejudice, and that fifty years from now some smart Randian disciple will see the implications and convert the thing into a horrible new Statist sect," and speculated that "life in a Randian Rationalist society would be a living hell."[49] From the accounts of those ex-members who survived the experience, life in the Rand cult truly did replicate Hell in miniature.

Yet Rothbard did not heed his own advice. He finished reading *Atlas Shrugged* on October 3, 1957, and did not hesitate to sit down and write Rand a perceptive and sincere fan letter that reveals the depth of his emotional reaction to her work:

> I have just finished your novel today. I will start by saying that all
> of us in the "Circle Bastiat" are convinced, and were convinced

very early in the reading, that *Atlas Shrugged* is the greatest novel ever written. . . .

This simple statement by itself means little to me: I have always had a bit of contempt for the novel form, and have thought of the novel, at best, as a useful sugar-coated pill to carry on agit-prop work amongst the masses who can't take ideas straight. A month ago, if I had said a book was "the greatest novel ever written," it wouldn't have been too high a compliment.

It is one of the small measures of what I think of *Atlas Shrugged* that I no longer pooh-pooh the novel. I have always heard my literary friends talk of the "truths" presented by novels, without understanding the term at all. Now I do understand, but only because you have carried the novel form to a new and higher dimension.[50]

His extravagant praise of "the almost infinite treasure house that is *Atlas Shrugged*" goes on for pages. As he read her novel, he sometimes felt a pang of

regret that all those generations of novel-readers, people like my mother who in their youth read Dostoievsky and Tolstoy, searching eagerly for they knew not what truths which they never quite found, that these people could not read *Atlas Shrugged*. Here, I thought, were the truths they were really looking for.[51]

This was, for Rothbard, a high compliment, his way of saying that the spirit that had driven David and Raya Rothbard to build a life in a new world of liberty and unlimited possibilities also animated *Atlas Shrugged*. It is doubtful that Rand, who always deprecated the importance of families—they weren't "rational," since you didn't join a family by choice—appreciated the accolade. He goes on to credit Rand with carving "out a completely integrated rational ethic, rational epistemology, rational psychology, and rational politics, all integrated one with the other." He is also "surprised that it astonishes even I who was familiar with the general outlines of your system. What it will do [to] the person stumbling upon it anew I cannot imagine."[52]

Rand's novel had so bowled him over that he determined to build bridges to a woman he had deliberately avoided, for reasons he tried to explain, to her and to himself, in what he called "the painful part of this letter." He frankly confessed that "most times when I saw you in person, particularly when we engaged in lengthy discussion or argument, that I found afterwards that I was greatly depressed for days thereafter." Generously blaming "a defect in my own character" to this aversion, he remarked: "Why I should be so depressed I do not know."[53]

He would find out—or remember—soon enough. Rothbard's own devastating critique of the Randian movement, "The Sociology of the Ayn Rand Cult," while it accurately portrays the Randians as a classic cult operation, does not mention his own experience with Rand and her followers.[54] The reason for this uncharacteristic omission underscores the accuracy of his trenchant analysis.

In the days immediately following the publication of Rand's blockbuster novel, Rand and Rothbard got along quite well. These two high-octane controversialists, who both loved to stay up all night discussing philosophy, politics, economics, and the latest movies, were naturally drawn together. The Rothbards would get to Rand's apartment sometime around 7 or 8 at night, and not get out until the first light slanted through the living-room window; then he and Joey would go down to the Automat and get breakfast, famished and exhausted by the endless discussion.

Rothbard's later writings on Objectivism emphasize the foibles of the Randian leaders and the personal idiosyncrasies of Rand, but it is clear that he understood and appreciated the emotional power of

Rand's fictional creations—and that, on first reading *Atlas Shrugged*, he experienced some of that power himself.

While *Atlas Shrugged* climbed to the top of the best-seller list, the critics savagely attacked the book; among the most intemperate was Patricia Donegan, writing in *The Commonweal*, a liberal Catholic weekly, who described Rand's magnum opus as "an outpouring of hate."[55] A month later, the magazine published Rothbard's reply, in which he attributes several "grave errors" to Donegan's review. To begin with, he says, the prurience implied in Donegan's interpretation of the characters' romantic entanglements is misplaced; the novel's heroine did not have three lovers at once, as Donegan averred: "Her three lovers are seriatim, and not simultaneous." That cleared up, Rothbard takes on Donegan's assertion that compassion (both the word and the concept) are entirely missing from Miss Rand's novel. To the contrary, says Rothbard, compassion plays "an important role" in *Atlas Shrugged*. The question is: compassion *for whom*? Rand's novel dramatized compassion "for heroic individuals tortured by looters and others who make them feel guilty for their very virtues." Unlike the morality of liberal Christianity the Randian concept of compassion is "for a man's fight against suffering, or against unjustly imposed suffering, rather than pity for suffering per se. And whereas Miss Donegan is perfectly correct that 'humility' has 'no place in the author's scheme of things,' charity does. But once again, it is charity for the sake of virtues," and not "the subsidization of vice." Far from being an "outpouring of hate," Rothbard writes that "the central theme of *Atlas Shrugged* is love of man's life."[56]

The Commonweal not only ran a reply by Donegan, who still saw something a bit suspicious in the heroine's performance in the romantic realm, but also another piece by the editors a few weeks later, in which they cite the Donegan-Rothbard controversy: "Ordinarily," they write, "the matter would have been left there, but since then we have seen an interview with the novel's author which provides an interesting footnote to the discussion." They then print excerpts from an interview with Rand conducted by Mike Wallace, in which he asks: "What thinker or philosopher living today in or out of America do you respect?" Her answer: "Not one." Wallace follows up with: "By your considered judgment, you are therefore the most creative thinker alive today?" Rising to the occasion, Rand replies: "If anyone can pick a rational flaw in my philosophy, I will be delighted to acknowledge him and I will learn something from him. Until then—I am."[57]

Such an extravagant flight of grandiosity might have served as a warning to Rothbard and some of his associates in the Circle Bastiat about what they were letting themselves in for, but this rather ominous portent either went unnoticed or ignored. In his fan letter to Rand, Rothbard had compared *Atlas Shrugged* to *Human Action*, and acknowledged that

> when, in the past, I heard your disciples refer to you in grandiloquent terms—as one of the greatest geniuses who ever lived, as giving them a "round universe"—I confess I was repelled: surely this was the outpouring of a mystic cult. But now, upon reading *Atlas Shrugged*, I find I was wrong.[58]

It took him less than six months to realize he had been right the first time. While his admiration for *Atlas Shrugged* was genuine, two other factors undoubtedly played a role in his sudden reversal. The first was the fact that a book, albeit a novel, explicitly advocating laissez-faire capitalism and the centrality of private property as the basic organizing principle of a free society, had shot to the top of the best-seller lists. In 1957, the few libertarian remnants of the Old Right had almost entirely faded away. Here, at last, were reinforcements: just when it seemed all was lost, the calvary was coming over the hill. While the Randians were gener-ally ill-read and in need of education in several key areas, Roth-bard obviously believed at this point that the Randians were edu-cable. This dramatic breakthrough for the mass dissemination of libertarian ideas seemed to confirm Rothbard's natural optimism, and he was reflexively sympathetic and even enthusiastic about the success of the book. If he sometimes went overboard in his enthusiasms, all he suffered was disappointment in the end; this time, however, the consequences would be more unpleasant.

Perhaps most importantly, however, Rothbard also hoped that the Randians could help him in another way. Virtually all of the top Randians in New York City were undergoing the rigors of "Objec-tivist Psychotherapy" as conducted by Rand's chief disciple, Nathaniel Branden, and as word of its miraculous effects reached Rothbard, the thought that he might solve one of his more pressing problems had some appeal. This is a recruiting technique common with many cults, which often assume a "therapeutic" guise, and in Rothbard, as we shall see, they had a customer blissfully and some-what naively unaware of just what he was getting into.

As a psychosociological phenomenon, cults have a structure of belief peculiar to themselves, a form which remains constant no matter what the content of the cultic ideology. First and foremost is the centrality of the supreme leader, the object of the cult, a person who embodies their doctrine, whatever that may be. But this doc-trine, in the case of a cult, has two aspects. First, there is the *exoteric*, or outer doctrine, which is espoused to the public. After drawing in recruits, these are gradually introduced to the *esoteric* doctrine, the inner truths, known only to the circle of initiates. In the case of the Objectivist movement, the exoteric doctrine was radical individu-alism, the prototype of which was the character of Howard Roark in Rand's 1943 novel, *The Fountainhead*. The esoteric doctrine, how-ever, was quite different—exactly the opposite of the egoist stance that attracted recruits in the first place. Rothbard contended that "the esoteric creed is: Ayn Rand is the greatest person who ever lived or ever shall live, and therefore everything she says is correct. And any deviation from what she says is affronting reason and reality and a cause for immediate excommunication by all the faithful. So the whole thing operates as a totalitarian religious cult with orders handed down from Rand to her top circle which was called in those days the 'senior collective.' "[59] As Rothbard cogently put it, the Rand cult "promoted slavish dependence on the guru in the name of independence; adoration and obedience to the leader in the name of every person's individuality; and blind emotion and faith in the guru in the name of Reason."[60]

While Rand certainly did nothing to discourage the cultic atmosphere that began to pervade her immediate circle, the real problem was her followers, as Bennett Cerf, her publisher at Random House for many years, observantly remarked in his 1977 autobiography.[61] In particular, her top lieutenant, Nathaniel Branden, a psychologist, and some twenty years younger than Rand, used his mentor's growing following to build up his roster of clients, swelling not only the ranks of his patients but also the coffers of the organization he founded to propagate Rand's philosophy, the Nathaniel Branden Institute (NBI). All of Branden's patients were required to take the lecture course, "Basic Principles of Objectivism," as part of their therapy. From Rand's living room to Branden's office and then through the doors of NBI—this conveyor belt method proved fantastically successful.

For a long time, Rothbard had been afflicted by a travel phobia, but he was determined to get over it, and on the recommendation of Rand he signed on with Branden as a patient. The relationship lasted less than six months: short but intense.

Membership in the New York branch of the Randian cult meant a continuous whirl of cult activity. Rothbard writes that "every night one of the top Randians lectured to different members expounding various aspects of the 'party line': on basics, on psychology, fiction, sex, thinking, art , economics, or philosophy. (This structure reflected the vision of Utopia outlined in *Atlas Shrugged* itself, where the heroes and heroines spent every evening lecturing to each other.)"[62]

It did not take very long for the sheer wear and tear of all this frenzied activity to fray Rothbard's relations with Rand. Failure to attend Randian lectures soon led to queries from the leadership: how is it that you choose not to spend virtually every waking moment with the most rational people in all of New York City, if not the world? In the cultic universe of the New York Randians, this was considered a reasonable question. "But what if," asked Rothbard, "as so often happens, one didn't like, even couldn't stand, these people?"[63] Then your days in the Randian movement were numbered. When it became obvious that Rothbard's fear of travel was not about to disappear under the moralistic fulminations of "Objectivist Psychotherapy," a mixture of mind-games and hectoring, as well as endless lectures and classes in "Basic Principles of Objectivism," Branden decided that Rothbard's problem was linked to other issues—for example, Rothbard's "irrational" choice of a mate. For how could Rothbard claim to be rational if he chose a mate whose belief in God violated the Randian principle of the primacy of reason? Wasn't one's sexual choice a reflection of one's deepest values, as Rand and the "Objectivist" school of psychotherapy taught? If Rothbard *really* wanted to turn his life around, throw off the neuroses and obstructions of the past like Atlas shrugging off the world, then he ought to schuck off his charming and devoted wife, JoAnn, and replace her with a more suitable Randian mate. Branden, and his hangers-on, who fancied that they knew all of the rational people in New York City, would be more than happy to nominate prospective candidates.[64]

In a letter to Richard Cornuelle, Rothbard relates that he began therapy with Branden because his psychologial ideas seemed very interesting, and Ayn practically promised a cure in a short period of time. "As time has progressed," however,

> I have become progressively more repelled by the whole setup; if you think that Ayn was bad before, you should see the situation now that Branden has organized a whole cult of swooning teenagers around Ayn and himself, a cult that gets a great deal of its power from Branden being their therapist. Recently, I became convinced that I would have to break off with Branden, when he began to lay down as a condition of my "cure" that I pester Joey to give up Christianity and adopt atheism, and that I give up such Christian friends as Leonard Liggio, Frank Meyer, etc. It was then that I realized what an absurd fanatic this fellow is.[65]

At one of the final encounters between Rand and Rothbard, the Randians decided to give poor Joey the benefit of a doubt, and a chance to redeem herself. "Let her read zee proofs," announced Rand. If Joey read these alleged proofs—the content of a lecture on atheism by Branden—and remained unconvinced, then that—in the Randian view—would be the final evidence of her irredeemable irrationality. Joey was duly escorted into a separate room, where she sat down and read through Branden's deadly dull prose, which showed no more understanding of religion or the religious impulse than a dog comprehends poetry. She remained unconvinced—and still married to Rothbard.[66]

COMING UP FOR AIR

But in the Rand cult, you didn't get away for long with such a show of defiance. Although Rothbard, in the wake of this last bizarre incident, was determined to break off all relations with the Objectivists, the "senior collective" did not look kindly on drop-outs. As if to underscore their own nuttiness, a short time later the Randians came up with a pretext for purging Rothbard on the grounds that he had "plagiarized" both the ideas of Ayn Rand and an unpublished paper by Barbara Branden in an academic paper that he was to deliver at a scholarly conference: it was his classic essay, "The Mantle of Science." Rothbard, in a point-by-point refu-tation of their claims, noted that the concepts claimed by the Ran-dians as their original creations dated back at least to the Scholastic scholars of the Middle Ages.*

The irony is that this accusation arose in the context of this par-ticular article, a major section of which is devoted to a proof of the concept of free will—the very issue on which Rand had clashed with Rothbard not so long ago. Having switched her position, Rand was now claiming that Rothbard had stolen *her* original ideas.

In a remarkably pompous seven-page single-spaced letter to Rothbard dated July 20, 1958, Nathaniel Branden accuses Rothbard

---

*The extensive file containing Nathaniel Branden's letters to Rothbard, and his replies, makes tedious and really rather sad reading. For example, Branden accuses Rothbard of lifting without attribution from Barbara Branden's unpub-lished dissertation, "Human Freedom and Human Mechanism" (unpublished master's thesis, New York University, 1956), and Rothbard cites another of his own, written and submitted to an academic journal in 1954. It is all very tiresome, and somewhat baffling, until we read the letters back and forth between various individuals associated with the principals, the mutual recriminations and emo-tional grandstanding, with former fast friends grandly excommunicating each other with extraordinary gusto. This bizarre behavior as the leitmotif of the Ran-dian movement has been extensively documented elsewhere; indeed, the Rand cult spawned a whole literature of recovery, a series of memoirs by her former associates, notably the Brandens, but including far too much other material to list here. *The Ayn Rand Cult* by Jeff Walker (Chicago: Open Court, 1999) is a virtual compendium of the various purges and excommunications that convulsed Rand's circle while she was alive, and continued to thin the ranks after her death.

of stealing the idea that man is born with no innate knowledge, that he must act in accord with his nature, and that reason rather than mystic intuition is his best guide to action. The alleged inventor and owner of these ideas, he informed Rothbard in no uncertain terms, was Ayn Rand. When Mises heard of this, he remarked that "I really did not know that the concept that man has no automatic knowledge of how to survive and that the task of his reason is to discover the values and virtues (the ends and means) needed to keep him alive was not known to mankind before the fall of 1957."[67]

Branden claimed to have gone over Rothbard's essay line by line and alleged that he had found almost a dozen instances where Rothbard had virtually paraphrased Galt's speech and Barbara Branden's thesis. If he really *had* gone over Rothbard's essay line by line and compared the texts, the truth would have been obvious even to Branden: not only is there no question of word-for-word plagiarism, but there are also significant stylistic and conceptual differences. Rothbard's clear, concise style, economical and punchy, is not anything like the hectoring and overdramatized Randian rhetoric. On the question of stealing the ideas Branden charged Rothbard with expropriating; the absurdity of the charge was well expressed by one of the organizers of the conference, Helmut Schoeck, the prominent Austrian economist and author of the classic *Envy*, who wrote that the claim of plagiarism was "fantastically ludicrous." The ideas in Rothbard's essay "are part and parcel of hundreds if not thousands of books and treatises which were published in the past sixty years, in some cases the past few hundred years." Branden claimed that Rothbard's example of a child with a gun illustrating the need to acquire knowledge had been lifted by Rothbard from Barbara Branden's thesis. This charge Professor Schoeck considered the "most ridiculous of all": the example of the child and the gun "can be found in every textbook in social psychology, social control and related subjects for the past sixty years or so. I have used this example spontaneously in many lectures. It is the most obvious one to come to the mind of anyone trying to make that point." Schoeck's advice to Rothbard: "Ignore these crackpots."[68]

It would have been easier to ignore Branden if he had not been Rothbard's therapist. For the past six months, Rothbard had confided his secrets, his longings, his anxieties, and poured out his heart secure in the knowledge that Branden's sense of professional ethics and propriety would forbid him to betray such a confidence. In a note to Richard Cornuelle, however, Rothbard reveals that "Branden has begun to tell other things concerning my therapy, things both true and false."[69]

Rothbard was upset if not unnerved by this disturbing incident, as his somewhat frantic letters to Mises and to Richard Cornuelle make clear. Aside from being subjected to the indignity of his therapist spreading stories about him, Rothbard also had to contend with the fact that two of his good friends, George Reisman and Robert Hessen, had taken Branden's side, and would no longer speak to him. The defection of these two veterans of the Circle Bastiat, and their endorsement of Branden's trumped-up charges of "plagiarism," was yet another painful aspect of this whole affair.

The combination of ideology and psychotherapy gave the Randian cult leaders the kind of power over their followers that not even the Stalinists wielded. This meant that Branden and his cadre of "Objectivist" psychotherapists had the goods on each and every one of their followers: their patients had divulged their most intimate secrets, some of which would doubtless have proved embarrassing if revealed. Under these circumstances, it wasn't hard for the leaders to keep them in line. For if Rand and Branden decided that this or that Objectivist had deviated from orthodoxy, was unrepentant, and had to be excommunicated from the group, then all this sensitive information was revealed at their subsequent "trial." The Grand Inquisitor at these bizarre proceedings was always Nathaniel Branden, with Rand as the chief judge and the rest of the Randian leadership as a kind of Greek chorus, dutifully echoing the pronouncements of their leaders.

Rothbard was duly invited to attend his own trial, when the time came, but he declined. He was tried *in absentia*, and, although the vote was not unanimous, the Randian "senior collective" expelled Rothbard from the World of Reason and into the Outer Darkness.

The short history of the Objectivist movement—a history of splits, excommunications, and internecine feuds of unrelenting ferocity—more than verified Rothbard's early indictment of the Randians as a "totalitarian religious cult" founded on emotionalism. Yet he understood and appreciated the appeal of Rand's novels, having experienced it himself. He saw the necessity of emotion as well as reason, art as well as scholarship, in the success of any movement for radical social change. In a discussion of "the balance of reason and emotion in the ideology and propaganda of the successful radical movements," Rothbard writes, "it seems clear that what the libertarian movement should strive for is an *integration* of reason and emotion, of enthusiasm and a passion for justice that stem from a rational understanding of libertarian doctrine. On the other hand, reason without emotion tends to be dull, mechanical, uninspiring, *boring*."[70]

This was the real source of Rothbard's initial attraction to *Atlas Shrugged* and Objectivism, and that of libertarians in general: the need for drama, glamor, myth, and symbol in politics. The Christian libertarians at *Faith and Freedom* had used the rhetoric, canons, and symbols of Christianity to buttress their arguments in favor of economic and personal freedom—and Rothbard was willing to go along with that, provided that he had a platform for his libertarian views. The Randians had used the rhetoric, canons, and symbols of a fiercely secular religion of their own invention as the basis of a similar political and economic stance—and Rothbard was willing to go along with that, too, until he was caught up in the orgy of psychological sadism perpetrated by Rand and her followers in the name of "reason."[71]

This explanation is true in a general sense, yet it obscures Rothbard's real attraction to the philosophy of his Randian allies, a factor entirely missing from his alignment with *Faith and Freedom*: there was never any question of Rothbard joining Fifield's church. He did join Branden's church, however briefly. Yet he was never fully drawn into the Rand cult in the sense that so many of the brightest libertarians were at the time, and it didn't take long for him to rebel against its strictures.

There is every evidence and every reason to believe that, at first, Rothbard took the fracas with the Randians very hard. The hope that "Objectivist psychotherapy" could rid him of his travel phobia had been dashed, and he was unable to even attend the symposium at which he was supposed to deliver his paper on "The Mantle of Science," held at Sea Island, Georgia. In a letter to the organizers of the conference, Rothbard wrote: "When I accepted your invitation last winter, I was convinced by the assurances of my therapist, Nathaniel Branden, to whom I had been going in an effort to rid myself of my phobia about traveling, that I would definitely be able to attend the conference because I would be cured of the phobia by this fall." By mid-summer, however, there had been no cure in sight and he explained to the conference organizers that he has explored various other avenues by which he might conceivably make the trip, all to no avail. It is quite a distraught letter, painful to read, especially when one realizes the extent of the psychological abuse inflicted by Branden on his trusting patient. The unusual fact that Rothbard was threatened with a lawsuit by his own therapist led to the public revelation of the intimate details of his psychological state. The ugliness of this incident is further illustrated by the fact that, in a letter to Branden, Rothbard makes it clear that it was Branden who first suggested that he make an effort to attend the conference and deliver his paper in person. It was Branden who convinced him that "there was a ninety-five percent chance of my being able to travel there." It was Branden who set this up as a test of Rothbard's ability to overcome his travel phobia—and then pounced with his phony charges of "plagiarism."[72] If anything illustrates the dangers of cultism, then this is it.

The problem with Objectivism was trenchantly diagnosed by Rothbard, who made the crucial point that "entering the movement through a novel meant that despite repeated obeisances to Reason, febrile emotion was the driving force behind the acolyte's conversion."[73] The emotional power of the Randian mythos drew many young people into contact with individualist and free-market ideas for the first time. "Almost all of the young people drawn to libertarianism in the 1960s and early 1970s came through the Randian movement," writes Rothbard, "drawn almost completely by the emotionalism of *Atlas Shrugged.* [Jerome] Tuccille's [1971 book] title *It Usually Begins With Ayn Rand*[74] was certainly correct for that period. The result of this large influx, however, was that the Randians tended to become fixated on the emotionalism, and on the personality cult of Ayn Rand." While this was not irreparable, another grave problem was that Rand's "youthful followers were actively discouraged from reading any divergent opinions, or, indeed, any of the facts of reality; each young individualist was encouraged to believe that he could spin out all theories and facts of reality from his own unaided mind," a mindset that "tended to fixate the libertarian youth at an immature level." The enforced ignorance of the Randian rank-and-file was a reflection of the top leadership: Rand herself rarely read anything more serious than a detective novel.[75] Her youthful acolytes seemed always to be rereading Rand's works—and little else. For someone who claimed to have created a complete philosophical system encompassing metaphysics, epistemology, ethics, and esthetics, Rand produced very little nonfiction writing. A long-promised nonfiction treatise on her philosophy was never written. Aside from a slender volume on the Objectivist theory of concept-formation, and various lectures and short essays culled from her magazine, the philosophical writings of Ayn Rand are rather sparse: a long essay, "For the New Intellectual," published in a book of the same title,[76] a lecture on "The Objectivist Ethics," reprinted in a collection of short pieces entitled *The Virtue of Selfishness*.[77] And that is *it*. (The official NBI "Recommended Reading" list included the works of Ludwig von Mises, with the caveat that Rand did not agree with Mises's "subjectivist epistemological views." This, of course, is a caricature of Mises's real views. Conflating epistemology with the methodology of economics, Rand and her circle demonstrated their monumental ignorance of both.)

Barbara Branden, in *The Passion of Ayn Rand*, quotes Rothbard as saying he is "in basic agreement with all [Rand's] philosophy" without sourcing the quote. She also makes the absurd and undocumented claim that Rothbard said "that it was [Rand] who convinced him of the theory of natural rights which his books uphold."[78]

The idea that Rothbard needed to be convinced of natural rights by Rand is almost as ludicrous as the delusion that Rand invented natural rights theory. Just as Rothbard's passion for justice predated the publication of *Atlas Shrugged* by many years, so the development of natural rights theory predated Rand by many centuries. This point is made, oddly enough, in Rothbard's fan letter to Rand about *Atlas Shrugged*, in which he acknowledges that

When I first met you, many years ago, I was a follower of Mises, but unhappy about his antipathy to natural rights, which I "felt" was true but could not demonstrate. You introduced me to the whole field of natural rights and natural law philosophy, which I did not know existed, and month by month, *working on my own as I preferred*, I learned and studied the glorious natural rights tradition.[79]

This reveals that Rand knew she owed more intellectual debts than the one she acknowledged to Aristotle. Rand clearly provided Rothbard with a few leads as to the direction his research might take, and that is what he acknowledges—not, as Barbara Branden would have it, that "it was [Rand] who convinced him of the theory of natural rights which his books uphold."

As the libertarian philosopher George H. Smith points out in *Atheism, Ayn Rand, and Other Heresies*, "Rand's theory of ethics is based on natural law, an approach that was exceedingly popular for many centuries (we find it in the ancient Stoics, for instance). As natural law ethics fell into disfavor, Rand was one among a minority of philosophers (mainly Aristotelians) who attempted to resurrect this tradition—although here, as elsewhere, Rand labored under the misapprehension that she was giving birth to a new approach, rather than breathing life into an old one."[80]

Rand's standing as *the* original libertarian natural rights theorist seems dubious at best, especially in light of Rothbard's revelation that she had to be talked out of her support for the concept of "eminent domain," that is, government seizure of private land. In a discussion of influences on Rand's thought, including the authors Rose Wilder Lane and Isabel Paterson, Rothbard remarks that "the last person I know of to convert Ayn Rand to anything was Herb Cornuelle. Apparently he converted her to being against eminent domain. She apparently had been for it because it was in the Constitution."[81]

Ms. Branden's contention that Rothbard was "in basic agreement" with the Randian creed is true in the narrow sense that they both were advocates of individualism and laissez-faire capitalism. Both believed in the possibility and necessity of a rational ethics. Where they differed was in their general approach to ideas. Rand's attitude toward the history of ideas and her own place in it is summed up in the pronouncement of Howard Roark, the hero of *The Fountainhead*, who declares "I inherit nothing. I stand at the end of no tradition. I may, perhaps, stand at the beginning of one."[82]

Unlike Rand, Rothbard was too widely read to believe that he had invented reason and individualism. He *had* inherited something: not only the insights of Mises and the Austrian School, but also the revolutionary optimism of Lord Acton, the intellectual and political heritage of classical liberalism, as well as the fighting spirit and stern anti-imperialism of the Old Right. He was proud to stand at the end of a long and glorious tradition.

Rothbard's foray into the eccentric exoticism of Ayn Rand and her followers was a diversion, really only a brief interlude, before he would embark on the next leg of his ideological odyssey, a journey that would take him beyond left and right, and create in the process a new synthesis: libertarianism. In the fantasy world of Rand and her acolytes, which was after all centered around the pronouncements of fictional characters and the events of a novel, the stark realism of such questions as the prospect of nuclear war did not come up for discussion. But in the real world, school-children practicing their air raid drills were told to "duck and cover," and their parents were building fallout shelters in the back yards of suburban America. Rand, a Russian immigrant and refugee from Stalin's terror, was a fanatical Cold Warrior who knew nothing about foreign policy, and so naturally wrote exten-sively on the subject. As the international situation worsened and war clouds loomed, Rothbard was increasingly worried and instinctively drew closer to his old friend Leonard Liggio, who had stayed aloof from the Randians and instead pursued his own contacts on the antimilitarist Left.

REEVALUATION AND RENEWAL: THE REVISIONIST INSIGHT

The old Circle Bastiat had dispersed, with Raico and Hamowy departing for Chicago. Ideologically, Rothbard and Leonard Liggio were utterly isolated in New York City, without resources of their own or any kind of organizational backing, without a platform or a literary outlet from which to raise high the banner of liberty. Anybody else would have given up the fight. Instead, he and Liggio embarked on a wide-ranging intellectual and ideological reevaluation of their previous position, and took a kind of intellectual inventory of their liabilities as well as their assets. Their chief asset, aside from the mighty theoretical edifice of Misesian economics, was the isolationist legacy of the Old Right: but, they asked, where had the Old Rightists gone wrong? What fatal flaw in their outlook led to their defeat? Rethinking the question of just who started the Cold War and who kept it going, Rothbard and Liggio concluded that "our older isolationism had suffered from a fatal weakness: the implicit acceptance of the basic Cold War premise that there *was* a Russian threat."[83] They adopted a view of Stalin that many of the ex-leftists in the conservative movement no doubt found familiar: one that closely resembled Trotsky's in that it depicted Stalin as narrowly concerned with building socialism in one country, the Soviet Union, at the expense of the Communist principle of "proletarian internationalism," that is, the duty of exporting Red revolution to other countries. Stalin's successors had hewed to the same nationalist line, and, furthermore, due to their increasing economic weakness, had almost frantically tried to stop the military build-up and achieve disarmament through negotiation. The United States had always successfully resisted, and American peace activists were routinely dismissed and smeared by the Right as Communist dupes or worse. The works of D. F. Fleming, William Appleman Williams, and Gabriel Kolko, put the libertarian insight that the greatest threat to American liberty is in Washington, D.C., in a new light. Rothbard and Liggio now agreed that "there was no Russian 'threat' ":

> The threat to the peace of the world, in Europe, in Asia, and throughout the globe was the United States Leviathan. For years, conservatives and libertarians had argued about the "external" (Russian) and "internal" (Washington) threats to individual liberty, with libertarians and isolationists focusing on the latter and conservatives on the former. But now we—Leonard and I—were truly liberated; the scales had fallen from our eyes, and we saw that the "external threat," too, emanated from Washington, D.C.[84]

This revisionist view of the global conflict was complemented by a developing revisionist perspective on the domestic front. Both Rothbard and Liggio had always considered themselves extreme right-wingers, an allegiance that had, up until this point, seemed entirely natural. But the first advocates of laissez-faire were on the Left—the seventeenth- and eighteenth-century liberals who rose up against monarchy, theocracy, and war, and overthrew the old order. Socialism, in this new schema, was a confused middle-of-the-road doctrine between pure liberty, on the Left, and unmitigated statism, in the form of throne-and-altar conservatism, on the Right. From this new analysis, Rothbard drew three corollary conclusions, simultaneously puncturing three key misconceptions widely held on the Right:

1. The concept of libertarians and conservatives as "natural"

allies was based on a myth. In the 1920s, libertarians Mencken and Nock, who battled Prohibition and exposed the lies of Versailles, were considered liberals. A decade passed, and these same old-style liberals were denounced as right-wing extremists for opposing the New Deal and FDR's road to war, and their allies were conservative businessmen, such as general Robert E. Wood, chief executive of Sears and Roebuck, who headed up the antiwar America First Committee. Rothbard's history lesson raised the possibility of a future alliance with the Left. The important change in Rothbard's thinking was that such a decision was, in any case, a tactical question, and not a matter of high principle: with the destruction of the Volker Fund, the last of his emotional and organizational ties to the Right had been broken.

2. The right-wing fear of Marxian communism was, as Rothbard puts it, "inordinate." As a confused and contradictory system, which expected a dictatorship to cause "the withering away of the State," socialism could not last; as Mises had demonstrated, the socialist plan for the economy leads to its inevitable collapse. Since socialism would be discredited and dethroned "before too many years had elapsed," there was nothing to fear from the Left: the real enemy was Bill Buckley and his trigger-happy crew of vengeful ex-Communists whose blood-lust would not be satiated until they had fired the first shots of World War III.[85]

3. The right-wing mythology that, before Franklin Delano Roosevelt, the United States was a free-market utopia, virtually devoid of government regulation, displayed a complete ignorance of history. Rothbard was at this point considering, if not actually writing, his pathbreaking contribution to economic history, *America's Great Depression*.[86] Here he applies the Misesian theory of the business cycle—as originating in bank credit expansion and subsequent malinvestment—to the story of the Great Crash. Blasting the conservatives' revered image of Herbert Hoover as the

ideological antipode to the hated FDR, Rothbard showed how
Hoover's program of public works and welfarism paved the way
for the New Deal revolution. The Hooverite cadre in conservative
circles were especially incensed by the book, as was the *New York
Times*, which sneered that "this book is so far to the right that . . .
the author criticizes the policies of former President Herbert
Hoover as being too radical and ascribes to him, with bitterness,
the start of the New Deal." As an example of "creeping conservatism," Rothbard's book should be read only in tandem with
something along the lines of Marx's *Capital*, for the sake of balance,
although "most readers probably find the middle a happier place
to be." This insipid critique averred that "Dr. Rothbard's completely laissez-faire economics will never capture public enthusiasm because it lacks a basic need in today's world—humanity."[87]

With the liberal left and the Hooverite right up in arms over
the book, Rothbard surely felt he was on the correct path: his
analysis of the role of big business in the rise of the modern welfare-warfare state offended the official mythology of both liberal
corporatism and its "conservative" twin brother. This new direction in Rothbard's research and thinking was influenced by a
group of left-revisionist historians who studied under William
Appleman Williams at the University of Wisconsin, most notably
Gabriel Kolko. In his book, *The Triumph of Conservatism*, Kolko
showed that the lords of Big Business, far from being martyrs to
the cause of free market capitalism and "America's Most Persecuted Minority," as Ayn Rand had put it, were actually the most
powerful and implacable enemies of laissez faire. The corporate
giants had not only favored the Progressive era regulations but
had also *originated* them in an effort to cartellize the markets.
Instead of a "persecuted minority," the corporate giants were, in
large part, a state-privileged elite. Far from championing free markets in principle or in practice, corporate barons had ruthlessly

used the blunt instrument of government to erect barriers to market entry and bludgeon their competitors into submission.[88]

It is typical of Rothbard that, in developing this new perspective, his excitement at the discovery and implications of new ideas ignored the practical question of how to communicate them, that is, through what medium. As JoAnn Rothbard succinctly put it, "Murray couldn't organize his way out of a paper bag," but he had the capacity to inspire those who could. In later years, he would attract many such men of action, lieutenants who mediated between Rothbard's exuberant optimism and the dreary reality of practical tasks. But they had yet to appear. Recalling that time, Rothbard writes: "Isolated and alone, Leonard Liggio and I nevertheless set out on what seemed to be a superhuman . . . task"—the consolidation of a tiny and scattered libertarian movement into a cohesive national group dedicated to their new "left-right perspective."[89]

Fortunately, there was one bright spot on the libertarian horizon: the emergence of the Freedom School, in the Colorado Rockies, as the center of a new libertarian activism. Established in 1956, the Freedom School was the brainchild of Robert LeFevre, a pacifist of the individualist anarchist persuasion and a colorful and charismatic man whose skills as a teacher gave him a great success in converting young people to libertarianism. As graduates of the Freedom School fanned out across the country, more than a few found their way to New York, including Edward Facey, Robert J. Smith, and Roy A Childs Jr. Alan Milchman, head of the Brooklyn Young Americans for Freedom, was won over, along with a sizable contingent at the University of Kansas, where the group was headed by Bob Gaskins and David Jackman. The addition of the Kansas group was particularly gratifying for Rothbard, since they put out a periodical, *The Standard*; the voice of the Old Right would at last be heard, and Rothbard's search for an outlet for his foreign policy views was, he thought, happily ended. The April 1963 issue of *The*

Standard contained reprints from Chodorov and Mises on the centrality of libertarian opposition to the war-making powers of the state, as well as an important essay by Rothbard, "War, Peace, and the State."[90] But student publications are even more ephemeral than student political organizations, and *The Standard* was soon defunct.

As 1964 rolled around and the candidacy of Barry Goldwater mobilized the Right in a frenzied crusade, Rothbard was frantic: his old enemies at *National Review* had their fingers much closer to the nuclear button than he had ever thought possible.

Without a forum to express his views, however, there was little he could do to stem the overwhelming tide of enthusiasm for Goldwater on the Right, even in the libertarian precincts of the movement. All he could do was write a letter to *The Innovator*, a small newsletter published in Southern California—at that time a major nexus of libertarian activism, such as it was—protesting their virtual endorsement of the 1964 GOP presidential candidate. On domestic economic issues, he pointed out, Goldwater was timid to a fault: "I would like, in fact, for you to point to one specific mainstay of the current statist system that Goldwater proposes to repeal."[91] The income tax, under a Goldwater regime, would not only stay intact but would retain its "progressivity." Social security would also remain sacrosanct, along with antitrust legislation; and besides that, the candidate's economic advisors were all Keynesians. Contrary to popular belief, Goldwater did not propose to dismantle the Tennessee Valley Authority, but only to sell the steam-generating plants to state governments. Even in the unlikely event that President Goldwater launched an authentic attempt to dismantle the statist order, "what in the world can he do on all these problems, when Congress would not be in any sense in Goldwaterite hands?" But as president, Goldwater would not be powerless:

There is one aspect of presidential power, however, where Goldwater would have, as president, almost unlimited freedom of
action. This, unfortunately, is in the field of foreign affairs. Here
the president can do almost anything he wants. And here is precisely the area where Goldwater and the conservative movement
are not only not libertarian, but the preeminent enemies of liberty
in our time. For the Goldwaterites are, first and foremost, aggressive and ardent champions of American imperialism [and] eager
advocates of nuclear war against the Soviet Union. They are the
big "button-pushers" of our time.[92]

Lyndon Johnson's now-infamous television attack ad, showing
a little girl cavorting in a field of flowers while nukes sent by the
evil Goldwater explode overhead, was denounced by "fair-
minded" liberals and remembered by conservatives as the political
equivalent of the Japanese attack on Pearl Harbor—but Rothbard
was delighted. At last, the Democrats were "zeroing in on the true
dimensions of the Goldwaterite menace."[93]

The role of the entrepreneur is to anticipate trends, or try to,
and thus be in on the ground floor when it is time to cash in.
Timing is everything, and the intellectual entrepreneur who is a
few steps ahead of history is likely, in time, to be rewarded. But
there is always a lull, a period when history has yet to catch up,
and the innovator is left alone to contemplate his isolation. It must
have been more than a little demoralizing, then, even to the ever-
optimistic Rothbard, when he realized that even among Mises and
the Misesians his political views were considered heretical if not
beyond the pale. It was during this period that he turned more
often to the genuine outsiders among his friends and correspondents, such as that old iconoclast Harry Elmer Barnes, for a sympathetic hearing: "Actually, though I'm personally very fond of
von Mises, and economically count myself a disciple of his and the

Austrian tradition, the political differences between myself and the other Misesians are so enormous that relations are getting pretty strained all around," he confided to Barnes. A few times a year, Mises's friends and disciples would gather in New York City for a dinner, with speakers and discussion, "and for the last couple of times, it has been me and one or two other mavericks against the crowd (including Mises), and the atmosphere is getting pretty strained." One source of the strain was the growing war hysteria of the Right, personified by the presidential candidacy of Barry Goldwater: "Last fall, I delivered a paper on [the Great Depression of] 1929, and used the opportunity to slam into Goldwater and the Goldwater Movement—which had a blockbuster effect on the assembled people (e.g., [Sylvester] Petro, Henry Hazlitt, et al.)." There had been another confrontation when one Professor Shenfield, a British economist, "delivered a long panegyric to Western Imperialism, and what a terrible thing it was that these ungrateful colonials had the gall to want the British, etc. kicked out." But the worst of it was that "the general trend of the audience was anti-Shenfield . . . for being too soft on the wogs, since he couldn't bring himself to advocate marching back in to 'protect private property.' " Rothbard's vocal and vigorous dissent in favor of "the old fashioned Cobdenite anti-imperialist position" had gotten him nowhere. "If not for a few congenial people like yourself and Baldy [F. A. Harper] around," he told Barnes, "the world would be pretty grim, intellectually and politically."[94]

It was, indeed, a grim prospect that awaited his trenchant and timely article, "The Transformation of the American Right," which could only find a home in the pages of *Continuum*, an obscure Catholic quarterly. "It almost takes a great effort of the will to recall the principles and objectives of the Old Right," he wrote, "so different is the current right-wing today." While the emphasis had been on "the Billy James Hargises, the Birchers, [and] the various crusaders for god and country," the lack of any real intellectual history of the American Right had obscured "an enormous and significant change in the very nature of the Right that has taken place since World War II." Yesterday's conservatives, Rothbard reminded his readers, were born in opposition to the New Deal and Roosevelt's unrelenting campaign to drag us into World War II. "The guiding motif of what we might call the 'old American Right' was a deep and passionate commitment to individual liberty, and to the belief that this liberty, in the personal and economic spheres, was gravely menaced by the growing power of the Leviathan state, at home and abroad.[95]

Whereas the heroes of the New Right were such champions of anti-Communism as Chiang Kai Chek, Francisco Franco, and Korean strongman Syngman Rhee, Rothbard recalled a time when "the intellectual heroes of the old Right were such libertarians as John Locke, the Levellers, Jefferson, Paine, Thoreau, Cobden, Spencer, and Bastiat." While Buckley and his cabal of ex-Communists and right-wing Social Democrats were calling for a preemptive war of "liberation" against the Soviet Union, Rothbard remembered the Old Right of Garet Garrett, John T. Flynn, and that cantankerous old America Firster Louis Bromfield, a novelist and screenwriter whose advice on the Korean crisis was that the U.S. should "withdraw entirely from an area in which we have no right to be and leave the peoples of that area to work out their own problems."[96]

Quoting from Bromfield, Nock, Chodorov, Garrett, and Congressman Howard Buffet (Senator Taft's 1952 midwest campaign manager and a personal friend of Rothbard's—and, yes, father of billionaire investor Warren Buffet), Rothbard's portrait of the Old Right was shot through with nostalgia for a movement that had disappeared at the very moment when it was most sorely needed. Rothbard writes that "these quotations give the flavor of an era that is so remote as to make it seem incredible that such views should have dominated the American Right-wing."[97]

In his *Continuum* piece, Rothbard made the vitally important— and prescient—point that the contemporary Right's hankering for a military confrontation with the Soviet Union was based, in part, on the assumption that "once communism 'takes over' a country, it is doomed, and its population might as well be written off to the eternal abyss." Such stark pessimism was shortsighted in the extreme, and "all the more curious in the light of the demonstrations by libertarian economists that socialism cannot provide a viable economic system for an industrial society." De-communization was not only possible, as in the case of Yugoslavia, but very probable; yet "the indifference to this problem on the Right is another indication of its concern: nuclear war. De-communization is to come about, not through a change in the ideas and actions of the Russian and other peoples, but, according to the Right, through their liquidation."[98]

Liberation through liquidation was a fate the peoples of the world managed to avoid; but at the time this was not at all certain. Indeed, with the Cold War heating up, and conflict breaking out in Africa, the Middle East, and Southeast Asia, the prospect of nuclear annihilation seemed a far likelier resolution to the Cold War impasse than what eventually came to pass. The specter of another world war—one that would dwarf the destructive power of the first two—is what motivated Rothbard to raise the standard of peace in a war-torn world. Yet in spite of the paucity of his readers, the unpopularity of his stance, and the fact that the cause of the Old Right seemed irretrievably lost, Rothbard was quietly optimistic. There were "some signs" that "thinkers are beginning to apprehend the dissolution of the old forms." The libertarian movement was beginning to stir; some conservatives were raising questions about the New Right takeover; and the eminent critic Edmund Wilson had come out with a polemic entitled *The Cold War and the Income Tax*. "Perhaps indeed," Rothbard concluded, "the country is ripe for a fundamental ideological realignment."[99]

As the Goldwater campaign went down to defeat—much to Rothbard's relief—the invincible complacency of postwar corporate liberalism seemed utterly justified. But the celebration of the "end of ideology" had been premature. By fall, the Free Speech Movement had emerged at the Berkeley campus, and the world was turned upside down. On April 17, 1965, tens of thousands marched on Washington demanding an end to the Vietnam war. The rollercoaster ride of the sixties had begun.

Rothbard was ready for it, ready to move on to new frontiers, new circles, new ways to influence the political culture—and, along the way, set in place the foundation stones of a mighty theoretical edifice, a new and radical paradigm that would inspire the birth of a newly independent libertarian movement.

NOTES

1. See Murray N. Rothbard, "Mises, 'Human Action': Comment," *American Economic Review* (March 1951): 181–85. See also Murray N. Rothbard, "Praxeology: Reply to Mr. Schuller," *American Economic Review*, December 1951, pp. 943-46.

2. Rothbard to Richard Cornuelle, 1 April 1954, p. 4. Emphasis in original.

3. Rothbard to Ludwig Lachmann, 14 February 1957, p. 4.

4. Murray N. Rothbard, "In Defense of 'Extreme Apriorism,' " *Southern Economic Review* (January 1957): 314–20.

5. Ibid.

6. Murray N. Rothbard, "The Mantle of Science," in *Scientism and Values*, ed. Helmut Schoeck and James W. Widgeons (Princeton, N.J.: D. Van Nostrand, 1960). Reprinted in Murray N. Rothbard, *The Logic of Action*, vol. 1 (Cheltenham, UK: Edward Elgar, 1997). Page numbers refer to this edition.

7. Cited in John T. Flynn, *The Roosevelt Myth* (San Francisco: Fox and Wilkes, 1998), p. 137.

8. Ibid., pp. 10–11.

9. Ibid., pp. 22–23.

10. Parker Thomas Moon, *Imperialism and World Politics* (New York: Macmillan, 1930), p. 58.

11. Murray N. Rothbard, "The Politics of Political Economists," *The Quarterly Journal of Economics* (February 1960): 659–65.

12. Ludwig von Mises, review of *Man, Economy, and State*, by Murray Rothbard, *New Individualist Review* (Autumn 1962): 41.

13. David Gordon, *Murray N. Rothbard: A Scholar In Defense of Freedom: A Bibliographical Essay* (Auburn, Ala.: Ludwig von Mises Institute, 1986), pp. 10–11.

14. Ibid.

15. Mises, review of *Man, Economy, and State*, p. 39.

16. Ibid.

17. Rothbard, "The Betrayal of the American Right," unpublished manuscript, pp. 179–80.

18. Ibid.

19. Rothbard to William F. Buckley Jr., 19 August 1956.

20. Ibid.

21. Ibid.

22. Rothbard to William F. Buckley Jr., 8 September 1959.

23. Ibid.

24. Rothbard, "The Betrayal of the American Right," 182.

25. Ibid.

26. Ibid.

27. Ibid., p. 183.

28. Edward C. Facey, "Conservatives or Individualists: Which Are We?" *New Individualist Review* (summer 1961): 24.

29. " 'National Review': Criticism and Reply," *New Individualist Review* (November 1961): 3.

30. Ibid., p. 4.

31. Ibid., p. 5.

32. William F. Buckley Jr., "Three Drafts of an Answer to Mr. Hamowy," *New Individualist Review* (November 1961): 9.

33. Ibid., p. 5.

34. Ronald Hamowy, "A Rejoinder to Mr. Buckley in One Draft," *New Individualist Review* (November 1961): 11.

35. Cited in Rothbard, "The Betrayal of the American Right," p. 186.

36. Rothbard to Richard Cornuelle, 11 August 1954, p. 1.

37. Ibid.

38. Ibid.

39. Ibid., p. 2.

40. Ibid.

41. Ibid.

42. Aside from the testimony of the Brandens, elaborated on in their numerous writing, the peculiar grimness of the Randians is acknowledged as a problem by some latter-day Objectivists. See David Kelley, *Truth and Toleration* (New York: Institute for Objectivist Studies, 1990). Kelley's emphasis on Rand's concept of the "benevolent sense-of-life" seeks to rescue Objectivism from the Objectivists.

43. Rothbard to Richard Cornuelle, August 11, 1954, p. 3.

44. See Barbara Branden, *The Passion of Ayn Rand* (Garden City, N.Y.: Doubleday & Co., 1986), pp. 255–79.

45. Rothbard to Richard Cornuelle, 11 August 1954, p. 3. Emphasis added.

46. Ibid., p. 4.

47. The original 1936 edition contained passages that were excised from later editions. On this and Rand's early Nietzscheanism, see Jeff Walker, *The Ayn Rand Cult* (Chicago: Open Court Publishing Co., 1999), pp. 275–77.

48. R. W. Bradford, "The Rise of the New Libertarianism," *Liberty* (March 1999): 43.

49. Rothbard to Richard Cornuelle, 11 August 1954, p. 3.

50. Rothbard to Mrs. Ayn Rand O'Connor, 3 October 1957.

51. Ibid.

52. Ibid., p. 2.

53. Ibid., p. 3.

54. Murray N. Rothbard, *The Sociology of the Ayn Rand Cult* (Burlingame, California: Center for Libertarian Studies, [1972] 1990).

55. Patricia Donegan, "A Point of View," *The Commonweal* (November 8, 1957): 155–56.

56. Murray N. Rothbard, "Communications," *The Commonweal* (December 20, 1957): 312–13.

57. "Note on a Bestseller," *The Commonweal* (January 3, 1958): 349.

58. Rothbard to Mrs. Ayn Rand O'Connor, 3 October 1957, p. 4.

59. Interview with Walter Block and Walter Grinder, "Rothbard Tells All," unpublished transcript in possession of author, p. 16

60. *The Sociology of the Ayn Rand Cult*, p. 5.

61. Bennett Cerf, *At Random* (New York: Random House, 1977).

62. Ibid., p. 10.

63. Ibid., p. 11.

64. Interview with JoAnn Rothbard.

65. Rothbard to Richard C. Cornuelle, 27 July 1958.

66. Interview with JoAnn Rothbard, July 1994.

67. Ludwig von Mises to Rothbard, 30 July 1958.

68. Helmut Schoeck to James W. Wiggins, 13 August 1958.

69. Rothbard to Richard Cornuelle, 27 July 1958.

70. Murray N. Rothbard, "Toward a Theory of Libertarian Social Change," pp.62, 67. Emphasis in original.

71. For a discussion of the secular mysticism of Rand and her followers, see Dr. Albert Ellis, *Is Objectivism a Religion?* (New York: Lyle Stuart, 1968).

72. Rothbard to Nathaniel Branden, 15 July 1958.

73. Rothbard, *Sociology of the Ayn Rand Cult*, p. 5

74. Jerome Tuccille, *It Usually Begins With Ayn Rand* (New York: Stein and Day, 1971).

75. Rothbard, *Sociology of the Ayn Rand Cult*, p, 6.

76. Ayn Rand, *For the New Intellectual* (New York: New American Library, 1961).

77. Ayn Rand, *The Virtue of Selfishness: A New Concept of Egoism* (New York: New American Library, 1964).

78. Barbara Branden, *The Passion of Ayn Rand*, p. 413.

79. Rothbard to Rand, 3 October 1957. Emphasis added.

80. George H. Smith, *Atheism, Ayn Rand, and Other Heresies* (Amherst, N.Y.: Prometheus Books, 1991), p. 202.

81. Block and Grinder, "Rothbard Tells All," p. 18.

82. Ayn Rand, *The Fountainhead* (Indianapolis: Bobbs-Merril, 1943), p. 25.

83. Rothbard, "The Betrayal of the American Right," p. 188.

84. Ibid., p. 190. While not in any way disparaging Liggio's contribution during this time, it was typical of Rothbard to be wildly generous in crediting others for his own insights.

85. Ibid., p. 194: "If ours—and Mises's—analysis was right, then socialism should fall apart before too many years had elapsed, and much more rapidly than the Old Order, which had had the capacity to last unchanged for centuries."

86. Murray N. Rothbard, *America's Great Depression* (Los Angeles, Calif.: Nash Publishing Co., 1963).

87. "Books of the Times: End Papers," *New York Times*, 17 October 1963.

88. Gabriel Kolko, *The Triumph of Conservatism* (Glencoe, Ill.: The Free Press, 1963).

89. Rothbard, "The Betrayal of the American Right," p. 197.

90. Murray N. Rothbard, "War, Peace, and the State," *The Standard* (April 1963).

91. Murray N. Rothbard, letter to *The Innovator* (August 1964).

92. Ibid.

93. Rothbard, "The Betrayal of the American Right," p. 199.

94. Rothbard to Harry Elmer Barnes, 8 May 1964, p. 4.

95. Murray N. Rothbard, "The Transformation of the American Right," *Continuum* (summer 1964): 220–31.

96. Ibid., pp. 222, 224–25.

97. Ibid.

98. Ibid., pp. 227–28.

99. Ibid., p. 231.

4

BEYOND LEFT AND RIGHT

For Rothbard, the sixties were a turning point, a coming of age, a breakthrough on two distinct but interrelated fronts: the professional and the political. In both realms, he would build on his continuity with the past, as the upholder of a long and proud intellectual tradition, to project a new synthesis that completed and corrected the original.

In early 1962, the organizational foundations of the tiny libertarian movement—such as they were—were shattered by the sudden and near-total collapse of the Volker Fund. As the chief promoter of libertarian scholarship in America, the fund had sought out and subsidized scholars such as Rothbard who would otherwise have been thrown back on their own scarce resources to carry on the battle for libertarian ideas as best they could, unaided and virtually alone. The fund made it possible for Mises, Hayek, Rothbard, and dozens of others to develop and advance libertarian views in the midst of an ideological climate implacably hostile to their ideas. This anchor vanished, one day, when the president of the fund dismantled the organization "in a fit of pique."[1]

The source of the problem was Dr. Ivan Bierly, a formerly libertarian member of the staff. Bierly had been converted to the doctrines espoused by the Reverend Rousas J. Rushdoony, whose ideology is an idiosyncratic mix of old-fashioned constitutionalism and Calvinist theocratic millennialism. According to Rothbard, Bierly was "convinced of the need for an elite Calvinist dictatorship, which would run the country, stamp out pornography, and prepare America for the (literal) Armageddon, which was supposedly due to arrive in a generation." Bierly convinced Harold Luhnow, the head of the fund, "that he was surrounded on his staff by a nefarious atheist-anarchist-pacifist conspiracy."[2]

When Luhnow pulled the plug, Rothbard was devastated. In a letter to F. A. "Baldy" Harper, who had been a key Volker Fund official, Rothbard exclaimed: "Wow! What an outburst of nihilism and irrationality!" The implosion of the Volker Fund not only illustrated the dangers of one-man rule, even in a private organization, it also "seems to me symbolic of what the Right-wing has become: a totally irrational, know-nothing movement." Furthermore, it was outrageous "that supposedly intelligent people could entertain for a moment the idea that you, I, or Ken [Templeton] are either pro-Communist and/or anti-Christian." Rothbard's usually high spirits were considerably lowered as he contemplated recent events: "We are left with neither a Volker Fund nor an Institute, and the world is to be abandoned to the know-nothings. Mutual commiserations are in order." He wondered if there was "any hope at all of a Phoenix rising from the ashes, or must we all, like Howard Roark, take jobs 'at the quarry.' " It was, he concluded, "depressing that such irrationality is loose in the world." For over a decade, he had counted not only on his fees from the Volker Fund, but also on the company and good advice of its various officials and employees. He could only depend on a few more months pay, and "it therefore looks as if I will soon have to start looking for another job."[3]

His last ties to the Right severed, Rothbard took stock of his position. Several attempts to obtain an academic appointment somewhere in the New York metropolitan area had been pursued over the years, without success. He had always supplemented his income from Volker with grants from various pro-free market foundations. The Earhart Foundation had granted him a substantial sum to work on *America's Great Depression*, and he had been doing part-time work for FEE since the late forties. He also worked as a speechwriter and researcher for Congressman Ralph W. Gwinn (R-New York), an Old Right stalwart. In addition to all this, he did research and consulting for a group called the Princeton Panel, run by Richard Cornuelle, a free-market educational program aimed at businessmen.[4] Toward the end of 1962, Rothbard received a "substantial" grant from the Lilly Endowment, where Ken Templeton had wound up, to write a general history of the United States.[5] The hunt for an academic position continued until 1966, when he finally found a position at the Polytechnic Institute of Brooklyn, teaching economics to engineering students two days a week. Thanking a correspondent for his good wishes on the new job, Rothbard confided that

> actually, there are some amusing elements: for one thing, the social science department is almost solidly Marxist, probably the only Marxist department in the country (outside of the Workers' School). Actually, this means—especially with the historians here, though things are considerably rougher with the economists—that I have less actual disagreements with them than with ordinary Liberal-Keynesians. For one thing, we can spend a good part of our time denouncing the latter, as well as the Center

Establishment. Part of the time they regard me as a black reactionary, but rather more of the time as a lovable Utopian.[6]

Rothbard did not mind teaching engineering students who took his class as part of their general education requirement, nor did he mind being surrounded by Marxists: having come of age at Columbia University in the postwar years, he was rather used to it. He found his job quite satisfactory because, for the rest of the time, he was free to pursue his own interests, and this gave him the leisure to take stock in another important sense.

A NEW STRATEGIC PARADIGM

In the political-ideological realm, Rothbard continued to follow what he called his "isolationist and antistatist guiding star," with one major difference: in following it, he had often tread a very lonely path. But at last the world seemed to be catching up to him. As a massive antiwar movement emerged in opposition to the Vietnam war, Rothbard and Leonard Liggio rejoiced. These two Old Rightists, emerging from the catacombs and rubbing their eyes, could scarcely believe what they saw: the biggest antiwar movement in modern times. While the old America Firsters disbanded their organization and ceased all activity after Pearl Harbor, the opposition to U.S. military intervention in Vietnam did not begin until the war was a few years old. From his perspective, Rothbard describes what he found to be truly heartwarming:

Here at last was not a namby-pamby "peace" group like SANE [Committee for a Sane Nuclear Policy], but a truly radical antiwar movement which zeroed in on the evils of American warmaking; and here was a movement that excluded no one, that baited neither reds nor rightists, that welcomed all Americans. . . . Here at last was an antiwar Left that we could be happy about![7]

Rothbard detected an "instinctive" libertarianism in the student critique of the university, with its many ties to the military-industrial complex and its status as a virtual adjunct of the state. Albert J. Nock's pessimistic assessment of mass education and government schools found its left-reflection in social critic Paul Goodman's analysis of the public school as a technocratic machine geared to the output of human widgets.

Yet his enthusiasm for the student rebellion—unlike Ayn Rand's ill-informed blanket condemnation—was not unambiguous. For years, conservatives had been "attacking the huge and swollen bureaucracies engaged in dispensing higher education, especially the gigantic and ever-burgeoning state universities." But no sooner had "a profound and widespread rebellion against this educational Moloch emerged and accelerated among the students trapped in these universities," then "the conservatives reacted in horror" and sought to stamp the movement out on the grounds that the students were "found to violate their tastes in clothes and hair styling." But the New Left was guilty of the same kind of inconsistency: they had "not realized that [California] Governor [Ronald] Reagan, by moving to cut the university's swollen budget, has acted to reduce the very gigantic university system that the students have properly denounced. And the New Left, in protesting against Reagan's proposal for charging [formerly free] tuition, has failed to understand that there is nothing progressive about forcing the taxpayers to pay for someone else's education. On the contrary, shifting the burden of payment to the student himself will give the student-consumer far more power over their own education, and ultimately over their own fate."[8]

A peculiar historical twist that must have delighted Rothbard

was that this challenge to corporate liberalism and internation-
alism was arising in the camp of the enemy: the right-wing Social
Democrats of the League for Industrial Democracy (LID), who, as
Rothbard put it, "represented the worst of Old Left liberalism."[9] As
the youth section of the LID, Students for a Democratic Society
(SDS), formerly the Student League for Industrial Democracy
(SLID) went sliding down the slippery slope, first rejecting the
Vietnam war, then condemning red-baiting, and finally rebelling
against the whole state-capitalist order, Rothbard saw an open-
ing—and was determined that libertarians would not be left out of
the action. He was particularly gratified that the Berkeley Free
Speech Movement boasted its contingent of libertarians, the
Alliance of Libertarian Activists, which, shoulder-to-shoulder with
SDSers, battled censorship of student publications and a haughty
pedagogic nomenklatura.

In the spring of 1965, the first issue of a new journal, *Left and
Right*—subtitled "A Journal of Libertarian Thought"—rolled off the
presses. Run on a shoe-string budget and published three times a
year, *Left and Right* was founded by coeditors Rothbard, Liggio, and
libertarian scholar and activist George Resch, for two reasons: to
educate libertarians as to the necessity of turning away from their
right-wing orientation and toward the burgeoning antiwar movement, and to reach out to the Left.

The first issue featured Rothbard's seminal essay, "Left and
Right: The Prospects for Liberty." Perhaps reflecting on what was
likely to be his own destiny, Rothbard remarks that Lord Acton,
the great nineteenth-century classical liberal, was "one of the few
figures in the history of thought who, charmingly, grew more radical as he grew older," and goes on to quote Acton's vivid contrast
between the Whig and the true liberal:

The Whig is governed by compromise. The Liberal begins the

reign of ideas. . . . One is practical, gradual, ready for compromise. The other works out a principle philosophically. One is a policy aiming at a philosophy. The other is a philosophy seeking a policy.[10]

"A philosophy seeking a policy" is a phrase that fairly sums up the history of libertarianism in the modern world, and also sums up, in its essence, the course of Rothbard's evolution as a thinker. For it was typical of Rothbard that he never was content to philosophize, but always took a hands-on approach to advancing his ideas. Like his ideological opposite number, Karl Marx, a thinker of similar importance, Rothbard was a system builder who passionately believed not merely in the possibility of eventual victory, but often seemed to imply that, given certain fairly safe assumptions, the triumph of liberty was practically inevitable. In both, this belief evoked activism rather than complacency. Like Marx, who took an active role in the formation of the First International, Rothbard often plunged head-first into the organizational life of the movement he inspired.

Writing at top speed, Rothbard turned out not only scholarly treatises but also a great body of political journalism, cultural commentary, and polemics of such deadly accuracy that their subjects never forgot, or forgave. Much of his best writing is addressed to his fellow libertarians, a kind of open letter. The "Left and Right" essay takes this form, patiently explaining to the partisans of liberty why they are not reactionaries but the only true progressives. Speaking directly to the Old Right remnant that had passed through the dark age of the New Deal and survived the postwar era, he pointed out that the main problem of those who call themselves conservatives and all champions of the free market in a collectivist age is that they have "long been marked, whether [they] know it or not, by long-run pessimism, by the belief that the long-run trend, and therefore time itself, is against them." This sense of doom is fully justified, he wrote, "for conservatism is a dying remnant of the *ancien regime* of the preindustrial era, and as such, it *has* no future." But the party of liberty has no use or reason for such fatalism, for "while the short-run prospects for liberty may seem dim, the proper attitude for the libertarian to take is one of unquenchable long-term optimism."[11]

A fundamental certainty that the cause of the right and the good must triumph was essential to the character of the man; central to his personality, as well as his ideology. Rothbard's optimistic temperament is given full expression in this important essay, in which he notes the *permanence* of the liberal revolution. The wave of eighteenth-century revolutions that swept away the Old Order of feudalism and mercantilism in Europe and the Americas had achieved a victory that was irreversible. For the first time, mankind had thrown off its shackles; the society of status was effectively abolished, along with the "divine right" of kings. Not only that, but the aristocratic hierarchy lost its economic privileges. The Industrial Revolution cemented the victory of (classical) liberalism in the sense that human psychology in the developed world had undergone a fundamental change:

> The liberal revolution implanted indelibly in the minds of the masses . . . the burning desire for liberty, for land to the peasantry, for peace between the nations, and perhaps, above all, for the mobility and rising standards of living that can be brought to them only by an industrial civilization. The masses will never again accept the mindless serfdom of the Old Order. Given these demands that have been awakened, the long-run victory is inevitable.[12]

Written in the spring of 1965 as the lead article of the first issue of *Left and Right*, this essay was the manifesto of a new libertarianism, a clarion call for a new turn in the road to a free society, one that required a complete break with the outmoded and ineffective strategy of the past. This implied not only a fresh course of action, but also inspired a novel perspective, a new and deeper understanding of the history of ideas. Typically, Rothbard did not hesitate to challenge assumptions so sacred that no one had ever thought to call them into question. He saw that the political spectrum, as defined in the contemporary meanings of "Left" and "Right," had gone entirely askew. In the struggle between liberty and power, the two eternal antagonists had, somehow, switched polarities. It was a startlingly original idea, unsettling not the least because it meant that libertarians were fighting on the wrong side of the barricades.

In 1965, this was not an idea that many conservatives were willing to hear. It was the height of the Cold War, and the "New Right" of William F. Buckley Jr., mobilized by his biweekly magazine, *National Review*, was completing its mastery of the movement. Purging all elements that might impede their path to power, the Buckleyites (with the notable exception of Frank S. Meyer, a *National Review* editor and Rothbard's good friend) only really cared about a single issue: their campaign to militarily confront and destroy the Soviet Union. As Buckley put it, "we have to accept Big Government for the duration—for neither an offensive nor a defensive war can be waged . . . except through the instrument of a totalitarian bureaucracy within our shores." Far from opposing confiscatory taxation, conservatives must support "the extensive and productive tax laws that are needed to support a vigorous anti-Communist foreign policy," including the "large armies and air forces, atomic energy, central intelligence, war production boards and the attendant centralization of power in Washington—even with Truman at the reins of it all."[13]

It was typical of Rothbard that he did not care that his radical thesis would alienate some, enrage others, and cause no end of trouble. That it would isolate him and subject him to all sorts of ill-informed attacks—even to the point of being red-baited!—did not deter or even discourage him.

Left and Right: The Prospects for Liberty was a watershed in his thought, and also an act of self-discovery. For his increasing baf-flement and isolation, as the Old Right gave way to the New, at being attacked as Moscow's pawn—and by those who, up until very recently, had taken their marching orders from *Pravda*—was, in the new paradigm outlined in his essay, explained if not excused. Without changing his fundamental position one iota, Rothbard had gone from being excoriated as a right-wing extremist to being branded a Communist dupe. The explanation for this was due partly to the fact that these epithets were issuing largely from the same group of people who had been prowar left-ists and Popular Frontists during the thirties and were now liberal anti-Communists. Whatever their various line shifts, the leftist cul-tural and political elites, who dominated the intellectual and polit-ical life of New York City, had always been consistent on two points: they were invariably prowar, and always pushing for the expansion of government power on every level. The young Roth-bard had, in large part, defined himself in opposition to this intel-lectual and political establishment; now, however, in unraveling the true history of the libertarian idea, he was reconnecting the tiny and beleaguered movement to its heritage and its historic mis-sion, and, in the process, redefining himself.

A key point made by Rothbard is that the Old Order had been *permanently* defeated by the classical liberal revolutions of the eigh-teenth and nineteenth centuries: there was no going back to the abso-lutism of the preindustrial era without giving up the comforts and conveniences of modern life—and to that the masses of people would never consent. No wonder conservatives were such pes-simists! Temperamentally, as well as politically, the American Right

of the late fifties and sixties was the antipode of the Rothbardian optimism that lights up the pages of the premiere issue of *Left and Right*.

This emphasis on the history of the movement for a free
society was continued and brought up to date in Leonard Liggio's
contribution to the first issue, "Why the Futile Crusade?", a
detailed and riveting account of the rise and fall of the (Robert A.)
Taft wing of the Republican party. While pointing out that Taft
himself constantly conciliated the internationalist wing of his
party, and deferred to it in many important instances, Liggio
acquaints his readers with the more consistent views of Taft's congressional lieutenants, such as Howard Buffett. In his lead essay,
Rothbard had reclaimed for libertarians their intellectual heritage;
Liggio's task was to orient them politically, to give them some
sense of where they ought to be going by telling the story of
where they had been. Alan Milchman's review of D. F. Fleming's
The Cold War and Its Origins[14] introduced the libertarian remnant
to Cold War revisionism. In the immediate postwar era, of course,
it had been conservatives who had championed historical revisionism, and only the conservative publishers Henry Regnery, the
Caxton Printers, and Devin-Adair would touch such revisionist
works as Harry Elmer Barnes's *Perpetual War for Perpetual Peace*[15]
or Charles Callan Tansill's *Back Door to War*.[16] Now the "historical
blackout," as Barnes called it, was extended and continued in the
era of the Cold War, with ostensible conservatives leading the
charge. Thus, revisionism was taken up once again by liberals and
the left, just as it had been in the years of post-Versailles liberal
disillusion, when the myth of German war guilt was exploded by
Nock, Mencken, Oswald Garrison Villard, and others then considered men of the Left.

Left and Right never had a circulation of more than a few thousand, but its influence on a whole generation of libertarians was to
effect an intellectual sea-change. Without funding, or promotion,

Left and Right found its way to pockets of libertarian supporters on campuses across the nation. From Berkeley to the University of Kansas to the University of North Carolina, libertarian student organizations inspired by Rothbard's call to reclaim their legacy as the "true" Left sprang up overnight—and suddenly libertarians were being noticed. Ronald Hamowy's article in the *New Republic*, "Left and Right Meet," publicized the Rothbardian "left-right" strategy, contrasting the free market anti-imperialist legacy of Spencer, Bastiat, Sumner, and Nock, with the hopped-up jingoism of the Buckleyites. While conservatives were intent on crushing civil liberties and defending a technocratic bureaucracy against its youthful charges, there was, Hamowy argued, a nascent libertarian spirit in the New Left revolt against the tyranny of the public school system and the state-subsidized and -controlled universities.[17]

In practical terms, the New Left movement afforded libertarians a chance to bypass the official institutions of the university, which had always been closed to them (witness Mises's isolation and humiliation at NYU). The movement also enabled them to utilize various counter and parallel institutions set up by the New Left: Rothbard and Liggio were particularly interested in the "Free University" phenomenon that sprang up briefly during the heyday of the New Left as a way to bypass the academic and political establishment. Liggio started teaching a course on the nature and history of imperialism at the Free University of New York; via this forum, and on the strength of *Left and Right*, Rothbard came into contact with the students of William Appleman Williams who lived in the vicinity of New York City: James Weinstein, Ronald Radosh, and Martin Sklar. The Free University course also launched Liggio on a new career as a New Left scholar and activist: he played a key role in the antiwar "Teach-in" movement, became an editor of the New Left journal *Leviathan*, and was put in charge of the American section of the Bertrand Russell Peace Foundation. The most notable achievement of the foundation was to organize a War Crimes Tribunal which judged the U.S. government guilty of crimes against humanity in Vietnam.[18]

Rothbard's intervention in New Left politics did not mean the abandonment of the Old Right: far from it, *Left and Right* was devoted to educating a new generation about the fact that such a movement had even existed. The third issue reprinted in its entirety Garet Garrett's philippic *Rise of Empire*, in which the author, a master polemicist and stylist of the Old Right, mourned the passing of the Old Republic and saw, in the shadow of that "pygmy" Truman, portents of an American Caesar. Such grizzled America Firsters as Harry Elmer Barnes and William L. Neumann were featured alongside Ronald Radosh and Conrad Lynn. *Left and Right* represented Rothbard's strategic conception of a Left-Right alliance against the tyranny of the Center. The smug complacency of the social democratic intellectuals, who proclaimed "the end of ideology," was shattered. His long and lonely guerrilla campaign against the status quo, begun in the immediate postwar era, was finally beginning to yield a few victories.

AMERICA IN THE SIXTIES—
A ROTHBARDIAN PERSPECTIVE

Rothbard's affiliation with and enthusiasm for the New Left during its heyday in the sixties has long been a lightning rod for his critics in the libertarian movement as well as among conservatives. The latter used it as a means to red-bait and otherwise smear his memory, while the former, in light of his later turn toward the Right, cite his pro–New Left writings as proof of inconsistency. Yet anyone who examines the record of his political commentary during this period in the context of his later writings can only note that it seems to echo, down through the decades, a single leitmotif: the centrality of human freedom.

One striking example among many is his cogent and clear exposition of independence in "The Principles of Secession," which appeared in a newspaper column written sometime in the summer of 1967.[19] Here he defends General Charles DeGaulle, who "has been reviled, derided, and hooted at by the entire American press for getting up in Quebec and shouting, 'Vive le Quebec Libre.' " While the general's dramatic gesture was an occasion for merriment in the United States, in Canada, and especially in Quebec this was taken quite seriously because "they knew that Canada is two nations, and that the British have been dominating the French in Canada ever since Britain invaded and conquered New France (as Canada was called) in the mid-eighteenth century." In view of this history, he asks: "Why shouldn't the French of Quebec have the right to secede from Canada and form their own nation, where their own language and culture prevails?" He goes on to point out that "none of the territorial boundaries of the current governments of the world are God-ordained; they are all products of historical forces, most of which were unjust and coercive." Libertarians, however, could object: "Wouldn't the French only be setting up a Quebec state, and why would this be better than a Canadian state?" In anticipating this criticism, Rothbard displays the strategic intelligence that imbues all his political commentary. "One answer," he writes, "is that decentralization is itself a good. . . . The more states the world is fragmented into, the less power any one state can build up, whether over its own hapless subjects or over foreign peoples in making war." Rothbard also avers "that as long as states exist it is a net gain to eliminate the tyranny of a state over a minority ethnic group." Aside from fulfilling the right of these minorities to be free of ethnic and religious persecution, support for the principle of secessionism advanced the libertarian agenda in another vitally important way: "For if one part of a country is allowed to secede, and this principle is established, then a subpart of that must be allowed to secede, and a subpart of *that*, breaking the government into ever smaller and less powerful fragments . . . until at last the principle is established that the individual may secede—and then we will have true freedom at last." This must move every libertarian to endorse secession movements wherever and whenever they may arise: and not only in Quebec, or Africa, or Scotland, or some other exotic locale, but right here at home in the United States. In this and other newspaper columns, Rothbard raised the prospect of an independent black republic seceding from the United States.

As the Black Power movement gained momentum, in the streets as well as in the media, and the "long hot summer" of 1967 razed cities to the ground, he defended the thesis that the spectacle of "tanks rumbling through the streets, buildings sprayed wholesale with machine-gun fire, . . . compulsory curfews and blockades imposed" on black neighborhoods from Los Angeles to Detroit dramatized a simple fact: "Negroes in America are, indeed, an occupied and colonized people," and therefore "we must give serious consideration to a solution which, baldly stated, seems absurd and ridiculous: the partitioning of the United States into white and Negro nations."[20]

In 1967, Rothbard had lamented "the tragedy of the southern defeat in the Civil War, for that defeat has buried the very thought of secession in this country from that time forward. But might does not make right, and the cause of secession may rise again."[21] Twenty-five years later, the cause did rise again when I personally heard Rothbard explain the same principles of secession—in virtually identical language—to a meeting of the Southern League (now the League of the South), which seeks the restoration of the old Confederacy. The audience had changed: the speaker had not. He was still at the same old stand, preaching an identical doctrine of self-determination, eagerly looking for chinks in the armor of the centralized state. What had changed was that instead of black neighborhoods being targeted and razed to the ground by "law enforcement" agencies, white separatists and Christian fundamentalists at Waco and Ruby Ridge were the quarry. The victims of state oppression had changed, but Rothbard's message was the same subversive refrain: *secede!*

Then and later, Rothbard opposed liberal integrationism. In a three-part column on the urban riots in the summer of 1967, he hailed the rise of black nationalism: "The Negro movement has come a long way from the days when compulsory integration was the goal and the NAACP was the leader. The old civil rights movement was thoroughly statist and modern-liberal; its goal was to use the arm of the federal and other governments to coerce whites into hiring, eating, and living with Negroes. The new movement, headed by [H.] Rap Brown and Stokely Carmichael of SNCC [Student Nonviolent Coordinating Committee], is totally and radically alienated from the government of the United States and the entire power structure." He was particularly taken with Brown's declaration that "the white man makes all the laws, he drags us before his courts, he accuses us, and he sits in judgment over us." "There speaks the voice of a true black nationalist," he wrote admiringly, and one with whom he could make common cause. In Rothbard's view, black separatism was the "inner logic of the continuing rebellions of the Negro ghettoes," and this was explicitly recognized by black activists at the National Black Power Conference held in Newark that year. The answer to the racial turmoil that engulfed the nation was not brute force, as the conservatives maintained; such a policy, Rothbard believed, would only provoke more violence and exacerbate the problem. Yet liberals were just as bad, if not worse in their way: "Nothing is deader than the Liberal solu-

tion of more federal funds, more playgrounds, interracial committees, and all the rest. Detroit was supposed to be the great model
home of Liberal Race Relations, with plenty of playgrounds," etc.,
"and Detroit suffered a week-long civil war and property damage
of $1 billion. Detroit murdered liberalism, and good riddance."[22]

The death of the old statist-oriented civil rights movement was
prefigured in the assassination of Martin Luther King Jr. Rothbard
deplored and condemned the assassination of King, "but no more
and no less than I deplore and condemn the murder of any man,"
noting that stores were not closed for a week nor were ball games
canceled when "the great black leader Malcom X" was killed by an
assassin's bullet. Why all the brouhaha over King? Because he
"was the major restraining force on the developing Negro revolution. All the more was this true because, in moments of crisis, he
relaxed his absolute nonviolence to come out in favor of the use of
violence by federal troops to put down Negro rioting." Riots
erupted in Washington, D.C., in the wake of King's death, and "we
were treated to the highly revealing picture of soldiers with
machine guns on the White House steps. The veil, the mask, the
illusion that the government rules by voluntary 'consent' of the
public was, in those photographs, stripped away, and we saw
clearly, some for the first time, that the government rules, in the
last analysis, by the gun and the bayonet—and by these alone."[23]

The government's war on American blacks had its parallel in
that same government's war on the Vietnamese. When the cities
erupted and blacks openly and massively rebelled against the government, the establishment was divided into "hawks" and
"doves," and there was talk of "search and destroy." Rothbard
cites one General Almerin C. O'Hara, commander of the New York
National Guard, who said he would "not rule out the use of any
weapon" to crush the urban rebellions. "Escalation once more
raises its ugly head," wrote Rothbard. When Lyndon Baines

Johnson deplored the July insurrection and declared violence "will not be tolerated," Rothbard could not contain his disdain. Johnson's statement, that "we will not endure violence; it matters not by whom it is done, or under what banner," was "a classic of its kind," said Rothbard, a "masterpiece of unconscious humor." Rothbard's guffaw was fairly audible: "It is a statement from a man in charge of the greatest violence-wielding machine, the mightiest collection of destructive power, in the history of the world. It comes from a man in charge of the day-by-day use of that power to bomb, burn, and napalm thousands of innocent women and children and old people in Vietnam."[24]

Four years into the Johnson presidency, Rothbard summed up LBJ's reign not as liberalism betrayed but as liberalism fulfilled: "By launching imperial war against foreign countries, by expanding the power of the state over the economy and the society, by bringing ever greater military control of society, Lyndon Baines Johnson is only following in the footsteps of his—and the intellectuals'—beloved mentors, Roosevelt and Truman. No wonder Lyndon feels puzzled and betrayed by the rancor of the liberal intellectuals."[25]

Liberal internationalism was still the great enemy, and, for all his potshots at conservatives, the main target of the curmudgeonly Old Rightist. In attacking the draft as slavery and rejecting the specious claim that an army of conscripts could be the defender of "freedom," Rothbard was updating the Old Right critique of FDR's determined push to get us into World War II: by indicting governments that "have been trumpeting far-off bogeys as an excuse for enslaving" their citizens, he was echoing the warning of America Firsters like John T. Flynn and Colonel Robert McCormick who saw that we would win the war against national socialism in the trenches only to succumb to it on the home front. "For at least two decades," wrote Rothbard, "we have been living in a society that has taken on all the characteristics of fascism. At home we have the fascist corporate state economy: an economy of monopolies, subsidies, and privileges run by a tripartite coalition of Big Business, Big Unions, and Big Government; and we have a military garrison state, with permanent conscription, tied to a permanent war economy fueled by armament contracts."[26]

In assessing the "revolutionary mood" of the nation's college campuses, Rothbard rejoiced in the fact that "it is almost impossible now to find any intellectual who either favors the war in Vietnam or who has anything but loathing for President Johnson." But there was more good news: "This opposition to the war and to the U.S. government has, in surprisingly many instances, deepened into opposition to all government whatsoever—into a truly libertarian insight into the nature of the state apparatus."[27]

The Cold War liberals Rothbard loved to hate were finally getting their come-uppance, and he could hardly contain his glee. Not only that, but the moribund Old Right, whittled down to a precious few, was making a comeback—or, at least, getting some long-deserved recognition. As Rothbard hailed SDS's break with his old enemies in the Social Democracy, and the turn toward a principled opposition to the Vietnam war, former SDS President Carl Oglesby published *Containment and Change*, which not only recalled the anti-imperialism of the Old Right, but also echoed Rothbard's call for a New Left–Old Right alliance against the common interventionist enemy. Citing Rothbard's *Continuum* article chronicling "The Transformation of the American Right," Oglesby quotes liberally from congressman Howard Buffett, Chodorov, Garrett, and General Douglas MacArthur in support of a noninterventionist foreign policy. In its opposition to war and centralization, the New Left, Oglesby argued, was "rootedly American," and, together with the rightist strand of libertarian isolationism, had the possibility of mounting a serious challenge to the ruling elite.[28]

In the spring of 1968, Rothbard saw a notice in the *Village Voice* advertising the creation of a new political party in New York, the Peace and Freedom party. His interest was aroused by the only two guidelines for membership: "One [was] the belief in peace, immediate withdrawal from Vietnam and [a] peaceful foreign policy" he recalled, and "secondly . . . every group and person should be able to run his own life, a very vague thing which anybody can agree with. So I figured, this sounds great."[29]

On the national scene, it was Hubert Humphrey versus Richard Nixon, a Cold War liberal versus a Cold War conservative. Alabama Governor George Wallace would get on the presidential ballot in all fifty states, but his Southern agrarian roots did not reach far enough to include the isolationist populism of Tom Watson. In Rothbard's view, "we needed an alternative," and "so I show up at a Peace and Freedom meeting. I just wandered in innocently," said Rothbard, a few years later, and one can almost hear the mischievous cackle that must have accompanied this statement. "And I was plunged into the vortex of left-wing politics; it was a lot of fun, it was a very fun thing." Libertarians opposed to electoral politics on principle "don't know what they're missing when they . . . reject the idea of party politics."[30]

Ever since his break with *National Review* and the conservative movement, Rothbard had been agitating for an alliance with the New Left on the basis of opposition to the Vietnam war and the domestic repression that accompanied that war. The Peace and Freedom party of New York was a kind of experimental laboratory in which it was possible to test the viability of this new strategy. Rothbard relates that the "interesting thing was that we had a little thing going where we had enough libertarians in there, in this little party, to have working control of at least half of the Faculty Club of the party. This meant that we were sort of in a power position in the party, even though we had only ten members. It was a crucial ten members."[31]

Libertarian leverage in the Faculty Club gave Rothbard delegate status to the regional body. Wading into that maelstrom of Marxist factions, he remarked, "I didn't know from nothing about any of these groups." He soon found out, making the discovery that, on a national scale, the whole Peace and Freedom operation was controlled by an obscure Trotskyist grouplet, the Independent Socialist Clubs, followers of one Hal Draper. "And it turned out that the Draperites had control of all the full-time organizing work, all the officers of the party, all the organizers who were traveling between states. . . . I didn't know this at the beginning." The Draperites, having put all of their hundred or so members into the budding young party from the very beginning, had what Rothbard called a "very peculiar" position. "They were in favor of no party," he explained, "they were in favor of waiting for the McCarthyites to come in. There was supposed to be a great influx of millions of Gene McCarthy's followers who were supposed to come in, whom they could then control. So they wanted to keep a very loose structure with nothing much going on." The Draperites had in tow entire chapters consisting mostly of hippies, "some left-wing anarchists, I think, also artists and people of that ilk, poster-painters. So I wasn't very congenial to any of these people."[32]

Chafing under the do-nothing regime of the Draperites, Rothbard and his intrepid band of antiwar libertarians sought allies to unseat the Peace and Freedom Party establishment—and found them in the Progressive Labor Party, which had formed its own faction of Peace and Freedom. As Rothbard explains it, "meanwhile it turned out that the Progressive Labor faction, even though they themselves obviously [operated under a] totalitarian structure, weren't really interested in controlling the [Peace and Freedom] party. They had their little *shtick* on the West Side; they had control of the West Side club; that's all they were interested in controlling, . . . and they were essentially interested in keeping their oar in and that's it. So, they also wanted a party. Since they wanted to keep their West Side club, they wanted a strict party with geographical units and a regular kind of party structure. So we formed an alliance."[33]

The dour Maoist ideologues of the Progressive Labor Party, and Rothbard's merry band of anarcho-capitalists were as unlikely allies as can possibly be imagined. Yet Rothbard at no point compromised his total commitment to private property and the free market for the sake of working with these people. He never supported statist measures, or any expansion of state power, and always made his own position on the issues unmistakably clear. The tactical benefits derived from this odd coupling gave the libertarians effective control of the joint PL-libertarian caucus when it came to the Peace and Freedom party platform. "I remember first we were the only ones to show up at the policy committee, [to] try and set the platform, because nobody was really interested for a long time." In alliance with the Maoists, "we drove through [a] platform more laissez-faire than anything since Andrew Jackson, total freedom in trade I remember, drastic reductions in taxes. Gold standard. The only thing they balked at, they refused to go along with abolition of rent control; that was sort of an article of faith to them. They were organizing tenants; they couldn't go along with that. It was a hilarious time. I remember one time the PL leader Jake Rosen—of course [he] knew what was going on [but] none of his followers really knew the score—and he was driving this thing through the caucus, [and] it comes to the plank about total freedom of trade and abolition of all subsidies, control and regulation of international trade—you know, this fantastic laissez-faire plank. So one of these PL characters says, hey, what's this, this looks like bourgeois free trade, and Jake says no, no this is an antimonopoly coalition. That took care of that. So it was a charming thing."[34]

What this illustrates above all is Rothbard's view of his political

activities as a kind of hobby—a vacation from the complex problems of theory that occupied the center of his attention. While he
was researching and making copious notes on his history of economic thought, writing *Power and Market*, contributing a biographical account of Ludwig von Mises for the *International Encyclopedia
of Social Sciences*,[35] and contributing an important essay on historical
revisionism to the memorial volume for Harry Elmer Barnes, he
took time out to engage in an activity that he indulged in for its
own sake, for the sheer pleasure of the experience. His activism not
only allowed him time off from the realm of abstract ideas, it also
allowed him to people-watch, to analyze and simply wonder at the
mysteries of human nature.

The Draperites, with their majority at the state convention,
ended up voting the libertarian–Progressive Labor platform planks
down; the Peace and Freedom party of New York broke up soon
after that, but not before providing the nascent libertarian movement in New York with its first taste of party politics. Rothbard later
summed up the experience by saying that the lesson to be learned
was to be "wary [of] political parties in general and left-wingers in
particular," but this was said in retrospect; at the time, Rothbard's
enthusiasm for the alliance with the New Left and libertarian visibility in the growing antiwar movement was at an all-time high.[36]

An important breakthrough for Rothbard's "left-right" alliance
was the publication of his "Confessions of a Right-Wing Liberal," in
the summer of 1968, in *Ramparts*, the glossy muckraking magazine
of the New Left, in which he summarized his own political evolution and proposed an anti-imperialist coalition of the New Left and
the Old Right against the prowar center. "Twenty years ago," confessed Rothbard, "I was an extreme right-wing Republican, a
young and lone 'Neanderthal' (as the liberals used to call us) who
believed, as one friend pungently put it, that 'Senator Taft had sold
out to the socialists.' Today, I am most likely to be called an extreme

leftist, since I favor immediate withdrawal from Vietnam, denounce U.S. imperialism, advocate Black Power, and have just joined the new Peace and Freedom Party. And yet my basic political views have not changed by a single iota in these two decades!"[37]

In this widely noticed piece for the premier magazine of the New Left, Rothbard covered much of the same ground as in his earlier article on "The Transformation of the American Right" in *Continuum*, and, later, in his unpublished book, "The Betrayal of the American Right." An interesting note on why "The Betrayal of the American Right" remained unpublished: Rothbard recalled that he wrote the original manuscript in 1971, and made additions in 1973: "It was scheduled to be published by Ramparts Press for January 1972 in its Fall 1971 catalog, but apparently they wanted me to make extensive changes which I refused to make. In 1973, it was supposed to be published by Bob Kephart's short-lived Libertarian Review Press, but when the editor there balked at the mixture of the personal and the historical . . . I withdrew it from consideration."[38]

Unlike the *Continuum* piece, the *Ramparts* article, though similar in subject, was told in the first person; Rothbard not only recounted the story of the Old Right but detailed his own journey from the Old Right to the New Left. He mourned the fate of the old liberals, who had allied with the pre–World War II Right—men like John T. Flynn, historian Charles A. Beard, and Harry Elmer Barnes—who were crowded out of the picture by the ex-Trotskyist James Burnham, former spy for the Kremlin Whittaker Chambers, Will Herberg, Eugene Lyons, J. B. Matthews, Frank S. Meyer, Willi Schlamm, and other defectors from Communism. In the old days "there was no question as to where the intellectual right of that day stood on militarism and conscription: it opposed them as instruments of mass slavery and mass murder." Then the rise of McCarthyism shifted the mass-base of the Right from the Midwest to the eastern seaboard, bringing in a whole new crowd "whose outlook on individual liberty was, if anything, negative." His critique of the Buckleyite Right, though similar in tone and content to the earlier piece, was considerably sharpened; longtime *National Review* editor Willmoore Kendall was described as "another repellent political theorist who made his mark in *National Review*" and whose view of "community rights" over individual rights led him to opine that "Socrates . . . not only *should* have been killed by the Greek community, whom he offended by his subversive criticisms, but it was their moral *duty* to kill him." Mencken, Nock, Jefferson, Thoreau, and Paine had given way to Burke, Metternich, DeMaistre, and Hamilton as the heroes of the Right.[39] Under the impact of the Cold War, American conservatives were shedding the last remnants of their libertarian spirit, and were even abandoning the free-market domestic program they once espoused. It was a great relief to Rothbard to have finally broken with these troglodytes.

Rothbard was now attending meetings of the Peace and Freedom Party, which had just nominated Black Panther leader Eldridge Cleaver for president, instead of the Constitution Party or "Students for Thurmond." Yet the apparent change in his politics was superficial. The important fact to remember is that, while his allies had certainly changed, his roster of enemies remained constant: the targets of his spleen were the same New Deal liberals and mandarins of Social Democracy who had declared the "end of ideology" in the fifties, and were now being rudely reminded of the complete inaccuracy of their prediction. In a delightful turn of events, Rothbard was using the far-left-wing *Ramparts* as a platform to accuse Buckley of having jettisoned his old libertarian friends and allies and "drawn ever closer to the liberals of the Great American Consensus." This explains "Buckley's ever-widening popularity in the mass media and among liberal intellectuals." Conservatives of Buckley's ilk "have come to agree that economic issues are unimportant" and to accept the "welfare-warfare state of liberal corporatism." With both liberals and conservatives united against the antiwar and Black Power movements, "no wonder that liberal Daniel Moynihan . . . should recently call for a formal alliance between liberals and conservatives, since after all they basically agree on these, the two crucial issues of our time!"[40]

In detailing the story of how "a tiny band of ex-rightist libertarians" came to found *Left and Right*, Rothbard unveiled the strategic thrust of his recent activities: "To make contact with libertarians already on the new left and to persuade the bulk of libertarians or quasi-libertarians who remained on the right to follow our example."[41] Though it is highly doubtful that much progress was made in reaching incipient libertarians among the legions of the New Left, there were many more on the Right who, shaken out of complacency by the tumult of the times, found Rothbard's argument persuasive. The *Ramparts* article caught the attention of Karl Hess, a Washington-based conservative Republican publicist who had been an aide and speechwriter to Senator Barry Goldwater during the 1964 presidential election. Hess had been associated with the founding of the American Enterprise Institute, and had also been a working journalist, in addition to his work as the number two official in the GOP after Goldwater's nomination. At that time, however, like so many during that era, Hess was in the middle of a personal as well as a political transformation that propelled him far afield from the life he had known.[42]

Hess contacted Rothbard, and a spirited discussion began that did not end until Hess declared his conversion to libertarianism in Rothbard's living room a few months later. As Hess relates in his autobiography:

> I had run into several laissez-faire capitalist economists and historians, notably Murray Rothbard and Leonard Liggio. An article by Rothbard in the left-wing *Ramparts* magazine, in par-

ticular, was an ideological eye-opener. It described anarchism, a position well to the right of Right and well to the left of Left. I had never really thought about or known much about anarchism (or libertarianism), but reading about it made me think that I hd been one all along. So, I wrote to Rothbard and he generously invited me to come to New York, stay in his apartment, and join the nightly get-togethers of what then seemed to be the entire libertarian anarchist movement.[43]

Hess's attraction to libertarianism, and to the then-burgeoning New Left movement, was to some extent based on his formerly conservative loyalties: as he put it, "The New Left that unfolded itself for me was as isolationist as my old hero, the late Senator Robert [A.] Taft of Ohio. But the New Left had the public relations sense to call it anti-imperialism."[44]

Shortly after that, Hess called a Washington press conference announcing his defection from conservative ranks and his sympathy for the New Left. The novelty of the headline grabbed the attention of newspaper editors all across America: EX-GOLD-WATER SPEECHWRITER JOINS SDS. This was followed by a spate of magazine articles, including Hess's "The Death of Politics," published in *Playboy*. The Goldwaterite who had grown a beard and given up a suit for plaid flannel shirts and blue jeans was suddenly a controversial figure. His announcement attracted considerable attention on the Right, especially among the student contingent, Young Americans for Freedom, a conservative youth group, which was befuddled by the success of the campus New Left and lived a withered and generally ineffective life in its shadow.

A MOVEMENT IS BORN

As the turbulent year of 1969 dawned, this time, the Rothbards' living room could no longer contain the entire libertarian movement that resided in New York City, and the Libertarian Forum was founded by Joseph Peden and Gerald Wolosz. Over sixty attended the first meeting held in a Chinese restaurant on the Upper West Side, coming from as far away as Buffalo, Delaware, and South Carolina. This was followed shortly afterward by the publication of the first issue of a new periodical, the *Libertarian Forum*, which listed Rothbard as editor, Hess as Washington editor, and Peden as publisher.[45] Issued in newsletter format, and promising its readers two issues per month, the preview issue, dated March 1, 1969, embodied the determined optimism of the Rothbardian mindset, declaring that it is high time for libertarianism to "become a movement and cease being merely an inchoate collection of diffuse and haphazard personal contacts."[40]

The *Libertarian Forum*, which lasted—despite gaps in its publishing history—until 1984, well after the New Left had dissolved into a maelstrom of bomb-throwing, was to become Murray's favorite form of writing, the unique brand of personal journalism that occupied many of his morning hours. This was, for him, the most enjoyable activity imaginable: not only to have opinions on a variety of subjects, but also to have the chance to express them, in print, with some regularity. The years of enforced silence, due to the inability of an Old Rightist to find literary sanctuary in the pages of a compatible periodical, were over.

The *Libertarian Forum* was not just a vehicle for Rothbard to express his views on a wide variety of topics, from Vietnam to the latest movies, with dollops of high theory, juicy gossip, and "movement" news thrown in the mix for good measure—although

it was indeed all that. Yet it was more. As an avid student of political strategy and tactics, he agreed with Lenin on the central
importance of the press in building a movement for radical social
change. Like Lenin, who built his Bolshevik party on the scaffolding created by his newspaper, *Iskra* (The Spark), Rothbard created the *Libertarian Forum* as the literary precursor of an organized
libertarian movement.

By the spring of 1969, it seemed to Rothbard that the libertarian
movement had entered a new stage, one that necessitated a more
formal organization, and the Radical Libertarian Alliance (RLA)
was constituted on May 17, on the occasion of the third meeting of
the Libertarian Forum in New York City. According to an account
published in the *Libertarian Forum*, the fact that police spies had
infiltrated this meeting had been revealed by "unimpeachable
sources" who "had read the report in sextupilicate of a cop spy at
the meeting."[47] Whatever the veracity of this report, the presence of
police spies at a political meeting was all too believable in the
hopped-up atmosphere of that time. The routine surveillance of
antiwar groups was stepped up in the sixties—as subsequent congressional investigations revealed—and the local "Red Squad"
was naturally interested in this latest cabal of malcontents. While
flattering to the organizers, in the sense that it implied they represented some substantial and immediate threat to the security of the
state, such surveillance was probably unnecessary: the leadership
of the RLA, consisting of budding young Rothbardian scholars
such as Walter Block, Roy A. Childs Jr., Wilson A. Clark Jr., and
John Hagel III, was far more interested in attending seminars on
Austrian economics than in learning how to make bombs. What
the RLA had to offer the youth of America was intellectually, but
not literally, explosive.

The explosion they caused was not a physical one, but an ideological one, and it occurred over the Labor Day weekend in St.

Louis, Missouri. The occasion was the national convention of
Young Americans for Freedom, and the cause of the fireworks was
a planned intervention by Rothbard in league with his RLA
activists. The idea was to take advantage of the functional tensions
that had been building in the YAF for some time over the issues of
war and the draft. Hess in tow, the RLA arrived in St. Louis armed
with the August 15, 1969 issue of *Libertarian Forum*, bearing the
bold headline: "Listen, YAF!"[48]

In the passion and logic of his argument—expressed in characteristically blunt and colorful language—this article shows Rothbard at his agitational and inspirational best, and it is worth quoting
the opening paragraphs in order to appreciate the rare talent of a
writer for whom the polemic was a highly developed artform:

> This open letter is addressed to the libertarians attending the YAF
> national convention in St. Louis this Labor Day weekend. Notice
> I said the *libertarians* in YAF; I have nothing to say to the so-called
> traditionalists (a misnomer, by the way, for we libertarians have
> *our* traditions, too, and they are glorious ones. It all depends on
> *which* traditions: the libertarian ones of Paine and Price, of
> Cobden and Thoreau, or the authoritarian ones of Torquemada
> and Burke and Metternich.) Let us leave the authoritarians to
> their Edmund Burkes and their Crowns of St. Something-or-
> other. We have more serious matters to discuss.
>
> In the famous words of Jimmy Durante: "Have ya ever had
> the feelin' that ya wanted to go, and yet ya had the feelin' that ya
> wanted to stay?" This letter is a plea that you use the occasion of
> the public forum of the YAF convention to go, to split, to leave
> the conservative movement where it belongs: in the hands of the
> St. Something-or-others, and where it is going to stay regardless
> of what action you take. Leave the house of your false friends, for
> they are your enemies.
>
> For years you have taken your political advice and much of

your line from assorted "exes": ex-Communists, ex-Trots, ex-Maoists, ex-fellow-travelers. I have never been any of these. I grew up a right-winger, and became more intensely a libertarian rightist as I grew older. How come I am an exile from the Right-wing, while the conservative movement is being run by a gaggle of ex-Communists and monarchists? What kind of a conservative movement is this? This kind: one that you have no business being in.[49]

From his self-confident cadence and ringing tone, it is clear that Rothbard knew that his words would have an effect. Within YAF, a large and aggressive libertarian faction had coalesced into an organized caucus, and was ready to challenge the Buckleyite leadership on two key points: the Vietnam war and draft resistance. As the only national right-wing youth organization, YAF had attracted the entire gamut of right-wing opinion, from traditionalists, and a few outright authoritarians, to "fusionists," Objectivists, and a growing number of libertarians. Hundreds of libertarian youth flocked to YAF during the sixties: radicalized by the war, a great many of these college and high school activists had been initiated into the libertarian movement via the novels of Ayn Rand. But Rand did not offer much in the way of a political outlet for her students of Objectivism. She apparently believed that, until the last philosophy professor agrees that "A is A" and the stain of Kantianism is thoroughly cleansed from the fabric of Western thought, it is "too soon" for political action. We must first win over the intellectuals to the virtues of Objectivist epistemology, the Randian leaders insisted: then and only then can we even think about changing the world.[50]

Abstention was not Rothbard's style. Instead, he not only plunged headfirst into the fray, but did so with a definite plan in mind—a strategy the first phase of which was completed in St. Louis. While the story of the St. Louis convention, at which a draft

card was publicly burned and fistfights broke out, has been told far
too often, it was indeed a pivotal event in the history of the modern
libertarian movement. Tensions built all weekend as the delegates
debated the burning issues of the day, and reached a violent climax
as it came time to vote on what position YAF should take on the
question of the draft. Chanting their derision of the draft-dodging
"laissez-fairies," the prowar, proconscription YAFers were enraged
as one young libertarian punctuated his remarks by igniting what
was purportedly a draft card. A mini-riot ensued. Suffice to say that
the plan—to split YAF and found an independent libertarian movement—succeeded. On the East Coast, the Pennsylvania-based
Society for Individual Liberty, and in the West, the California Libertarian Alliance, coalesced with local circles and campus-based
groups throughout the country: this was the core group that would
go on, in 1972, to launch the Libertarian Party.

In the meantime, however, the emergence of Karl Hess as the
Youth Leader of a radicalized and growing libertarian movement
was reflected not only in the pages of the *Libertarian Forum*, where
his "Letter From Washington" column appeared, but also in the
mainstream press. Both the *New York Times*[51] and *Newsweek*[52] ran
articles on the ideological odyssey of the Goldwaterite-turned-
hippie; while the former piece was respectful, the latter piece was
to Rothbard's mind "snide and supercilious. But," he averred, "in
the annals of public relations, 'every knock is a boost,' so long as
the name gets spelled right, and not only is Karl mentioned, but so
too is our own little, no-budget *Libertarian Forum*—our first breakthrough into the mass media!"[53]

With Rothbard as the theoretician, and Hess as the man of
action, we see the emergence of a pattern that would be repeated,
in all its variations, down through the years. Rothbard, the system-
builder, could not undertake the task of building a movement.
There had to be a division of labor. Given the shortage of libertar-

ians in the previous decade, there had been no question of such a division, short of dividing one person into two. Now, however, the movement was growing by leaps and bounds, and the division of intellectual labor was not only possible but urgently necessary.

Rothbard's "Listen, YAF" had been accompanied by an advertisement in the *Libertarian Forum* proudly announcing—"Hear Ye! Hear Ye!"—a Libertarian Conference over the Columbus Day weekend, October 10–12, 1969, at the Hotel Diplomat, in New York City. The featured speakers were Rothbard and Hess, with panelists including Walter Block, Roy A. Childs Jr., Walter Grinder, Leonard Liggio, Joe Peden, Robert J. Smith, and YAF convert Jerome Tuccille. "And so," Rothbard wrote, "we're on the march. Onward and upward."[54]

Onward, yes, but not always upward. The conference, as the headline in a subsequent issue of *Libertarian Forum* put it, represented "Two Steps Forward, Two Steps Back" for the libertarian movement. It was, wrote Rothbard, "a wild and woolly time, both exciting and dull, wonderful and a shambles."[55]

What is striking in Rothbard's account of the conference is his own ability to stand aside from the emotional and intellectual investment already made and judge the results of his own decisions, both personal and ideological. "In contrast to the P. R. snow jobs handed out by other conference organizers, attesting to the joy and grandeur abounding at their meetings, this will be a candid, unvarnished report and appraisal of the Conference. Our readers deserve no less." Knowing Rothbard, they expected no less.[56]

From Friday night until Saturday afternoon, Rothbard's delight at the attendance of over 200, virtually all of them out-of-towners, knew no bounds. "We, the organizers of the Conference, looked out across this sea of faces and hardly recognized a soul," wrote Rothbard. "It was a great and historic moment."[57]

The range of interests and talent in the growing cadre of young

Rothbardians is evident in the packed schedule of lectures and panels. Rothbard gave an overview of the libertarian system, covering natural rights and the structure of property rights. Laurence Moss, then a graduate student at Columbia University, delivered a speech called "Economics of Sin," Jerry Tuccille announced his conversion to anarchocapitalism, and Mario J. Rizzo, then an honors senior in economics at Fordham University, gave what Rothbard thought was a "brilliant" paper that stood Marx on his head. Rizzo argued that the Marxist analysis of profits as an index of exploitation, while invalid as a critique of laissez faire, is indeed applicable to the corporate state, where profits are, increasingly, an index of state privilege. The revisionist insights of Kolko and others into the role of big business as the chief instigator and architect of the regulatory state, married to a pure free-market perspective, opened up the possibility of a radical alternative to Marxism.

The importance Rothbard and his circle attached to history and to promoting the idea that modern libertarianism represented but the latest development in a movement rooted in a long tradition was reflected in the subjects addressed by many of the speakers. Walter Grinder, then a graduate student at New York University, traced the origins of the Cold War. Leonard Liggio regaled his audience with a biographical sketch of Edward T. Atkinson, the laissez-faire economist who founded the Anti-Imperialist League during the Spanish-American war. The subject of Dale Grinder's "learned, witty, and illuminating paper" was "U.S. imperialism in China and the Far East, 1880–1920."[58]

Rothbard was in his element, the world of ideas, and reveled in the sight of his most intelligent and original students expanding and developing the boundaries of the libertarian paradigm. But not everyone was so happy. Rothbard reports an "undercurrent of rebellion" rumbling "from various 'Young Turks' who, apparently restive at the having to follow trains of thought for more than one paragraph, began to gripe about the 'overstructuring' of the conference, and to call for general 'rapping' (open discussion)."[59]

In recalling the nearly forgotten argot of the sixties, the verb to "rap" seems to sum up all the ephemeral silliness of that era: it means to engage in endless and aimless "dialogue" in order to reach a collective "consensus." The problem was that his method did not lead to consensus but to polarization and split.

As a measure of his affection and desire for continued friendship with Hess, Rothbard did not name these "Young Turks," but it was clear enough to anyone who had attended the conference. By this time, Hess and his comrades of the libertarian Far Left were not interested in learned discussions of foreign policy, the history of libertarian opposition to war, or the problem of developing a strategy for intervening in the antiwar movement. Clad in the Viet Cong–Mountain Man garb popular at the time, Hess and his hippie minions were not interested in discussions of *any* kind. What they wanted was *action*.

Jerome Tuccille's hilarious description of Hess's role at that convention captures the spirit of the man and the times:

> Now an apparition in olive-green battle fatigues materialized in the corridor, surrounded by a personal entourage of sartorial imitators.
>
> "It's him. He's arrived," a voice called.
>
> "Who's arrived?"
>
> "The Field Marshall of the Revolution."
>
> . . . There he was, the funkiest looking revolutionary in fifty states, with a wardrobe fresh off the rack of Abercrombie & Fitch. Combat boots laced to the top with rawhide strips . . . khaki shirt opened to the third button so his chest hairs stuck out . . . and, [the] *piece de resistance*, a green Fidel Castro fatigue cap with a black and red Wobbly button pinned over the peak. All in all, an easy two hundred clams' worth of proletarian garb.[60]

That night, Tuccille recounts, the Field Marshal of the Revolution "poured forth a message to match his attire: Strike! Assault! Direct action against the state!"

> "Which side of the barricades will you be on when the chips are down?" Hess asked hard-eyed from the podium, menacing the profit-mavens and other right-wing libertarians in the audience. He had perfected a way of asking questions so that they sounded like threats. "There is no neutral ground in a revolution," Hess continued. . . . "You're either on one side of the barricade or the other."[61]

Like Fidel exhorting his revolutionary regiments into battle, Hess urged the conference to abandon all this empty talk and launch an assault on nearby Fort Dix. Why talk about it, why not just *do it*! We have to "live liberty," guys, and that means putting our lives on the line. A good third of the conference participants marched out of the hotel and into the streets, whooping and chanting, with Karl Hess leading the parade. Thus was left-libertarianism born.

Poor Murray! In what was virtually a one-man crusade to stem the tide of leftist hysteria, he kept his head and argued with the conference organizers to keep the event going. The next day, an audience of about fifty listened as Rothbard, Tuccille, and Liggio criticized the frenzied leftism of Hess and his "lifestyle libertarianism." But as the warriors against the Leviathan returned from Fort Dix, a new kind of frenzy permeated the conference: a frenzy of fear. Rothbard writes that "it became evident that the hotel room, the hotel lobby, and the street outside were suddenly crawling with plainclothes cops, their badges and their guns bulging prominently from their supposedly civilian attire."[62]

Hess, who had been staying with the Rothbards, went into hiding in an apartment provided by Walter Block, who at the time owned some New York City real estate. There were rumors that

Hess was under surveillance by federal authorities, and the New York City "Red Squad" was hot on his trail.

The disastrous finale of the conference, in which the leftist contingent took to the microphone, and—in hysterical and obscene terms—berated the rest of the attendees for not letting themselves be gassed at Fort Dix, marked the effective end of Rothbard's political alliance with Hess. Despite the fact that Hess's name remained on the *Libertarian Forum* masthead until mid-May of 1970, the bulk of Rothbard's fire was increasingly directed at what he called "the threat of ultraleftism." Right after the conference fiasco, he devoted a series of articles to attacking the economic fallacies of anarcho-communism, exposing the developing nihilism and radical egalitarianism of the New Left, and, in mid-March, 1970, declaring its death in "The New Left, RIP."[63]

Hess continued his leftward course. With the IRS after him for refusing to pay taxes, he gave up all his property and could not work for a living. According to his own account in *Dear America*, Hess's motive in refusing to pay taxes was pure loathing for the IRS officials he came in contact with during an audit. In his 1975 book, he describes the moment he decided to become a tax resister:

> Several things about such a moment. It comes, like anger, quickly and without much warning. It usually reflects your general disposition and not any particularly exact need of that disposition. It is not, in short, a utilitarian anger, it is simply an anger. . . . Without making any extravagant claims for the practice, I can only say that I chose, face-to-face with these prime agents of the state, to tell them "No."[64]

In other words, he did it on impulse, not just for ideological reasons but "because [he] got mad."[65] It was the spirit of the times. Karl Hess and his radical Left-libertarian cohorts held that allegiance to libertarianism as a political ideology was not enough: one had to "live liberty." This meant rejecting not only state authority, but moral authority, and all social conventions. At a time when everyone was tuning in, turning on, and dropping out, this was not exactly an original position to take, but certainly it was popular at the time.

Hess abandoned the central precept of libertarianism, private property rights, when he joined the New Left back in the sixties, and never really returned to it. While his position seemed to evolve, in a sense he failed to return to the movement he renounced for SDS and the Black Panthers, never disavowing the hostility to the free market revealed in *Dear America*. Even as he drew closer to the Libertarian Party near the end of his career, he did not stray very far from the utopian syndicalism of his SDS days. But his real loyalty was to the counterculture: for Karl Hess, the sixties never really ended.

On the other hand, Rothbard was a man of the Old Culture: he believed it was possible to be a revolutionary, an anarchist, *and* lead a bourgeois life. Respectably dressed, if a bit rumpled, in his signature bow-tie, white shirt, and jacket, Rothbard was immune to the blandishments of the sixties youth culture, preferring the odes of Cicero to the howls of Alan Ginsberg and the music of the Baroque to that of the Beatles.

In distancing himself from Hess, Rothbard did not give up his left-right strategy: the Vietnam war dragged on, and the country had yet to cast the Nixonian incubus from its breast. He continued to lambast the twin evils of U.S. imperialism and Nixonian economics in the pages of the *Libertarian Forum*, but added to this isolationist-antiinflationist brew was his increasing criticism of the New Left, not only of its political excesses but also of its cultural excrescences, such as women's liberation and the various victimologies that were then in their infancy. When one New Left leader took him to task for not genuflecting before the feminist icon, complaining that Rothbard did not understand that women are victims of "male colonial oppression" and have to separate themselves from men in order to "get their sisterhood together," Rothbard flung up his hands and cried: "O judgment, thou hast fled to brutish beasts, and men have lost their reason!"[66]

Rothbard's casting out of the sixties counterculture was completed with the publication of "Freedom, Inequality, Primitivism, and the Division of Labor," in which he skewered the egalitarian and primitivist themes that animated the New Left. The "natural inequality of ability and of interest among men must make elites inevitable," he wrote, and we must "accept the universal necessity of leaders and followers. The task of the libertarian," then, "is not to inveigh against elites which, like the need for freedom, flow directly from the nature of man." Coercive elites are artificial aristocracies who maintain their power through the offices of the State. Once this power is rolled back, however, "we will discover 'natural aristocracies' who will rise to prominence and leadership in every field."[67]

POWER AND MARKET

In this blaze of activity on behalf of libertarianism as a movement, one would think that little time or energy would be left to pursue the goal of developing libertarianism as a theory. But all the ideological fireworks, libertarian conferences, political pamphleteering, and strategic shifts of the moment did not even begin to exhaust Rothbard's intellectual energy. At the height of all this activity, he was preparing for publication the book that has become a key cornerstone of the Rothbardian system, a comprehensive critique of the role of the state in the economy: *Power and Market*.[68]

Originally intended as the third volume of *Man, Economy, and State*, the book was radically condensed and shoehorned into the two-volume format by the publisher, Ed Nash, of the Nash Publishing Company. Nash was a Randian type who thought the book was "too anarchistic" as well as being too long. The original manuscript of *Man, Economy, and State*—all nineteen-hundred pages of it—had been completed in 1959. But when Rothbard sent it in to the Volker Fund, Harold Luhnow, the head of the fund, balked at the sheer size of it, while Ivan Bierly fought to have it published. They agreed that it needed a tough editor, and the manuscript was sent to Volker Fund associate Frank Meyer, whose verdict was that it was a great book—of twelve-hundred pages. The problem, Meyer averred, was not just its length, but the anarchist implications of the third section. The first chapter of that section is a rigorous proof that security can be provided through private means and that the state misallocates resources here as in other cases. Of course, Rothbard did not come out and say anarchism is the answer. He was satisfied to show that state provision of goods and services, including security, cannot work and relies fundamentally on the imposition of violence—and letting his readers draw their own conclusions. Meyer objected to mixing radical political conclusions with straight analysis, and stressed the length problem, but in addition to this, a major reason for cutting nearly one third of the manuscript was that,with the Cold War in full swing, conservatives like Meyer were not about to challenge the massive militarization of American society by endorsing the privatization of national security.

Going beyond the Misesian insight that men act to achieve their values and that they employ various means to achieve certain ends, Rothbard rejected the implication of "value-free" praxeology that the matter of *which* values to choose is completely arbitrary. Roy Childs went overboard, in his review of *Power and Market*, in calling Mises "a frank ethical nihilist," but in any case the utilitarian stance actually taken by Mises was far from satisfying for Rothbard. Members of the Circle Bastiat recall that he differed with Mises's utilitarianism from the beginning. Rothbard not only believed in the necessity of a rational ethic, but, in *Power and Market*, he also laid the foundations for one on land cleared by his predecessors. In *Human Action*, Mises makes a concession to statism that, uncorrected, could have eventually resulted in the unraveling of a systematic theory of the free market. "He who in our age opposes armaments and conscription is . . . an abettor of those aiming at the enslavement of all," wrote Mises. Furthermore,

> the maintenance of a government apparatus of courts, police officers, prisons and of armed forces requires considerable expenditure. To levy taxes for these purposes is fully compatible with the freedom the individual enjoys in a free market economy.[69]

Aside from contradicting Mises's other writings on the subject, in which he opposes conscription because it means that "war socialism has replaced the market economy," this passage had always been considered "off" by Mises's more attentive students. It turns out that—unknown to Rothbard—the original text of *Human Action* contained no such paragraph. Thanks to the discovery of Mises's missing papers and manuscripts in a Soviet archive in Moscow, the restored and only complete edition of *Human Action* was published in 1999. The restored edition clarifies Mises's consistent opposition to conscription.[70]

In the seven chapters of *Power and Market*, Rothbard systematizes a fully consistent libertarian argument against government intervention in human affairs in any form or circumstance. As a polemic against the idea that the state is a necessary precondition for liberty, the first chapter is unanswerable in its inexorable logic and unmatched in the precision of its language. Pointing out that "it was the fallacy of the classical economists to consider goods and services in terms of large *classes*," and that modern economics has "demonstrated that services must be considered in terms of *marginal units*," he concluded that a reversion to the earlier method would result in the discovery of "a great myriad of necessary, indispensable goods and services, all of which might be considered as 'preconditions' of market activity. Is not land room vital, or food, . . . or clothing, or shelter? Can a market long exist without them? . . . Must all these goods and services therefore be supplied by the State and the State only?"[71]

In chapter two, Rothbard presents a systematic examination of government intervention in social relations, classifying any and all instances of state coercion under that heading. The consequences of coercion, both direct and indirect, are examined in the context of three categories: autistic, binary, and triangular. The first category is created when the state commands "an individual subject to do or not to do certain things when these actions directly involve the individual's person or property *alone*." In this case, the aggressor receives no tangible benefit from the coercion. "Binary" intervention occurs when the aggressor, the state, compels an "exchange between the individual subject and [it]self, or a coerced 'gift' to [it]self from the subject." This is highway robbery, another word for taxation, or conscription, or other forms of enslavement. In the case of "triangular intervention, the state either compels, restricts, or bans exchanges between a *pair* of subjects. Here Rothbard analyzes the relationship between intervention and conflict, individual "utility" and resistance to invasion, the true nature of democracy, and a host of other questions.[72]

In chapter three, Rothbard demolishes the case for triangular intervention—price controls, licensing, quality and safety standards, immigration laws, child labor laws, antitrust, conservation laws, and so forth. A typical example of his ruthless logic is his cri-

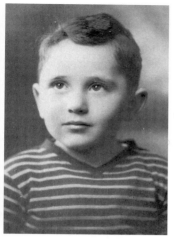

Murray was a bright and intellectually voracious child.

In 8th grade, Rothbard enrolled in the Birch-Wathen School, located in midtown Manhattan, where he blossomed; here he is at graduation, making the valedictory speech.

David Rothbard, an immigrant, shared with his son a deep commitment to American values in both culture and politics.

Rothbard was very close to his parents throughout their lives, particularly to his mother, Raya.

By the early 1950s, when this picture was taken, Rothbard was working for the Volker Fund, and had already begun his magisterial *Man, Economy, and State.*

"By the time I got to graduate school," Rothbard recalled, "I didn't argue purely as a laissez-faire theorist—but I was getting there."

Rothbard married JoAnne ("Joey") Schumacher in 1953; she was, he once wrote, "the indispensable framework."

Williamson Evers (left) and Rothbard celebrate the founding of the Cato Institute in 1978; Evers is proudly holding up *Inquiry*, Cato's magazine.

By the mid-fifties, Rothbard had gathered a small group of libertarians called the "Circle Bastiat." Here he is with Ralph Raico (right), the Circle's "Major Poet."

Llewellyn H. Rockwell Jr. (right), founder of the Ludwig Von Mises Institute, gave Rothbard a platform after the break with the Cato Institute.

A Rothbard lecture was an unforgettable experience. Speaking with a minimal amount of notes, he entranced his audience with his wide-ranging knowledge and charmed them with his humor.

Rothbard speaking at a Ludwig von Mises Institute seminar.

tique of economic protectionism, in which he asks the vital question: If you are going to choke off trade, why stop at national borders? If the inhabitants of a nation benefit from such "protection," then why not extend these alleged benefits to the inhabitants of a particular state, or a particular city, or, in the end, a particular *farm*? In this devastating analysis, Rothbard shows that protectionism, as an economic theory, is pure solipsism.

Chapters four and five deal with two forms of "binary" interventionism: taxation and government spending. Both distort the free market, and shape human society in ways that, instead of preventing conflict and exploitation, make both inevitable. Government, he proves, cannot be run on a "business" basis: unlike a voluntary exchange, in which both parties benefit (otherwise no transaction would occur), the relationship of subjects to the state must, by its nature, involve victims and victimizers, the vanquished and their conquerors.

Mises devotes a mere six pages of *Human Action* to the issue of taxation, claiming that such a concept as a "neutral tax" is possible. Rothbard, on the other hand, conducts a comprehensive and merciless dissection of all the arguments, both economic and moral, for taxation. Of particular interest is his analysis of the roots of the search for a "just tax" in the parallel search for a "just price" of a good or service. While the latter concept has long since been abandoned by modern economists, the former is still pursued by politicians and economists alike. The exciting sixth chapter of *Power and Market*, entitled "Antimarket Ethics: A Praxeological Critique," lays the foundations for the libertarian ethical theory that Rothbard later buttressed and expanded on in *The Ethics of Liberty*. Here he examines every possible philosophical-ethical objection to the free market, from the viewpoint of altruism, Aristotelianism, Thomism, and other positions, ranging over a wide variety of issues such as the relation between morality and human nature, the question of equality, the problem of security, the concept of "luck," the issues of charity, poverty, human rights versus property rights, and "economic power" versus political power.

In the final chapter, Rothbard points out that, under cover of "objective" social science, unspoken ethical assumptions are in force, and are utilized as a rationale for a whole range of statist measures. In and of itself, economics cannot posit an ethical theory, "but it does furnish existential laws which cannot be ignored by anyone framing ethical conclusions."

While Rothbard is hard on ostensibly free-market economists who accept state intervention in certain areas as a matter of course, *Power and Market* is, in the context in which it was published, an assault on the liberal-Left consensus that dominated the domestic politics of the day. It was an era in which a Republican president imposed wage and price controls and his Democratic successor declared a war on poverty—one that, ultimately, wreaked almost as much havoc, destruction, and social dislocation as the shooting war the United States was losing in Southeast Asia. To question the welfare state was permissible only if, like Hayek, you qualified your case and spoke in ambiguous language. But to question the legitimacy and necessity of government itself was to defy the sixties paradigm: the absolute necessity of a bloated and centralized state, to protect Americans not only from the threat of Communism abroad, but the threat of chaos at home.

Rothbard initially warned in the *Libertarian Forum* of the possibility of the coming anti-Leftist backlash and massive repression, but by the end of 1970 he was writing that "the prospect of civil war that seemed to be looming on the horizon, a war in which fascist repression would have crushed a vociferous Left, seems now but a ghost of the past. The center still holds, and more strongly than it has for several years."[73]

FOR A NEW LIBERTY: THE MOVEMENT COMES INTO ITS OWN

In summing up his experience with the New Left, Rothbard is honest with himself and posterity: "Looking back over the experiment of alliance with the New Left," he writes,

> it also became clear that the result had been in many cases disastrous for libertarians; for, isolated and scattered as these young libertarians were, the [Wilson] Clarks and the [Alan] Milchmans and some of the Kansas group were soon to *become* leftists in fact, and in particular to abandon the very devotion to individualism, private property rights, and the free-market economy that had brought them to libertarianism, and then to the New Left alliance, in the first place.[74]

While the New Left had become completely crazed, and was, at any rate, as good as dead, the possibility of a rapprochement with the Right was completely out of the question. Conservatives were still locked in the deadly embrace of Bill Buckley and his legion of ex-Communist Cold Warriors. President Nixon had just appointed the editor of *National Review* to the Advisory Commission of the U.S. Information Agency, the chief Cold War propaganda arm of the United States government; this was Buckley's reward for purging the conservative movement of any and all elements "who might disturb Conservatism in its cozy sharing of political rule. Hence, by 1968, with the exception of Frank Meyer, who still adhered to Ronald Reagan, all conservative doubts about the greatness and wisdom of Richard Milhous Nixon had been effectively stilled" thanks to the efforts of Buckley and Co.[75]

In surveying the ideological landscape after the seismic shock of the New Left had worn off, Rothbard saw that the conservative-liberal coalescence of the postwar era had reasserted itself: "We now face an America ruled alternately by scarcely differentiated wings of the same state-corporatist system." And yet, in characteristic fashion, he writes: "But this is no reason for despair."[76]

Despair was the farthest thing from Rothbard's mind in the spring of 1971, as the patient work of the last fifteen years at last seemed to be bearing fruit. The mainstream media, bored with the increasingly grim shenanigans of the burnt-out New Left remnants, began to focus on libertarianism. After an article on libertarianism appeared in *The Nation*, Rothbard published no less than two articles on the *New York Times* opinion page in quick succession[77] and the avalanche of publicity that followed was truly awe-inspiring: *Newsweek*, *Time*, *Playboy*, *Esquire*, the *Wall Street Journal*, the *National Observer*, and the *Washington Post* all published articles on libertarianism The magazine of the War Resisters League, *WIN*, published a special issue on libertarianism, featuring articles by Rothbard, Liggio, Hess, and others.[78] Suddenly, libertarians were everywhere, even on television,[79] and columnists and writers of Sunday supplements were acquainting their readers with the views of Murray N. Rothbard.

This spate of publicity led to the offer, by Macmillan, for Rothbard to write a book outlining the libertarian political philosophy, and he sat down and wrote what is probably the best-known (and best-selling) of all his works, *For a New Liberty*.[80] Written in a clear, concise, and colorful style, *For a New Liberty* is a programmatic work that fully lives up to its subtitle: "The Libertarian Manifesto." Part I, "The Libertarian Creed," includes an admirably boiled-down explanation of natural rights as the basis of property and exchange; the nature of the state as "the supreme, the eternal, the best organized aggressor against the persons and property of the mass of the public";[81] the inevitability of oligarchy, no matter what *form* the state takes, no matter how "democratic" its pretensions, in spite of any and all constitutions ever written; and the vital role of the Court Intellectuals as the legitimizers of state authority.

Of particular note is the fact that Rothbard starts out by, first, neatly disposing of utilitarianism as a possible foundation for a philosophy of liberty. "Suppose a society which fervently considers all redheads to be agents of the Devil and therefore to be executed whenever found," he writes:

> Let us further assume that only a small number of redheads exist in any generation—so few as to be statistically insignificant. The utilitarian libertarian might well reason: "While the murder of isolated redheads is deplorable, the executions are small in number; the vast majority of the public, as non-redheads, achieves enormous psychic satisfaction from the public execution of redheads. The social cost is negligible, the social psychic benefit to the rest of society is great; therefore, it is right and proper for society to execute the redheads."[82]

Indicting the tax system as theft pure and simple, Rothbard notes, "To add insult to injury, the individual taxpayer, in filling out his tax form, is also forced by the government to work at no pay on the laborious and thankless task of reckoning how much he owes the government."[83]

Describing the guilt-by-association tactics of the anti-"isolationist" historians, Rothbard writes: "If not actively pro-Nazi, 'isolationists' were at the very least narrow-minded ignoramuses ignorant of the world around them, in contrast to the sophisticated, worldly, *caring* 'internationalists' who favored American crusading around the globe."[84]

The undertone of a mordantly mischievous humor that runs through Rothbard's prose enlivens the text of this and virtually all of his books—just as it enlivened conversation with the man himself. As a writer, he used to great advantage his vast store of knowledge, the achievement of a lifelong literary omnivore. Drawing on these immense resources, motivated by a passion for the cause and sheer joy in the act of literary creation, he wrote several learned works at top speed and in relatively rapid succession; from this point in his life onward, Rothbard produced the equivalent of at least one multivolume set every few years. This formidable literary capacity was sharpened and given its characteristic style by the ironic tone, sometimes gentle, often not, a bittersweet note that was the perfect counterpoint to the author's otherwise sunny optimism.

The essential and deep-seated nature of this optimism was reflected in Rothbard's unreconstructed radicalism, both in theory and style, which lent his works a certain boldness: "Empirically," he writes in *For a New Liberty*, "the *most* warlike, *most* interventionist, *most* imperial government throughout the twentieth century has been the United States."[85]

For a New Liberty was written as a programmatic document, but instead of the abstract propagandism that is the chief pitfall of such works, the book is firmly anchored in the real world, not only by the author's sense of history and wealth of empirical data but also by the final chapter, devoted to presenting "A Strategy for Liberty." Here was a man who could discourse on the intricacies and personalities of the current New York City mayor's race just as long and learnedly as he could hold forth on the subjective theory of value or the history of natural law theory. Buckley's sneering characterization of Rothbard as the impractical anarchist professor, busily spinning gossamer castles in mid-air, turns the truth on its head: Rothbard was, in fact, among the most hard-boiled of realists, whose optimistic temperament never for a moment clouded his political judgment. After some three-hundred pages of presenting the philosophical, political, and economic principles underlying the free society, what Rothbard wants to know is: "Now that we have the truth, how can we achieve victory?"[86]

He was practical, but no pragmatist. The opening paragraphs of Rothbard's discourse on strategy make the case for a consistent radicalism, citing William Lloyd Garrison, the libertarian anti-slavery activist of the 1830s, whose stance toward slavery paralleled Rothbard's stance toward the state: "Urge immediate abolition as earnestly as we may, it will, alas! be gradual abolition in the end. We have never said that slavery would be overthrown by a single blow; that it ought to be, we shall always contend."[87]

Rothbard confronts strategic theory in the same way he approaches economics: in a systematic manner deduced from basic axioms, and illustrated by a wealth of historical examples. The need for a movement, the role of internal education, the meaning and methods of both "left" and "right" deviations from the libertarian "plumbline," and the vital question of which groups to target in the struggle for liberty—these and other issues are raised and effectively answered in a stunning tour de force that employs "Crusoe economics"–style analysis, backed up by masses of historical evidence, and all of it illustrated by his capacity for the vivid anecdote.

Rothbard was particularly concerned with strategy at this point, for the simple reason that the libertarian movement was taking off: developing a strategic perspective was as necessary as a driver learning to steer.

The growing success of libertarianism as an organized movement seemed to energize him as never before: in literary terms, Rothbard was entering one of the most productive periods of his life. Before the seventies were over, he had written and published a book-length series on the statist origins of the movement for public schools, *Education, Free and Compulsory*,[88] and a five-volume history of the American Revolution, from the first colonization to the Boston Tea Party to the counterrevolutionary schemes of Federalism.[89] He also wrote a whole brace of major essays, including "Ludwig von Mises and the Paradigm of Our Age,"[90] in which he

applied Thomas S. Kuhn's theory of paradigms, or thought-sys-
tems, as explicated in *The Structure of Scientific Revolutions*,[91] to
explain, on the occasion of Mises's ninetieth birthday, the reason
for his mentor's persistent "outsider" status. He also wrote "Egalitarianism as a Revolt Against Nature," a classic essay in which the
most cherished assumption of economists and ethicists, "equity,"
is challenged and demolished.[92] This does not even take into
account the ten book chapters published in various anthologies in
the period 1971–76, including "Freedom, Inequality, Primitivism,
and the Division of Labor" (1971), in which he disposes of "back to
nature" Marxists then gaining currency;[93] "Herbert Hoover and the
Myth of Laissez-Faire" (1972), a classic of Hoover revisionism,[94] in
which this conservative Republican icon is unmasked as a precursor of New Deal corporate statism; "War Collectivism in World
War I" (1972), a masterly analysis of the effects of war on culture as
well as on economics and politics;[95] and "The New Deal and the
International Monetary System" (1976), a revisionist economic history of the confluence of politics, war, and monetary policy.[96] But
even this by-no-means complete list does not include the entirety
of his output: during this time he also wrote a regular column in
Reason magazine, just then coming into its own, and another
column for *The Individualist*. He also made contributions to *Human
Events*—among them "The Movie Hero Is a Vital Part of American
Culture"[97]—as well as pieces in miscellaneous libertarian periodicals. Finally, there is the *Libertarian Forum*, in which he commented
on the passing scene.

The prolific output of this prodigious intellect was a natural
wonder: he was like a one-man ideological movement, a combination theoretician, propagandist, strategist, journalist, and political
streetfighter—except that it wasn't a one-man movement anymore.
Libertarianism was about to break through to the surface of public
consciousness and take its place on the modern American scene.

In 1972, the Libertarian Party was founded. Its first national convention consisted of a get-together of a few dozen delegates in David F. Nolan's living room, in Denver. Rothbard was, at first, cool to the existence of the LP. While he certainly approved the organization of a political party dedicated to the libertarian ideal, he did not have high hopes for *this particular* party, whose leaders were young, inexperienced, and unfunded.

The date of Rothbard's reversal on the question of whether to organize a libertarian political party is certain: the weekend of March 30–April 1, 1973, when the Free Libertarian Party of New York held its first state convention at the Williams Club in Manhattan. "While tempted," Rothbard confessed in the *Forum*, he "had held aloof" from the LP. "But to this old political warhorse, the firebell of a Convention proved too much to resist."[98]

Not only did he attend the convention, but he also joined the LP and was thus able to vote and engage in the give-and-take of internal debate and discussion. It was, as subsequent history would reveal, a fateful decision, one that would eventually come to consume a great deal of his time, energy, and attention.[99]

He was skeptical, at first, and he admits to "trepidation about what the convention would bring" in the weeks prior to the gathering. "In the first place," he writes, "it has been my usual experience that when more than five libertarians . . . gather together to meet, it is high time to look for the nearest exit." Haunted by "the memories of all the Crazies who had flooded into the 1969 libertarian conference in New York," Rothbard wondered "what joy and/or pain would this new turn bring?"[100]

The answer was: plenty of both.

During the long interregnum of the fifties, when the mandarins of postwar liberalism declared "the end of ideology," Rothbard had been an unreconstructed Old Rightist of the second mobilization, a young McCarthyite who yearned to take back his party and his country from the Eastern establishment. Submerged in the deepest, darkest catacombs of the Right, libertarians like Rothbard had emerged, in the sixties, to the sight of a massive antiwar movement and a deep and growing popular disillusionment with government. Confronted with the post-Nixon blurring of political boundaries and the growing ideological convergence of the two major parties, it seemed to Rothbard that the strategy of submersion or "entrism" in a larger movement was no longer necessary. By this time, a sizable cadre of libertarians had been built up, including not only a growing number of aspiring economists, the second generation of the American branch of the Austrian School, but also a number of activists and rank-and-filers, most of whom were personally unknown to Rothbard—a new and refreshing development, that seemed to augur well for his conviction that it was high time for the libertarian movement to strike out on its own, with its own independent organizations and institutions, and under its own banner.

In the strategy section of *For a New Liberty*, Rothbard discourses on the important question of which groups in society offered libertarians the most promising field for recruitment; he came out solidly in favor of orienting toward "Middle America." This was in marked contrast to left-libertarians, such as Hess, who still looked to the counterculture as the vehicle for libertarian social change. Rothbard's incontrovertible thesis was also contrary to the expectations of libertarians weaned on Rand, who imagined that reality would replicate the plot of *Atlas Shrugged*, in which heroic businessmen go on strike and, as the novel's dust jacket proclaims, "stop the motor of the world." But in fact, as Rothbard points out, big business was very often the author and chief beneficiary of government regulation of industry. Citing Domhoff, Kolko, and other revisionist historians of the "progressive era," Rothbard writes that these reforms "were designed to create what they did in fact create:

a world of centralized statism, of 'partnership' between government and industry, a world which subsists in granting subsidies and monopoly privileges to business and other favored groups."[101]

Fortunately, as Rothbard pointed out, not all big businessmen were recipients of state privilege and champions of the status quo. While "expecting the Rockefellers or the legion of other favored big businessmen to convert to a libertarian or even a laissez-faire view is a vain and empty hope," he wrote, "this is not to say that *all* big businessmen, or businessmen in general, must be written off." Regulation benefits some at the expense of others, and these others, "especially those remote from the privileged 'Eastern Establishment,' " are "potentially receptive to free-market and libertarian ideas."[102]

When he wrote those words, Rothbard naturally could not have known that one such businessman, the scion of one of America's wealthiest families—whose family heritage and temperament rendered him remote indeed from the sociopolitical circles of the Eastern elite—would soon arise as the sponsor of the libertarian movement, and, specifically, of its Rothbardian wing. His patronage would propel Rothbard and his movement, over the next few years, to an entirely new and heretofore undreamed of level of success.

NOTES

1. Rothbard, "The Betrayal of the American Right," unpublished manuscript, p. 187.

2. Ibid.

3. Rothbard to F. A. Harper, 22 March 1962. Harper was also devastated by the breakup of Volker: its $17 million of assets were slated to go to the Institute for Humane Studies, headed by Harper. But the Fund was dissolved before this was finalized, and, as Rothbard tells it, IHS "was sud-

denly out on the street as a pure and lovable libertarian research organization. For the rest of his life, Baldy Harper struggled on as head of IHS."

4. See Rothbard to Ludwig M. Lachmann, 14 February 1957.

5. Rothbard to Ivan Bierly, 12 December 1962.

6. Rothbard to Gordon Tullock, 1 October 1966.

7. Rothbard, "The Betrayal of the American Right," p. 201.

8. Murray N. Rothbard, "Education in California," Pine Tree Features, n.d. This was the first of a series of fifty-eight newspaper columns written for Pine Tree Features, which was run by the pacifist–LeFevrian outfit, the Rampart Institute, in Colorado. The Rothbard bibliography compiled by Carl Watner describes this material as "fifty-eight typewritten articles, circa 1967–68, in possession of Robert Kephart; publication information not yet ascertained," the columns were published in the *Santa Ana Register* by R. C. Hoiles, a devoted LeFevrian and the publisher of Freedom Newspapers chain in Southern California.

9. Rothbard, "The Betrayal of the American Right," p. 202.

10. Murray N. Rothbard, *Left and Right: The Prospects for Liberty* (San Francisco: Cato Institute, 1979), p. 8.

11. Ibid., p. 1. Emphasis in original.

12. Ibid., p. 26.

13. William F. Buckley Jr., "A Young Republican's View," *Commonweal* (January 25, 1952).

14. D. F. Fleming, *The Cold War and its Origins* (New York: Doubleday and Company, 1961).

15. Harry Elmer Barnes, ed., *Perpetual War for Perpetual Peace* (Caldwell, Idaho: Caxton Printers, 1953).

16. Charles Callan Tansill, *Back Door to War* (Chicago: Henry Regnery Company, 1952).

17. Ronald Hamowy, "Left and Right Meet," *The New Republic* (March 12, 1966).

18. Rothbard, "The Betrayal of the American Right," p. 202. According to Rothbard, Liggio was also briefly managing editor of the *New York Guardian*, a leftist weekly, but "he was purged for 'taking the capitalist road' in trying to cut costs."

19. Murray N. Rothbard, "Principles of Secession," Pine Tree Features (June–August 1967).

20. Rothbard, "Principles of Secession," Pine Tree Features, n.d. [July–August 1967].

21. Murray N. Rothbard, "Civil War in July, 1967 Part I," Pine Tree Features.

22. Murray N. Rothbard, "Civil War in July, 1967, Part III," Pine Tree Features.

23. Murray N. Rothbard, "Martin Luther King," Pine Tree Features, n.d. [May 1969].

24. Ibid.

25. Murray N. Rothbard, "LBJ—After Four Years," Pine Tree Features, n.d. [November 1968].

26. Murray N. Rothbard, "The Coming American Fascism," Pine Tree Features, n.d. [1967].

27. Murray N. Rothbard, "The Revolutionary Mood," Pine Tree Features, n.d. [1968].

28. Carl Oglesby and Richard Shaull, *Containment and Change* (New York: Macmillian, 1967), pp. 166–67.

29. Interview with Walter Block and Walter Grinder, "Rothbard Tells All," unpublished transcript in possession of author, p. 38.

30. Ibid.

31. Ibid., pp. 38–39.

32. Ibid.

33. Ibid., p. 39.

34. Ibid., p. 40.

35. Murray N. Rothbard, "Biography of Ludwig von Mises," *International Encyclopedia of Social Sciences* 16 (1968): 379–82.

36. Block and Grinder, "Rothbard Tells All," p. 40.

37. Murray N. Rothbard, "Confessions of a Right-wing Liberal," *Ramparts* (June 15, 1968).

38. Rothbard to Thomas Fleming, 21 March 1991. The editor was Gary Alexander.

39. Rothbard, "Confessions of a Right-wing Liberal." Emphasis in original.

40. Ibid.

41. Ibid.

42. See Karl Hess, *Mostly on the Edge: An Autobiography* (Amherst, N.Y.: Prometheus Books, 1999).

43. Ibid, p. 185.

44. Ibid, pp. 191–92.

45. The newsletter was originally called *The Libertarian*, but, starting with the fourth number, was forced to change its name when a New Jersey-based periodical, which no one had ever heard of, claimed first rights to the name.

46. "Why 'The Libertarian,' " *The Libertarian* (March 1, 1969): 1.

47. The Movement Grows," *Libertarian Forum* (June 1, 1969): 1.

48. Murray N. Rothbard, "Listen, YAF," *Libertarian Forum* (August 15, 1969): 1–2.

49. Ibid.

50. This fierce sectarianism applied only to those closest to Rand's own position, and did not prevent her from penning endorsements of Richard Nixon and Gerald Ford.

51. "Goldwater Aide Now A Radical, Adopts Anarchism Philosophy," *New York Times*, 28 September 1969.

52. "Ideologues: You Know He's Right," *Newsweek*, 29 September 1969.

53. Murray N. Rothbard, "We Make The Media," *Libertarian Forum* (October 15, 1969).

54. Ibid.

55. Murray N. Rothbard, "The Conference: Two Steps Forward, Two Steps Back," *Libertarian Forum* (November 1, 1969).

56. Ibid.

57. Ibid.

58. Ibid.

59. Ibid.

60. Jerome Tuccille, *It Usually Begins With Ayn Rand* (New York: Stein & Day, 1971), pp. 117–18.

61. Ibid., 121.

62. Rothbard, "The Conference: Two Steps Forward, Two Steps Back."

63. Murray N. Rothbard, "The New Left, R.I.P.," *Libertarian Forum* (March 15, 1970).

64. Karl Hess, *Dear America* (New York: William Morrow, 1975), p. 91.

65. Ibid.

66. Murray N. Rothbard, "Death of the Left," *Libertarian Forum* (December 15, 1970).

67. Murray N. Rothbard, "Freedom, Inequality, Primitivism, and the Division of Labor," *Modern Age* (summer 1971).

68. Murray N. Rothbard, *Power and Market: Government and the Economy* (Menlo Parl, Calif.: Institute for Humane Studies, 1970).

69. Ludwig von Mises, *Human Action* (Princeton, N.J.: Yale University Press, 1949), p. 282.

70. Ludwig von Mises, *Human Action: Scholar's Edition* (Auburn, Ala.: Ludwig von Mises Institute, 1999).

71. R. A. Childs, Review of *Power and Market, Libertarian Forum* (15 November 1970): 4–6 footnote.

72. Ibid.

73. Murray N. Rothabrd, "The Elections," *Libertarian Forum* (November 15–December 1, 1970).

74. Rothbard, "The Betrayal of the American Right," p. 208.

75. Ibid., p. 209.

76. Ibid., p. 211.

77. Murray N. Rothbard, "The New Libertarian Creed," *New York Times*, 9 February 1971, and "The President's Economic Betrayal," 4 September 1971.

78. Murray N. Rothbard, "Know Your Rights," *WIN* (March 1, 1997): 6. This is a minihistory of the "right-wing" libertarian movement, focusing on the Old Right–libertarian opposition to imperialism and war.

79. Rothbard appeared on NBC's *Today Show*, and did several radio interviews.

80. Murray N. Rothbard, *For a New Liberty* (New York: Macmillan, 1973).

81. Ibid., p. 48.

82. Ibid., p. 25.

83. Ibid., p. 95.

84. Ibid., p. 279.

85. Ibid., p. 287. Emphasis in original. In the 1978 edition of the book, brought out under the auspices of the Cato Institute, that passage is immediately followed by the exculpatory phrase: "Such a statement is bound to shock Americans," and attributes such prudery to "intense propaganda by the Establishment." The original version contained no such *mea culpa.* The change was made at the insistence of Cato Institute officials, who seemed to believe that mentioning the shock evinced by Rothbard's statement would somehow alleviate it.

86. Ibid., p. 297.

87. Cited in ibid., p. 302.

88. Murray N. Rothbard, *Education, Free and Compulsory* (Wichita, Kansas: Center for Independent Education, 1972).

89. Murray N. Rothbard, *Conceived in Liberty: Vol. I: A New Land, A New People, the American Colonies in the Seventeenth Century* (New Rochelle, N.Y.: Arlington House, 1975); *Conceived in Liberty: Vol II: A "Salutary Neglect": The American Colonies in the First Half of the Eighteenth Century* (New Rochelle, N.Y.: Arlington House, 1975); *Conceived in Liberty: Vol III: Advance to Revolution* (New Rochelle, N.Y.: Arlington House, 1976); *Conceived in Liberty: Vol. IV: The Revolutionary War, 1775–1784* (New Rochelle, N.Y.: Arlington House, 1979). The story of the fifth volume, in brief, is that Rothbard dictated the text onto an early version of the long-playing record, for which the technology rapidly became obsolete, and the text was never transcribed. The record was eventully misplaced.

90. Murray N. Rothbard, "Ludwig von Mises and the Paradigm of Our Age," *Modern Age* (fall 1971): 370–79.

91. Thomas S. Kuhn, *The Structure of Scientific Revolutions* (Chicago: University of Chicago Press, 1970).

92. Murray N. Rothbard, "Egalitarianism as a Revolut Against Nature," *Modern Age* (fall 1973): 348–57.

93. Murray N. Rothbard, "Freedom, Inequality, Primitivism and the Division of Labor," *Modern Age* (summer 1971): 226–45.

94. Murray N. Rothbard, "Herbert Hoover and the Myth of Laissez-Faire," in *A New History of Leviathan*, edited by Ronald Raosh and Murray N. Rothbard (New York: E. P. Dutton, 1972), pp. 111–45.

95. Ibid., pp. 66–110.

96. Murray N. Rothbard, "The New Deal and the International Monetary System," in *Watershed of Empire: Essays on New Deal Foreign Policy*, edited by Leonard Liggio and James J. Martin (Colorado Springs: Ralph Myles, 1976), pp. 19–64.

97. Murray N. Rothbard, "The Movie Hero Is a Vital Part of American Culture," *Human Events* (June 15, 1974): 16.

98. Murray N. Rothbard, "Present At The Creation," *Libertarian Forum* (April 1973).

99. To what end, is left for the reader to judge.

100. Rothbard, "Present At The Creation."

101. Rothbard, *For a New Liberty*, p. 314.

102. Ibid., p. 314.

5

1700 MONTGOMERY STREET

Rothbard had mixed feelings about the invitation from multi-billionaire Charles Koch to spend the weekend at a ski lodge in Vail, Colorado. The purpose of the occasion was to discuss the future of the libertarian movement, and Rothbard was naturally pleased at the prospect of Koch's financial support to a number of projects he had in mind. But Rothbard—not the skiing type, to say the least—was uneasy: he had the distinct impression that the skiing lodge would be perched on the very peak of the mountain, a prospect he found fairly daunting. It was only after Joey explained that, no, the skiers go *up* the mountain via a ski lift, with the lodge safely ensconced in the valley at the *foot* of the mountain, that he agreed to go.[1]

Though born to great wealth, Charles L. Koch did not just sit back and enjoy the fruits of his father's labors, but insisted on expanding the family fortune until it became one of the biggest in the country and the world: shared among the brothers, Fred, Charles, David, and William, the sheer scale of the Koch corporate assets—concentrated in oil pipelines, natural gas, cattle, and engineering—still placed them among the top twenty-or-so of the Billionaire's Club. Their father, Fred C. Koch, had been an Old Right stalwart and a founding member of the John Birch Society, serving on its national council. Charles had inherited not only the money, but some measure of the politics, and was a generous (but judicious) donor to conservative causes of a libertarian bent. Koch Industries had awarded Rothbard a full-time research grant, from 1974–75, to write *The Ethics of Liberty*, including a grant for secretarial help. An entire division, albeit relatively small in comparison to the rest of the Koch empire, was given over to the propagation of Kochian ideology, with one or another corporate functionary overseeing the operation, as Koch increasingly took up the libertarian cause: funding the Institute for Humane Studies, originally founded by F. A. Harper in 1961, and taking up where the late and much-lamented Volker Fund had left off.

THE CATO INSTITUTE: THE EARLY YEARS

Rothbard's relationship with this apparatus was volatile from the start. While he had a lovable personality, he could be irascible when crossed, and in his later years this tendency would become more pronounced. Yet at this point he had not developed the lasting animosities that would come to dominate his relations with the Kochian bureaucracy. Imbued with hope that the libertarian circles scattered throughout the country could become an effective intellectual and political force, Rothbard faced the ingrained pessimism of conservative bureaucrats terrified of making too many waves.

The first skirmishes are documented in an internal policy memo from former Volker Fund apparatchik Kenneth S. Templeton to Koch lieutenant George H. Pearson, in which Templeton sneers at

Rothbard's proposal to establish a scholarly journal to advance libertarian scholarship. In his memo, Templeton affected the pose of one too precious to dirty his hands in the mire of "activism," a word he always adorned with quotation marks. Not only did Templeton fail to find this a persuasive proposal, but he accused Rothbard of seeking to build a coterie of followers and promoting an ideological movement. He opposed Rothbard's strategy of developing the cadre of an ideological movement, and instead championed infiltration and cooperation. The Templeton memo epitomizes everything Rothbard disliked about academia: the phony facade of "objective" or "pure" scholarship, allegedly "value-free," like physics or the study of biology; the implicit snobbery, that looked down its "scholarly" nose at grubby "activism."[2]

Templeton was skeptical that Rothbard could simultaneously function both as an old-fashioned public intellectual and a research scholar capable of producing books like *Man, Economy, and State* and *America's Great Depression*, even if he were to give up the *Libertarian Forum* and his cadre-movement strategy. In retrospect, Templeton clearly underestimated Rothbard, who not only continued his activism, but whose best and most productive years were still ahead of him.[3]

Rothbard had nothing but contempt for this posture of the "disinterested" social scientist. Fourteen years earlier, he had penned a stinging retort to this conceit in his classic essay, "The Mantle of Science." Today's social scientists, having shunted aside the old-fashioned idea that a rational ethics is possible,

> have taken to smuggling in arbitrary, *ad hoc* ethical judgments through the back door of each particular science of man. The current fashion is to preserve a facade of *Wertfreiheit*, while casually adopting value-judgments, not as the scientist's own decisions, but as the consensus of the values of others. Instead of choosing

his own ends and valuing accordingly, the scientist supposedly maintains his neutrality by adopting the values of the bulk of society. In short, to set forth one's own values is now considered biased and "nonobjective," while to adopt uncritically the slogans of other people is the height of "objectivity." Scientific objectivity no longer means a man's pursuit of truth wherever it may lead, but abiding by a Gallup poll of other, less informed subjectivities.[4]

In the war between liberty and power, Rothbard was not "neutral"—and neither, it turned out, was Charles Koch. Templeton lost this struggle with Rothbard, as Koch underwent a radicalization, was converted to the Rothbardian strategy, and summoned Rothbard to the mountain. There, amid the snowy peaks of Vail, Rothbard made his pitch.

Over the course of a weekend, in the winter of 1976, Rothbard and the heir to one of the largest family held corporations in the nation talked late into the night. As the roaring fire in the elaborate stone fireplace burned down to flickering embers, Rothbard outlined the need to organize and systematize the burgeoning libertarian movement and to bring order out of chaos.

The Libertarian Party had coalesced around the presidential candidacy of Roger MacBride, a television producer whose *Little House on the Prairie* series was a big hit. MacBride had captured the hearts of libertarians when, as a Republican elector from the state of Virginia, he had bolted ranks and cast his vote for John Hospers, the party's first presidential candidate. But the party was plagued by a lack of funding, almost insuperable obstacles to ballot status, and the inexperience of the founding leadership. Furthermore, the general flakiness and counterculturalism of a large section of the LP rank-and-file was a source of never-ending irritation to Rothbard. He was, at this point, thoroughly exasperated with the crankery that flourishes in the hothouse atmosphere of any and all radical movements—and that seemed especially at home in the libertarian subculture of the seventies. As 1976 dawned, his "From the Old Curmudgeon" column in the *Libertarian Forum* announced his "New Year's Wish for the Movement"—a year-long moratorium on the eccentricities that bedeviled the organizations and individuals that made up much of the libertarian movement.

For one, he was thoroughly "sick and tired of reading about how we should all stock up a year's supply of dried beans, and backpack it to the hills. Fellas, I've got news for you: I ain't eating any dried beans, and I ain't back-packing it to the hills. I will stick to the market, crippled though it may be, and continue to dine in plush urban comfort on Pepsis, vodka martinis, and veal parmigiana."[5]

A similar interdict was placed on that old libertarian pipedream, starting a "New Libertarian Country": "One would think that if man can really learn from experience, then the total and abject failure of each and every one of these cockamamie stunts should have sent all of their supporters a message: namely, to come back to the real world." He was also looking forward to a ban on "psychobabble": "Wouldn't it be great? A whole year of nothing, not a word, not a peep, about 'open relationships,' 'growing as a person,' 'getting in touch with your feelings,' 'nonauthoritarian relations,' 'living free,' and all the rest of the malarkey." Appalled by the ignorance of the typical Libertarian Party activist, who knew no more about the world than was depicted in science fiction novels, he called for "a year's abstinence" from what seemed to be the primary or even sole reading material of the modal libertarian.[6]

He was particularly annoyed, and even angered, by the rise of a "left" opposition to the MacBride candidacy within the Libertarian Party. In Rothbard's view, their objection to MacBride was not ideological, but *cultural*: he wore a suit and tie, was a "real world" person, and therefore was suspect in the eyes of the militant hippie faction. The 1975 nominating convention had been the scene of a strong challenge from this element, and Rothbard feared a replay of the "leftist" fervor of the sixties, which he believed would isolate and alienate the movement from its real constituency: the great middle American majority. The movement was still experiencing a hangover from its sojourn into the New Left, and badly needed a corrective.

The question of strategy had always preoccupied Rothbard. It was the subject of many a late-night gabfest in the days of the old Circle Bastiat, and, as the biweekly (and, later, monthly) record of the *Libertarian Forum* shows, a point of great contention and confusion in the libertarian movement at large. Rothbard did not just have very definite opinions on the subject, but, in his typical fashion, he approached the problem in a systematic way. He had published a multipart series on strategic issues in the obscure *Libertarian Connection,*[7] but now he and a greatly expanded circle of friends and allies put their energies into examining every aspect of this vital issue. A private seminar was held in New York City, with the attendees all writing papers on various aspects of the subject: Koch utilized his familial experience and wrote a paper on the John Birch Society, and also a paper on the Fabian Society, the British socialist group. Joseph R. Stromberg's contribution was "Fabianism and Social Change: The Perpetuity of Gradualism"; Williamson Evers took on "Lenin and His Critics on the Organization Question," while Edward H. Crane III gave an "Analysis of the Prospects for the Libertarian Party."[8]

This informal symposium was really part of an ongoing discussion, begun in the early seventies by Rothbard, Koch, and George Pearson, when they put together a prospectus for a new libertarian organization, the Libertarian Society. The proposed organization was modeled on the John Birch Society, not only in its top-down hierarchical structure, but even down to pledging that "reading rooms" would be established in an outright imitation of the American Opinion bookstores set up by the Birchers in cities across the country. This society would coexist with the Libertarian Party in a kind of symbiosis, as the brain set on the party's broad shoulders. While Koch, Pearson, and Rothbard had agreed to form an "Initial Committee," none of these three was a political organizer, and the idea lay dormant until the spring of 1976, when Pearson sent Ed Crane a copy of the prospectus, and reported on a meeting with Rothbard and Koch in which the idea of the Libertarian Society had been revived. A list of possible executive directors is part of the memo, with Crane topping the list.[9]

Crane, a young broker from San Francisco, had just been elected chairman of the Libertarian Party. Imposing at least a semblance of order and routine on the party machinery, Crane made short shrift of the "crazies," as Rothbard called them. Tough-minded, and with an air of command and competence, Crane was impressive, and Rothbard was enthralled. In a letter to Crane, Rothbard outlines his strategic theory—the goal of victory, the need for cadre, the "pyramid of ideology"—and endorses the concept of organizing a Libertarian Society along the lines suggested in the prospectus. "Now, we have quite a few scholars in the libertarian movement," wrote Rothbard,

> (although not as much, of course, as we should have), and we have a large, amorphous, and often nutty rank-and-file; but we have almost no one with organizing ability. This makes you, Ed, a unique and extremely scarce resource; not only are you the best person I can think of to head a Libertarian Society effort, but you are also the *only* one, and I know that Charles [Koch] feels the same way. This is not said to flatter you, but simply as a bald statement of existing reality.[10]

This view of Crane as the instrument by which libertarian ideas would be realized in the world was a function first performed by Hess, and later by others. Now Crane would play the crucial role of the activist disciple in a drama that began on a high note, trumpets blaring.

Shortly after that sojourn in Vail, the Cato Institute and allied organizations began to take shape. The Institute was named by Rothbard after the *Cato's Letters*, a series of pseudonymous polemics published in the period leading up to the American Revolution and written by John Trenchard and Thomas Gordon. Their series of fiery libertarian pamphlets are often cited by historians as a major catalyst of the revolutionary upsurge. it was also thought, among the founders of the institute, that the allusion to Cato the Elder couldn't hurt. Not only did it give the organization a patrician air, but the name conjured up other classical allusions. The old Roman senator, after all, had ended every speech with the famous imprecation against Rome's ancient enemy: "Carthage must be destroyed!" Insert "the state" in place of the Carthaginians, and the name conjures the Rothbardian spirit that imbued the founders of this new intellectual enterprise.

The headquarters of the Libertarian Party had been moved to San Francisco, with Ed Crane firmly in charge, and Cato soon followed. By early 1977, the Cato Institute was ensconced at 1700 Montgomery Street, in a three-story glass-and-steel building at the foot of picturesque Telegraph Hill.

This had been Rothbard's dream: a libertarian thinktank. The liberals had any number of public policy organizations, and the conservatives had the Heritage Foundation, as well as a number of lesser thinktanks and foundations, but not since the neutering of the Foundation for Economic Education had there been a full-fledged full-service libertarian thinktank, with a resident staff and an academic program that could attract the best students from all over the country. The Cato Institute, however, was more than that; it was a more sophisticated (and tax-exempt) version of the Libertarian Society outlined in the early prospectus. Cato was meant to be a libertarian brain trust, with the official Libertarian Party as only one branch of a larger movement that would penetrate academia, journalism, the world of publishing, and enter the popular consciousness. Backed by Koch's generosity, Cato would be on an equal footing with the Brookings and Heritage institutes, and any of the other Washington-based thinktanks that dominated the policy wonk scene—and all *without* moving to D.C., epicenter of the Leviathan.

Rothbard's own contribution to the strategic symposium was a blockbuster. His book-length manuscript, "Toward a Theory of Libertarian Social Change," elaborated on a fully worked out strategic theory: The need for a movement, the concept of cadre, the necessity of calling for the abolition of state power as quickly as possible, the twin deviations of opportunism and sectarianism, the nature of ideological entrepreneurship, the question of leadership, the role of reason and emotion in building a movement, the error of the infallible party, and a historical analysis of the Old-Right libertarian movement from the early fifties. All this and more was packed into nearly two hundred richly footnoted pages.[11]

As we have seen, Rothbard was no ivory tower philosopher; for him, the Misesian injunction that economics (and all the social or "soft" sciences) result from purposeful human action was reflected in his lifelong commitment to the libertarian movement. He did not merely write about economics, politics, and his vision of liberty, but made strenuous (and often lonely) efforts to translate his libertarian ideals into reality.

As an economist, historian, and philosopher, Rothbard's monuments are *Man, Economy, and State, The Ethics of Liberty*, the four-volume history of the American Revolution, and the posthumously published two-volume set, *An Austrian Perspective on the History of Economic Thought*. But "Toward a Theory of Libertarian Social Change" is clearly the book he had the most fun writing, and it shows: Rothbard's narrative flow never breaks as he takes the reader on a historical tour of revolutions and radical politics, drawing examples from both Left and Right, and utilizing a praxeological or "value-free" analysis to draw the lesson for today.

The book was written in April of 1977 as a privately circulated memo and distributed to the inner councils of the newly organized Cato Institute. The cover page contained the following note:

STRICTLY CONFIDENTIAL

Not to be quoted, discussed or circulated without the written or otherwise expressed permission of the author.

Rothbard was not the author of this note, although at the time he allowed himself to be convinced that it was necessary. What was in one sense Rothbard's most immediately useful book, "Toward a Strategy for Libertarian Social Change" was deemed too "hot" for general circulation; even to Rothbard's closest friends and collaborators, it seemed axiomatic that any book that quoted Lenin and objectively analyzed the strategic and organizational methods of both Marxism and right-wing authoritarians (as well as the American revolutionaries, classical liberals, and others) was bound to offend all the wrong people.

It was only natural, given human nature and especially the nature of such a small and tightly knit movement, that such a pledge of confidentiality would arouse widespread notice, not only among libertarians, but among their declared enemies. Not long after it was written, the book's existence was revealed in an article in *National Review*, which implied that Rothbard was an admirer of Lenin and that he was promulgating a conspiracy of anti-American revolutionaries who sought to subvert the very foundations of the Republic, if not Western civilization.[12]

Libertarianism was smeared as "opposed to all conservative traditions, to tradition itself" and libertarians were portrayed as the cadre of a dark conspiracy to "subvert the freedom movement." The idea that Rothbard denied "the legitimacy of any social authority" was a lie, and not a very effective one, as even the mildly skeptical could turn to his voluminous works for evidence to the contrary. Indeed, in the libertarian canon, social authority (as opposed to state authority) is the only legitimate authority, as Albert Jay Nock and his disciple Frank Chodorov long ago pointed out. Rothbard inherited and elaborated this position, which he cogently expressed in an appreciation of the thought of Frank S. Meyer, who sought to fuse the libertarian love of liberty with the conservative concern for virtue and respect for tradition:

> It would be a false and perverted rationalism to say that any custom which cannot be proven on some other ground to be "rational" must go by the board. We can then conclude as follows: (a) that custom must be voluntarily upheld and not enforced by coercion; and (b) that people would be well advised (although not forced) to begin with a presumption in favor of custom, other things being equal. In a world, for example, where every man takes off his hat in the presence of ladies, an individual should be free not to do so, but at the risk of being generally considered a boor.[13]

National Review's caricature of libertarianism as a demonic ideology that envisioned the destruction of the family, the liquidation of all social conventions, and a war of all against all dovetailed nicely with the Buckleyite effort to portray libertarians as communist dupes: on foreign policy, "the libertarian position is indistinguishable from the Communist position."[14] Most of *National Review*'s bile was directed at Cato's opposition to the policy of global interventionism and massive "defense" spending. The article was larded with carefully edited quotes from the strategy memo citing Lenin, and the Rothbardian conspirators were portrayed as a Fifth Column that was undoubtedly receiving orders directly from Moscow via Rothbard. It was a pathetic and generally ineffective polemic that was nevertheless given at least some weight by Cato's refusal to make Rothbard's memo public. Even long after the policy of secrecy proved counterproductive, in view of the sinister imputations of the *National Review* article the memo remained in the archives—only to be uncovered some fifteen years later as further evidence of the author's prolific versatility. Rothbard's book-length memo deserved to have been openly published and distributed as widely as possible within the occasionally flaky and strategically retarded libertarian movement, instead of hidden away for the private delectation of the Cato vanguard. "Toward a Theory of Libertarian Social Change" is a masterful manifesto and political manual for activists, written from the perspective of a great libertarian theoretician who was also a hardboiled political realist, a manuscript that shows Rothbard, the philosophical man-of-action, at the top of his form.

Some of the references to various groups and individuals are obscure even to libertarians of the present day. Yet Rothbard is a writer whose central concern was never journalistic minutiae, but the underlying principles that govern the ebb and flow of current events. He was, above all, a great teacher, a talent that is showcased in this still-unpublished work. Here Rothbard expounds on the absolute necessity of the libertarian cadre—a combination full-time activist and ideologue—and explains the nature, function, and nurturing of the species, which up until that point in time, the spring of 1977, had been a rare creature indeed. Suddenly, with the help of one of the wealthiest families in the United States, if not the world, the number and quality of these practically nonexistent creatures would be increased a hundred-fold. Rothbard's discussion of the need for and key function of a periodical press, his emphasis on the importance of a vital youth movement as a barometer of a movement's health, and his insistence on the need for cadre-development through a process of internal education and the nurturing of libertarian scholars, all foreshadowed the birth of various spin-offs and wholly owned subsidiaries of the Cato group: *Inquiry*, a biweekly "outreach" magazine; *Libertarian Review*, a "movement" magazine; Students for a Libertarian Society (SLS), the youth arm of the movement; and a full academic program of Cato fellowships, scholarly conferences, and week-long summer seminars, which attracted the cream of the libertarian crop.

If the writing of "Toward a Theory of Libertarian Social Change" had a practical purpose, it also had a broad theoretical goal: to set out a theory of libertarian social change in a historical context. Few libertarians had attempted anything like this since the days of the eighteenth-century French classical liberals, who first formulated a "class analysis" that pitted the state against the people (a concept stolen by Marx and distorted for his own ends). In the section entitled "Good Guys and Bad Guys," Rothbard analyzes how ideological movements from the far Left to the far Right have utilized this Manichean scenario to their advantage. He points out the economic and other fallacies inherent in the Marxist model of economic classes in conflict, and explodes the myth of fascism as "status resentment" of the "enraged bourgeoisie."

Rothbard's masterful presentation of the libertarian theory of class analysis is particularly cogent today, when any attempt to explain events in a coherent way is attacked as a "conspiracy theory." Rothbard indicts "contemporary libertarians and classical liberals" for failing to "*identify* the specific members of the ruling class—a coalition led by certain big-business groups allied to technocratic intellectuals and labor union leaders." Far from being the result of intellectual error, the statist system, in Rothbard's view, is the product of an extremely lucrative intellectual racket: "Statism," Rothbard points out, "is in the rational self-interest of the exploiters. In contemporary America, it is in the self-interest of the business groups and labor unions who gain privileges, cartels, and subsidies galore from the state, and of the intellectuals and technicians who form the state-controlling bureaucracy. . . . It is this general truth, and the particular concrete facts that constitute it, that must be continually exposed to the public."[15]

Particularly insightful is his wide-ranging discussion of the role of reason and emotion in political organizing, as well as the concept of "ideological entrepreneurship" as "an art and not a science that can be learned by rote." The key to success, he believed, was in understanding the relation of this art to the need for strategic flexibility.[16]

He draws an analogy between the need for a strategic framework in politics and "the function of the price mechanism within the economic system." Although warning that "the analogy should not be carried too far," Rothbard makes the original and vitally important point that a strategic orientation or theory allows the ideological entrepreneur to

> [allocate] scarce resources among competing goals. In other words, strategy enables a political movement to undertake a systematic and explicit ordering of priorities which in turn enables the movement to allocate its scarce human and financial resources in the most efficient manner possible.[17]

Rothbard maps the contours of his ideological universe by identifying the libertarian "center" as a kind of golden-mean between the two basic deviations from libertarian principles. The two great temptations that seek to lure libertarians off the straight (and often narrow) path of principled politics are what Rothbard defines as opportunism on the Right, and sectarianism on the Left. Both, says Rothbard, are rooted in pessimism, an abandonment of the idea that the ultimate goal of libertarianism, the radical devolution of the state, is possible. The left-sectarian retreats into a shell of rhetorical phrasemongering and ultimatistic demands, while the right-opportunist tries to sneak libertarian principle in by the back door, hiding, denying, and even actively subverting ultimate libertarian goals in the name of some imagined short-term gain.

The discussions of Lenin as a model of entrepreneurial flexibility in his willingness to go against the received wisdom—often demonstrated in his opposition to the "orthodoxy" of his most devoted followers—foreshadowed the denouement of this episode in Rothbard's life. But for now, at least, everyone was reading from the same script, as written by Rothbard. In the final pages of "Toward a Theory of Libertarian Social Change," the author rejects an alliance with the remnants of the New Left and formulates an interim strategy based on the premise "that libertarians' natural allies, for the current historical period, are the (moderate) liberals, who, in any case, dominate the media and opinion-moulding groups, rather than the conservatives or the extreme Left."[18]

In understanding the significance of the Cato years—really only two, from 1978 to 1980—in Rothbard's life, it is necessary to look back on his experience, and that of his revered libertarian mentors. The previous generation of Old Right libertarians, in confronting the Leviathan, had looked at the task of rolling it back as well-nigh impossible: the best they could hope for, they thought, was to carry on a successful holding action. Their job was to stay at their posts, stick their fingers in the dike, and hold back the flood waters of collectivism. When they tired and fell away, a new generation—fewer, always fewer—would take their place, and each generation would see the floodtide rise higher—until, inevitably, all were engulfed.

This was the mindset of such lyrical pessimists as Garet Garrett, whose classic essay on the New Deal, "The Revolution Was," was described by Rose Wilder Lane as essentially saying, "there's nothing to do now, but sit and keen, wail with Garet for the happy past that is no more and can never be again." Lane added, "That attitude irritates me to near the point of frenzy."[19] While Rothbard admired and honored Garrett, his own outlook, as we have seen, was fundamentally different. Up to this point, however, it had been hard for Rothbard to argue against those who pointed to the looming colossus of big government and declared that libertarianism was a futile crusade. He had made a convincing theoretical case, in "Left and Right: The Prospects for Liberty," against the dark visions of libertarians such as Mencken and Albert J. Nock, who held out no hope for the human race, except in a tiny "Remnant" that would carry on the traditions of liberty and human civilization in splendid isolation.

The whole course of Rothbard's career so far had been animated by an attempt to break out of that isolation. While the case for optimism was all worked out in theory, in practice it was quite a different story. Over the years, he often complained, in print and in private, that while what the Marxist tacticians used to call "the objective conditions"—the appeal of the libertarian message—were "ripe, indeed a little over-ripe," the "subjective conditions" (the means to get this message out) lagged far behind. In 1976, libertarian institutions on every level, from the scholarly to the political, were still in the seedling stage.

Then someone poured a large amount of a very good fertilizer on this freshly planted crop. With the infusion of Koch's millions, the subjective factor had finally caught up to the objective conditions. Rothbard was unleashed—and so were the Rothbardians, virtually all of whom were called on to fill various editorial, academic, and administrative posts in this burgeoning apparatus of libertarians.

Williamson Evers, chosen for the key spot as editor of *Inquiry*, was a close friend and associate of Rothbard's. Evers had been discovered, during the sixties, by Ronald Hamowy, then teaching at Stanford University, who reported that one of his more precocious students had the disconcerting habit of quoting, verbatim, from the works of Murray N. Rothbard. It was the beginning of an important friendship, one bound not only with a mutual love of liberty, but a genuine affection evident in their copious correspondence. In these letters is the spirit of camaraderie that Rothbard had hoped to find in the Libertarian Party, intensified by a mutual devotion to principle, informed by a love of learning, and lit up with flashes of Rothbardian humor, and, literally, bursts of song. When Murray and Joey came out to California, instead of moving to San Francisco where the Cato Institute was located, they chose to live in Palo Alto, near Evers, who dutifully drove his mentor to the office each work day. It was a morning ritual enjoyable to both, and it was clear at the time that young Bill was Rothbard's favorite.

If Evers was the "good boy" of the Rothbardian circle, then perhaps the "bad boy" or "problem child" of the lot was the brilliant but erratic Roy A. Childs Jr. It had not always been so. Roy had been among the most precocious and radical of the young Rothbardians in the early days in New York. As a young student from Buffalo, Childs had come to New York City and was immediately elevated to the role of "boy wonder" with the publication of his audacious "Open Letter to Ayn Rand" in which he attacked the Randian concept of limited government and made the case for anarchocapitalism.[20] As an editor of *The Individualist*, and then of *Books for Libertarians* and the *Libertarian Review*, Childs was a flamboyant character whose charm, high-powered intellect, and booming voice stood out in any crowd. He was complex, brilliant, often moody, and wildly ambitious. He was also a prolific writer who could turn out a piece on any topic from Austrian economics to the inside story on the latest Third World hotspot with skill and dispatch. He was instrumental in converting scores of libertarians, who had come into the movement from Objectivism, to anarchocapitalism, in disabusing them of the notion that big business was in any sense "America's persecuted minority" as Ayn Rand put it, and in furthering their education on the role of U.S. foreign policy in the rise of the Total State. He played a key role as secretary of the Radical Libertarian Alliance, and helped coalesce and merge the local and regional groups into the Society for Individual Liberty, which later formed the basis of the Libertarian Party.

Childs once told a newspaper reporter that Murray considered him "sort of an intellectual son," and this was true for many years.[21] But Roy was no acolyte: he was not the type to defer to authority, and he often challenged his mentor—who, fortunately, was usually delighted to argue fine points of libertarian theory with his young friend well into the night. Rothbard and Childs had much in common, not only ideology but also in their basic approach to ideas and to the world. Both were independent intellectuals who disdained the ivory tower and both were determined to fight for their ideas in the cultural-political arena. Unlike most libertarian intellectuals, who tended to be somewhat otherworldly, Childs was a hard-headed realist, well read and well versed in current affairs. He was an ideologue, but not a narrow-minded single-track type, and had a wide range of knowledge and interests— classical music, film, fiction: in short, the pleasures of life, which he seemed to have an unlimited capacity to enjoy. In this sense,

Childs was a Rothbardian temperamentally as well as ideologically, and this was the real basis of their friendship.

But there was a wild side to Roy. The Rothbards once let him stay in their New York City apartment during a long absence—with the one proviso that he stay out of a certain room. When they returned, they discovered that not only had he not stayed out of the room, he had actually *rented it out* to someone![22] They were angry—but not for long. Childs's friends, including the Rothbards, put up with his peccadilloes, and perhaps even encouraged him with their indulgence. Why did they do it? Childs was a vastly entertaining human being. His sense of fun, combined with his enormous erudition, made him a delightful companion; his air of being a savvy New Yorker, combined with his youthful idealism, resulted in a kind of sophisticated innocence that could be very appealing, and people sought him out. Childs could charm the birds out of the trees, and he knew *everyone*—not only libertarians, but a vast network of scholars, journalists, writers, publishers, musicians, and accomplished people in many different realms, with whom he kept in constant touch by telephone and letter.

Over the years, the wild side of Childs began to predominate. His problems with alcohol, and his increasingly serious weight problem gave rise to a continuing threat to his health, which in turn affected his mental equilibrium. His health problems undoubtedly contributed to his inability to write his first book, which was going to be called "Liberty versus Power," in spite of signing at least one book contract and spending the advance. He also had a stormy romantic life, one dramatic enough to make for a good-sized novel, and this combined with his frustrations as a writer made for an increasingly unhappy "Roychick," as the Rothbards affectionately called him.

The lift in Roy's spirits at being elevated to the editorship of the revamped *Libertarian Review*, which Koch bought from Robert D. Kephart and moved out to sunny California, did much to restore his health, both physically and psychologically. But his relationship with Rothbard, while still friendly, was increasingly overshadowed by a new factor: his growing enmity to Williamson Evers, who was also an "intellectual son" of Rothbard's—and, it seemed, the favored one.

Ralph Raico, now a professor of history at Buffalo State College, in New York, took a leave to come to California and edit the "back of the book" of *Inquiry*, and Ronald Hamowy was hired on as a consultant. Leonard Liggio was also installed in an office at 1700 Montgomery, as was David Theroux (who later went on to found the Independent Institute), as head of Cato's academic program, along with Robert Formaini, an economist, who went on to work for the Federal Reserve Bank.

A few hundred feet down the road, in a converted warehouse at 1620 Montgomery Street, the various satellites of Cato revolved in a constant flurry of activity: *Libertarian Review*, where Roy Childs held court, and two activist organizations, the Libertarian Party, and Students for a Libertarian Society (SLS). Various Cato apparatchiks commandeered the Libertarian Party office: Chris Hocker, former salesman; David Boaz, an elegant, quietly articulate young man; Eric Garris, an ex-New Leftist and local libertarian activist, whose organizing skills were as legendary as his ability to make trouble; and the affable and capable Bob Costello, who hailed from Chicago, had a business background, and was charged with the Herculean task of getting the LP on the Californian ballot. Then there was Milton Mueller, the bespectacled youth leader, who had the look of an ascetic and an academic air. Mueller had been imported from Illinois, where he had proved himself toiling in the vineyard of the local Libertarian Party, to head up Students for a Libertarian Society.

Libertarian Review—and Roy's whimsical attitude when it came to running an office—was my own doorway into this libertarian hothouse. I had been active in the libertarian movement since the tender age of fourteen, when I carried on a vigorous correspondence with young East Coast libertarians who would later come to play a prominent part on the movement: Lanny Friedlander and I consulted by mail on his plans for the publication of a libertarian magazine that he had decided to call *Reason*; the big attraction here was that this was to be printed, not mimeographed. I devoured the first issues as soon as they arrived in my mailbox, twelve-to-sixteen-page issues stapled together, with real photo-offset covers. I joined Young Americans for Freedom, as well as the Liberty Amendment National Youth Council, where I ran into David F. Nolan, who would go on to found the Libertarian Party.[23] As a militant Randian, imbued with the sectarian spirit of Objectivism, I split from YAF months before the famous Columbus Day confrontation between the libertarians and traditionalists and formed my own organization, Young Radicals for Capitalism: through ads in the *Innovator*, an early libertarian newsletter, and some publicity in *Commentary on Liberty*, the voice of the Libertarian Caucus in YAF, I somehow managed to recruit a chapter of fifty-plus members at the University of Michigan before anybody realized that the "YRC National Office" was in reality a sixteen-year-old kid and his typewriter. Never having attended a single libertarian meeting, except for an occasional foray into New York City to attend lectures at the Nathaniel Branden Institute, I was only marginally aware of Murray N. Rothbard as the author of books on economics; in his role as a libertarian activist, I only knew about his 1964 letter to the *Innovator* attacking Goldwater as a warmonger, an idea that struck me as odd, in part because of where it appeared: The *Innovator*, after all, was supposed to be a right-wing magazine.

In 1978, when *Libertarian Review* opened its San Francisco office, I was a twenty-seven-year-old Libertarian Party activist and aspiring writer. The news that a libertarian magazine had actually arrived in town motivated me to hit the typewriter, turn out an article, and march down to 1620 Montgomery Street to submit it in person. Childs not only accepted the article, but also decided, on the spot, that I would make an ideal editorial assistant.

All of these individuals, as varied in background and demeanor as they were, had one thing in common: all answered to Ed Crane. This was not due only, or even primarily, to his key role as the link between Charles Koch and the network of libertarian organizations that benefited from Koch's largesse, but also to Crane's own charisma and will to get things done. A classic man-of-action, Crane did not mince words or suffer fools gladly. In this, he was very much like the man he acknowledged—at the time—to be his mentor and the leading theoretician of the libertarian movement. Crane was a "real world" person, with a strong business background, pragmatic yet principled, who was fond of little mottoes like "conservative in form, radical in essence," and knew how to play political hardball. To Rothbard's delight, Crane and his "real world" associates scattered the libertarian *luftmenschen*[24] to the winds. The way was cleared to make libertarianism a political and ideological force to be reckoned with.

I didn't realize at the time what a great privilege it was to have stumbled into this exotic world of libertarian activism, where ideas were the coin of the realm and our lives revolved around the progress of a great cause. Here, gathered together in one place, were the finest libertarian scholars: Rothbard, Liggio, Raico, and Hamowy. This foursome alone possessed enough intellectual firepower to constitute the equivalent of an entire army. Add to this the mischievously lighthearted energy of Roy Childs, the inexhaustible enthusiasm of youth, and an almost unlimited budget, and the result was the modern libertarian movement at the very apex of its early success.

Before the factional stormclouds descended on our sunlit California utopia, the united libertarian movement was beginning to be taken seriously not only as an intellectual credo, but, for the first time, as a political force in California politics. Edward E. Clark's 1978 campaign for governor, masterminded by Crane, and enthusiastically supported by all of us, garnered a stunning 5.5 percent of the vote, the highest statewide vote for a third party candidate in many years. The pundits began to sit up and take notice, and the San Francisco Libertarian Party began to play a visible role in local politics. A bookstore, Libertarian Books and Periodicals, was set up in a central location on San Francisco's Market Street; its visibility and accessibility were emblematic of our conception of grassroots organizing.[25]

The late seventies were an extraordinarily productive period for Rothbard: volume 3 of his *Conceived in Liberty* was published, along with a revised edition of *For a New Liberty*. Writing columns for *Reason* and *Libertarian Review*, in which he commented on current events, Rothbard also made a major contribution to the history of economic thought with his article, "New Light on the Prehistory of the Austrian School,"[26] which first broached the theme of what was to later blossom into his massive *History of Economic Thought*: that the Catholic Scholastics, as the precursors of the Austrian subjective value theory, represented a higher stage of development than what came later, namely Adam Smith, the alleged "founder" of classical economics and modern free-market thought. In the title of this piece, the author clearly meant to conjure the revisionist spirit of Professor Sidney Bradshaw Fay's "New Light on the Origins of the World War." In 1920, the publication of Professor Fay's famous three-part series in the *American Historical Review* sparked a debate that led to a major reversal in scholarly (and popular) opinion on the causes and consequences of World War I. Rothbard clearly hoped to spark a similar debate and reevaluation of the history of economic thought, but this would have to wait until the publication, some years later, of his great master work, in which this theme is fully developed. For now, the "New Light" article was a condensation that outlined his basic argument. Again, in the quarterly *Modern Age*, he prefigured the themes of his magisterial *History*. In "Ludwig von Mises and the Paradigm for Our Age," Rothbard raises the idea of the "paradigm" first introduced by the historian of science Thomas A. Kuhn. Instead of an ever-upward-and-onward view of the historiography of science, Kuhn proposed a paradigmatic conception, wherein all scientific data is filtered through the dominant scientific paradigm, until the frequent appearance of anomalies throws the system in crisis, and, after a struggle, a new paradigm emerges triumphant. Rather than a series of ascending steps, knowledge progresses in fits and starts, revolutionary "leaps" and degenerative declines; knowledge is not only gained, but also lost. This was the case not only with the Scholastics, but with their modern successors, the Austrian School of economics.[27]

His purview also included economic history: "The New Deal and the International Monetary System" is an important essay in which Rothbard traces the evolution of an Anglo-American alliance of central banks into an international monetary system, or banking cartel, as the prototype of a world central bank.[28]

In addition to his regular articles for *Inquiry*, including many book reviews, Rothbard edited the *Journal of Libertarian Studies* and published several major articles in its pages, including some of the material that would later be incorporated in his 1982 book *The Ethics of Liberty*.[29] To top it all off, he kept up a running commentary in the monthly *Libertarian Forum*, which came out regularly if often late.

Ken Templeton, it turned out, was wrong: it *was* possible for Rothbard to write serious books, edit a scholarly journal, write commentary for the *Forum* and other venues, take an active part in the libertarian movement, and *still* find time to gossip with his friends, read voraciously, and generally enjoy life to the fullest. His enjoyment was considerably enhanced by the fact that the major media were beginning to take notice of the surging libertarian movement. *Newsweek* opined that the libertarian student movement was the hottest thing on the block, and political analysts began to take note of the new libertarian phenomenon, including (and especially) those who considered themselves its enemies. *National Review* ran an article on the libertarian movement, which asserted that an anti-American anarchist cabal, funded by a billionaire, was "subverting the freedom movement"; the hit-piece quoted from the unpublished strategy memo, but only enough to horrify its readers with the fact that Rothbard took Lenin seriously as a strategic thinker.[30] On the Left, too, there was unease over this alliance of a "right-wing anarchist" and a radicalized billionaire, with Noam Chomsky reportedly worried about the growing libertarian influence, and young leftists fuming over the campus visibility of SLS.

THE SPLIT

These attacks from outside forces tended to unite the Cato group and gloss over their differences: but when Robert Poole and his neo-Randian contingent at *Reason* magazine wrote letters to *National Review* saying, in effect, that the Buckleyites were right—but not about *them*—the first signs of a fissure began to appear. While the public response to the conservative attacks, and the betrayal of their "libertarian" fellow-travelers was fierce and unequivocal, there were private recriminations. Ed Crane was committed to building a movement based on his concept of what he often called "reasonable radicalism," a paradigm that seemed mainly stylistic at the time. Rothbard's intellectual flamboyance was bound to clash with the Brooks Brothers conservatism of Crane, who was now in a position where he had to defend every incendiary word Rothbard had ever

written. What at first appeared to be a difference owing to temperament and a contest of contrasting styles and personalities soon
widened into an all-out ideological war. In the case of Crane, as in
others, idealization soon turned to demonization when Rothbard's
great expectations were dashed on the rocks of reality.

The first open disputes were centered around SLS, the student
wing of what we affectionately called "the Kochtopus"—and, later
on, not so affectionately. At this point I was a writer and organizer for
SLS, and had already achieved my main claim to fame in the annals
of LP history as the founder of the Radical Caucus (RC) and its
bimonthly periodical, *Libertarian Vanguard*, a publication that looked
like a leftist tabloid, and, initially at any rate, was written in a style
that the *Whole Earth Catalog* described as an "intense vehemence."
Born as the result of a generalized inchoate rebellion against the libertarian status quo, the RC was originally composed of myself, Eric
Garris, and Bob Costello. (In Bob's defense, it must be said that he
joined only out of friendship, rather than political agreement, and
soon dropped out.) Having no other "role models" to work from, like
generals fighting the last war, we aped the attitudes and even the
typefaces and graphics of the New Left at their most *rrr*-revolu-
tionary. What charmed Rothbard was that, without having read his
secret strategy memo, except what had been revealed in *National
Review*, we had evolved a crude version of the cadre-style organizational principles espoused in that document. Like Rothbard, we took
the concept of strategy seriously, we realized the importance of
internal education and the libertarian press, and we cared deeply
about the issue of war and peace. Soon after the first issue of *Libertarian Vanguard* had shocked the delicate sensibilities of the Libertarian Party elders—as, of course, it was meant to—I received a letter
from Rothbard, who kindly complimented us on our efforts, and
indicated that he and Evers were interested in joining the RC.

That the author of *Man, Economy, and State* was putting himself on the same level with a motley crew of ill-read and ill-bred "radicals" did not impress us at the time. All we knew or cared about was the political advantage this would give us in our internal manueverings in the Libertarian Party. We soon discovered, however, the *real* advantage: close proximity to one of the greatest minds of this century, and one, moreover, that was *accessible* to us. For Rothbard's high intelligence, while fully matured, was nevertheless quite *playful* in a way that naturally appeals to the young. Most of all, we loved arguing with him because he did it so well. Each meeting of the Radical Caucus Central Committee, held every couple of weeks at the height of our activity, was, for us, a learning experience, and Rothbard was unsurpassed as a teacher.

It would be a mistake to center a discussion of Rothbard's activities during the Koch era, roughly from 1976 to March of 1981, in the context of the Radical Caucus; as an organization, the RC never amounted to much, and, as his correspondence shows, it was never taken all that seriously by Rothbard. Yet one document that resulted from our deliberations, the RC's ten-point program, is relevant to understanding the central thrust of Rothbard's politics, and a major reason for the coming split in the Cato organization. The sixth point, "Populism," instructs libertarians to seek to win over "the great majority of Americans," and clearly points to the prospect of radicalized Middle Americans as the key to a libertarian victory. In the extended and often heated discussion in which we hammered out our program, Rothbard insisted on the inclusion of this point, as against the ethnocultural particularism favored by the RC "Left," led by Garris and myself.

This populist orientation set him apart from the Cato leadership, personified in Crane, and represented a decisive shift away from the strategy enunciated at the end of "Toward a Theory of Libertarian Social Change," which concluded "that our natural allies, for the current historical period, are the (moderate) liberals, who, in any case, dominate the media and opinion-moulding groups, rather than the conservatives or the (extreme) Left."[31] Yearning for a constituency outside of the media and the middle-class liberals they catered to, Rothbard was already beginning to chafe under the strategic constraints imposed by his own memo. While the liberal media constituency would gladly support libertarians on social issues, like drug legalization and abortion, he realized they would never sit still for the systematic dismantling of the welfare-warfare state that would be the swift result of a Rothbardian revolution.

The first hint of trouble came over the campaign by Roy Childs and Milton Mueller to introduce an ideological "innovation" into libertarian theory: the idea that nuclear power is *per se* unsafe and inherently statist, and that therefore all nuclear power plants should immediately be shut down. Mueller took up with the scientist Dr. John Gofman, big in the burgeoning antinuclear movement of the late seventies. Gofman wrote several articles for *Libertarian Review*, Rothbard and Evers responded, and the issue became a *cause celebre*. Rothbard skewered the antinukers in "Capturing the Masses: A Skit," a one-act farce he wrote up in an idle moment and which effectively captures the SLS mindset. "The scene is a warehouse in San Francisco, serving as common headquarters for the *Libertarian Monthly* . . . and the Libertarian Youth League, its campus organization. A dozen LM and LYL youth are gathered . . . for their weekly meeting. The Youth Leader, head of LYL, is making his report:

> YOUTH LEADER: . . . our basic strategy is quick victory, the seizing of power in America. We will do it by going to various parts of the masses and showing them that their *seemingly* statist views in different areas are *really* libertarian. But *their* ideas are emotional, fragmented, *ad hoc*: *we* can offer them a mighty intellectual system, starting with "A is A," self-esteem, and property rights, and ending up with their favorite statist conclusions.[32]

The youth leader is clearly Mueller, LYL is SLS, and the *Libertarian Monthly* is *Libertarian Review*. Rothbard mocks them mercilessly for tailing after every campus leftie fad of yesteryear, from the boycott of Nestle to the South Africa divestment movement. This excursion into the dramatic arts—like his previous effort in this realm, "Mozart Was A Red," a pastiche based on his experience in the Rand cult[33]—brings to mind Rothbard's comment on H. L. Mencken as the sort of individualist "who can—from that same dedication to truth and liberty—enjoy and lampoon a society that has turned its back on the best that it can achieve."[34]

As to whether Childs, who knew better, ever meant to seriously argue—as Mueller did—that nuclear power (or *any* technology) can be characterized politically, is highly doubtful. What is clear is that he used the Mueller-Gofman hypothesis as a kind of prod to enrage Evers and goad Rothbard into launching an all-out attack. This was not long in coming.

Employees of single-donor nonprofits follow the moods and movements of their benefactor like flowers in a field, their faces turned toward the sun. At Cato, Crane, as the veritable voice and instrument of Koch, was the sun, and his employees were satellites who revolved obediently around him.

All but Rothbard and Evers. In a letter to Evers, written at the end of the four-year factional war for control of the Libertarian Party, Rothbard relates, with considerable feeling, the genesis of that epic struggle, and recalls that "four years ago, it was just the two of us, totally isolated . . . battling against a mighty concentration of money, full-time professionals, organs of opinion, and power. . . . We launched the battle out of desperation, because there was nothing else to do: I don't think either of us thought we were going to win. And yet we did it. If I were a religious man, I would say that Providence was shining down on our efforts, as the victory seems almost miraculous . . . think of it, Williamson, we took on a billion dollars and beat it!"[35]

While there were several preliminary brushfires and skirmishes, the Sarajevo of 1700 Montgomery Street was Ed Clark's 1980 presidential campaign—backed by Koch's money and Crane's "expertise"—which refused to come out for measures that, today, seem entirely uncontroversial, such as the abolition of the income tax and dismantling the IRS. Instead of "ending welfare as we know it," the libertarian Clark merely suggested not adding more people to the rolls. In a letter to Clark, Rothbard pointed out that the 20 percent cut advocated by Clark was *less* than the 33 percent touted by Kemp-Roth: "If Libertarians stand for anything, it is drastic tax cuts, and for us to be outflanked by the Reaganites on taxes passeth my understanding." After taking up yet more Clarkian points of departure from the libertarian plumb line—on drugs and internal campaign organization, for example—Rothbard got down on his hands and knees: "Ed, this is a very serious situation," he wrote, "and I plead with you to reconsider your course."[36]

Clark did not reconsider. If Crane had somehow thought that Rothbard would stick to high theory, not interfere in real-world politics, and go along with the program, it was a serious miscalculation. Rothbard went public with his criticisms: both the *Libertarian Forum* and *Libertarian Vanguard* started blasting away at Clark. When Clark went on *Nightline* and was asked by Ted Koppel to sum up libertarianism in a short soundbite, Clark uttered a fatal phrase that gave credence to Rothbard's critique: "Low-tax liberalism," Clark earnestly replied, thus setting off a round of factional warfare that, four years later, had reduced the membership of the Libertarian Party by at least half and destroyed it as an effective political force.

While the Clark campaign was the major arena of contention between Rothbard and his ex-disciples in the Cato leadership, the dispute soon spread to other areas. The hiring of a Chicago School economist by Cato, at Childs's instigation, and what Rothbard characterized as the sudden downplaying of Austrian economics by Cato and affiliated scholarly programs was seen as part of the pattern of sellout. Rothbard was convinced that Crane and his lieutenants had made a conscious decision to throw principle overboard in the pursuit of power, money, and respectability.

Rothbard's fury knew no bounds. He was determined to fight, no matter what the price. And he fought *hard*, neither asking for nor giving any quarter. He privately complained that Crane and Koch were intent on reducing him to the status of a totem, to be rolled out on official holidays and lauded for his radicalism, and then put back on the shelf. It was, he said, a fate he had no intention of enduring in silence.

The intensity of Rothbard's vituperation mystified many people, even many of those who basically agreed with his analysis of the Crane operation as an opportunist sellout—including myself. It was only years later, in researching this work, that I came to understand the full meaning of and motive behind Rothbard's actions during this time. In a letter to Robert Kephart answering the latter's criticism of a particularly inflammatory screed against the Cato group in the *Libertarian Forum*, Rothbard answered the common complaint, "Yes, but why do you have to get so *personal*?"—and reflected on the connection between this fight and all the others:

> Bob, older and wiser heads . . . have been giving me similar advice all my life, and I'm sure all that advice was right. Ralph Raico was on the phone the other day with Joey and they were both ruminating about my life, and Ralph said, "Murray has never been careful." No question about it. When I was a young libertarian starting out, I was advised by Leonard Read: "Only be critical of bad measures, *not* of the people advocating them." It's

OK to criticize government regulation, but not the people advocating them. One big trouble with that is that then people remain
ignorant of the ruling class, and the fact that Big Business often
pushes regulatory measures to cartelize the system, so I went
ahead and named names. In the late 1960s, when *New Individualist Review* was flourishing, I helped (unwittingly) [to] destroy it
by writing an article pointing out that Herbert Hoover was not a
laissez-fairist but a statist and the founder of the New Deal. That
got me the undying enmity (to this day) of Glenn Campbell, Art
Kemp, and other Hoover worshippers and also helped ruin *New
Individualist Review*.[37] Why did I do it? Because I couldn't stand
the injustice of all these people admiring Hoover when he didn't
deserve it (to say the least).

Then, when I became an anarchist, I was advised, similarly:
"Forget this anarchist stuff. It will injure your career, and ruin
your scholarly image as a laissez-faire Austrian." I of course
didn't follow that perfectly accurate advice. Then, come the late
1950s, I was advised by friends: "For god's-sakes, forget this
peace crap. Stick to economics, that's your scholarly area anyway.
Everybody's against this peace stuff, and it will kill your scholarly image, and ruin you with the conservative movement."
Which of course is exactly what happened. And then: "Don't
attack [Chicago School economist Milton] Friedman directly. Just
push Austrianism." And "don't push Austrianism too hard, so
you can be part of one big free-market economics family."

. . . So you see, Bob, my deviation from proper attention to
my career image is lifelong, and is too late to correct at this point.
I'm sure that if, in Ralph's phrase, I had been "careful," and followed wise advice, I would now be basking in lots of money,
prestige, and ambiance. . . .

Why did I consistently take the wrong course? I like to think
that the main reason is one that moved me a great deal when I
read about it in [Torsten] Gardlund's life of the great Swedish
"Austrian" economist, Knut Wicksel. Wicksel was asked: "Here

you are, a great economist, and yet you're getting yourself always into trouble, and ruining your scholarly image, because of all the crazy radical things you're doing." (For example, Wicksell was put in jail for a while for advocating repeal of anti-birth control laws.) . . . And Wicksel answered simply: "Because nobody else was doing it."

For me that summed it up. If there had been lots of libertarians who were anarchists, lots who were antiwar, lots who named names of the ruling elite, lots attacking Hoover, Friedman, etc., I might not have made all these choices, figuring that these important tasks were being well taken care of anyway, so I may as well concentrate on my own "positioning." But at each step I looked around and saw indeed that nobody else was doing it. So therefore it was up to me.[38]

In the case of the Libertarian Party, "it was simply not in me to walk away from what I believe to be the most important focus of libertarian activism without putting up a fight."[39] And nobody else was doing it.

This extended reflection on the pattern of his life throws the spotlight on the man behind the paradigm. While not disdaining the concept of success, in the professional and financial sense, a passion for justice assigned him other priorities. The first of these was truth, which he dared speak to Power. For that he paid a high price: but he was willing to pay it. Yet it was fair to ask, at the time, whether Rothbard wasn't overstating his case. The dividing line between the personal and the political was hard to discern: it is no easier in retrospect. While the subsequent political evolution of the two factions led them down diverging roads, this was by no means apparent then. Both personal and ideological issues were at the root of the sustained factional warfare that tore the libertarian movement apart in those years. Yet who is to say, especially at this late date, which was cause and which was effect; it was, in any event, a self-reinforcing cycle of personal and ideological clashes that eventually culminated in a factional Armageddon.

It is fair to say that this struggle against what he called the "Crane Machine" engaged much of Rothbard's attention from 1979 to 1983, but it did not consume him as it did so many of those around him. He wrote and published two books during this period—*The Ethics of Liberty*[40] and *The Mystery of Banking*[41]—in addition to several major scholarly articles, and was simultaneously researching a book on the progressive era in American history. How he managed this level of productivity while engaged in this increasingly acrimonious dispute is a testament to the scale of his intellectual gifts: he was a giant among pygmies, too large to be consumed by the struggle with his errant followers.

Yet the level of stress had an undoubted effect on Rothbard's health: around this time he developed angina, an affliction of the heart. The pills prescribed by his doctor banished the chest pain he was experiencing, harbinger of an underlying condition that would not resurface for a decade. In the meantime, however, there was plenty of time to savor the sweetness of life, particularly the sweetness of victory over his erstwhile disciples.

The long factional struggle reached its climax at the Libertarian Party's 1983 national convention. Preparations for this signal event were feverish, with both sides lining up delegates and emitting streams of propaganda touting their presidential candidate and attacking the opposition. The Crane forces backed Earl Ravenal, a professor of international affairs at Georgetown University, and a well-known and respected foreign policy analyst. Rothbard and his allies, who were by now organized in the "Coalition for a Party of Principle," rallied around "Anyone But Ravenal." There was much agonized deliberation over the proper embodiment of the insurgents' cause. Evers and Rothbard finally settled on Gene Burns, a radio talk show host who claimed to be a libertarian. An interview with the prospective candidate was published in *Libertarian Vanguard*, and it looked as if he was going to be our man.[42] Then, lightning struck in the form of a newsletter put out by the "Libertarian Defense Caucus," a tiny prointerventionist grouplet, and mailed to all delegates, in which Burns expressed support for U.S. military intervention in Nicaragua, and averred that we oughtn't to wait for the Sandinistas to cross the Rio Grande before we "send in the 82nd Airborne."

The candidacy of Earl Ravenal had put me in a dilemma. By any objective measure, Ravenal was far more qualified to run for the office of president than anyone we could come up with. Here was a respected, reasonable, but radical critic of bipartisan internationalism, who would no doubt be inclined to put the issue of war and peace front and center in his campaign. Yet it was unthinkable that we could support the candidate of the hated Crane Machine—wasn't it?

The next meeting of the RC Central Committee was a stormy one. Evers was put on the carpet, and the questions came fast and furious: What happened to your man Burns? Why didn't you tell us he is a warmonger? Poor Bill spent the next couple of days trying to get a "clarification" out of the would-be candidate, but Burns wouldn't backtrack. In desperation, Evers turned to David Bergland, a Southern California lawyer and onetime fireman, who had been the party's gubernatorial candidate. A nice guy and a libertarian stalwart, Bergland was just not in Ravenal's league. Eric and I were dispirited: the Bergland candidacy underscored the cynicism and destructiveness of the factional war. But what was our alternative? It was too late to come up with a third candidate, and so we went to the convention reluctantly committed to Bergland.

It took me less than twenty-four hours to realize that there was indeed an alternative to voting along factional lines—and that was putting the long-term survival of the party and the movement above short-term factional maneuvering.

Eric and I were not alone in this. For many months, Scott Olmsted, the editor of *Libertarian Vanguard*, and Colin Hunter, a successful Silcon Valley entrepreneur, had loyally supported the Rothbard-Evers line on the factional struggle, in spite of the strenuous arguments of the Raimondo-Garris minority that the battle had lost whatever ideological character it once had. But our constant criticism had had a cumulative effect, and by the time we all got to the convention they were ready to be won over. I sent out a feeler to the Ravenal people, who were quick to respond: a meeting with the candidate, and the assurances of the Cato leadership, convinced us to do the unthinkable and come out for Ravenal.

With the majority of the RC Central Committee behind me, Eric and I decided to stage our coup in a public forum: the next day's Radical Caucus meeting, ostensibly organized to make plans for our first national conference and boost Bergland. Instead, we used the meeting as a platform to announce that the majority of the RC Central Committee had voted to endorse Ravenal. I made this announcement at the start of the meeting while Eric handed out leaflets explaining our reasons in detail. I then raised for the first time in public the issues that had previously been discussed in private meetings of the RC leadership: the factional war had become an obsession, and blinded us to the real politics of the choice before us. At this, Evers was on his feet and shouting. For a moment, it looked as if the meeting might degenerate into total chaos, but order was eventually restored and the question was thrown open to the floor. Evers made a passionate speech, but could barely finish it for the flood of emotion that seemed to wash over him; he ended his remarks literally in tears. As for Rothbard, I had never seen him so angry. "I would like to deliver a statement at this time," he said, "and since it is very short, I would appreciate the courtesy of not being interrupted. The minimal requirement of any caucus—whether it be Bolshevik, or Menshevik, redneck . . . or sewing circle—is that you don't criticize your caucus comrades in public. Justin's public attack on Evers and myself is such a gross violation of this requirement that I am not sure at this point that the Radical Caucus exists at all, much less ready for a National Conference. Right now, it looks more like a snake pit than a caucus. Secondly, I want to emphasize as strongly as I know how that the minute the Radical Caucus endorses Earl Ravenal is the minute it has my resignation. That resignation will be irrevocable."[43]

Right after that cathartic meeting, the RC Central Committee held its last session, easily the most raucous to date. Rothbard berated us while Evers sat stone silent. This was an outrage, a despicable betrayal, the proverbial stab in the back: we had sold out for "high positions" in the Ravenal campaign! I pointed out to Rothbard that, when he was in the majority, we had gone along loyally with the program, but privately argued for our own position. Now that we were the majority, it was time for him to observe "caucus discipline" and support Ravenal.

Faced with a choice between political correctness, RC-style, and the prospect of continued Koch-Crane control of the LP, Rothbard did not take long to make a decision: he practically jumped out of his chair: "That's it! I'm outta here!" He stormed out, Evers following in his wake.

It was a very tight race the next day on the convention floor. As the roll call of the states resounded throughout the hall, there was a breathless silence before the chair announced the vote totals. It was a horse race right down to the wire. Rothbard sat there, his notepad in hand, scribbling down the numbers as the votes were announced, while Evers raced from one delegation to another, lining up votes and muttering into a walkie-talkie. In the end, Bergland squeaked by with a two-vote majority.

As the reality of what had happened began to sink in, the Ravenal delegates got up, as if at a prearranged signal, and walked out, not bothering to stay for the vote for party officers. The message was loud and clear: you wanted the Libertarian Party—now take it.

Rothbard was glad to take it. His attitude toward his erstwhile comrades and disciples was colorfully expressed in a letter to Evers: "And so, the proper, if private response to the flight of the Crane Machine and . . . the imminent withering away of the Radical Caucus Central Committee, should be the old song we used to sing at camp: 'We hate to see you go, We hate to see you go, We hope to hell you never come back, We hate to see you go.' "[44] That more than half the talent and virtually all of the money had left the party en masse did not seem to bother him in the least: perhaps he consoled himself with the old Leninist maxim on the necessity of the Bolshevik split with the Mensheviks: "Better fewer but better."

Celebrating his triumph, he exults that "the time has come for a quiet but intense two-man celebration. We've done it, Williamson. Against all the odds, the lone battle that we launched 'against the world' four years ago is just about over. We've done it; we've Brought the Mother Down."[45]

LIBERTARIANISM AND NATURAL LAW: *THE ETHICS OF LIBERTY*

The intensity of Rothbard's involvement in the Libertarian Party did not detract one iota from his intellectual energy; as we have seen, his literary output throughout this period can only be described as prolific. Of the major projects that came to fruition during this period, *The Ethics of Liberty*, published in 1982, was his most elegant work yet, and, in a certain sense, his most ambitious.

Rothbard's *Ethics* defines and defends against all comers the methodological, moral, and political foundations of libertarian law, derived from natural law. While *The Ethics of Liberty* outlines the concept and history of natural law, it is not a prescription for personal morality, but instead sets out to construct a social ethic: libertarianism as a political philosophy.

Citing James Sadowsky on the crucial distinction between the right to take a particular action and the morality of that action, Rothbard sets the tone by averring that political philosophy cannot tell you whether or not to have an abortion, if you ought to get a divorce, or what the meaning of life is. It can only tell you what is (or ought to be) allowed, not what is correct or desirable.

The elegance of this work is in its seamless derivation of just property rights from natural law utilizing classic "Crusoe economics": starting with Crusoe, alone on an island, Rothbard establishes the right of self-ownership as inherent in the nature of humans as thinking, acting, choosing beings. Introducing Friday onto the island, Rothbard then outlines how the market economy arises from natural law; that is, from the nature of human beings and the fact that they must produce in order to live. The rigor of his arguments is impressive, demolishing all possible objections with its implacable logic. Covering the nature of aggression, criminality as coercion, the problem of land theft, children and rights, property rights and the theory of contracts, lifeboat situations, and the "rights" of animals, Rothbard applies the general principles of libertarian political theory to specific cases. In Part Two, "The State Versus Liberty," Rothbard defines the state as a gang founded on theft that defends its monopoly over a given territory by means of terrorism and intimidation, and, in the next chapter, points out its inner contradictions: in particular, the intellectual contradictions of the laissez-faire believers in limited government. For those who consider anarchism to be a product of fuzzy thinking and impractical idealism, these chapters on the nature of the state are required reading: the hard logic and relentless realism of Rothbard's portrayal of the state as "a vast engine of institutionalized crime and aggression" makes a powerful case for anarchocapitalism. Particularly important to Rothbard, and to posterity, is the chapter entitled "On Relations Between States." Employing the methodology of Crusoe-economics, he analyzes the question of war and peace, just and unjust wars, retaliation and reparations, the morality of weapons of mass destruction, and the nature of imperialism. In raising the banner of Old Right isolationism in the middle of a treatise on political philosophy, Rothbard neatly sums up the unique moral perspective of a libertarian foreign policy:

> The libertarian is interested in reducing as much as possible the area of state aggression against all private individuals, "foreign," and "domestic." The only way to do this, in international affairs, is for the people of each country to pressure their own State to confine its activities to the area which it monopolizes, and not to aggress against other state monopolies—particularly the *people* ruled by other states.[46]

In Part Four, "Modern Alternative Theories of Liberty," Rothbard takes on the utilitarians, Mises (on "value-free" economics), Isaiah Berlin's confusion of freedom with power, F. A. Hayek's muddled conception of nonviolent "coercion," and Robert Nozick's "immaculate conception of the state." Having demonstrated the justice and theoretical viability of a stateless condition of perfect liberty, the author gives us, in the final section, his "theory of strategy for liberty." It is a theoretical elaboration and clarification of many of the concepts first explored in "Toward a Theory of Libertarian Social Change," shorn of the historical examples, and stripped down to essential principles. Rothbard's strategic conception is a centered radicalism that accepts and agitates for any and all reductions in state power. The need for cadre, the necessity of abolitionism, the pitfalls of planned destatization, the nature and origins of "left" and "right" deviations from the plumbline position, the case for libertarian optimism—here, in a stunning feat of integration, is a concept of strategy that unites theory and practice, seamlessly woven into the rest of his argument. The effect of this chapter, with its hard-edged realism and long-range perspective, is to erase all prejudices against anarchism as necessarily utopian.

Rothbard's intention was not to construct a personal morality based on natural law, but to "elaborate that subset of the natural law that develops the concept of natural rights and that deals with the people sphere of politics, i.e., with violence and nonviolence as modes of interpersonal relations. In short, to set forth a political philosophy of liberty."[47]

Hans-Hermann Hoppe, in his introduction to the 1998 edition, calls *The Ethics of Liberty* "Rothbard's second *magnum opus*." It is, he writes, "the second pillar of the Rothbardian system," which "explains the integration of economics and ethics via the joint concept of property." While modern social scientists mainly denied the possibility of a rational ethics, "Rothbard sought and found support for his contention regarding the possibility of a rational ethic and the reintegration of ethics and economics based on the notion of private property in the works of the late Scholastics and, in their footsteps, such 'modern' natural rights theorists as Grotius, Pufendorf, and Locke." Hoppe makes the important point that, while these ideas had rarely been expressed with such rigor and clarity, "Rothbard did not claim that these fundamental principles of just conduct or proper action were new, or his own discovery, of course." Rothbard was far too well read in the social sciences to believe that that he was the first to advance the theory of self-ownership, or that he alone had explored its implications. In this sense, he was "a preserver and defender of old, inherited truths," not a revolutionary firebrand but a restorer of lost knowledge: "his claim to originality, like that of Mises, was one of utmost modesty."[48]

Yet, as Hoppe shows, Rothbard's contribution was considerable. While the tradition he sought to resurrect and perfect goes back to antiquity, his facility with the axiomatic-deductive method gave him the intellectual tools to shape not only rigorous arguments and proofs, but also to build "a more systematic, comprehesive and consistent ethical doctrine or law code than anyone before him."[49]

While some of the material (on punishment, for example) appeared earlier, most of the book was written at the height of the factional struggle inside the Cato Institute and the Libertarian Party. That he was capable of writing one of his greatest works while at the same time pouring so much energy into the faction fight is a testament to his prodigious talent, his capacity for work, and his ability to focus on the task at hand to the exclusion of all else, as well as a tribute to his emotional equilibrium. Nor was his scholarly output restricted, during this period, to a single book: he was researching a book on the Progressive Era, which was partly completed; a section of this material was published in the *Journal of Libertarian Studies* as "World War I as Fulfillment: Power and the Intellectuals."[50] Here he examines the important role of religion in the rise of the modern welfare state, specifically the key impetus of post-millennial pietism as the driving force behind a whole raft of statist measures, including prohibition, government regulation of business, and the Germanophobic sentiment leading to America's entry into World War I. Rothbard's writings on the Progressive Era, which have never been put together in a single volume, are a rich vein of analysis that contemporary scholars, libertarian or whatever, would do well to mine. In a fascinating narrative that unfolds like the plot of a novel, Rothbard documents his thesis with the fascinating stories of the men, and especially the women, who led the Progressive movement: ministers, social workers, intellectuals, and other professional do-gooders, whose zeal to remake America in the image of an (often secularized) God was rooted in a theological vision in which humanity would be the agency that would establish the Kingdom of God on earth. These themes were intimately linked to another project he was also energetically working on: what was to become the two-volume *History of Economic Thought*.

Sometime in the early eighties, the Cato Institute packed up and moved to Washington, D.C., to eventually become the premier libertarian–conservative policy thinktank.

Rothbard, for his part, took an entirely different road. He was now approaching sixty, an age when people are supposed to be mellowing out, relaxing, and generally coasting along on the accomplishments of the past. Not Rothbard. Instead of mellowing into the Grand Old Man of the Libertarian Party, he began to develop a mindset that would eventually lead him to abandon the great bulk of the movement (which he referred to in one letter to Evers as "Our Beloved Party") that he had fought so hard to "save." Instead of coasting along on the intellectual energy and achievements of the past two decades, he began to develop a new strategic orientation, a new perspective on the fast-changing currents of world history that would lead him back to familiar territory: back to his Old Right roots.

In *Left and Right: The Prospects for Liberty*, he had cited Lord Acton, "one of the few figures in the history of thought who, charmingly, grew *more* radical as he grew older."[51] With those words, Rothbard was writing his own epitaph.

NOTES

1. Interview with JoAnn Rothbard.

2. Ken S. Templeton, "Memo to George Pearson," 1 May 1974.

3. Ibid.

4. Murray N. Rothbard, "The Mantle of Science," in *Scientism and Values*, edited by Helmust Schoeck and James W. Wiggings (Princeton, N.J.: D. Van Nostrand, 1960), pp. 159–80.

5. Murray N. Rothbard, "My New Year's Wish For The Movement," *Libertarian Forum* (December 1975).

6. Ibid.

7. Murray N. Rothbard, "Libetarian Strategy," pts. 1–5, *Libertarian Connection* (February 10–August 9, 1969).

8. "These are cited in Murray N. Rothbard, "Toward a Theory of Libertarian Social Change," unpublished manuscript in possession of author, 1977. Others may have contributed to this symposium.

9. Pearson to Crane, 5 May 1976.

10. Rothbard to Crane, 5 May 1976.

11. Murray N. Rothbard, "Toward a Theory of Libertarian Social Change."

12. *National Review* (June 8, 1979).

13. Murray N. Rothbard, "Frank S. Meyer: The Fusionist As Libertarian," *Modern Age* (fall 1981): 352–63.

14. Ernest van den Haag, "Libertarians and Conservatives," *National Review* (June 8, 1979): 725–39.

15. Rothbard, "Toward a Theory of Libertarian Social Change," pp. 43–48. Emphasis in original.

16. Ibid., pp. 56–62.

17. Ibid.

18. Ibid., pp. 170–71.

19. Garet Garrett, *The Revolution Was* (Caldwell, Idaho: Caxton, 1952). Roger Lea MacBride, ed., *The Lady and the Tycoon: The Best of Letters of Rose Wilder Lane and Jasper Crane* (Caldwell, Idaho: Caxton, 1973), p. 126.

20. Roy A Childs Jr., "Objectivism and the State: An Open Letter to Ayn Rand," *The Rational Individualist* 1, no. 10 (August 1969).

21. Scot Sublett, "Libertarians' Storied Guru," *Washington Times*, 30 July 1987.

22. Interview with JoAnn Rothbard.

23. The Liberty Amendment was a proposed constitutional amendment that would have not only abolished the income tax, but also forbidden a long list of federal activities.

24. A favorite Rothbardian epithet, Yiddish for "people of the air," denoting light-minded bohemians and n'er-do-wells.

25. The bookstore survived for nineteen years, its fortunes rising and falling with those of the libertarian movement. The last libertarian tenants at 1800 Market Street were forced out in 1998, when the city of San Francisco declared the whole block a "redevelopment zone," bought the dilapidated building at an inflated price, and turned it over to a gay "nonprofit" to build a multimillion-dollar government-subsidized Gay Community Center.

26. In Laurence Moss, ed., *The Foundations of Modern Austrian Economics* (Kansas City: Sheed and Ward, 1976), pp. 52–74.

27. Murray N. Rothbard, "Ludwig von Mises and the Paradigm for Our Age," *Modern Age* (fall 1971).

28. Murray N. Rothbard, "The New Deal and the International Monetary System," in *Watershed of Empire: Essays on the New Deal Foreign Policy*, ed. Leonard P. Liggio and James J. Martin (Colorado Springs: Ralph Myles, Publisher, 1976), pp. 19–64.

29. Murray N. Rothbard, "Robert Nozick and the Immaculate Conception of the State," *Journal of Libertarian Studies* (winter 1977).

30. Lawrence V. Cott, "Cato Institute and the Invisible Finger," 8 June 1979, pp. 740–42.

31. Rothbard, "Toward a Theory of Libertarian Social Change," pp. 170–71.

32. Murray N. Rothbard, "Capturing the Masses: A Skit," unpublished manuscript, undated 1979–80, p. 1.

33. Murray N. Rothbard, *Mozart Was a Red* (Burlingame, Calif.:

Center for Libertarian Studies, 1996). This was written much earlier, sometime in the late fifties.

34. Murray N. Rothbard, "H. L. Mencken: The Joyous Libertarian," *New Individualist Review* 2, no. 2 (summer 1962): 16.

35. Rothbard to Evers, 20 March 1983.

36. Rothbard to Edward E. Clark, 5 January 1980.

37. Ralph Raico, the editor of the *New Individualist Review*, says this is "not really so." Letter to the author, 12 March 1999.

38. Rothbard to Robert Kephart, 14 April 1983.

39. Ibid.

40. Murray N. Rothbard, *The Ethics of Liberty* (Atlantic Highlands, N.J.: Humanities Press, 1982).

41. Murray N. Rothbard, *The Mystery of Banking* (New York: Richardson and Snyder, 1983).

42. "Interview with Gene Burns," *Libertarian Vanguard* (August 1983).

43. Rothbard's notes, in possession of author.

44. Rothbard to Evers, 19 March 1983.

45. Rothbard to Evers, 20 March 1983.

46. Murray N. Rothbard, *The Ethics of Liberty*, p. 193.

47. Rothbard, *The Ethics of Liberty*, p. 25.

48. Murray N. Rothbard, *The Ethics of Liberty* (New York: New York University Press, 1998), pp. xvi–xvii.

49. Ibid, p. xviii.

50. Murray N. Rothbard, "World War I as Fulfillment: Power and the Intellectuals," *Journal of Libertarian Studies* (winter 1984).

51. Rothbard, *Left and Right: The Prospects for Liberty*, pp. 7–8.

6

A NEW BEGINNING

A lthough Rothbard had won the battle for the soul of the Libertarian Party, it was a Pyrrhic victory. From 1980 to 1983, the libertarian movement had been consumed by a knock-down drag-out factional brawl. When it was over, the Libertarian Party was a shadow of its former self; the party's 1984 presidential candidate, David Bergland, received some 220,000 votes, about a quarter of Clark's 1980 vote total. In the absence of Crane, the "Coalition for a Party of Principle" splintered and the factional wars continued. Only this time, instead of such earthshaking questions as abolitionism versus gradualism, or the requirements of a libertarian foreign policy, the burning issues were: Who will be the new national chair? Where will the headquarters be located? Who will run the ballot drive? These fights centered almost exclusively around personalities; ideology had almost completely dropped out of the picture.

But not as far as Rothbard was concerned. While he loved intrigue, and was very much concerned with who held what party post, he watched over the ideological health of his Beloved Party

257

like a doting and often stern father. In a 1984 letter to Mike
Holmes, then editor of the *Libertarian Party News*, Rothbard takes
the time and effort to write a detailed two-page critique of the
activities of the Placer County (California) Libertarian Party. In the
wake of the party's poor showing in the presidential election, Libertarian Party loyalists were then touting the alleged success of
party activists at the *local* level as the real measure of the LP's
value. Holmes had sent him a large packet of literature and clip-
pings, but Rothbard was not too impressed. In reviewing the
Placer County LPers' literature and public statements on two key
local issues, Rothbard noted "on Roads they are abysmal, on the
Courthouse they are weak." On the Road Question: "Mike, they
don't have to advocate selling the roads. But neither is it permissible for them to attack the incumbent statist supervisors for cutting the county road budget!" As for the Courthouse, "the Placer
LP team at least did not take an evil position," he remarks, with an
almost audible sigh, "but it was certainly weak."[1]

The Placer County case "illustrates a basic problem with the
LP," he continued. "As we have grown older as a Party, from hippies in their twenties to real world people holding jobs in their
thirties, we have been gaining in solidity and respectability and in
people with influence in their communities. Great. But the flip side
of this is that we are in danger of losing ideological purity" which
youth "often brings us but which jobholders tend to be a bit weak
on." Bemoaning the loss of many libertarian organs of opinion,
including *Inquiry*, and the "desperate" need for internal education,
he is at a loss as to "how we can tackle this long-range but vital
problem . . . but at least we should think hard about it."[2]

Rothbard had plenty of time to think about this and other issues
now that he was back in New York, back to teaching, and back to a
more familiar environment. And there is much evidence that he did
indeed think hard about his relationship with the Libertarian Party.

While it was still his "Beloved Party," there is every reason to believe that it was rapidly becoming *less* beloved. Rothbard was more than a little annoyed that the Bergland campaign had taken up the banner of the Equal Rights Amendment—a sin for which he had excoriated Clark and Crane. Although he had supposedly "won," Rothbard was fighting the *same* battles, and hints of boredom, irritation, and his increasing exasperation with the organized libertarian movement throughout 1985, presage his growing conviction that the Libertarian Party was a dead end. Still flush with victory and high hopes for the LP, in the summer of 1984, no detail was too small to require Rothbard's attention. In a letter to Evers, he contemplates the ouster of a party official and comes up with a list of eleven possible replacements.[3] Less than two years later, his tone is considerably testier, and he opens a letter to Evers with a complaint: "I'm a bit confused," he writes. "Why, with all the great problems facing our nation, problems on which the LP National Committee has taken no stand or resolution, *why* do we need a lengthy, sixteen-part resolution on tort law reform?"[4]

It would take a while for this ambivalent attitude to resolve itself. In the meantime, Rothbard stuck it out, and in this he had the increasingly important assistance of Llewellyn H. Rockwell Jr.

THE LUDWIG VON MISES INSTITUTE: A LIFELINE

Rockwell, a Boston-bred protege of conservative stalwart Neil McCaffrey, nurtured his love of radical free-market thought while working as senior editor at Arlington House Publishers, which had brought back several editions of Mises's books. He first met Rothbard in 1975, and immediately felt that they were two kindred spirits. At the time, Rockwell was working for Hillsdale College, a bastion of free-market scholarship, and he tried to get Rothbard invited as a speaker. "But that was ruled out immediately," says Rockwell. "I was told that he might be a fine economist, but he was a loose cannon" and "inherently dangerous since he was an independent intellectual unconnected to the apparatus of official conservatism."[5]

Rockwell was the editor of *Private Practice*, where he worked to apply the insights of the Austrians to the economics of health care, and later chief aide to Congressman Ron Paul (R-Texas). In 1982, with the blessing of Margit von Mises, he founded the Ludwig von Mises Institute. As the increasingly important center of the Austrian School of economics in America, the Mises Institute was a lifeline to Rothbard in the post-Koch era. Rothbard accepted the position of vice president for Academic Affairs in 1982. Three years later, a project very dear to Rothbard's heart, the *Review of Austrian Economics*, came to fruition, thanks to Rockwell. The institute's summer seminars in Austrian economics drew many of the best students from across the nation, where they listened, rapt, as Rothbard displayed the wide range of his erudition in a full schedule of lectures and seminars. Speaking with minimal notes, Rothbard entranced his audiences with the sheer massiveness of his knowledge and charmed them with his humor. For Rothbard, the Mises Institute was everything the Cato Institute should have been: with only a fraction of Cato's relatively gargantuan budget, the Mises Institute was reaching more students with a hardcore Austrian message. This made Rothbard *very* happy. In the early eighties, Koch-dominated organizations had a virtual monopoly in the realm of libertarian thinktanks, pouring millions into their various projects. The founding of the Ludwig von Mises Institute not only broke that monopoly but also acquired its single greatest asset: Rothbard.

Shortly after setting up shop, Rockwell says he received a phone call from George Pearson, of the Koch Foundation: "He said that Mises was too radical and that I mustn't name the organization after him, or promote his ideas." Pearson reportedly told him that Mises was "so extreme even Milton Friedman doesn't like him." The new Kochian turn was completely away from the hard-edged antistatism of Mises and Rothbard and toward a softer, more accommodating approach. "If I insisted on going against their *diktat*, they would oppose me tooth and nail." But there was another dimension to the new Kochian dispensation. As Rockwell ignored the threats and went ahead with his plans to give Rothbard a platform, more calls came in from the same circles: "All urged me to dump Murray and then shun him, if I expected any support."

Whatever else one may say about Lew Rockwell—and his adversaries in libertarian and conservative circles have not been shy about expressing their opinions—nobody believes he is easily intimidated. As he went ahead with his plans, setting up the *Review of Austrian Economics*, compiling a list of editors and contributors, letters and calls poured in from those associated with Koch-dominated organizations: "They resigned and swore eternal enmity," Rockwell testifies. After losing some big donors, and facing the prospect of an indefinitely delayed *Review of Austrian Economics*, Rockwell was taken aback. "It was," he says, "my baptism by fire into the world of research institutes."

Far from being intimidated, the threats had the exact opposite of their intended effect. In true Rothbardian fashion, Rockwell was not discouraged but emboldened by this storm of opposition. The *Review of Austrian Economics* came out in 1986 and put out ten volumes, now succeeded by the higher profile *Quarterly Journal of Austrian Economics*. Starting out on his dining-room table, Rockwell brought the Ludwig von Mises Institute into the nineties with its own building adjacent to the campus of Auburn University, five periodicals, and an extensive academic program that is placing hardcore Misesians in economics departments from coast to coast.

But in the meantime, the going was rough. Reflecting on what motivated the avowed enemies of the institute, Rockwell asks: "Why would a multibillionaire care if the Institute existed or not? I mean, we were a gnat compared to his water buffalo. It's a mystery that even today I do not entirely understand."[6]

The explanation for the virulence of these attacks is in the personal enmity that Rothbard's break with the Cato group had aroused on both sides. This was but the latest outbreak of the factional war that had been decimating the libertarian movement since 1983—a struggle with which Rockwell would soon become all too familiar.

On the political-ideological front as well, Rockwell was increasingly playing the role once assigned to Crane, the intellectual entrepreneur and man-of-action who could create the institutions necessary to the nurturing of libertarian scholarship and activism. Writing to Evers excitedly with the news that the *New York Times* was publishing his article on farm subsidies, Rothbard ascribed to Rockwell the qualities of intellectual entrepreneurship he had written about in "Toward a Theory of Libertarian Social Change": "intuiting that the *Times* would be sympathetic to my Menckenesque blast at the farmers for always whining to the government for aid and getting it . . . he sent it to them, and they're publishing it!" While Rockwell had known Rothbard for years, by the mid-eighties the two were beginning to enter a collaboration that enabled the embattled old warrior to receive at least some of the honor that was his due. "More and more, by the way," wrote Rothbard, "I'm impressed with Rockwell; not only a great guy, but also a top-notch organizer, an energetic entrepreneur in our field, and a sound hard-core person who appreciates scholarship. . . . Also he learns about people very fast, being 'radicalized through struggle.' In a sense, he is the person Crane was supposed to be in 1976."[7]

Starting out with a minimum of capital and his own steely determination, Rockwell built the Mises Institute with the blessing of Mises's widow, Margit, and gave the Austrian School its voice in America and throughout the world. The first-ever all-Austrian conferences for teachers and students, the *Review of Austrian Economics*, the *Austrian Economics Newsletter*, the publication of books, not only classics but also new and pioneering works by such up-and-coming scholars as Hans Hermann-Hoppe and David Gordon—these achievements marked Rockwell as the quintessential Rothbardian, the man who could deliver where others had failed. It was a friendship and intellectual partnership that would endure for the rest of Rothbard's days.

It was most gratifying that, finally, after teaching at Brooklyn Polytechnic since 1966, with only a two-year hiatus in California, Rothbard finally achieved the kind of professional recognition that was long since past due. In 1985, he was appointed S. J. Hall Distinguished Professor of Economics at the University of Nevada at Las Vegas. While still maintaining their New York City base of operations, the Rothbards again headed out West, and Murray soon settled into his new teaching position with more than a little satisfaction.

On the political-ideological front, however, all was not rosy. As early as the summer of 1986, there were rumblings from Rothbard that he was sick of the libertarian movement as a cultural phenomenon. In a letter to Bergland, his longtime factional colleague, Rothbard exhibits more than a little irritation with the "laid-back" California tone of the LP pamphlets written by Bergland. While the text is formally correct, Rothbard writes that he "was led by your articles, however, to some ruminations on strategy. It seems to me that a lot of our literature is geared to 'free spirits,' to people who don't want to push other people around, and who don't want to be pushed around themselves. In short, the bulk of Americans might well be tight-assed conformists, who want to stamp out drugs in their vicinity, kick out people with strange dress habits, etc. And, if so, we won't win if we make our pitch exclusively to a minority of free spirits whom we ourselves may culturally or esthetically agree with, and thereby lose the tight-assed majority."[8]

Rather than address the nation as if it were composed solely of hippies, California surfers, and other "free spirits," Rothbard wondered why the Libertarian Party failed to speak to the Great American Middle Class. As the 1988 presidential election loomed, Rothbard, Rockwell, and Burton S. Blumert, a longtime libertarian activist and friend of the Rothbards, began to push the candidacy of Congressman Ron Paul as the LP nominee.

Although a Republican, Paul had always been close to the LP, frequently appearing at their events, and there had been speculation over the years that he would one day seek the party's presidential nomination. That year, 1988, was a trying one for Rothbard, as the cultural eccentricities of his Beloved Party went beyond the irritating to encompass the maddening. The opposition to Paul coalesced around Russell Means, the American Indian leader and activist who had made a national reputation as a militant advocate of the Native American cause—a militance that had often escalated into violence or the threat of it. Means had suddenly decided that he was a capital-"L" Libertarian, and, with no record of libertarian utterances (let alone activism) declared his candidacy for the LP presidential nomination. Every "free spirit" in the party gathered 'round his banner, and the fight was on.

Rothbard, for his part, was thoroughly fed up with the *luftmenschen*, who, he was convinced, were driving "real world" people away from the Party and the movement. For all too many years, he had endured the unendurable and put up with what he called "the Crazies": the ultraleft crazies of the New Left era, who had turned the first national libertarian conference into a shambles; the "lifestyle" crazies of the anti-MacBride opposition, who had objected to the 1976 presidential candidate's suit and tie; and now the hostile reaction of these *luftmenschen* to Congressman Paul and his wife, Carol, who "are the sort of Americans to set the crazies' teeth immediately on edge." The ideological critique of the opposition—which boiled down to the fact that Paul personally opposes abortion—was "a camouflage for their bitter cultural hostility to a middle-class person with a steady income and a real-world job."[9]

Paul won the nomination, but only after a bruising convention battle that split the party into warring factions whose struggle persisted long after the November election. Ron Paul had more than tripled Bergland's pathetic vote total, tempering the party's leftish edge and reviving the organization's flagging finances. Yet Paul was consistently attacked in the wake of his success (indeed, *because* of his success) and Paul's people were unceremoniously dumped from leadership positions.

Rothbard had lost before, and there was nothing preventing him from going into opposition once more, and battling the forces of opportunism and sectarian error that threatened his Beloved Party. But not this time. Aside from being thoroughly fed up, Rothbard's decision to leave the Libertarian Party was motivated by events outside the microuniverse of the LP: the domestic political consequences of the dramatic implosion of Communism in the Soviet Union and Eastern Europe. As the Berlin Wall fell, the "experts" dithered and tried to explain why not a single one of them had expected it, while the dean of the Austrian School of economics in America sat back and smiled; Mises had predicted the implosion in 1920 in his famous article on the impossibility of economic calculation in a socialist society.[10]

As early as 1954, Rothbard had written that "as a longterm threat . . . we should have no fear of military conquest by the Russians, or by the Chinese either. They began as backward countries and, since we know communism to be a relatively inefficient economic system, we need not worry about their offensive military might."[11] In *Left and Right: The Prospects for Liberty*, he was even more explicit. The crisis of statism, he explained in 1965,

> becomes particularly dramatic and acute in a fully socialist society; hence the inevitable breakdown of statism has first become strikingly apparent in the countries of the socialist (i.e., communist) camp. For socialism confronts the inner contradiction of statism most starkly. Desperately, socialism tries to fulfill its proclaimed goals of industrial growth, higher standards of living for the masses, and eventual withering away of the state—and is increasingly unable to do so through its collectivist means. Hence, the inevitable collapse of socialism.[12]

While it was years before the domestic political consequences of the Communist cataclysm were apparent, Rothbard had, as early as 1983, roiled the inner councils of the Radical Caucus by noting, approvingly, that the nation was in for a bout of "right-wing populism." His critique of the Clark campaign, though cloaked in "radical" rhetoric, was essentially a conservative one: that Crane was catering to "middle class liberals."[13]

RETURN TO THE OLD RIGHT

Rothbard's cultural conservatism and his growing revulsion at the sight of the left-libertarian *luftmenschen* coincided with the reappearance of the Old Right on the political scene. For years, Rothbard had been on the road, in exile from his real political-ideological home, which had disappeared off the map sometime in the mid-fifties. With the end of the Cold War, the Old Right had reappeared, like Atlantis rising from the depths. As Rockwell put it, in "The Case for Paleolibertarianism," "conservatives are questioning not only foreign intervention, but the entire New Deal-Great Society-Kinder Gentler apparatus." Celebrating the developing split on the Right, he made the case for a new turn, a new strategic vision for the post–Cold War era:

> This conservative crack-up represents an historic opportunity for the libertarian movement. The Cold War ruptured the Right; now the healing can begin, for Lord Acton's axiom that "liberty is the highest political end of man" is at the heart not only of libertarianism but of the old conservatism. There are differences, but their number is lessening and none of them is so broad as to prevent intelligent exchange and cooperation.[14]

This departure from the Rothbardian policy of the past three decades was radical enough. But Rockwell (and, standing behind him, Rothbard) did not stop there. Not only was it time to "restore the old concord" with the Right, but, before this could occur, it was also necessary to "delouse" the libertarian movement. The millions who sympathize with libertarian *ideas* "are put off by the Woodstockian flavor of the movement. *Hair* may have left Broadway long ago, but the Age of Aquarius survives in the LP." This countercuturalism is "deadly baggage" that must be dumped, or else "we will miss the greatest opportunity in decades."[15]

The howling chorus of protests and denials that greeted Rockwell's article proved that he had struck a nerve: but Rothbard and Rockwell did not stay around long enough to hear it. Libertarians had never been all that interested in or knowledgeable about foreign affairs, and hardly seemed to notice the enormous domestic political implications of the end of the Cold War. On the other hand, in the conservative movement change was in the air: the "isolationism" of the Right was back in full force, and this was the decisive impetus behind Rothbard's new strategic shift. Shortly after the publication of what amounted to a "Dear John" letter to the Libertarian Party, Rothbard and Rockwell established a new journal, the *Rothbard-Rockwell Report*, announcing their split not only from the LP but from the movement itself. The editors of the Report considered themselves *paleo*-libertarians. The "paleo" prefix means recovering lost history, or, in modern parlance, getting back to your roots, and that is precisely what Rothbard and Rockwell intended to do: the Old Right was back, and it was up to them to take full advantage of this sudden opening on the Right. After all, nobody else was doing it.

The *Libertarian Forum* was for all intents and purposes defunct, the last issue having been dated September-December 1984. Now, the old tradition was revived, and Rothbard again sallied forth against the enemies of liberty, not only statists of every hue and persuasion, but also "libertarian" deviationists and con artists galore. He had sorely missed his mornings writing the *Forum*; what more could anyone like Rothbard want than the luxury of getting to express his opinions in print, every month or so, freely and at length? He approached his task with his usual gusto, writing on subjects ranging from the Bosnian civil war to the lurid details of the latest libertarian scandal. The *Report* was soon required reading not only for libertarians, but also for Beltway conservatives eager to learn what the right-wing populist heartland was thinking.

The other regular outlet for Rothbard's political and economic articles was *The Free Market*, monthly journal of the Mises Institute. Every month, starting in 1985, Rothbard exposed the economic fallacies, theoretical mumbo-jumbo, and government propaganda that props up the statist system. Collected after his death and published as *Making Economic Sense*,[16] these articles were short masterpieces that, as examples of the art of persuasion, are models of clarity, precision, and the jargon-free, distinctively Rothbardian style, fearlessly polemical, wryly ironic, and insightful on many levels at once. For all too many students, even students of economics, the mere thought of reading a text having to do with the subject is enough to induce a yawn. The excitement generated by Rothbard, however, is in his ability to pull abstract theory down to earth, and thus make it more accessible as well as far more interesting. A good example is his 1987 *Free Market* article, "The Consequences of Human Action: Intended or Unintended?" in which he points out the problem with the Hayekian theory celebrating capitalism's productivity and beneficence as "the consequences of human action, not human design." Aside from making the relatively obvious point that this ignores the reality that we can never *really* know the intentions of economic actors, in all their psychological complexity as unique individuals, Rothbard explores another level of meaning: the real-world *consequences* of the theory of "unintended consequences." "Arcane methods of methodology," he writes,

> often have surprising political consequences. Perhaps, then, it is no accident that those who believe in unintended and not intended consequences, will also tend to whitewash the growth of government in the twentieth century. For if actions are largely always unintended, this means that government just grew like Topsy, and that no person or group ever willed the pernicious consequences of that growth. The Hayekian perspective cloaks the self-interested actions of the power elite in seeking and obtaining special privileges from government, and hereby impelling its continuing growth."[17]

What is called "the dismal science" is lit up by Rothbard's sardonic wit. Detailing the anticompetitive horrors of California's "farm committees" (i.e., cartels) that legally block smaller, lower-quality fruit from reaching the market, Rothbard mocked the chairman of the ten-man Peach Committee, who invoked taxpayer-financed "focus groups" to argue that "this is what the consumers want." Rothbard jeered, "save your money, fellas. I can predict the result every time: consumers will always prefer larger peaches to smaller ones, just as given the choice, they would prefer a Cadillac to a Geo. Given a choice of receiving a gift, that is, without having to pay for the difference. And price, of course, is the point of the whole deal." The Peach Cartel reveals just *whose* welfare is being served by the "welfare state." In its essence, the system amounts to "the government cartelizing and restricting competition, cutting production, raising prices, and particularly injuring low-income consumers, all with the aid of mendacious disinformation provided by technocrats hired by the government. . . . Bleating hypocritically about how the policy is all done for the sake of the consumers," the hirelings of power reaped the profits of their public service—and surely *these* particular consequences were not unintended.[18]

Rothbard's passion for justice framed his analysis of state-capitalism, in which he insisted on identifying the culprits—the "Bad Guys," as he put it in "Toward a Theory of Libertarian Social Change"—who benefit from the system. This same passion also informed his political commentary, and this, combined with his power elite analysis—"no ruling class has ever resigned"—enabled him to home in on statist trends long before anyone else knew what was going on. Years before the Clintonian assault on local school autonomy and the growing clamor of the "national standards in education" movement, Rothbard spotted this trend in the Bush administration. While massive federal intervention has resulted in the meltdown of the educational system in this country, "the Neocon Welfare State would finish the job: expanding budgets, nationalizing teachers and curricula, and seizing total control of children on behalf of the state's malignant educational bureaucracy."[19]

In defending entrepreneur Michael Milken from the liberal lynch mob in the late eighties, Rothbard's power elite analysis again provided the key insight in understanding the meaning of current events. Quoting financier-philanthropist David Rockefeller's remarks on Milken's "extraordinary income" which "inevitably raises questions as to whether there isn't something unbalanced in the way our financial system is working," Rothbard demanded to know:

> How does Rockefeller have the brass to denounce high incomes? Ludwig von Mises solved the question years ago by pointing out that men of great inherited wealth, men who get their income from capital or capital gains, have favored the progressive income tax, because they don't want new competitors rising up who make their money on personal wage or salary incomes.

Addressing his adversary directly, Rothbard continues:

> And yes, Mr. Rockefeller, this whole Milken affair, in fact, the entire reign of terror . . . raises a lot of questions about the workings of our political as well as our financial system. It raises great questions about the imbalance of political power enjoyed by our existing financial and corporate elites, power that can persuade the coercive arm of the federal government to repress, cripple, and even jail people whose only "crime" is to make money by facilitating the transfer of capital from less to more efficient hands. When creative and productive businessmen are harassed and jailed while rapists, muggers, and murderers go free, there is something very wrong indeed.[20]

There *is* something very wrong, and Rothbard's power elite analysis—a kind of intellectual microscope, in which he focuses in on details and locates patterns that are otherwise invisible—coupled with his extensive research into economic history, enabled him to get to the core of it.

A good example of the Rothbardian microscope in operation is

his 1994 book, *The Case Against the Fed*, which tells the story of the
most secretive, and certainly the most powerful government
agency of them all: how it came to be, who was behind its creation,
how it wields its enormous power—and who benefits.[21]

For the ordinary citizen, the Federal Reserve is a mystery
wrapped in an enigma, as inscrutable as the look on Alan
Greenspan's face as he drones before a Congressional committee.
In clear, nontechnical prose, illuminated as usual with flashes of
biting wit, Rothbard demystifies the Federal Reserve system: not
only its functioning as a banking cartel, and a giant Ponzi scheme
based on the fraud of fractional reserve banking, but also its origins as a massive power play by leading factions of the American
financial elite. Rothbard's analysis of twentieth-century U.S. economic history as a great power struggle between economic elites,
between the House of Morgan and the Rockefeller interests, was
the application of methodological individualism and Austrian economic theory to the problem of power. Using these indispensable
tools of the libertarian scholar, Rothbard formulated a trenchant
analysis of the American elite and the history of the modern era.

The twin themes of *The Case Against the Fed* and another work,
published in book form at this time, *Wall Street, Banks, and American
Foreign Policy*,[22] developed out of a lifetime of economic and historical writing. In the former work, the author relates the history of
how the Federal Reserve System came to be foisted on the unsus-
pecting American people by a high-powered alliance of banking
interests. His analysis is clear, concise, and wide-ranging, covering
the nature of money, the genesis of government paper money, the
inherent instability (and essential fraudulence) of fractional reserve
banking, and the true causes of the business cycle (bank credit
expansion). As Rothbard explains in his economic writings, the key
is in understanding that money is a commodity, like any other, and
thus subject to the laws of the market. A government-granted

monopoly in this, the very lifeblood of the economic system, is a recipe for inflation, a debased currency—and the creation of a permanent plutocracy whose power is virtually unlimited.

In *Wall Street, Banks, and American Foreign Policy*, Rothbard applies this analysis to the international arena. Rothbard's integration of economic history—the full story of the elite-led-and-financed movement to establish the Federal Reserve system—with the interplay of events leading up to two world wars is documented in detail. In these two books, the Rothbardian power elite analysis comes into full and fascinating play. After the long battle to create a central bank in the United States, the high priests of high finance finally seized and consolidated control of domestic economic policy. It only remained for them to extend their dominance internationally and approach the achievement of their final goal: the Keynesian dream of a world central bank, and a single global currency that can be inflated at will. The system of institutionalized embezzlement that is fractional reserve banking would then be foisted on the entire globe. Defying the interdiction on all discussion of two key policy-making organizations, the Council on Foreign Relations, and, later, the Trilateral Commission, Rothbard underscores their vital role as the activist arm of the ruling elite.

These two bastions of the corporate and political establishment have been seized upon by the new populist Right as the virtual embodiments of the power elite, and rightly so. It is only by reading Rothbard, however, that this insight is placed in its proper historical perspective. For the fact of the matter is that, as Rothbard shows, long before the founding of the CFR or the Trilateral Commission, there was a power elite in this country; that elite will likely endure long after those organizations are gone or transmuted into something else.

As he explained in his classic pamphlet "What Has Government Done to Our Money?", *The Case Against the Fed*, and in many other works, the power and wealth of the financial and political elites in this country rests on insupportable and inherently unstable foundations: a fractional reserve banking system in which only 10 percent of the actual deposits are on hand at any one time. "Bankers are inherently inclined toward statism," he declared in the opening paragraph of *Wall Street, Banks, and American Foreign Policy*:

> *Commercial bankers*, engaged as they are in unsound fractional reserve credit, are, in the free market, always teetering on the edge of bankruptcy. Hence they are always reaching for government aid and bailout:
>
> *Investment* banks do much of their business underwriting government bonds, in the United States and abroad. Therefore, they have a vested interest in promoting deficits and in forcing taxpayers to redeem government debt. Both sets of bankers, then, tend to be tied in with government policy, and try to influence and control government actions in domestic and foreign affairs.[23]

Clearly distinguishing himself from the *Wall Street Journal* wing of the conservative movement, Rothbard cast a jaundiced eye on the ascension of Alan Greenspan to the chairmanship of the Fed. When Fed Chairman Paul Volcker was rumored to be on the outs, the financial press moaned and groaned that the stability and confidence of the world economy hinged on his continuance in office. When he finally left, Volcker was consigned to the anonymity reserved for all ex-Fed chairmen, and no longer praised as Atlas bearing the weight of the world economy on his broad shoulders. The appointment of a new Atlas in the person of Alan Greenspan, Rothbard noted, had been greeted with hosannas from all points on the political spectrum. What makes the chairman of the Fed so widely and automatically beloved? "To paraphrase the famous answer of Sir Edmond Hilary, who was asked why he persisted in climbing Mt. Everest, it is because the Fed chairman is there. The very existence of the office makes its holder automatically wonderful, revered, deeply essential to the world economy, etc." This "air of majesty and mystery" is a smokescreen generated to mask the essential bankruptcy of the system.[24]

The Greenspan appointment had a special irony for Rothbard. Greenspan had been part of Ayn Rand's inner circle, thirty years earlier, and Rothbard had known him to be one of the most devout cadre of the Objectivist cult. While, in theory, the Objectivists were devoted to the gold standard, and while, in theory, Greenspan was opposed to the Fed's very existence, in practice, as Rothbard pointed out, he was a conservative Keynesian. While the *New York Times* and other establishment organs noted Greenspan's formal adherence to Randianism and laissez-faire, they correctly pointed out that, as the *Times* put it, this belief exists "only on a high philosophical plane." As a "laissez-faire pragmatist," Rothbard noted, Greenspan "is only in favor of the gold standard if all the conditions are right: if the budget is balanced, trade is free, inflation is licked, everyone has the right philosophy, etc." Since the likelihood of these things coming to pass simultaneously is almost nil, "never are one's 'high philosophical principles' applied to one's actions. It becomes almost piquant for the Establishment to have this man in its camp." According to Rothbard, "the establishment has good reason to sleep soundly with Greenspan at our monetary helm. And as icing on the cake, they know that Greenspan's 'philosophical' Randianism will undoubtedly fool many free-market advocates into thinking that a champion of their cause now perches high in the seats of power." Behind Greenspan's reputation as a "student of Objectivism," his real allegiances were less "philosophical" and more down-to-earth; as a longtime member of the Trilateral Commission, and as a board member of J. P. Morgan & Co. and Morgan Guaranty Trust, here was a man the establishment could trust.[25]

Another case of a "free-market" mask hiding the corporatist reality was the North American "Free Trade" Agreement (NAFTA). Rothbard nailed NAFTA as mercantilism, pure and simple, a regional trade bloc whose economic practices are no freer than that of the European Community. So you want free trade? No problem. All the establishment "has to do is repeal our numerous tariffs, import quotas, anti-'dumping' laws, and other American-imposed restrictions on trade." Rothbard also raised the key issue of the great chink in the armor of the U.S. Constitution, in which "every treaty is considered 'the supreme law of the Land.' " He warns that "if we must be wary of any treaty, we must be particularly hostile to a treaty that builds supranational structures, as does NAFTA." Lamenting the failure of the Bricker Amendment* introduced by Old Right Republicans in the mid-fifties in an attempt to plug this particular hole in the ramparts, Rothbard pointed to the evil "side agreements" that delivered American business to the tender mercies of a multinational bureaucracy.[26]

In opposing NAFTA, and exposing it for the mercantilist scam that it was and is, Rothbard and the Mises Institute stood virtually alone among ostensibly "free-market" luminaries and thinktanks. (Even the Libertarian Party, under the tutelage of Bill Evers, jumped on the NAFTA bandwagon, albeit with a long litany of qualifications and caveats.) Their only allies were to be found on the "reactionary" Right, not only Patrick J. Buchanan but a group of rightist intellectuals associated with the Rockford Institute in Rockford, Illinois.

Rothbard's alliance with the "paleoconservatives" of the Rock-

---

*Introduced in the Senate by Senator John W. Bricker in February 1952, the "Bricker Amendment" to the Constitution sought to eliminate the power of treaties to override the constitution and protect American sovereignty by establishing that "a provision of a treaty which conflicts with this constitution shall not be of any force or effect."

ford Institute was an important, and, for him, gratifying development of the post–Cold War realignment on the Right. The first contact was made by Rothbard when he wrote to Tom Fleming— editor of *Chronicles*, the Rockford Institute's monthly magazine— and the latest victim of a neoconservative hit squad. Fleming had published an article by the talented Bill Kauffman, novelist and idiosyncratic libertarian, that praised Gore Vidal as a man of the Old Right.[27] For this, *Chronicles* and its publisher, the Rockford Institute, were attacked by Midge Decter and Norman Podhoretz as "enemies" who harbored anti-Semitism. Fleming was smeared as a "nativist" because he upheld the small-town traditions of Southern agrarianism against the cosmopolite pretensions of Northeastern urban elites.

The casual observer might ask: But what has any of this got to do with anti-Semitism? In the objective world that most people live in, the answer is: Nothing. In the perfervid world of the New York intellectuals, typified by Podhoretz and Decter, the answer is: Everything. Because, you see, such words as "cosmopolite" or even "urban" are *code-words* for Jews, since (it is alleged) Jews tend to congregate in cities. Therefore, to attack cities is a hate crime, a vicious act of anti-Semitism. Fleming had *really* stepped over the line, however, when he had allowed praise of the Podhoretzes' pet hate to reach the printed page. Years ago, Vidal had earned their eternal enmity by pointing out to them, in public and in print, that to judge virtually all foreign policy questions on the basis of "Is it good for Israel?" is to effectively sign on as a "fifth columnist."

Rockford rebutted the smear campaign with the simple truth: not a single anti-Semitic statement or inference had ever appeared in *Chronicles* or any other Rockford publication, and to say otherwise was a mortal insult to the many Jewish writers, editors, and readers of *Chronicles*. But the concerted campaign to smear Fleming and destroy the Rockford Institute did not let up; instead,

it escalated onto the front page of the *New York Times*. The neoconservatives enlisted Richard John Neuhaus, a Lutheran minister
who headed Rockford's Center for Religion and Society, head-
quartered in New York City. Neuhaus had long been at odds with
Fleming. As one Rockford official put it, "Neuhaus badmouthed
Rockford to our donors, while spending our money hand-over-
fist." Neuhaus was promptly fired, and soon found the lock on the
center's office had been changed. Wailing to the *Times* that he and
his belongings had been literally thrown out into the street,
Neuhaus and his neoconservative allies denounced this act of self-
defense as "ill-mannered."[28]

On reading this account of the latest bloodsports of his old
enemies, the content of Rothbard's thought processes are not hard
to imagine: "Are we to be spared nothing?" To hear *this* from the
same people who think nothing of destroying someone's career on
the basis of a trumped-up charge of "anti-Semitism"! Rothbard
wrote to Fleming, extending his sympathy and support, and a
lively correspondence ensued. This was followed by long telephone conversations, then a meeting that led to the formation of a
new organization: the John Randolph Club. Named after John
Randolph of Roanoke—the fiery orator and colorful character of
colonial America who declared "I love liberty, and hate
equality!"—this by-invitation club of paleoconservative journalists, publicists, and academics held its first conference in 1992. The
resounding success of this opening to the Right put Rothbard in an
expansive mood. In those days, he would often remark to me,
"Isn't it great that we're finally out of the Libertarian Party?" He
found the company of conservatives far more personally congenial
than the company of Libertarian Party activists who, as a group,
tended to be boorish.

The excitement of so many new contacts, of finding a new audience for his ideas and building new friendships was tempered by

the death of a friend from the old days. When Roy Childs died in the summer of 1992, Rothbard was shocked, but not surprised. Roy's demons had been getting the best of him, lately, and his health problems had been getting worse for years. When Cato went east after the split, Roy went, too, but with a heavy heart. He loved San Francisco, a city whose playfulness and easygoing nature reflected his own, and hated to leave. But *Libertarian Review* was no more, and *Inquiry* followed it into oblivion soon after. What was Childs, who used to refer to himself as *"The* Editor," to do? There was nothing for the editor to edit. While Cato seemed the logical place for a man of his talents—and ambition—he was far too eccentric to fit into the Beltway, and was by this time quite ill. After a brief stint at Cato, he went to work as the editorial director of Laissez-Faire Books, a libertarian book service operated by his good friends Howie and Andrea Rich. Both Howie and Andrea knew he was in serious trouble, and did everything they could to help him regain his health and his equilibrium. Despite being afflicted with diabetes, an increasingly serious weight problem, and any number of other ailments, he still managed to continue writing: his reviews for the Laissez-Faire Books catalog, written during this difficult period, were little gems which, strung together, would read like a capsulized intellectual history of the recent past as seen through the prism of a witty, erudite, and passionate partisan of liberty. Although by this time he was having a lot of difficulty getting around, Childs kept in touch with a far-flung and diverse network of friends by phone and letters—nor had he given up on his youthful ambition of becoming a public figure of some renown. When he heard that John Stossel, the television host and producer, needed someone to appear on a show about "discrimination" against overweight people and debunk the idea of "fat peoples' rights," he jumped at the chance. Not only did he appear on the show and do a memorable job—"Let's face it," he quipped, "I'm no blonde surfer. Is it 'discrimination' that I can't get a date?"—but he became friendly with Stossel. Stossel has since gone on to become the libertarian star in the television firmament, with a number of libertarian-oriented television specials to his credit—a role that Childs had often imagined playing. But by the summer of 1992, he was in no condition to even leave his apartment. Childs knew it was time to make a decision: through the intervention of friends, including Charles Koch, he went to the Pritikin clinic in Miami to lose weight, recover his health, and get on with his life. Sadly, it was not to be. He died on June 12, 1992, in his room at Pritikin.

"After Roy died," wrote Rothbard to a mutual friend, "someone said that Roy was the last of the Old Libertarians, the old neo-Randian synthesis before the big paleo-nihilo split. A perceptive point. I am glad that Roy and I had pretty much reconciled in the last year [or] two; the last time he called it was about two weeks before he died."[29] The Rothbards attended the memorial meeting in New York City, organized by Andrea and Howie Rich, where people who had not seen each other for years—and with good reason—all sat together in the same room in solemn tribute to their departed friend without a trace of the old rancor.

If, for Rothbard, the death of Roy Childs marked the end of an era, the passing of the Old Libertarians into the storied history of the movement, then the birth of a new libertarianism was marked by another signal event that took place around this time: the Gulf war. George Bush's crusade for the "New World Order," the first major overseas adventure by the United States in the post-Soviet era, did not sit well with many conservatives, notably Patrick J. Buchanan. *Chronicles* was savage in its opposition to the war, with Fleming and columnist Samuel Francis particularly outspoken. The same crew that had taken out after Fleming over the Neuhaus affair now unleashed their wrath on Buchanan. As in the case of Rockford, a concerted effort was made to silence and essentially destroy Buchanan. In both cases, the attempted character assassination failed.

Rothbard leapt to Buchanan's defense in the pages of the *Rothbard-Rockwell Report*, and soon joined the Buchanan Brigades, Pat's "peasants with pitchforks" rising against the eastern establishment of the Republican Party. It was just like old times again! The resurrected Old Right, diverse but united, was once again leading a nationwide rebellion against the arrogant Eastern elites. Rothbard was an honored guest among the Buchananite contingent at the 1992 Republican National Convention, where he had a wonderful time in the company of Phyllis Schlafly and thoroughly enjoyed Buchanan's defiant speech—so hated by the media and loved by the populist masses. In one of his last published articles, however, Rothbard chided Buchanan for being a classic case of the old adage that people (and especially politicians) often concentrate on those issues in which they have the least expertise; in Buchanan's case, this is undoubtedly the realm of economics, for example, trade policy. Rothbard had followed his isolationist star into the Buchanan coalition, but was increasingly disturbed by Buchanan's remark about not caring one whit about what "dead Austrian economists" have to say on the subject of trade policy, which struck Rothbard as beyond the pale.

It was the highlight of a good year, at a high point in Rothbard's life. Not only had he finally given up his strategical wanderlust, which had taken him far afield from his Old Right origins, and returned to his roots; not only had he, at last, abandoned the albatross of the Libertarian Party, but he was finally beginning to achieve the professional recognition that had been denied him for years. In 1994, the Ingersoll Prize, awarded by the Rockford Institute to recognize writers "whose works affirm the fundamental principles of Western civilization" and given in the past to such luminaries as Mario Vargas Llosa, Wendel Berry, Muriel Spark,

Octavaio Paz, V. S. Naipul, Russell Kirk, Robert Nisbet, and Forrest McDonald, was presented to Rothbard. The prize, which came with a cash gift of $20,000, meant much to a man whose Heraculean labors on behalf of liberty had thus far brought him very little in the way of tangible rewards.

His appointment as the S. J. Hall Distinguished Professor of economics at the University of Nevada, in Las Vegas, had given Rothbard a great psychological and professional lift; in a 1987 interview with the *Washington Times*, Joey Rothbard said it was "deeply satisfying for her husband to be in a real economics department with actual colleagues."[30] Up until 1991, his relations with those colleagues had been properly collegial: his department head had consistently awarded him with evaluations of good to excellent in the yearly reports. But in 1991, with the ascension of Professor Mark Thayer as head of UNLV's economics department, the honeymoon was over.

On a cold day in March 1992, Rothbard complained in a letter that "this is the winter of my discontent." Describing chairman Thayer in a most uncomplimentary manner, he goes on to evoke the humiliation of having to read Thayer's trumped up "evaluation," which grudgingly graded him as "satisfactory." Thayer made it clear, however, that Rothbard had barely escaped a more direct rebuke—one, perhaps, to be delivered in the future.[31]

In every area of Thayer's evaluation, very restrained praise is invariably followed by a direct slap in the face; for example, while professor Rothbard's general performance has been satisfactory, "he had only limited contact with most economics students" and he was admonished that he needed to "teach more students."

This slap really stung; he *had* been "teaching more students" until Thayer and his faculty allies succeeded in abolishing the M.A. program that attracted students of Austrian economics from around the country. For now, the academic bureaucrats had let

Rothbard off with a warning. "However," wrote his evaluator, in the future, he must "be available as a role model for junior faculty." To this, Rothbard replied, "I maintain that the best way I can serve as a 'role model' is to be allowed to go about my business as a scholar and teacher without being subject to harassment. Collegiality has to be a two-way street."[32]

Rothbard never coveted the honors heaped on other far less worthy scholars; all he ever wanted was to be left alone to do his work. Alas, this modest desire was never really fulfilled, and he spent many precious hours in his later years fulminating against his academic enemies and fighting their seemingly endless machinations. His correspondence during this period is filled with references to their down-and-dirty tactics; in one bizarre case, a prospective student, attracted to UNLV on the strength of Rothbard's books, was actively discouraged from attending the university by one of Rothbard's enemies on the faculty. The would-be student traveled a long distance to visit UNLV's economics department: "What I received was a very condescending three-hour lecture on why I did not want to learn anything about Professor Rothbard's views."[33]

While Rothbard succeeded in getting Thayer's initial draft evaluation modified on certain points, the charges still left him open for future attack. He refused to sign on to the evaluation and chose, instead, to attach a separate comment. Both documents would go to the administration, that is, to the office of the Dean, which was far more favorable to Rothbard than the head of his own department. "So the war continues," he remarked wearily to Lew Rockwell.[34]

That Rothbard had to defend his scholarship, and particularly his productivity, against the assault of then-chairman Thayer, "whose claim to fame," as one wag put it, "was that he had coauthored a journal article concerning the various strengths of sunscreen," was an indignity he could not and would not abide. On

September 18, 1992, an open letter to the economics department signed by Rothbard, Hans-Hermann Hoppe, and Clarence Ray, declared that they were "seceding" from the Department of Economics, and proposed a new Economics Department in the College of Liberals Arts. "For years we have been subjected to systematic mistreatment in this department," they wrote. "There has been continuing denigration of our research, of our teaching, and of our service." While acknowledging that "part of this schism is based on personality differences," the letter pinpointed "very different ways of regarding the discipline of economics" as being at the core of the dispute. "The majority of the department is committed to economics as a quantitative and econometric science; we, on the other hand, look at economics as far more of a qualitative and philosophic discipline." The letter translates the principle of secession, so often argued in Rothbard's political writings, into the terminology of academic politics, pointing out that the majority approach is more suitable to a business school, while the Austrian philosophic orientation was ideally situated in a Liberal Arts curriculum. The final paragraph goes on to state some general principles, ending with the kind of rhetorical flourish that endeared Rothbard not only to his friends but also to his enemies: "Peaceful separation would be better for all of us," the letter continues. "It would be welcomed by the university authorities. It would mean that the Department of Economics is willing to set aside personal vindictiveness in behalf of the good of all. If, after centuries of enmity, the Czechs can let the Slovaks go in peace, surely the Department of Economics at UNLV can do no less."[35]

Both the tragic and heroic aspects of Rothbard's last years are intertwined with his experience at UNLV. In an evocative memoir of Rothbard the teacher, Douglas French, a student in Rothbard's "History of Economic Thought" course, compares listening to a Rothbard lecture to "being a passenger in a high-speed car chase.

With facts and ideas streaming at us, Murray would suddenly change direction, heading down a path that seemingly took us away from our destination, but never did. He knew exactly where he was going. I hung on with the rest of the class, furiously trying to take down every word." French was no libertarian ideologue—at least, not until he walked into Rothbard's class: "Most libertarians discovered Murray Rothbard by reading *The Ethics of Liberty*, *For a New Liberty*, or one of his many other books or articles. My discovery started with the following entry in the University of Nevada Las Vegas 1990 fall course catalog: 'History of Economic Thought, instructor—Rothbard.' "[36]

Popular with his students and always in great demand for his time, Rothbard "never talked down to me or any of his students," writes French, and "often asked as many questions as he answered." Yet this great teacher and scholar, who won the hearts and minds of his devoted students, "was anything but revered by most of the economics faculty at UNLV," French relates. "The rest of the department resented the 'east end of the hall,' where Murray, Hans-Hermann Hoppe, and a couple of free-market sympathizers had their offices on Beam Hall's fifth floor."[37]

Like any human being, Rothbard must have had his moments of doubt and demoralization, but we are not privy to these. The ebullient floodtide of letters written at the height of the intramural warfare at UNLV documents Rothbard's irrepressible fighting spirit. His unflagging optimism may have been due, in some part, to his sense of humor and fun-loving personality; who else would have compared a proposal to create a new Economics Department with the sundering of Czechoslovakia?

His optimism was reinforced by the psychic reward of seeing libertarian ideas, and the insights of the Austrian school, take root and spread, not only in academia, through the determined efforts of the Mises Institute, but in the wider political culture. The 1994 congressional elections, in which a whole generation of radical Republicans were swept into office on an anti-government platform, confirmed the optimism that had been his fuel through all the years of ideological isolation and near despair. Rothbard was jubilant. First, the fall of the Kremlin, now the federal Leviathan, would be next. In the *Rothbard-Rockwell Report*, and in private conversation, Rothbard expressed the view that we might just be entering the first phases of a revolutionary situation. It was a great time to be alive.

The shattered expectations of the early eighties had finally given way to the renewal of hope as the nineties dawned. Rothbard was at the very height of his powers, and his stature as a scholar and political theorist was rapidly rising. Unburdened of the albatross of the Libertarian Party, which for years had weighed heavily around his neck, his natural optimism blossomed into a certainty that the great hope of his youth—the rise of a great populist tidal wave that would topple the ruling elites— was on the horizon. In his famous 1992 speech to the John Randolph Club, Rothbard exulted in the return of the Old Right and examined the revolutionary possibilities inherent in its reappearance. He started out by quoting that grizzled old warrior of the original Right, Garet Garrett:

> There are those who still think they are holding a pass against a revolution that may be coming up the road. But they are gazing in the wrong direction. The revolution is behind them. It went by in the night of depression, singing songs to freedom.[38]

What is needed, then, said Rothbard, is a *counter*revolution led not by conservatives but self-conscious radicals of the Right. This, he reminds us, was indeed the stance of the old, pre–World War II Right, which he broke down into three groups: (1) the "extremist" individualists and libertarians, such as Garrett, H. L. Mencken, Albert Jay Nock, and Rose Wilder Lane; (2) right-wing Democrats of the Jeffersonian mould, such as Senator James A. Reed of Missouri; and (3) "moderate New Dealers, who thought that the Roosevelt New Deal went too far, for example Herbert Hoover." United against the centralizing and statizing domestic policies of FDR and his Brain Trust, the Old Right coalition also opposed the campaign to drag us into World War II and refused to endorse the militant interventionism of the elites, which amounted, "in the prophetic words of Charles A. Beard, to waging 'perpetual war for perpetual peace.' "[39]

Rothbard explains how and why the primacy of the foreign policy debate realigned the political spectrum, with right-wing internationalists such as Lewis W. Douglas, a New Deal opponent, now landing in FDR's camp, and veteran isolationists of the left, such as Beard, Harry Elmer Barnes, and John T. Flynn "gradually but surely becoming right-wingers in the course of their determined opposition to the foreign New Deal." As opposed to the homogenized and militarized conservative movement of the Cold War era, with its fierce purges of dissident groupings such as isolationists, Randians, and libertarians, the Old Right was a veritable peaceable kingdom. Within the overall framework of opposition to war abroad and socialism at home, there were certain "charming disagreements" which could be boiled down to differing answers to the question: "How much of existing government would you repeal?" The minimum demand was repeal of the New Deal, while "others would press on to abolition of Woodrow Wilson's 'New Freedom,' " including the abolition of the Federal Reserve and the income tax. Still others, Rothbard among them, "would not stop until we repealed the Federal Judiciary Act of 1789 and maybe even think the unthinkable and restore the good old Articles of Confederation."[40]

At a time when the Right was getting in touch with its Old Right roots, Rothbard was getting in touch with some of his own personal roots, fondly recalling his youth as the sole right-winger in a Marxist-leftist milieu: in those days "as middle-class Jews in New York, my relatives, friends, classmates, and neighbors faced only one great moral decision in their lives: should they join the Communist Party and devote one hundred percent of their lives to the cause, or should they remain fellow travelers and devote only a fraction of their lives?"[41]

"I found the Old Right in 1946," he told his paleoconservative audience, "and was happy there for a decade." Clearly he was looking forward to another decade of amicable relations with his newfound conservatives allies, a revitalized Old Right, older and wiser in its reconstituted form. Decentralized and without a "party line" but united on key issues, the reborn movement of his youth would have to resolve some fundamental strategic questions. The Marxists had posed the question in terms of which group would be the agency of social change, but Rothbard posed it in a slightly different form: "The relevant question for the right-wing is the other side of the coin: Who can we expect to be the bad guys? Who are agents of negative social change?"[42]

He chuckled at this point, as did his audience, at this casual reference to their self-conception as an oppositional movement, a movement in search of enemies, even of scapegoats: for Rothbard thought that the elites who rule this country should indeed be made into scapegoats, and made to pay for their crimes. The question was: Who are the biggest enemies of liberty? "Basically," said Rothbard, "there have been two answers on the Right: (1) the unwashed masses, and (2) the power elites." Rothbard relates that "very early I concluded that the big danger is the elite, and not the masses," for, even granting the worst fears of conservatives who despise the "mass man," most of these average Joes just don't have time for political shenanigans. They have to work for a living, and spend most of their time and energy on the daily business of life, and their only interest in politics is sporadic. Those who have time for politics are the professionals: "the bureaucrats, politicians, and special interest groups dependent on political rule." Their livelihood depends on politics, and so they are active twenty-four hours a day.

The elites rule over and exploit the great majority of average Joes, taxing and ripping them off, and living like kings on the accumulated plunder: but why do the people put up with it? Here Rothbard raises "what I like to call the mystery of civil obedience." Such diverse thinkers as David Hume, Etienne de la Boetie, and Ludwig von Mises pointed out that "precisely because the ruling class is a minority" in the long-run it cannot rule by force alone. The first requirement of any government is legitimacy in the minds of the governed, and this is the role of the intellectuals—to provide it. Weaving their apologias for state power, the intellectual class imbues the populace with—"as the Marxists used to say"— "false consciousness," and for this they are amply rewarded with perks, prestige, and power. The problem confronting the Right, or any group seeking to challenge the status quo, is to penetrate the hypnotic state induced by this "false consciousness," and awaken the masses to the true nature of their rulers.[43]

The only alternative is the "educationism" of Hayek, which declares that ideas, being the crucial element of success, must filter down through a hierarchy, "beginning with the top philosophers, then academics, and finally to journalists and politicians, and then to the masses." This "very gentle and genteel" strategy, while it suits its practitioners admirably, does not suit the needs of a movement that seeks to preserve and extend liberty. First, because the Hayekian strategy "at best will take several hundred years," but in addition there are several "blockages" that imperil this "trickle-down" theory. Thus, for example, many scientists are aware of the unscientific nature of the environmentalists' claim that man is a veritable plague upon the earth, "yet somehow it is always the same few hysterics that are exclusively quoted by the media." This invariably occurs because "the intellectual classes may be part of the solution, but also they are a big part of the problem." For the most part, they are heavily invested in the power and legitimacy of the state, and to spend all one's time convincing them to turn on their masters seems a fool's errand.[44]

Another related strategy is the "Fabian" alternative, which Rothbard describes as "quiet persuasion," not in the groves of academe, but in Washington, D.C., in the corridors of power. This technique is modeled after the old Fabian Society, which "gently pushed the British state into a gradual accretion of socialist power." But this strategy is flawed, when pursued by libertarians and others who want to decrease state power, because "what works to increase state power does not work in reverse." The Fabians nudged the British government in the direction it was already traveling. In agitating for less government within a state apparatus whose natural impulse is to expand, "the result is far more likely to be the state's co-opting and Fabianizing" the libertarians themselves "rather than the other way around."[45]

While Rothbard certainly did not think that intellectuals should be discounted as potential allies, he thought the focus of antigovernment agitation had to be on middle-class America. But this did not mean a policy of caution and restraint: "The proper course for the right-wing opposition must necessarily be a strategy of boldness and confrontation, of dynamism and excitement, a strategy, in short, of rousing the masses from their slumber and exposing the arrogant elites that are ruling them, controlling them, taxing them, and ripping them off."[46]

But how can such a strategy be called "conservative"? For decades, liberals had been denouncing anyone who wanted to abolish the New Deal or the Fair Deal with cries of "But that's not genuine conservatism, that's radicalism." Rothbard was prepared to concede the point: To the charge of "radicalism" he proudly pleaded guilty. Nothing less than this sort of radicalism could break the old pattern of right-wing acquiescence to the gains of the Left. Every left-wing "great leap forward," every advance toward collectivism since the New Deal, has been followed in the political cycle by a conservative "backlash" in which the gains of the Left are not repealed but preserved (and often extended). "When are we going to stop playing their game," he asked, "and start throwing over the table?"[47]

But what exactly does this mean—and how could it occur? Rothbard illustrates by giving an example from history: "Quick now: who was the most hated, the most smeared man in American politics in this century? He was not a libertarian, he was not an isolationist, he was not even a conservative; in fact, he was a moderate Republican. And yet he was so universally reviled that his very name became a generic dictionary synonym for evil." Rothbard's answer: Joe McCarthy. While the liberal-conservative consensus had been approval of McCarthy's goals but condemnation of his methods, Rothbard disdained his goals but found him admirable precisely because of his confrontational methods. The "unique and glorious thing about McCarthy" was that he "was able, for a few years, to short-circuit the intense opposition of all the elites in American life: from the Eisenhower-Rockefeller administration to the Pentagon and the military-industrial complex to liberal and left media and academic elites." If the Hard Right was going to triumph, then these were the enemies that had to be humbled, and McCarthy had done it, even if only briefly.

The intellectual left, Rothbard noted, had responded to the spectre of McCarthyism with a smear campaign that dwarfed any conceived by "Tail Gunner" Joe. In an influential book, *The New American Right*, edited by Daniel Bell, a consortium of prominent leftist sociologists and polemicists (some of whom were to mutate into the "neoconservatives" of the nineties) pronounced the verdict on McCarthy and his followers: they were victims of "status resentment," motivated by anger and hatred of their betters, and mentally unstable in a potentially dangerous mode.[48]

With the presidential campaign of Patrick J. Buchanan, who had raised the banner of America First and played Lindbergh to George Bush's FDR during the first Gulf War, the dreaded Radical Right was back in full force, and the smear brigade was back at the same old stand. Once again "status resentment," "paranoia," and the ubiquitous smear-word, "extremism," were diagnosed by the spin doctors of the chattering classes. Pat's "peasants with pitchforks" were denounced as bigots, anti-Semites, and even Francoists. One of Buchanan's chief attractions for Rothbard was the quality of his enemies; the elites hated Pat, and still do, largely for the same reasons they hated McCarthy: for his blunt, uncompromisingly angular stance, his combative style, and his ability to short-circuit the power of the elites.

For the first time in many years Rothbard saw that it was possible to bypass the elites and appeal directly to the people: this is why he supported Buchanan, and later Ross Perot. He saw that the range of "respectable" thought had narrowed to the point where the left and right-wing versions of social democracy had effectively merged—and that it was high time for an alternative to emerge. With Bolshevism dead, the main enemy was now Menshevism—the "soft-Marxism" of social democracy embodied in the modern welfare-warfare state: "We are now trapped, in America, inside a Menshevik fantasy, with the narrow bounds of respectable debate set for us by various brands of Marxists."[49]

Could the social democratic consensus be broken? With the rebirth of the Old Right in the nineties, Rothbard believed that the grip of the elites could be shattered, and the terms of the debate shifted. He saw a great political realignment taking shape, one that would shake the federal Leviathan to its very foundations. The whole point of the paleoconservative movement was to challenge the tired leadership of establishment conservatism and replace it with a new, vital, and radicalized cadre of shock troops who would confront the American imperium and rally the people to their cause. Two years before the Republicans gained a congressional majority in the 1994 elections, Rothbard was predicting and seeking to guide the coming upsurge of right-wing populism, convinced that, this time, it would short-circuit the power of the elites long enough to topple them.

"When I was growing up," said Rothbard, "I found that the main argument against laissez-faire and for socialism was that socialism and communism were inevitable: 'You can't turn back the clock.' But the clock of the once-mighty Soviet Union, the clock of Marxism-Leninism . . . is not only turned back, but lies dead and broken forever." Yet this is where our task begins rather than ends. Recalling that one of the authors of the Bell volume said, "in horror and astonishment, that the Radical Right intends to repeal the twentieth century," Rothbard's response, his voice dripping with sarcasm, was:

> Heaven forfend! Who would want to repeal the twentieth century, the century of horror, the century of collectivism, the century of mass destruction and genocide, who would want to repeal *that*? Well, we propose to do just that! . . . We shall break the clock of social democracy. We shall break the clock of the Great Society. We shall break the clock of the welfare state. We shall break the clock of the New Deal. We shall break the clock of Woodrow Wilson's 'New Freedom' and perpetual war. We *shall* repeal the twentieth century."[50]

The optimism that had enabled him to endure many long years of isolation—as a grade-school anti–New Dealer in a socialist milieu, as an Old Rightist on a campus where the Right was represented by Norman Thomas, as an isolationist at the height of the Cold War, as a principled libertarian in a party of opportunists— now burst forth in his writing and in his life. He was more productive, more successful, and more at home in the world than ever before. He had followed what he called his "antistatist and isolationist guiding star," often alone and against every kind of obstacle, to finally arrive at the day when he delivered the keynote speech at the "Costs of War" conference put on by the Mises Institute in late May 1994. It was a signal event. It was the first major gathering of antiwar, anti-imperialist conservatives since the dissolution of the America First Committee in 1941. Scholars and writers associated with the Rockford Institute, the Mises Institute, and the Center for Libertarian Studies, convened to hear talks from distinguished speakers such as Paul Fussell on "The Culture of War" and Ralph Raico on "Rethinking Churchill." The turnout was fantastic, the speakers exciting, and the trip to Stone Mountain, just outside the Atlanta conference site, was memorable. Good food and the joys of Southern hospitality were a pleasant prelude to the finale: Rothbard's speech that evening on "America's Two Just Wars: 1775 and 1861." Speaking without notes, peppering his talk with humor and personal anecdotes, Rothbard prefaced his disquisition on just war theory with a personal observation: "During my lifetime," he said, as the sun set over Stone Mountain,

> my ideological and political activism has been focused on opposition to America's wars, first because I have believed our waging them to be unjust, and, second, because war, in the penetrating phrase of the libertarian Randolph Bourne in World War I, has always been "the health of the state," an instrument of the

aggrandizement of state power over the health, the lives, and the property of their subject citizens and social institutions.[51]

When it was over, the audience stood and cheered. It was the climax of a successful and important event. As we sat around afterward, basking in the glow and sipping our coffee, Rothbard turned to me and said, "Isn't this great, Justin? I mean, just think back only few short years ago, when we were in the LP: we were stuck in some seedy hotel with a bunch of libertarian wackos explaining why foreign policy matters." Turning to look at the crowd that filled the meeting room, he added, "Justin, we've definitely come *up* in the world!"

Indeed we had. These were salad days for Rothbard, and he was ready to make another great effort, and set to work on completing the great project that had been in the making all these many years: turning boxes of accumulated notes into the thousands of manuscript pages of his monumental *History of Economic Thought.*

The great tragedy is that Rothbard did not have much time left. At the Mises Institute's summer seminar, held that year at Claremont College, in California, he complained of an inability to sleep. Back in New York, he consulted a doctor he had seen on a talk show, whose *shtick* was that hospitals were giving far too many tests to patients, and that most of these procedures were unnecessary. His views fed into Rothbard's general suspicion of doctors. Eight years earlier, in a letter to Evers on the subject of tort reform, he had declared himself "implacably opposed to Epsteinian pro-doctor views. I believe that doctors are, by and large, a group of highly paid butchers and murderers, and that much of their sins are *not* questions of contract or voluntary assumption of risk, but torts to the hilt." As proof of the medical profession's perfidy, Rothbard related the story of how his brother-in-law was advised by his physician to take certain anti-high-blood pressure pills. Upon finding that every time he took one he lost central vision in one eye for hours, he communicated his concerns to his internist and to an eye-specialist; both told him to ignore it, and take his pills, assuring him that the symptoms were meaningless and ephemeral. In a few weeks, he permanently lost his vision in that eye, and when he later pointed out to his physician that the Physicians' Desk Reference mentions eye problems as a possible symptom of the pill, the doctor said, "Gee, you're right." Williamson, these bastards have to feel the full majesty of the law.[52]

Another doctor suggested he go to Roosevelt Hospital, but Rothbard was adamantly opposed: his last interaction with this institution had been a disaster, when a medical orderly had grumbled at his "bumpy chest" which got in the way of carrying out some medical procedure—as if he had intentionally raised those bumps to make her life more difficult. It was a cold autumn in New York, and the weather bothered him. He knew he was getting weaker, but neither he nor Joey nor any of his friends knew that he was suffering from heart failure.

On January 7, 1995, Joey had an appointment at an optometrist's shop about half a block from their apartment. At around three that afternoon, Rothbard was on the phone talking to Lew Rockwell, and Joey reminded him as she sailed out the door that he had said he would accompany her to get her new glasses. Ten minutes later, Rothbard came into the store and told the clerk that his wife was inside getting fitted for glasses, and that he would like to get his glasses tightened while waiting for her. Tightening Rothbard's spectacles in a back room, the clerk heard a crash. By the time he came running into the front, Rothbard was unconscious. Emergency paramedics were on the scene very fast, but to no avail. All measures to revive him failed. He was taken to Roosevelt hospital, where he died a few hours later.

A memorial meeting was held in New York City, where over one hundred of Rothbard's friends and admirers gathered, several in the same room together for the first time in years, and paid tribute to the man whose enormous influence on their lives and ideas they were only just beginning to realize and fully acknowledge.

Chief among his enemies, William F. Buckley Jr. took advantage of the occasion to smear Rothbard in the guise of an "obituary," raising the same old lying canard about how, when Nikita Khrushchev visited America in the sixties, Rothbard allegedly bounded down the stairs of his apartment building, presumably to throw bouquets in the wake of the Soviet dictator.

Rothbard's former allies in and around the Libertarian Party reacted with their usual lack of either sense or taste. Of many summations of Rothbard's life printed in the avowedly libertarian media, the most ignorant was one fanzine writer who remarked that if libertarianism had been the status quo, the supposedly "contrarian" Rothbard would have been a socialist—thus betraying complete unfamiliarity with Rothbard's personality and his ideas. And in Washington, D.C., the president of a prominent libertarian thinktank turned quite pale when an aide, interrupting a seminar in progress, told him the news of Rothbard's passing.[53]

The cliché that genius must die before being recognized is unfortunately all too applicable in Rothbard's case. This is due, first of all, to fanatical hostility to the most consistent advocate of free markets and property rights by precisely those people whose business it is to hand out awards, fellowships, academic appointments, and other goodies, to intellectuals who go along with the program. The establishment Rothbard lambasted was hardly likely to honor him—living or dead.

But his friends and adherents, while honoring Rothbard, in

many ways overlooked his unique genius. This was due, in part, to his proximity. Only his absence gave them the perspective to realize the enormity of what had been lost. There was, however, another reason for this underappreciation of Rothbard's quality of mind: his own struggle to find a literary project equal to the scope of his erudition. While a glance at the footnotes of Rothbard's works published during his lifetime hints at the breadth and depth of his knowledge, nothing could have prepared anyone for his two-volume *History of Economic Thought*, published in 1997. For the first time, the full range of Rothbard's enormous erudition was employed in a theme broad enough to encompass the wide reach of his knowledge. It was the capstone of his life's work, the jewel in the crown of his scholarly achievements, and he had been working on it or thinking about it, in one form or another, at least since the fall of 1949, when he first wrote Mises and urged him to write a *Dogmengeschichte* "that would properly evaluate all of the contributions to economic thought."[54]

Mises left the task for him, however, and he took it up with his usual thoroughness: Rothbard's research notes would fill several volumes with illuminating and trenchant commentary, complete with full citations. But the *History* is more than a triumph of scholarship: it is the fullest expression of the defiant humanism at the core of "Austrian" or Misesian economics. The *History* allows its readers to see the whole pattern of economic thought superimposed on an elaborately colorful backdrop of religious, ethical, cultural, and political ideas.

If the system or paradigm that Rothbard spent his life constructing is thought of in terms of a towering edifice, a many-leveled structure majestic in its complexity, then the *History* stands at the apex, a penthouse with more rooms than anyone could explore in a lifetime, filled to overflowing with treasures of lost knowledge, both forgotten and suppressed.

The *History* is infused not only with the encyclopedic erudition of a true polymath but also with Rothbard's personality. He spent a long time thinking about it, reading and making notes, and after a while the book became an essential part of him, of his life as a writer and economist: he clearly considered it his life's work. As such, it deserves an extended examination, and a chapter all its own.

NOTES

1. Rothbard to Mike Holmes, 30 December 1984.
2. Ibid.
3. Rothbard to Evers, 1 August 1984.
4. Rothbard to Evers, 12 May 1986.
5. Interview with the author.
6. Interview with Llewellyn H. Rockwell Jr.
7. Rothbard to Evers, 16 May 1986.
8. Rothbard to David Bergland, 5 June 1986.
9. Murray N. Rothbard, "Life or Death in Seattle," *American Libertarian* (August 1987).
10. Ludwig von Mises, "Economic Calculation in the Socialist Commonwealth," in *Collectivist Economic Planning,* ed. F. A. Hayek (London: Routledge and Sons, 1935), pp. 87–130.
11. Aubrey Herbert [Murray N. Rothbard], "The Real Aggressors," *Faith and Freedom* (April 1954): 23.
12. Murray N. Rothbard, *Left and Right: The Prospects for Liberty*, p. 26.
13. Cited in Justin Raimondo, *Reclaiming the American Right*, p. 215.
14. Llewellyn H. Rockwell Jr., *The Case for Paleolibertarianism and Realignment on the Right* (Center for Libertarian Studies, 1990), p. 4; originally published in *Liberty*, January 1990.
15. Ibid.
16. Murray N. Rothbard, *Making Economic Sense* (Auburn, Ala.: Ludwig von Mises Institute, 1995).

17. Murray N. Rothbard, "The Consequences of Human Action: Intended or Unintended?" *The Free Market* (May 1987).

18. Murray N. Rothbard, "By Their Fruits," *The Free Market* (October 1992).

19. Murray N. Rothbard, "The Neocon Welfare State," *The Free Market* (September 1992).

20. Murray N. Rothbard, "Michael R. Milken vs. the Power Elite," *The Free Market* (June 1989).

21. Murray N. Rothbard, *The Case Against the Fed* (Auburn, Ala.: Ludwig von Mises Institute, 1994).

22. Murray N. Rothbard, *Wall Street, Banks, and American Foreign Policy* (Burlingame, Calif.: Center for Libertarian Studies, 1994).

23. Rothbard, *Wall Street*, p. 1. Italics in original.

24. Murray N. Rothbard, "The Mysterious Fed," *The Free Market* (October 1991).

25. Murray N. Rothbard, "Alan Greenspan: A Minority Report on the Fed Chairman," *The Free Market* (August 1987).

26. Murray N. Rothbard, "The Nafta Myth," *The Free Market* (October 1993).

27. Bill Kauffman, "Gnawing Away at Vidal," *Chronicles* (March 1989).

28. For the paleoconservative view of this dispute, see Paul Gotfried, *The Conservative Movement*, rev. ed. (New York: Twayne Publishers, 1993), pp. 144–45. For the neoconservative view, see David Frum, *Dead Right* (New York: Basic Books, 1994), pp. 134–35.

29. Rothbard to Robert D. Kephart, 13 June 1992.

30. Scott Sublett, "Libertarians' Storied Guru," *Washington Times*, 30 July 1987.

31. Rothbard to Llewellyn H. Rockwell Jr., 5 March 1992.

32. Murray N. Rothbard, "Comment on Chairman Thayer's Annual Evaluation," 19 March 1992.

33. Jeff A. Neumayer to Rothbard, 25 August 1991.

34. Rothbard to Llewellyn H. Rockwell Jr., 18 March 1992.

35. Murray N. Rothbard, Clarence Ray, and Hans Hermann-Hoppe, "Memo to the Department of Economics," 18 September 1992.

36. Douglas French, "Rothbard the Teacher," *Liberty* (May 1995): 14–15.

37. Ibid.

38. Garet Garrett, *The Revolution Was* (Caldwell, Idaho: Caxton Printers, 1945), p. 1.

39. Murray N. Rothbard, speech to the John Randolph Club, 18 January 1992.

40. Ibid. The Federal Judiciary Act of 1789 gave federal judges power to decide disputes between persons living in different states.

41. Ibid.

42. Ibid.

43. Ibid.

44. Ibid.

45. Ibid.

46. Ibid.

47. Ibid.

48. Daniel Bell, ed., *The New American Right* (New York: Criterion Books, 1955); revised edition, *The Radical Right* (New York: Anchor Books, 1964).

49. Rothbard, JRC speech.

50. Ibid.

51. Murray N. Rothbard, "America's Two Just Wars: 1775 and 1861," in *The Costs of War: America's Pyrrhic Victories*, edited by John V. Denson (New Brunswick, N.J.: Transaction Publishers, 1997), p. 119.

52. Rothbard to Evers, 12 May 1986.

53. Not long after, this same thinktank president, in a television interview conducted by John McLaughlin, denied the major influence of Rothbard on libertarian thought not once but *three* times, instead citing Hayek and Milton Friedman.

54. Rothbard to Ludvig von Mises, 22 September 1949.

7

THE CAPSTONE

The *History*, as we have seen, was there almost from the beginning. In answer to Rothbard's letter, Mises explained that "what separates the various 'schools' of economics from one another is their epistemological approach" and went on to outline his own plans for covering the subject in the seminar. However, he did not promise to write the work on the history of economic thought that Rothbard had suggested in his letter; instead, he wrote: "I hope that you will soon finish your thesis and will have time enough to begin to write a great book on the problems you refer to in your letter."[1]

Whether or not Rothbard decided then and there to take up his task is impossible to say, but in any case his conception of this work seems to have been present very early on. The actual writing, apart from notes, was begun sometime in the early seventies. As we have already noted, a kind of *precis*, or condensation of the essential concept, was published in the form of a brief article, "New Light on the Prehistory of the Austrian School," in 1976.[2]

303

Rothbard began to flesh out his theme in the early eighties, when, at the suggestion of economist Mark Skousen, he agreed to write a history of economic thought. Skousen arranged for publication through the Institute for Political Economy.

All was not smooth sledding, however. In a 1983 letter, Rothbard complains of "a crisis in my *History of Economic Thought* book." The publisher wanted the manuscript by the end of summer, and his editor insisted that Rothbard "stress the post–[Adam] Smith era. So I realized that the only way *that* can be done—and also, as he wants, to keep the book fairly short—is to scrap the wonderful and beautiful stuff that I have written up till now, and to write what *he* wants—what Joey calls for short 'the Ten Great Modern Economists,' and then hope that there will be enough time to link the two books up into one. If not, I may wind up with "one short book" and a larger, much broader book on the whole shebang."[3]

Luckily for future generations of libertarians, as it turned out, he did not scrap the beautiful and wonderful stuff that makes up the first volume. Instead, as he writes in the acknowledgments, "after pondering the problem . . . I told [the editor] that I would have to begin with Aristotle, since Smith was a sharp decline from many of his predecessors."[4]

"The whole shebang" is a good way to put it, for this is about the only phrase that does justice to Rothbard's theme. As he puts it in the introduction, "these volumes are very different from the norm." Rejecting the narrowly "economic" in favor of presenting the philosophical, religious, and political context in which economic theories are formulated, Rothbard created a vivid panorama of the history of thought: not just economic thought, but *all* social thought.

This theme was a logical outgrowth of the Misesian view of economics as a branch of praxeology, that is, the study of human action, which also includes psychology, history, ethics, political economy, and all the social (or "soft") sciences. A history of economic thought from an Austrian perspective would have to view its subject through this multifaceted prism, and could not be shoe-horned into a few hundred pages. Such a project would have to be a massive undertaking, the work of a lifetime. For any other scholar to take up such a challenge would be an act of hubris—even if they worked on nothing else. Rothbard took on the task *in addition* to his regular outpouring of books, scholarly articles, political commentary, and miscellaneous writings.

Not all the towering figures in the history of ideas were good teachers; genius tends to make its bearers impatient with ordinary people who do not make connections as quickly or in quite the same way. The idea of limiting an "Austrian" history of economic thought to the so-called ten great economists shows how little understood the praxeologic method is, even by alleged Misesians. However frustrating this might have been for Rothbard, such woeful ignorance, far from deterring or discouraging him, merely made him all the more determined to educate such people, and raise them up, as it were, to his level of understanding. This impulse to correct error—and to not only correct it, but to offer a complex and closely reasoned alternate paradigm—is what made him a great educator.

Against the "Great Man" theory of economic history, in which "Adam Smith created economics, much as Athena sprang full-grown and fully armed from the brow of Zeus," Rothbard counterposes a new paradigm that takes into account the endless complexity of human experience. Proclaiming his ideological allegiance at the very start, the author declares that "this work is an overall history of economic thought from a frankly 'Austrian' standpoint," that is, from the point of view of an adherent of the 'Austrian School' of economics. And "not only that," he continues, "this perspective is grounded in what is currently the least fashionable though not the least numerous variant of the Austrian School: the Misesian' or 'praxeologic.' "[5]

In the realm of methodology, the great achievement of Ludwig von Mises was to rescue economics from the scientistic conceit, whose deluded adherents see economics as a "science," that, like physics, is ever-increasing its knowledge and accuracy, perfecting its analysis toward complete understanding. This ever-onward-and-upward view of economic history, says Rothbard, is demonstrably false. There is such a thing as "lost knowledge"; history can (and all-too-often does) take a wrong turn, and can be diverted by error down an incorrect and destructive path.

Citing Thomas Kuhn's *Structure of Scientific Revolutions*, Rothbard points out that not even the "hard" physical sciences follow this "romantic, Panglossian" ever-ascending course. Debunking what Rothbard calls "the Whig theory of history" in the sciences, Kuhn showed that science did not develop in this way. A paradigm, once selected, is rarely challenged or tested; only when the number of anomalies and contradictions proliferate does the dominant paradigm go into "crisis." Then the old paradigm is overthrown, and a new one takes its place. It is not necessary to hold with Kuhn's nihilist view that all paradigms are equally valid (or invalid) "to realize that his less than starry-eyed view of science rings true both as history and as sociology."[6]

If the modernist prejudice that "later is better" is not even applicable to the "hard" physical sciences, then it is even *less* relevant to the study of the "soft" sciences, including economics, where a variety of factors, such as politics, religion, and ethics, influence the ebb and flow of economic ideas. Against the dominant paradigm in the history of economic thought, which purports to show that each and every school and tendency has made its unique contribution to the overall progress of economic science, Rothbard saw that "economics can and has proceeded in contentious, even zigzag fashion, with later systemic fallacy sometimes elbowing aside earlier but sounder paradigms, thereby redirecting economic thought down a totally erroneous or even tragic path."[7]

The "Few Great Men theory of economic history" starts with Adam Smith, the alleged founder not only of free-market economic theory, but also of economics *per se*. "Short shrift was given to anyone unfortunate enough to precede Smith." Yet Rothbard reveals a rich tradition—from the ancients (Greece, Rome, China), to the medieval scholastics. Rothbard shows, in fascinating and richly documented detail, that economic thought did not begin, or even reach its height, with the career of an eighteenth-century British Calvinist: "It all began, as usual, with the Greeks," the first discoverers of the concept and principles of natural law.

HELLENIC HERITAGE: THE GREEKS AND NATURAL LAW

Since economics had not yet separated itself out from the other sciences, Rothbard's view of ancient Greek economic thought is seen through the lens of culture and the philosophers. Plato is the archetypal totalitarian-mystic, the original oligarchist and precursor of all the vanguard parties to come. According to the Platonic school, dominant early on, the "limitations" imposed by natural law are intolerable, and therefore the goal is to "transcend" them. Alienated from his true self—which is eternal, transcending time and space—man is constantly trying to regain this godlike state. Overcoming this "alienation" has been, as Rothbard vividly demonstrates in the next five hundred or so pages, the motive and overriding purpose of scores of religious and ideological movements, from the Protestant Reformation to the secularized millennialism of Marx and the Communist movement—including the postmillennial pietist prophets of economic and social reform in America.

In spite of continuous and persistent error, and especially Plato's baleful influence, the progress of economic science made a giant leap forward with the advent of Aristotle, who, though continuing the Hellenic anticommercial bias, launched an effective polemic against Plato's oligarchical collectivism. Aristotle pointed out that the monolithism of Platonic society violates the natural law of human diversity. Since both parties benefit from any voluntary exchange, Platonic economics would punish both producers and consumers. In a detailed refutation of communal property, Aristotle argued that private property is more productive and more conducive to social peace. Also, private property is the inevitable adjunct of natural law, and thus cannot be abolished by government edict. The greatest of the Greek philosophers also made this important point: the system of private property affords men the chance to act morally, according to Aristotelian lights; that is, to practice philanthropy. Under Platonic communism, no such opportunity arises. Aristotle opposed Plato's idea that strict limits ought to be put on the accumulation of wealth by any individual, and believed that the inculcation of the aristocracy's asceticism in the general population was the only way to curb the unchecked desires of people for wealth and material possessions.[8]

Aristotle shared with Plato the aristocratic bias against commerce, and this Attic scorn for the entrepreneur had an enormous influence in later centuries, all of it unfortunate in the extreme. As Rothbard points out, Aristotelian thought was the philosophical basis of the Thomistic tradition. Through Saint Thomas Aquinas and his successors, the medieval proscription against "money-lending"—charging interest on loans—was based on the Aristotelian misconception of money. While recognizing the utility of such a commodity, Aristotle nonetheless condemned money-lending as "unnatural" on the grounds that it is "barren" and cannot, in and of itself, produce wealth. Therefore, the Greek aristocrat concluded, the charging of interest on a loan is "unnatural" and immoral. As Rothbard shows in subsequent chapters, it took generations of Thomist scholastics, through the early Middle Ages and right up until the late Renaissance, before the dire consequences of this Aristotelian error were undone.

Rothbard's irrepressible iconoclasm comes to the fore in his discussion of the unfortunate Pythagorean influence on Aristotle's economics, which infuses it with unnecessary mathematical terminology. "The only dubious benefit of this contribution," writes Rothbard, "was to give many happy hours to historians of economic thought attempting to read sophisticated modern analysis into Aristotle." But great thinkers, however elevated their greatness, "can slip into error and inconsistency, and even write gibberish on occasion. Many historians of thought do not seem able to recognize that simple fact."[9]

Rothbard skewers Aristotle's discussion of the reciprocity of exchange in the *Nichomachean Ethics*: Aristotle tells of an architect who exchanges a house for the shoes produced by a shoemaker, and goes on to posit, "the number of shoes exchanged for a house must therefore correspond to the ratio of builder to shoemaker. For if this be not so, there will be no exchange and no intercourse." Rothbard's response is: "Eh? How can there possibly be a ratio of builder to shoemaker? Much less an equating of that ratio to shoes/houses? In what *units* can men like builders and shoemakers be expressed? The correct answer is that there is no meaning, and that this particular exercise should be dismissed as an unfortunate example of Pythagorean quantophrenia."[10]

The effort by many to claim Aristotle as the forerunner of the labor theory of value is here debunked as "an elaborate wild goose chase." This homing in on a particular paragraph of the *Ethics* would prove extremely problematic for the science of economics in later centuries, as it includes Aristotle's dictum that for an exchange to take place, diverse goods and services "must be equated." According to Aristotle, for two people to exchange two different products, their value must be equal, otherwise the exchange would never have taken place. This is plain wrong, as the economists of the Austrian School were to point out centuries later. Products have no inherent worth; their market value is determined by the *preferences* of diverse consumers. As Rothbard argues, far from implying an equation of value, the exchange implies a "double inequality of subjective valuation."[11]

In the realm of methodology, Aristotle was a precursor of the Austrian School, in that he at least implicitly realized that the basis of all economics and philosophy consists of a few axiomatic concepts and can be imputed from these, the foremost being the necessity of human action. Rothbard cites the little-known work, the *Topics*, in which Aristotle lays out his philosophical analysis of human ends and means. These means, which he classifies as "instruments of production," garner their worth from the fact that their end product is useful to people. If a good is very desirable, then the means to produce it acquires its high value from this fact. He then proceeded to impute a series of ever more complex economic theories from axiomatic concepts: the necessity of human action, the pursuit of human ends by marshaling scarce means, the primordial fact of human diversity and inequality.

The Aristotelian roots of the Austrian School, and of free-market economics in general, are documented, at length, throughout these two volumes. As a philosophic system based on the supremacy of reason and the rules of logic, Aristotlianism provided the conceptual framework and context for much of the economic thought of the next two thousand years. But in the period immediately following Aristotle, that is, after the fourth century B.C.E., "the rest of the ancient world, and even Greece before and after these centuries, was essentially a desert of economic thought."[12] In spite of the fact that advanced economic institutions existed in China, Mesopotamia, and elsewhere—perhaps even more advanced, in some ways, than in Aristotle's Greece—little or no economic thought emerged from these civilizations. As Rothbard puts it, "here is an important indication that, contrary to Marxists and other economic determinists, economic thought and ideas do not simply emerge as a reflex of the development of economic institutions."[13]

How, then, to explain this relatively brief but spectacular flowering of economic thought in ancient Greece? The answer is in the broadly philosophic outlook of the early Greeks, who sought to derive truth from a few self-evident axioms, that is, in the methodology of the Greek philosophers. Aristotle, unlike today's positivists, believed in the objective existence of natural law; on this foundation of universal and apodictic truth, the epistemological structure of post-Hellenic European civilization was built. In the great edifice of Hellenic thought, there were many rooms, but all were held up by the same pillars of reason and logic; all were part of the great house of what the Austrian School called praxeology, that is, the study of human action, with economic science as a subset of this broad field. In the modern world, however, in which information is fragmented into "bits" and the positivist model of "empirical" evidence is used to "test" economic theory under "laboratory conditions," the wisdom of the philosophers is replaced by the phony "science" of the positivists with their pocket calculators, their computer models, and all the conceits of modernity.

But the world would be spared the rule of these nerds for two millennia; meanwhile, the death of Aristotle meant the decline of Hellenic economic thought, and of philosophical thought in general. Against the proprivate property doctrines of Democritus and Aristotle, Diogenes, the first Cynic, preached that money is the root of all evil; in pursuit of virtue, he lived in a barrel and he and his followers took a vow of poverty. While old Diogenes is a revered figure, who has come down to us as the image of a wise man perpetually searching for truth, Rothbard reveals that he was virulent in his view of man as a degraded creature. Prometheus, the hero who defied the gods and brought fire to mankind, was to Diogenes a villain; the growth of human knowledge, and progress itself, were, in the view of the Cynics, evils and not gifts.

The zigzag decline of Greek philosophy underwent a zig with the rise of the Stoics, who explicitly attacked egalitarianism—"Nothing can prevent some seats in the theater from being better than others," quipped Chrysippus, a leading Stoic—and countered the dictum of Diogenes that "money is the root of all evil" with one of their own: "the wise man will turn three somersaults for an adequate fee."[14]

The Stoics were the first to systematize the natural law as it applies to *individuals*. With the political decline of the Greek city-states, and the demise of the *polis*, the Stoics were set free to apply the natural law not to a small tribe but to the whole of mankind; and to construct an ethic as a universal standard against which all states are judged. "For the first time," writes Rothbard, "positive law became continually subject to a transcendent critique based on the universal and eternal nature of man."[15]

Rothbard traces the Aristotelian-Stoic influence from the later Roman Stoics: the famous Roman statesman and rhetorician, Cicero, and the Roman jurists who framed the legal tradition that was the basis of the English common law. While no real economic thought can be said to have existed at this point, some Roman jurists declared that property rights are inherent in the natural law. In an important sense, then, it was this spirit that moved Cicero to "contribute to Western thought a great antistatist parable":

> Cicero told the story of a pirate who was dragged into the court
> of Alexander the Great. When Alexander denounced him for

piracy and brigandage and asked the pirate what impulse had led him to make the sea unsafe with his one little ship, the pirate trenchantly replied, "the same impulse which has led you [Alexander] to make the whole world unsafe."[16]

KAUDER'S THESIS: CULTURE, ECONOMY, AND STATE

The richness of anecdote and analysis, the transparency of the language, the scope of the research, and the lightning flashes of wit that illuminate these two volumes are impossible to summarize. That material so densely packed with information can be transmitted with such a stylish touch is, in itself, no mean literary achievement. Yet, in the face of so much material—our analysis has so far concerned itself only with the first thirty pages!—the author also manages to not only maintain but intensify his focus, while drawing the reader into a compelling narrative. In this, the age of hyperpole, books are routinely described as "monumental." In the case of the *History of Economic Thought*, however, the term is truly applicable in the sense that, both in style and content, this book is Rothbard at the very apex of his form, not only as a writer but as a teacher and theoretician. In the very broad sweep of this magisterial work is the embodiment of his method: not economics as a fragmented pseudoscience, but as a field integrated with politics, ethics, religion, and philosophy; in short, not a "hard" and narrow science, like physics, but a much broader and "softer" one—the "science" of what it means to be human.

In reading the *History of Economic Thought*, then, we are simultaneously reading a history not only of philosophy, and politics, but most importantly of religion. Here we encounter the controversial and, as Rothbard proves, entirely correct thesis of economic historian

Emil Kauder, so central to this work—that Adam Smith, far from being the founder of economics, was the author of a major error that diverted the field away from a proto-Austrian subjective utility theory of value that emphasized relative scarcity, and substituted the labor theory of value. Not only the Spanish and Italian scholastics of the Middle Ages and the early Renaissance, but also the French economists of the eighteenth century had a far more sophisticated conception of the market than Smith: the earlier pre-Smithian emphasis had been on subjective valuation, entrepreneurship, and prices fluctuating with demand. Smith changed all that. He shifted the focus of economics to a labor theory of value and, as Rothbard put it, "a dominant focus on the unchanging long-run 'natural price' equilibrium, a world where entrepreneurship was assumed out of existence." Kauder's historical analysis would grant Smith the dubious honor of being "a necessary precursor of Karl Marx."[17]

Kauder's thesis, however, is much broader than the debunking of Adam Smith. As Rothbard relates in his introduction, Kauder's theory posed the question: "Why is it, for example, that the subjective utility tradition flourished on the Continent, especially in France and Italy, and then revived particularly in Austria, whereas the labor and cost of production theories developed especially in Great Britain?" Kauder attributed the difference to the profound influence of religion: the scholastics were, of course, Catholics, and France, Italy, and Austria were Catholic countries. Furthermore, these economists influenced by Catholicism "emphasized consumption as the goal of production and consumer utility and enjoyment as, at least in moderation, valuable activities and goals. The British tradition, on the contrary, beginning with Smith himself, was Calvinist, and reflected the Calvinist insistence on hard work and labor toil as not only good but a great good in itself, whereas consumer enjoyment is at best a necessary evil, a mere requisite to labor and production."[18]

Catholicism, distinguished by its relatively humanistic doctrines, translated into the idea that the goal of production is consumption, that consumption is not sinful, and life is to be enjoyed. Lodged in this mental context is the implication that economic values are subjective—since different things are enjoyed by different people.

In the Protestant ethos, however, the doctrinal and emotional atmosphere is quite different, as is the resulting economic theory. To begin with, Protestantism was a rebellion against the alleged slackening of the true (original) spirit of Christ in His Church. Particularly galling to the rebels was the sophisticated economic analysis of the Spanish scholastics, who—by the mid to late Middle Ages—had swept away the medieval ban on charging interest for a loan ("usury") in all but the most formal sense. Second, the Calvinist emphasis on labor as a good in and of itself—toil to the glory of God—was conducive to the labor theory of value, which imputed some inherent measure of worth to the products of man's labor. The economic implications of the Protestant-Catholic free will debate ought to be clear enough: if, as the original Calvinists asserted, man is predestined to walk a certain path, if the elect are chosen not by their acts but by the unknowable will of God, then surely the economic choices of such creatures are similarly predestined. Unlike the Catholic theorists of the natural law tradition, the Calvinist and Lutheran ideologues rejected reason as the framework of ethics, and instead insisted on divine revelation as the only path to truth. "If reason cannot be used to frame an ethic," writes Rothbard, "this means that Luther and Calvin had to, in essence, throw out natural law, and in doing so, they jettisoned the basic criteria developed over the centuries by which to criticize the despotic actions of the state." The stance of the Protestant sects, at least at first, was that "the powers that be are ordained by God, and that therefore the king, no matter how tyrannical, is divinely appointed and must always be obeyed."[19]

The statist agenda of Protestantism coincided with the goals of "secularist apologists for an absolute state" and "these two seemingly contrasting groups were closer than merely having the same enemy. In many ways, they were twins and not simply fortuitous allies."[20]

In the age of the rising nation-state, absolutist monarchs and their court intellectuals found the Protestant return to early Christian "purity" to be to their advantage. The seizure of church property, the abolition of a rival center of power, the chance to set up a new, state-run church: throughout northern Europe, the Protestant revolution moved to seize power, throw out the church—and usher in even more radical millenarian sects, such as the various groups of Anabaptists, whose radical communism and militant murderousness is described in detail by Rothbard in his chapter on "Protestants and Catholics."

While the original doctrines of Luther and Calvin were highly conducive to state-worship, persecution of Protestants in Catholic countries, particularly France, led to the development of libertarian theories of resistance to state authority in Protestant circles. Forced to abandon the Calvinist doctrine of unconditional obedience to the king, Huguenot writers reconstructed a natural rights theory of popular sovereignty. In contrast to the much-touted thesis of sociologist Max Weber, which traced the rise of capitalism to the rise of Protestantism (or Calvinism), Rothbard makes the point that "the popular idea of Calvinism as 'modern' and revolutionary, as the creator of radical and democratic thought" is grossly oversimplified. What really happened is that Calvinism, originally statist and absolutist, "only became revolutionary and antityrannical under the pressure of opposing Catholic regimes, which drove the Calvinists back to natural law and popular sovereignty *motifs* in Catholic scholastic thought."[21]

Rothbard's critique of the Weberian thesis is that it ignores the real roots of capitalist development in the early Italian city-states, as well as in Antwerp and southern Germany. The Rothbardian thesis is precisely the opposite of Weber's. As Rothbard puts it in his discussion of the differences between the Calvinist and Catholic visions:

> The focus, then, both in Catholic countries and in scholastic thought, became very different from that of Calvinism. The scholastic focus was on consumption, the consumer, as the goal of labor and production. Labor was not so much a good in itself as a means toward consumption on the market. The Aristotelian balance, or golden mean, was considered a requisite of the good life, a life leading to happiness in keeping with the nature of man.[22]

In economic terms, the southern European Catholic culture "emphasized the joys of consumption, as well as of leisure, in addition to the importance of productive effort." On the other hand, the wintry Calvinists of the north stressed "a rather grim emphasis on work and on saving" and condemned leisure as "idleness." All of which "fitted with the iconoclasm that reached its height in Calvinism—the condemnation of the enjoyment of the senses as a means of expressing religious devotion." Anyone else would have simply left it at that: a simple statement of his argument, with no further evidence offered. In a typical Rothbardian flourish, however, the author illuminates his subject with a flash of insight: "One of the expressions of this conflict," he writes, "came over religious holidays, which Catholic countries enjoyed in abundance. To the Puritans, this was idolatry; even Christmas was not supposed to be an occasion for sensate enjoyment."[23]

Here is the clincher that makes the case—a vivid and unforgettable example that brings home the centrality of culture and religion to the evolution of economic thought. Under the accumulated weight of evidence—and it is considerable—Rothbard shows that militant asceticism, from Plato's dictatorship of the philosopher-kings to the postmillennial pietism that energized the Progressive Era "reforms" of American capitalism, whenever and wherever it arises is inevitably a rationale for tyranny and invariably an occasion for blood-letting on a massive scale. This is a major theme of the *History of Economic Thought*, which runs through all of Rothbard's writings, both major and minor: the importance of human enjoyment, of values, of *pleasure* in life, and therefore in economics.

MACHIAVELLI AND MERCANTILISM: A LESSON FOR TODAY

A complete and thorough survey of the material covered in this thousand-page-plus *magnum opus* would at least double the size of this modest volume, and is, in any case, beyond the scope of the present work. Having whetted the reader's appetite for the real thing, there is space only to describe the highlights, and one that stands out is Rothbard's section on Machiavelli.

In and of itself, this section could stand alone as a masterpiece of integrative analysis. Here Rothbard subjects the "value-free" pose of the modern social scientist to the rigors of a libertarian class analysis, and the results are revealing: "There is a profound sense, too, in which Machiavelli was the founder of modern political science. For the modern 'policy scientist' . . . is a person who has put himself quite comfortably in the role of advisor to the prince or, more broadly, to the ruling class. As a pure technician, then, this counselor realistically advises the ruling class on how to achieve their goals, which, as Machiavelli sees, boils down to . . . maintaining and expanding their power." There is, however, one important sense in which the two differ: "For Niccolo Machiavelli never had the presumption—or the cunning—to claim to be a true scientist because he is 'value-free.' There is no pretend value-freedom in Old Nick. He has simply replaced the goals of Christian virtue by *another* contrasting set of moral principles: that of maintaining and expanding the power of the prince." The section on Machiavelli is entitled " 'Old Nick': preacher of evil or first value-free political scientist?" at the end of which Rothbard concludes that Machiavelli "was *both* the founder of modern political science *and* a notable preacher of evil." This is followed by a fascinating survey of sixteenth-century absolutist thought, in which Machiavelli's followers and outright imitators sought to gain the ear of the prince with similarly amoral advice.[24]

The mercantilist economics that accompanied the rise of the European nation-state, from the sixteenth to the eighteenth centuries, is described by Rothbard as: "a system of state-building, of Big Government, of heavy royal expenditure, of high taxes, of . . . inflation and deficit finance, of war, imperialism, and the aggrandizing of the nation-state. In short, a politicoeconomic system very much like that of the present day, with the unimportant exception that now large-scale industry rather than mercantile commerce is the main focus of the economy."[25]

This raises an interesting point, which will be raised again, and that is: To whom is the *History* addressed? Surely a work of this kind, dealing as it does with a specialty subtopic of economics, the history of economic thought, is of interest chiefly to other scholars, and, perhaps, *only* to them. That would be true if the author of this work were anyone other than Murray N. Rothbard. In Rothbard's case, as we have seen, scholarship—like toil of any kind—was not an end in itself, but only a means to an end: the pleasure of living in a free society, or at least in a society where the prospect of such freedom is not too distant. The *History* is a long and complex narrative that can be read on many levels. In addition to addressing an audience of scholars, economists, and intellectuals in general, in this passage (and in many others) Rothbard was speaking directly to libertarians, as he so often did, and, through them, to Everyman.

As Rothbard shows in his detailed description, the political landscape of seventeenth-century France bears more than a passing resemblance to our own. Not only the lavish and brazen corruption of the ruling elite, but especially its artistic pretensions and vaunting. The story of the origins of the revered French Academy in the mercantilist schemes of Jean-Baptist Colbert, King Louis XIV's economic advisor, as well as the various other artistic cartels, such as the Academy of Painting and Sculpture—"given a legal monopoly of art instruction"—is related by Rothbard in riveting detail. Not even music and the theater were immune from Colbertian cartellization. Money poured into the arts in the form of various subsidies and subventions. "Writers, artists, scientists, historians, philosophers, mathematicians, and essayists" were all feeding, in large numbers, at the public trough:

> It was a subvention that put to shame any contemporary national endowment for the humanities or national science foundation. The outpouring truly subverted any sort of spirit of independence that French intellectuals might have attained. The mind of a whole nation had been subverted.[26]

Again, the analogy to our own time, with an entire class of court intellectuals living off the largesse of the state, is painfully obvious. If the past is any guide, however, perhaps all is not lost. Parallel to this history of error was a growing reaction to the excesses of the absolutist state, which reached its apogee in the outlandish extravagance of Louis XIV, the so-called Sun-King. Rothbard takes us on a historical guided tour of the protolibertarian movements of the seventeenth and eighteenth centuries, from the "croquants' rebellion" against confiscatory taxation in

1636 to the laissez-faire theorists and economists who arose to challenge the mercantilist status quo.[27]

A well-organized and articulate opposition to *Colbertisme* and the Machiavellian conception of the state and its rulers arose in France, dedicated to free trade, *laissez-faire*, and limited government. Much of this was centered in the Roman Catholic clergy, which reasserted the Aristotelian-Thomistic tradition, and made a special point of driving home the key connection between imperialism and war as the engine of and rationale for domestic tyranny, especially ruinous taxation. In an anonymous pamphlet, written in the form of an open letter to the king, the greatest and most radical of the clerical antiabsolutists, Francois de Salignan de la Mothe, Archbishop Fenelon of Cambrai, blamed the Sun King's ministers for leading His Radiance astray:

> They have increased your revenues and your expenditures to the infinite. They have elevated you to the heavens . . . and impoverished all of France so as to introduce and maintain an incurable and monstrous luxury at court. They wanted to raise you on the ruins of all classes in the state, as if you could become great by oppressing your subjects.[28]

The evil ministers, concludes Fenelon, are determined to destroy their enemies, no matter what the cost to the nation or the crown. The minions of the Sun King have made the king's name "odious" because they have not wanted citizens but "only slaves," and have "caused bloody wars." They have driven loyal subjects to rebellion "by exacting from them for your wars, the bread which they have endeavored to earn with the sweat from their brows."[29]

As religious instructor to the king's mistress and tutor to the Duke of Burgundy, grandson of Louis XIV and second in line to the throne, Fenelon was in an excellent position to wield influence, and he used it to the utmost. The young duke was soon Fenelon's devoted disciple, and the pro–*laissez-faire* Burgundians at court pinned all their hopes on the duke's ascension to the throne. Fenelon's political novel, *Telemaque*, was written as an educational text for the young duke. In it, a young prince named Telemaque wanders the ancient world in search of advice on how to govern. Invariably, the advice proffered was: *laissez-faire.* "Above all," said a character called Mentor, a wise Phoenician, "never do anything to interfere with trade." In the mythical land of Salente, "the liberty of commerce was entire," and trade "was similar to the ebb and flow of the tide."[30]

The young Duke of Burgundy's education was further enhanced by Fenelon's engagement of Francois Le Blanc, author of a major book on monetary theory, to write a treatise on the consequences of state action in the foreign policy realm. Fenelon believed "war is the greatest of evils,"[31] and was determined to stamp the young duke with the antimilitarist imprimatur. Unfortunately, Le Blanc died before his tome could be completed.

The death of the Grand Dauphin, son of Louis XIV, meant that the Duke of Burgundy was next in line. Fenelon and the Burgundians were exultant. Their joy was short-lived, however, as the Duke of Burgundy was struck down by measles the next year, along with his wife and eldest son. This section again raises the question of whom Rothbard is really addressing in the *History of Economic Thought*. For here, in the middle of a historical narrative, the author takes time out to speak directly to the libertarian cadre of the future: "The tragic end of the Burgundy circle," he writes, "illuminates a crucial strategic flaw in the plans, not only of the Burgundy circle, but also of the physiocrats, Turgot, and other laissez-faire thinkers of the later eighteenth century. For their hopes and their strategic vision were invariably to work within the matrix of the monarchy and its virtually absolute rule. The idea, in short, was to get into court, influence the corridors of power, and induce the king to adopt libertarian ideas and impose a laissez-faire revolution."[32]

In writing those lines, it is hard to imagine that Rothbard did not have his erstwhile comrades at the Cato Institute in mind. Their strategy of going after the elites, of "cozying up to Power," as Rothbard put it, was precisely that of Fenelon's: a court cabal hoping to pull off a palace revolution. He knew, and not only theoretically, but from his own experience, all about the unfortunate consequences of such a strategy. "Reliance on the good will of the king, however, suffered from several inherent defects," continued Rothbard, intent on impressing this lesson indelibly on the minds of future libertarian students of strategy,

> One, as in the case of the Duke of Burgundy, was reliance on the existence and good health of one person. A second is a more systemic flaw: Even if one can convince the king that the interests of his subjects require liberty and laissez-faire, the standard argument that *his own* revenue will increase proportionately to their prosperity is a shaky one. For the king's revenue might well be maximized, certainly in the short run and even in the long run, by tyrannically sweating his subjects to attain the maximum possible revenue. And relying on the altruism of the monarch is a shaky reed at best. For all these reasons, appealing to a monarch to impose laissez-faire from above can only be a losing strategy.[33]

Rothbard did not just leave it at that, but, typically, suggests "a far better strategy" which, in his view, would have been to "organize a mass opposition from below among the ruled and exploited masses." Unfortunately,

> the erudite and sophisticated laissez-faire thinkers of the seventeenth and eighteenth centuries . . . would have rebuffed such a suggested strategy as certainly inconvenient and probably

lunatic. . . . Not least of all, men of influential and privileged status themselves are rarely inclined to toss all their privileges aside to engage in the lonely and dangerous task of working outside the inherited political system.[34]

This is the obverse of Rothbard's optimism, the sense that, while the ultimate victory of liberty may be all but inevitable, in the short run it seems as if liberty's partisans are not only few in number but also faint of heart. This feeling, often a sinking one, that "nobody else is doing it"—whether upholding the praxeologic or Misesian school of Austrian economics, or preserving the legacy of the Old Right, or pointing out the conservative statism of Herbert Hoover as the real precursor of the modern welfare state—meant that it was up to him, personally, to fill the gap. His great achievement is that he managed to fill so many gaps in such a relatively short lifetime.

The growing sophistication and popularity of laissez-faire economics, and the revival of natural law as the conceptual framework for the new libertarianism, was exemplified by the laissez-faire utilitarians who appeared on the scene at the tail-end of the Sun King's long reign. Unlike all-too-many alleged "libertarians" today, the laissez-faire French theorists knew that war, as Rothbard put it, is "the standard excuse for maintaining the crippling interventions of government." Exploitation and war were the natural consequences of statism, said the laissez-faire economist Pierre le Pesant Sieur de Boisguilbert, while harmony and peace were the result of markets unregulated by royal decree.[35]

The French utilitarians saw the market as the economic outcome of natural law allowed to operate free of coercion and distortion. The great advance here was that such theorists as Paul Seigneur de Belesbat and Pierre le Pesant de Boiusguilbert were in harmony with the new mechanistic cosmologies of Isaac Newton and others of the late seventeenth century. As opposed to the mysticism of

Fenelon, theirs was a rationalist creed, "not in itself anti-Christian," but "it certainly replaced the ascetic aspects of Christianity with an optimistic, more man-centered, creed; and also it was consistent with the rising religion of deism, in which God was the creator, or clock-winder, who created the mechanism of the universe and its self-subsistent natural laws, and then retired from the scene."[36]

Toward the end of his life, and especially as he was focusing on completing the *History of Economic Thought*, there was much speculation that Rothbard had suddenly found religion, and there were rumors that he had converted to Roman Catholicism. As Joey Rothbard put it, "if only it were so."[37] The above-quoted view of a God who has, perhaps, "retired from the scene," seems closest to his most sympathetic view of religious doctrine. The speculation about his embrace of the church was fueled by his praise of the Catholic scholastics as the precursors of the Austrian economists, and his embrace of Kauder's religiocultural thesis will only add more fuel to the fire. But his real views on the nature and importance of religion in human affairs were more complex than that. In a 1990 letter, he attacked the antireligious, and especially anti-Christian, stance of the typical libertarian. Strategically, it is obvious that a militant atheism will only alienate the great majority of Americans, and so insistence on this point will doom the libertarian movement to impotence. "But there is also the question of principle," he continued:

> I am convinced that it is no accident that freedom, limited government, natural rights, and the market economy only really developed in Western civilization. I am convinced that the reason is the attitudes developed by the Christian Church in general, and the Roman Catholic Church in particular. One, in contrast to Greek thought, where the city-state . . . was the locus of virtue and action, Christianity, with its unique focus on (a) the *individual* as created in

the image of God, and (b) in the central mystery of the Incarnation, God created his Son as a fully human person—[this] means that each individual and his salvation is of central divine concern.

Rothbard went on to point out the key role played by the Christians who took over the libertarian aspects of Roman civil law and property law, and the Christian Scholastics. Add to this the transnationality of the Church, the fact that

it was not tied to any one king or state and therefore served as a vital check upon state power. The concept of tyrannicide and of the right of revolution was developed by Catholic Scholastics. Locke (and his followers in the American Revolution) was a Protestant (Anglican) Scholastic, developing and sharpening Catholic Scholastic doctrine. Thus, even though I am not a believer, I hail Christianity, and especially Catholicism as the underpinning of liberty. (And also of art, music, and architecture, but that's another topic.)

In the same letter, he reiterates his atheism: "On the religion question, we paleolibertarians are not theocrats," he writes. "Obviously, I could not be myself, both as a libertarian and as an atheist." However, he continued, the left-libertarian hostility to religion, based as it is on ignorance and the bitterness of "aging adolescent rebels against bourgeois America," is "monstrous."[38]

Rothbard's attitude toward religion, and especially Catholicism, illustrates an interesting point: here is a man attacked by his enemies for being "intolerant" who could hail a doctrine he did not share as the "underpinning of liberty." Some intolerance! Rothbard's mind, far from being narrowed by ideology, was broadened by the depth of his commitment to liberty. In his lifelong battle against statism, Rothbard embraced all possible allies, and took his victories where he could find them.

In assessing the British mercantilist writers, Rothbard continues his theme of the vital importance of religion in the development of economic thought. Unlike the scholastics, Calvinists, and Catholic royalists of France, the Anglicans upheld the view that the king and God were one and the same. It was a stance rooted in the origins of Anglicanism as an instrument in the hands of a king to assert his dominion over the church. This merging of the temporal and the spiritual represented the extreme wing of royalist thought from early in the sixteenth century to the beginning of the seventeenth. As in heaven, so on earth, or, as Rothbard writes: "the 'governmental' and social ranking alleged to exist in the heavenly sphere must be duplicated in earthly government and in social life."[39]

SIR FRANCIS BACON: A REVISIONIST VIEW

Another Rothbardian theme permeating the *History* is historical revisionism. Here we learn that "Sir Thomas Smith, rather than his associate Sir Thomas Gresham (c. 1519–79), was responsible for the first expression of 'Gresham's law' in England."[40] We also get the real scoop on the alleged "economic liberalism" of the famous Chief Justice Sir Edward Coke, held up by the English Marxist historian Christopher Hill as the fountainhead of England's *laissez-faire* activists. In the Marxist view, Coke's supposedly "antimonopoly" decisions "were an expression of the alleged commitment of a rising class of puritan merchants to economic liberalism and laissez-faire."[41] Rothbard shows that Coke's entire political career was based on his support of mercantilism, not laissez-faire, and makes the important point that Coke wanted the Parliament, rather than the king, to administer the mercantile state.

Rothbard's puncturing of yet another inflated reputation, that of Sir Francis Bacon (1561–1626), is the author at his polemical best.

Lauded by the French *Encyclopedie* as "the greatest, the most universal, and the most eloquent of all philosophers," and honored to this day as a giant of social thought, Bacon's status as the "prophet of empiricism" makes him a prime target of this "Austrian" history of economic thought. As "the prophet of primitive and naive empiricism, the guru of fact-grubbing," Bacon was a "metaempiricist" whose role was to exhort *everybody else* to go out and collect the facts, just the facts, *all* the facts, "and knowledge, including theoretical knowledge, will rise phoenixlike, self-supporting and self-sustained, out of the mountainous heap of data."[42]

Bacon divided all knowledge into two categories, divine and natural. In the first category, information was received as *revelation*, directly through God and His agents. On the other hand, knowledge of the natural world could only be garnered via the empiricist method of "induction," by which, as Rothbard describes the process, "enormous masses of details could somehow form themselves into general truths."[43]

Such a method, Rothbard points out, is

> completely wrong about how science has ever done its work. No scientific truths are ever discovered by inchoate fact-digging. The scientist must first have framed hypotheses; in short, the scientist, before gathering and collating facts, must have a pretty good idea of what to look for, and why. Once in a while, social scientists get misled by Baconian notions into *thinking* that their knowledge is "purely factual," without presuppositions and therefore "scientific," when what this really means is that their presuppositions and assumptions remain hidden from view.[44]

The world was either matter or spirit. In the former case, knowledge "was purely sensate and empirical," or else, in the case of the latter, arrived at through divine revelation. In both cases, reason was ruled out of order.[45]

In the Baconian worldview, then, the natural law of the Catholic scholastics and their Protestant sympathizers was thrown out, and replaced by ethical relativism. Without natural law, the brakes on state power and its application were broken, and the state was given the red light to roll over individual citizens.

Rothbard's thesis that Bacon's renown is because "he succeeded in capturing the *Zeitgeist*; [that] he was the right man for his notions at the right time" is backed up with considerable evidence, most startling of which is Bacon's involvement in the perfervid world of seventeenth-century mysticism. Bacon's "scientific" pretensions have recently been pricked, Rothbard points out, by the revelation that he was a member (or sympathizer) of the mystical-alchemist Rosicrucian Order. The Rosicrucians, who based their doctrines on the mystical hermetic writings and what they imagined to be the Jewish Cabala, believed that Adam's sin was not in gaining knowledge but in refusing it. This knowledge, or Ancient Wisdom, is still accessible to man through magic and the enlightened wisdom of rulers who, "possessed of this divine knowledge, will guide man to perfection and happiness by fulfilling his true God-like nature."[46]

It was a time when "occult 'knowledge' was definitely part of the new spirit of the age," and also, as Rothbard points out, it was necessary to update and modernize "the simple-minded proclamation of the absolute power and glory of the English king." Bacon's "scientific realism," writes Rothbard, "was perfectly suited to the new task."[47]

Bacon, an admirer of Machiavelli, consciously modeled his political writings after the style of Old Nick, addressing himself directly to the king and acting the role of a general counselor—a role he played in real life. In reviewing Bacon's career as a statesmen who was born into Britain's power elite, Rothbard points to this as among the chief reasons for Bacon's inflated reputation as a social and scientific theorist. In a vivid account of Bacon's colorful career, Rothbard emphasizes Bacon's role as writer of official apologias, and chronicles his rise to power as Keeper of the Royal Seal, and then Lord Chancellor. Bacon was accused of bribery, and convicted, confessing but also claiming that taking bribes "never affected his judgment, and that his own 'intentions' remained forever 'pure.' Judging him by his own empirical method, however, one may be permitted to be skeptical of such 'metaphysical' notions."[48]

Rothbard's discussion of the Baconian movement in England is a fascinating survey of numerous personalities, all of them colorful, and the effect is to give the reader an overview of the "enlightened" intellectual elite of seventeenth-century England. These were the followers of the "new science," a mix of real scientists and their camp followers. While the Baconians were known as "the favorite philosophers and theoreticians of the puritan country gentry," as Rothbard puts it, they were

> never truly committed to any particular form of government. Like Bacon himself, they could flourish under an absolute monarchy. Monarchy, republic, Parliament, Crown, Church—all these forms of government made no particular difference to these "scientific," "value-free" would-be rulers of the nation.[49]

The Baconians, as polymorphous "seekers after the main chance," as Rothbard bluntly phrases it, adaptable to any regime as long as it is "sufficiently statist"—and provided they have "ample scope for [their] dreams of power and 'science' "—were a wild and wacky bunch, immersed in numerological and kabbalistic mysticism and cultism. They imagined themselves to be an "invisible college," and went in for the occult as just another branch of "knowledge" to be "scientifically" investigated. As Rothbard relates, "the seventeenth-century enthusiasm for the sciences, building upon the quasiunderground age-old numerological mysticism of the hermetics and cabala tradition, led to an arrogant frenzy of enthusiasm for quantitative and mathematical study of social life as well, among the scientists and especially their cheering sections." Rothbard then cites the eminent Harvard sociologist Pitirim Sorokin's 1956 book *Fads and Foibles in Modern Sociology* in referring to this frenzy, "from that day to the present, as 'quantophrenia' and 'metromania.' " Rothbard's hilarious account of the founding of the Royal Society and its veritable orgy of useless and obsessive record-keeping of meaningless "data" traces the modern quantophrenic tendency back to its Baconian roots.[50]

The reigning philosophers of the day—Baruch Spinoza, René Descartes, Gottfried Leibniz, Isaac Newton—were constructing what Sorokin describes as "a universal quantitative science, *Pantometrika*, with its branches of *Psychometrika*, *Ethicometrika*, and *Sociometrika*." The Baconian contribution to *Sociometrika* was Sir William Petty's *Political Arithmatic*, a Baconian tract that disdained intellectual arguments in favor of focusing solely on "number, weight, and measure," a slogan that appeared with maddening regularity throughout Petty's works. Here is the first occurrence of the modern "data"-obsessed "social scientist," who, armed with his infallible statistics, purports to measure social and economic interactions down to the hundredth percentile.

Petty—whose interesting life Rothbard captures in all its baroque detail—was the author of a proposal, in his *Political Arithmetic*, to forcibly transfer the populations of Ireland and Scotland to England, in the name of increasing labor productivity. It is particularly delightful to discover here that Jonathan Swift the satirist directed his most famous barbs at the Baconians, whose pomposity certainly made them vulnerable to ridicule.

In *Gulliver's Travels*, Rothbard points out, Swift effectively lampooned the crazed scientists of Laputa and elsewhere who were putting in effect what would now be called the Baconian 'research program.' " In *A Modest Proposal*, Swift parodied the pompous style and faux-mathematical precision of the numerology-obsessed Petty. Mocking the statistical mysticism of Petty's text, in which he seriously proposed subsidizing the birth of children to unmarried Irish women (again, in the name of increased labor productivity), Swift offered his own modest proposal, similarly salted with statistical verities. Reckoning "the number of souls in this kingdom" at "one million and a half," and making deductions for the well-off, the deaths, the miscarriages, and other factors, Swift then arrives at the figure of "a hundred and twenty thousand children of poor parents annually born." Arguing that there is no way to support these children, Swift then declares that he has heard it from an American in London that a one-year-old baby makes "a most delicious, nourishing, and wholesome food, whether stewed, roasted, baked, or boiled." As Rothbard puts it, "Swift then goes on to demonstrate, in the best value-free, numerological, empiricist Pettyite manner, the economic advantages of selling 100,000 children per annum to be eaten."[51]

The revival of "political arithmetic" in the modern era, in the form of "econometrics," awaits the birth of another Swift to parody its pretensions to "scientific" exactitude. These neo-Baconians (or, reaching back farther still, neo-Pythagoreans), eager to establish some theoretical precedent for their brand of numerological economics (aside from Rosicrucianism), have latched on to the writings of Charles Davenant, whom Rothbard describes as "an attorney who spent his life scrambling for the main chance." Rothbard's biographical sketch of Davenant, like many of the portraits that hang in this gallery of rogues and heroes, correlates character with ideology. Deposed from his post of commissioner of excise by the Revolution of 1688, Davenant took up his pen in defense of the cause nearest and dearest to his heart: his own financial interest. As Rothbard puts it, "all of his publications centered around special pleading for his own political interests, a quest for subsidy or for resuming his high post in the government." His *Essay upon the Ways and Means of supplying the War* urged an increase in the excise tax, "coincidentally Davenant's own area of expertise." Davenant's next campaign was launched to secure employment with the East India Company: a series of books defending the East India trade against the "bullionists" and proto-protectionists. But a job was not forthcoming until 1698, when the East India Company finally rewarded him and he regained his lost political positions, becoming commissioner of imports and exports in 1703. Davenant, a devout advocate of "political arithmetic," devoted his writings largely to politics after the restoration of his political fortunes, and, as Rothbard puts it, his stance "shifted with the political winds," the one consistent theme being his relentless scramble for the main chance. Rothbard relates that "he ended his career generally scorned and trusted by none," broke and living off the generosity of an old friend, the Duke of Chandos.[52] If not for the sudden "discovery" of Davenant's "law of demand," offered without proof in his *Essay Upon the Balance of Trade* (1699), "Davenant would be a forgotten and no-account minor mercantilist writer."[53]

Before getting into the canonization of Davenant by the high priests of modern econometrics, the function and beauty of these mini-biographies, such as the one of Davenant, is worth noting. "History," wrote Rothbard in the introduction, "necessarily means narrative, discussion of real persons as well as their abstract theories, and includes triumphs, tragedies, and conflicts, conflicts which are often moral as well as purely theoretical."[54] The personalities of the economists, the circumstances of their lives, their ambitions, their politics, their religious beliefs—Rothbard believed that all these factors, far from being peripheral, to be included in a history of economic thought for the sake of "color," have had a decisive impact on the course of economic science. Mercantilism, itself a coalition of special pleaders—each claiming subsidies, privileges, monopolies, and other entitlements—was a system well-suited to a man like Davenant. His career as a political and intellectual mercenary embodies the economic "principles" of mercantilism, such as they are.

As for Davenant's alleged discovery of the so-called law of demand—the contention that scarcity of, say, wheat, will not merely raise the price, "but that the effect will be a definite quantitative relation"—Rothbard disposes of this absurdity in a few paragraphs. Davenant's famous tables of prices, even if they were based on precise and complete statistical evidence, would only hold true for those years, in those locations, and only as a subjective reflection in the minds of the consumers at a given moment in time.[55]

As the arithmetical apologists for the status quo gave way to the English Civil War of the 1640s, the rise of the first mass libertarian movement, the Levellers, marks a milestone in the history of the struggle for liberty. The Leveller program—free markets, free press, freedom of religion, and free trade—lost out to the Cromwellians, much to the detriment of the republican cause, which collapsed after Cromwell's death. The Rothbardian theme of the key influence of the Catholic scholastics as the continuators of the Aristotelian–Thomistic natural law tradition comes into play in his discussion of John Locke, the great libertarian theorist whose influence in the colonies a century later would result in the first successful libertarian revolution.

ZIG AND ZAG: FROM CANTILLON TO SMITH

Rothbard's biographical sketch of Locke dramatizes his conception of how economic and political thought evolve: not as static doctrines, or paradigms, operating in a vacuum, but competing ideas operating in a context of give-and-take. In discussing Locke's debt to Lord Ashley, the first Earl of Shaftsbury, a leader of the classical liberal movement of the day—who, it turns out, converted Locke to a natural rights–libertarian philosophy—Rothbard complains that the significance of this relation "has been hidden all too often by historians who have had an absurdly monastic horror of how political theory and philosophy often develop: in the heat of political and ideological battle." The prevailing attitude seems to be that it is necessary to construct "an idealized image of Locke the pure and detached philosopher, separate from the grubby and mundane political concerns of the real world."[56]

This, as we have seen, was the exact opposite of the approach taken by Rothbard; just as he did not detach economics from politics, religion, and cultural ideology, so he did not believe the scholar had to detach himself from life. Rothbard, the warrior-scholar who plunged into the middle of every important controversy of his times, did not consider the real world to be either grubby or mundane but infinitely and endlessly exciting.

This dynamic understanding of how the history of ideas, and particularly economic ideas, zigged and zagged its way down to the present day is reflected in another unique aspect of the *History of Economic Thought*. In apologizing for the "unwonted length" of his work, Rothbard writes that it is "much longer than most since it insists on bringing in all the 'lesser' figures and their interactions."[57] Understanding the key role played by these so-called lesser figures is central to understanding Rothbard's conception of how ideas, and not only economic ideas, evolve. While Jonathan Swift is well known, the real subject of his most famous satires is completely obscure: yet Rothbard, in discussing the politicoeconomic origins of the Swiftian satires, not only writes a riveting narrative, he puts the actions and ideas of individuals in their social and political context, weaving a rich tapestry of bright colors and complex multileveled patterns—and demonstrating, in practice, the superiority of the praxeological approach in economics and all the social sciences.

In Rothbard's hands, "the dismal science" becomes an intellectual adventure fraught with all the elements of the human drama; not only the power of ideas but the power of human emotions: love, hate, greed and asceticism, God and the Devil—all are important (and frequently decisive) factors in the history of economic thought.

Rothbard's survey of the rising hard money and laissez faire theorists of the eighteenth century culminates in his chapter on Richard Cantillon, upon whom Rothbard confers the title of "the father of modern economics." Not the deified Adam Smith, mind you, the god of today's moderate conservatives, but "a gallicized Irish merchant, banker, and adventurer who wrote the first treatise on economics more than four decades before the publication of the *Wealth of Nations*."[58]

Cantillon deserves the title of the "first economist" because he pioneered the method of separating economics from theology and moral philosophy. However important ethics and religion may be, says Rothbard, this isolation of purely economic matters was necessary in order to break out of the mercantilist morass."[59] Before the role of government or the proper ethics to govern economic transactions could be discerned, the basic principles of the market—the how and why of its workings—had to be discovered and analyzed.

Cantillon's *Essai sur la nature du commerce en general*, is the first systematic examination of the market process.[60] In going beyond the scholastics, he built on the Aristotelian tradition in deducing general principles from axiomatic concepts, and using what Mises called "thought-experiments" to test his basic premises. As Rothbard puts it, "human life is not a laboratory, where all variables can be kept fixed by the experimenter, who can then vary one in order to deter-

mine its effects. . . . But the theorist can analyze cause and effect relationships by substituting mental abstractions for laboratory experi-
ments." These "thought-experiments" start out with simple models
that progress to successively higher levels of complexity. If the reader
can recall Sieur de Boisguilbert, who, in dramatizing the relation
between specialization and trade, came up with the simplest
example of two workers, a wool-producer and a grower of wheat,
and extended his example to successively larger areas (a small town,
a province, a nation, and, finally, the entire world). Cantillon took this
method in his *Essai* and applied it in a bold and illuminating fashion.

As France was a nation of great landed estates, the product of
feudal conquests and royal decrees, Cantillon's ingenious premise
conceives the entire world as a single megaestate, with a single
monopoly landowner who directs the economy by simply giving
orders, while everyone else obeys. Cantillon makes a single modi-
fication of his model: the land is farmed out to various renters who
produce various products. This changes the function and status of
the landlord. These producers, now in the position where they
must trade with each other, are no longer adjuncts of the royal
landlord, but free agents, entrepreneurs who must exist in the context of competition and the price system. In successive stages of
ever-increasing complexity, Cantillon analyzed the genesis of the
free-market economy, including the development of money as a
commodity that is also a vital instrument of exchange.

Rothbard shows that Cantillon, far from embracing the idea of
intrinsic value, presaged the later insights of the Austrians, developing and elaborating the old scholastic view of prices as the result
of subjective valuations. Again anticipating the Austrians, Cantillon focused on the pivotal role of the entrepreneur as the bearer
of uncertainty, the risk-taker whose income is dependent on variable factors. As the catalyst of economic activity, Cantillon's entrepreneur is the great balancer of supply and demand (*contra*

Schumpeter, as Rothbard makes a point of emphasizing, who characterized the entrepreneur as a "disruptive" personality type).

Cantillon's contribution was largely forgotten, his insights recreated by the Austrians, with interest in his work revived by F. A. Hayek (who wrote the introduction to the 1931 German edition of the *Essai*). The reason the economics profession seems to have forgotten all about its real founder is that, as Rothbard puts it, "modern economics is a set of formal models and equations purporting to fully determine human behavior, at least in the economic realm." There is no room here for uncertainty, entrepreneurial or otherwise, because such concepts cannot be "compressed into determinate mathematical models." If, however, it *is* possible to produce a set of equations with the predictive power of entrepreneurial insight, then would this not obliterate the concept of entrepreneurship itself? "Economic theory," writes Rothbard, "must choose between formally elegant but false and distorting mathematical models, and the 'literary' analysis of real human life itself."[61]

In his theories of money, trade, entrepreneurship, value, and price, Cantillon was "the first to show in detail that all parts of the market economy fit together in a 'natural,' self-regulative, equilibrating pattern": government intervention only impedes the operation of a flawless mechanism.[62] Further illustrating his theme that the direction of economic thought is not always upward-and-onward, Rothbard notes that Cantillon's pre-Austrian analysis of how the entry of new money profits the first recipients at the expense of later recipients is much more sophisticated than the Lockean quantity theory of money (upheld to this day by monetarists and neoclassicists).

Rothbard's biographical account of Cantillon underscores the Kauderian theme of this work: that the southern Catholic countries of Europe, and not Protestant England—*contra* the conventional wisdom—were the real seedbed of laissez-faire. As Rothbard clearly

shows in this account of Cantillon's achievements, it was a gallicized Irishman who was not only the first writer who thought about
economics systematically, but who was also a direct influence on the
French Physiocrats, A. J. R. Turgot, David Hume, and even Adam
Smith—"a man whose hyperdeveloped sense of his own originality
prevented him from citing or recognizing many predecessors."[63]

The advent of Smith as the "great man" of economics, the
superhuman founder and fountainhead of economic thought,
eclipsed Cantillon's vital role, and, indeed, of all economic thought
before the arrival of the great one. This "erasure," says Rothbard,
"enabled Smithian classical economics to take hold and dominate
economic thought for 100 years." Smith-worship "deflected" economics from the subjectivist–natural law–Aristotleian-Thomistic
traditions of Continental thought to the "British paradigm" of
Smithian so-called classical economics, which was (and is) "mired
in aggregative analysis, cost-of-production theory of value, static
equilibrium states, artificial division into 'micro' and 'macro,' and
an entire baggage of holistic and static analysis."[64]

In illustrating the politicoeconomic doctrines of the mid-eigh-
teenth-century French physiocrats, Rothbard relates the story of
how Dr. Francois Quesnay, the founder of this sect, answered the
complaint of the Dauphin of France that it was hard being a king.
Not at all, said Quesnay: " 'What then,' asked the Dauphin, 'would
you do if you were king?' 'Nothing,' was the straightforward,
stark, and magnificently libertarian answer of Dr. Quesnay."[65]

The French physiocrats were a well-organized movement, with
their own journals, *salons*, and cadre of propagandists: the writings
of Quesnay and his followers were widely read, and, with
Quesnay as doctor to the king's mistress, Madame de Pompadour,
and his chief lieutenant, the Marquis de Mirabeau, a famous
author, physiocracy gained prominence among the intellectuals.
At the core of their belief-system was a reverence for agriculture as

the heart and soul of the nation; since *land* is the end-all and be-all of economic activity, the *only* productive factor, all occupations outside of farming were "sterile." In spite of their generally consistent support for the free market, and their opposition to mercantilist controls, their contributions to technical economic analysis were a step down from Cantillon. The physiocrats upheld a confused "cost of production" theory of value, anticipating the Smithian labor or intrinsicist theory that ignores the subjective valuations of the consumer, and also upheld usury laws. Not quite as bad, but surely "more irritating nowadays" is Dr. Quesnay's *Tableau economique* (1758), which Rothbard describes in his inimitable fashion as "an incomprehensible, jargon-filled chart purporting to depict the flow of expenditures from one economic class to another." Not taken too seriously when it was first published, "it has been rediscovered by twentieth-century economists, who are fascinated *because* of its very incomprehensibility. All the better to publish journal articles on!"[66]

In characterizing the physiocrats as a "sect," Rothbard's description of them recalls nothing so much as his strikingly similar depiction of Ayn Rand's "Objectivist" cult. Like Rand, Dr. Quesnay was practically deified by his followers: "In no way did the cult aspect of the physiocratic group show itself more starkly than in the adjectives used about their master. His followers claimed that Quesnay looked like Socrates, and they habitually referred to him as the 'Confucius of Europe.' "[67]

Aside from the personality cult centered around the charismatic figure of the founder and chief theoretician, another similarity to the Randians is the physiocrats' strategic perspective: like the Randians, who, although ostensibly "radicals for capitalism," believed in working within the corridors of power, the physiocrats based their whole strategy on the possibility of converting the king to an understanding of the virtues of laissez-faire. While radically opposed to the mercantilist underpinnings of the monarchy, the physiocrats did not for a moment entertain the possibility that the royal authority would, could, or should be overthrown. As improbable as it seems, this strategy of converting the king worked in a couple of instances: the margrave of Baden, a German statelet, was converted to physiocracy and eagerly implemented its doctrines in his domain. Quesnay's other fans of royal blood included King Gustavus III of Sweden, Leopold II, Duke of Tuscany and later Austrian emperor, and Joseph II, also of Austria. Rothbard notes one encounter between the fervent margrave and his physiocratic guru, Mirabeau, in which the former asks whether "the physiocratic ideal was making sovereign rulers unnecessary." Mirabeau blanched, and "sternly" reminded his young pupil that the power of the monarch, while limited, would still be considered legitimate.

Going far beyond the physiocrats in the brilliance of his technical analysis was A. R. J. Turgot (1727–81), whose economic writings were a mere fraction of his output, which dealt mostly with history, philology, and the natural sciences. Born to an important family which had traditionally served as royal advisors, his brief but brilliant contributions to economic theory prefigured, in method and conclusions, the insights of the Austrian School: not only his advocacy of free trade, both domestically and internationally, but his technical analysis of the market process. Turgot's deductive methodology utilizes the thought-experiment, and Crusoe economics, and through this analysis comes up with a far more sophisticated view of the market economy than the alleged father of free-market thought, Adam Smith: Turgot anticipates, in an embryonic form, the Austrian view of costs as profits foregone, time-preference, the subjective view of prices, and the importance of expectations in the market. While afflicted with the land-mysticism of the physiocrats, to some degree, Turgot conceded that other factors of production must naturally coexist with the soil, namely, labor and time. In the kind of revelation that Rothbard relished—in which it turns out that an obscure and largely forgotten figure is really responsible for some remarkable achievement, usually attributed to someone else—Turgot also formulated an analysis of the law of diminishing returns "which would not be surpassed, or possibly equaled, until the twentieth century."[68]

Rothbard's critique of Adam Smith is the heart of this volume, dramatically illustrating two major themes of this work: not only the Kauder thesis but also, in a clear vindication of the Kuhnian "paradigm" theory, that economic thought was deflected by Smithian influence from the correct proto-Austrian path and onto a tangent that led directly to Marxism. The first great problem with Smith was his division of labor into "productive" and "unproductive," with the former being restricted to labor on material goods, as opposed to consumer goods. This "amounted to a bias in favor of investment in capital goods, since a stock of capital goods by definition has to be embodied in material objects." On the other hand, consumer goods are meant to be used up, that is, enjoyed, by consumers. The reason for this capital investment bias was rooted in Calvinist theology. As Rothbard writes, "Adam Smith's Presbyterian conscience led him to value the expenditure of labor *per se*, for its own sake, and led him to balk at free market time-preferences between consumption and saving."[69]

The Smithian blacklist of allegedly unproductive workers includes not only servants, and (in Smith's words) "players, buffoons, musicians, opera-singers, opera-dancers, etc.," but also churchmen, doctors, lawyers, and "men of letters of all kinds."[70]

Smith's adulation of capital goods was not limited to their durability: a house was not considered by Smith to be "productive." Smith was interested only in *capital* goods, that is, goods that would generate more wealth. Luxury was denounced by Smith, with what Rothbard characterizes as "Calvinistic scorn," as biologically damaging to the human species, resulting in a lower birth rate. Smith also denounced high profits as diverting capitalists from the straight and narrow. High profits, as Smith put it, "destroy that parsimony which in other circumstances is natural to the character of the merchant."

While everyone but the Marxists today dismisses the Smithian labor dichotomy as archaic, and of no consequence, his theory of value as presented in *The Wealth of Nations* is even more archaic— and we are still experiencing the disastrous consequences. Smithian value theory, Rothbard points out, was a "degeneration," not only a descent into intrinsicism after centuries of progress on the subjectivist road, "but also a similar degeneration" from Smith's own unpublished lectures.[71]

After centuries in which value had been determined by utility and scarcity, Smith "sharply and hermetically separates and sunders utility from value and prices, and never the twain shall meet." Not only that, but Smith drops out the concept of scarcity altogether: "And with scarcity gone as the solution to the value paradox, subjective utility virtually drops out of economics, as well as does consumption and consumer demand. Utility can no longer explain value and price, and the two sundered concepts will reappear in later generations as left-wingers and socialists happily prate about the crucial differences between 'production for profit' and 'production for use' "—the echo of Smith's dichotomy between value-in-use and value-in-exchange. And so the concepts of value and price, in *The Wealth of Nations*, take a fateful and fatal shift away from subjective utility and toward the idea of a "natural price" existing in the netherworld state of "equilibrium."[72]

Rothbard's analysis of the technical flaws in the Smithian approach is fascinating, even for the layman, but in Smith's defense it might be said that the real reason for his fame is his defense of the market against government intervention, that is, his political stance. But even on this score, reveals Rothbard, Smith is sorely lacking. A dedicated believer in the "martial virtues," whose devotion to the military glory of the nation-state led him to condone the Navigation Acts, "that bulwark of British mercantilism," Smith was at the diametrically opposite pole from the French advocates of laissez-faire, who understood all too well the necessary connection between war, taxation, and absolutist rule.[73] In addition to militarism, public education was another necessity, because, thus enlightened, as Smith wrote, the people are "less apt to be misled into any wanton or unnecessary opposition to the measures of government." Smith a free marketeer? Not when he called for regulation of bank paper (no small denominations, please!) while condoning fractional-reserve banking, public works, government coinage, a government post office, the outlawing of payment-in-kind, and some restrictions on exports. To this partial list add the taxes Smith called for, including higher taxes on land and the erection of tax-barriers to trade. The capstone of his tax program was a progressive income tax, many years before Marx made it a key plank in the Communist platform.[74]

Another major legacy of trouble we inherit from Smith is all the whining about "alienation" supposedly resulting from the division of labor and increasing specialization. In addition, Smith reverted back to the prescholastic era in calling for a revival of the laws against usury, proposing an interest rate ceiling of 5 percent. The whole point of this was to drive capital out of the hands of "wasteful" consumers, spendthrifts, and seekers-after-sinful-luxury, and into the hands of sober and frugal businessmen who, in deference to the great god Parsimony, would invest it in yet more capital goods. So much for the free-market time-preferences of autonomous consumers!

And so "the real story is almost the opposite"—as Rothbard puts it—from what the conventional wisdom about Adam Smith would have us believe. Instead of the monumental founder of the modern science of economics and a giant of free-market thought, Smith was, in the Rothbardian phrase, "an outstanding example of the Kuhnian case in the history of a science" in which true knowledge, instead of being gained, is *lost*.

In reviewing the scope and detailed analysis of the first volume of the *History*, my purpose here is not only to acquaint the reader with the interlocking themes of this work, but also to give some insight into the personality and purposes of its author. To anyone who knew Rothbard, the man, his focus on the unfortunate consequences of a dour, pleasure-denying, anticonsumptionist Calvinism-run-amok is no mystery. How else would one expect the (usually) easygoing and mildly hedonic Rothbard, a sunny optimist, to react to such a dark doctrine? His focus on the "forgotten" figures of economic thought, besides illustrating a key point that the interaction of ideas is in large part the catalyst of evolving social thought, also gives Rothbard the opportunity to sound off on one of his favorite themes: the unrecognized genius whose views are suppressed or ignored, only to be uncovered years later as a great and original contribution. In this familiar narrative, which is told in several different forms in the *History*, Rothbard was perhaps imagining one possible outcome of his own story.

If so, he was exhibiting his typical modesty. For the publication of the first volume of the *History* alone would have banished the possibility of obscurity; the publication of the second volume, *Classical Economics*, ensures the author a prominent place in the annals of social thought. It is beyond the scope of this present work, however, to engage in a detailed analysis of all Rothbard's works; I will therefore leave it to the reader to pick up where I have left off, and investigate for first-hand Rothbard's masterful survey of the Smithian movement, the career and works of J. B. Say, Jeremy Bentham, John Stuart Mill, and David Ricardo; so, too, his in-depth analysis of the evolution of monetary and banking theory.

We turn now to the second half of volume 2 for Rothbard's exhaustive analysis of Marxism (chapters 9–13) because, in the first place, these chapters are particularly fascinating and well written, and, second, because his integration of the Kauderian and Kuhnian themes into his treatment of Marxism and communism is unique and deserves elucidation.

MESSIANIC COMMUNISM: MYSTIC AND SECULAR

We have already seen, in Rothbard's discussion of the Anabaptist sects, how the early pre-Marxian communist doctrines flourished as a result of the religious turmoil of the sixteenth century. The pre-Marxist communist movement also included a secularist wing, which came to the fore especially during the French Revolution: Rothbard cites the works of two communist writers, the aristocrat Gabriel Bonnot de Mably (1709–85), elder brother of the famous laissez-faire liberal Etienne Connot de Condillac, and Giovanni Morelly, author of *Le Code de la Nature* (1755).

A prolific and popular writer, Mably was a radical egalitarian who believed that moral incentives could replace material incentives under a communist system. Instead of profits and wages, the winners in the new communist society would garner medals, ribbons, and other paraphernalia signifying the honor and esteem of their fellows. His other suggestion was that, even if communist society produced less due to a lack of incentives, society would just have to make due with less—a position eerily similar to the ecosocialist environmentalists of today.

While Mably believed that mankind was too corrupt to adopt his ideal communist system, Morelly thought that private property was an unnatural excrescence and that if mankind's true nature were allowed to surface the institution of private property would wither away. In Morelly's communist utopia, private property would not exist and the state would manage all the affairs of men: the nature of an individual's employment, the care of his children, the food that he eats, and the clothing that he wears—all would be provided for and determined by the state. As Rothbard describes Morelly's monomaniacal fantasies: "All buildings must be the same, and grouped in equal blocks; all clothing is to be made out of the same fabric"; in short, the secular pre-Marxian communist utopias were actually nightmarish dystopias where, as Alexander Gray, Scottish historian of economics, put it, " 'no sane man would on any conditions consent to live, if he could possibly escape.'"[75]

Yet history shows that there is hardly a cause so repellent or absurd that it has not found partisans to rally 'round its banner; the dogmas of the pre-Marxian communist theorists—especially Morelly's sartorially challenged socialism—found adherents amidst the turmoil of the French Revolution. In 1795, one Francois Noel Babeuf founded the Conspiracy of Equals, a secret revolutionary communist organization inspired by the writings of Morelly and others. In their manifesto, the Conspirators state their goal: "We demand real equality, or Death." These were not dreamy-eyed utopians who planned to go off somewhere and set up a voluntary commune, but armed utopians who envisioned violent revolution. Their manifesto declares that "we are willing to sweep everything away. Let all the arts vanish, if necessary, as long as genuine equality remains for us."[76]

Certainly the arts—along with all the rest of the great achievements of human civilization—would vanish if the Conspirators' program were ever carried out. In the Babeuvist society of the communist future, all property would be collectively owned and stored in communal storehouses, to be "equitably" distributed by the Babeuvist "superiors"—a proviso that provokes Rothbard to remark that "apparently there was to be a cadre of 'superiors' in this oh so 'equal' world!" Gone is the naive Rousseauan/Mablyian belief in man's innate nobility of spirit buried beneath the surface of private property and market relations, a New Socialist Man just waiting to burst forth to the surface. Prefiguring Lenin, Babeuf's strategy was to organize a vanguard party of professional revolutionaries that would seize power and set up a totalitarian dictatorship. Like the utopian communists, the Babeuvist revolutionaries envisioned their egalitarian paradise of the future down to the last detail, even to the eating arrangements: "All meals would be eaten in public in every commune," writes Rothbard, "and there would, of course, be compulsory attendance for all community members." And what do Babeuvists do for fun? According to their own utterances, "all private entertainment," Rothbard informs us, "would be 'strictly forbidden,' lest 'imagination, released from the supervision of a strict judge should engender abominable vices contrary to the commonweal.' "[77]

The Babeuvist conspirators were smashed by the police when they tried to recruit in the French army; Babeuf was arrested in 1796, and executed the following year. Yet the Babeuvist spirit did not die with him, but instead gave rise to a neo-Babeuivist party led by a member of the Conspiracy of Equals, Filippo Buonarotti, who managed to remain at large through the intervention of his friend, Napoleon. Buonarotti spent the rest of his life trying to set up an international Babeuvist organization. His widely read 1828 book, *The Conspiracy for Equality of Babeuf*, revived the Babeuvist cause in the minds of socialist radicals everywhere.

The two competing strains of communism are contrasted in his portraits of two representative young communists of the time, the English Christian socialist John Goodwyn Barmby, and Theodore Dezamy, whom Rothbard tells us was "greatly admired by Marx." Barmby, whose approach to communism was frankly mystical, wrote "communist hymns and prayers," conceived a plan to build "communitariums," in effect, a Communist Church "all directed by a supreme communarchy headed by an elected communarch and communarchess. Barmby repeatedly proclaimed 'the religion of Communism,' and made sure to begin things right by naming himself 'Pontifarch of the Communist Church.' "[78] To this more-than-slightly wacky tendency must be added the Fourierists, the Owenites, and the various and sundry Icarians and other utopian sects who each sought to establish model communist communities based on the egalitarian fantasies, architectural tastes, and dietary idiosyncrasies of the founders. None of these intentional communities lasted more than a few years.

At the opposite pole from these dreamy utopians was the tough-minded and infinitely more dangerous Dezamy, a militant atheist and propounder of ideological purity and organizational discipline. Dezamy, the proto-Lenin of the early communist movement, denounced what Rothbard calls "the quasireligious poetic and moralistic" tendency in communism, as typified by Etienne Cabet's utopian novel, *Voyage to Icaria*. And there was to be no more sentimentality about the means by which the communists were to attain their noble ends: a communist revolution must be immediate and total, with the abolition of money and all property following soon afterward. There was to be no more bourgeois nonsense about national culture and linguistic autonomy: the "universal nation" would speak a universal language and such divisive capitalist institutions as the family would be abolished.

Rothbard makes the vitally important point that these two strands of communist thought, the utopian-mystic and the ostensibly "scientific," were never clearly demarcated. Dezamy, for all the militance of his ostensible atheism, laced his rhetoric with the language of a chiliastic messianism, speaking of "this sublime devotion which constitutes socialism" and urging errant supporters to reenter "the egalitarian church, outside of which there can be no salvation."[79]

In Rothbard's theological-political taxonomy, the "secularized" version of communism that evolved into Marxism was essentially the same postmillennialist apocalyptic doctrine that, as Rothbard puts it, "would seize control of most of the Protestant churches in the northern United States during the nineteenth century." Their goal was "to use state power to coerce morality and virtue and then establish the Kingdom of God, not only in the United States but throughout the world."

Ostensibly secular, Marxism, by Rothbard's lights, is in a class with the "immedietist" postmillennialists encountered in the first volume: the Anabaptists, Munzterites, and others who aimed at not only achieving pure communism immediately but also asserted the necessity of an apocalyptic bloodbath, in which the earth would be cleansed of all but the elect, that is, the members of the communist sect.

On the other hand, the postmillennialist Christian messianism of the mainline Protestant churches during the nineteenth century—Rothbard, citing historian Jean B. Quandt, characterizes a prominent postmillennialist economist as "having divinized the state and socialized Christianity"—represents the "gradualist" wing of the postmillennialists, who sought power "in less violent and precipitate a fashion."[80]

In any case, whichever wing of the postmillennialists we are talking about, their emergence on the world stage spelled trouble for the cause of liberty; in Rothbard's phrase, they have "caused grave social and political trouble by 'immamentizing the eschaton,' in the political philosopher Eric Voegelin's phrase." In the Voegelinian view, the attempt to drag down the "eschaton"— the Kingdom of God—to an earthly level (and thus "immamentize" it) is responsible for all the mischief of the modern world.

This was the heresy of the Anabaptists, the messianic Christian predecessors of the modern socialist movement: Their doctrine of the elect completed the transformation of the Christian concept of salvation from the original Catholic-Thomist view of individual souls saved by acts of mercy and contrition to the *collective* and predestined salvation of the elect, tapped by God (or, in the Marxist version, by History) to usher in the new millennium, the Kingdom of God on earth. This is "a long way from the orthodox Christian, Augustinian stress on the individual soul."[81]

Rothbard outlines three major currents of thought that intersected both messianic communism (mystic and secular) and the millennialist religious movements of the time: (1) the concept of the elect as the necessary catalyst of the events leading up to the establishment of the Kingdom of God on earth; (2) the idea of the apocalypse, "a bloody Armageddon of the Last Days," shared by both German and Dutch Anabaptists of the sixteenth century as well as Karl Marx; and, (3) in contrast to the nutty utopian socialists, with their intricately detailed blueprints of life in the communist paradise—where even the architecture, fashions in clothing, and eating arrangements (including the menu!) are all laid out in advance—both Marx and the religious messianists left the specifics of their respective Kingdoms of God on earth rather vague. In one of his more arresting analogies, the author attributes this to the realization that the "spelling out the details of one's ideal society removes the crucial element of awe and mystery from the allegedly inevitable world of the future. In the same way," he continues,

> science fiction movies lose their glamour and excitement when, in the second half of the film, the mysterious, powerful and previously invisible monsters become concretized into slow-moving green bloblike creatures that have lost their mysterious aura and have become commonplace.[82]

Marx's vagueness as to the shape of the future communist paradise, beyond assuming superabundance, played a vital strategic role, not only in imbuing the communist activists with the awe and mystery appropriate to a religious crusade, but in giving them the tactical flexibility to seize and keep power. Yet there is another reason for Marx's reticence, reflected in the history of the one essay where he addresses this question. "Private Property and Communism" remained unpublished during his own lifetime, and understandably so; for in it, as Rothbard points out, Marx admitted that, come the victory of the Reds, the worst nightmares of the anti-Communists would come true. In Marx's inimitable phrase: "In the same way as woman is to abandon marriage for general prostitution, so the whole world of wealth, that is, the objective being of man, is to abandon the relation of exclusive marriage with the private property owner for the relation of general prostitution with the community." In this stage of "raw communism," Marx admits that "envy and a desire to reduce all to a common level" will animate the great historical changeover to communism. Here again Rothbard recalls "the monstrous regimes imposed by the coercive Anabaptists of the sixteenth century," whose orgiastic rites of communal lust erased the line between religion and psychopathology.[83]

Out of this cathartic maelstrom, by means of the magical "dialectic," the tumultuous first phase of the world communist revolution will give way to the higher stage of pure communism. What distinguishes the second from the initial "raw" stage of communism is that, in its higher form, the division of labor will be abolished. Such a division is impossible, because for Marx, being a Hegelian, individuals did not exist; only mankind as a collective organism is real. To Marx, the division of labor was evidence of man's tragic division against himself, his "alienation" from his own true nature, which could only be realized under communism. And we mean not just alienation in the Smithian sense, of being estranged from the product of his own labor and on account of specialization, but in a metaphysical sense; that is, in the Hegelian sense of being estranged from God.

Here, again, Rothbard returns to his Kauderian thesis of the important and often decisive impact of religious thought on the development of economic thought. Just as the theology of the Last Days (eschatology) has had a formative influence on the development of economic and political thought, Rothbard shows that the theology of the First Days (the branch of theology known as "creatology") has had an equally important influence. Why did God create the universe? This is the question creatology poses. Orthodox Christians, Catholic and Protestant alike, answer: Out of His unlimited love and benevolence. The answer of Gnostics, or, as Rothbard puts it, "of heretics and mystics," is: "out of a felt need and imperfection."[84]

The doctrine at the heart of this heresy, then, is that man—"the collective organic species, of course, not any particular individual"—is alienated from God, and constantly seeking reunion. Rothbard traces this dialectical theology—with its three stages of unity, split, and reunion—back to Plotinus, the Greek Platonist philosopher, who railed against any sort of diversity or multiplicity, which, in mankind, is manifested in individualism. Such nonconformists, says Plotinus, are "deserters from the All."[85]

Rothbard contrasts this heretical doctrine of metaphysical alienation with the orthodox Judaeo-Christian view, which, in Adam's Fall, locates the moment of man's *moral* estrangement from God. In Christianity, in the life and death of Jesus, the divine reconnects itself to the human, and man's alienation is abated, if not ended. In any case, the path to salvation is opened, and the elimination of alienation is possible.

In the Platonic-mystic view, individual salvation is not an option. Instead, in the view of the Platonist-mystics, most of them heretics from Christianity, salvation concerns only "man with a capital M," as "a collective blob or organism."[86]

MARX, HEGEL, AND FAUST

This mystic creatology was kept alive during the medieval era by various Christian heretics, who believed in a woozy sort of pantheism, and underground gnostic sects, who longed for reunion with God, or "the One." The goal of this mystic discipline was to empty the vessel of the self so that it might be filled with God. The writings of the German cobbler and mystic Jacob Boehme, whose vision of Nothing transmuting into Something by means of a catalytic *nisus,* were a rich source for the later Idealist philosophers to mine—even aping Boehme's penchant for capitalization. In an aside, Rothbard notes: "It was, by the way, typical of Hegel and his Idealist followers to think that they add grandeur and explanation to a lofty and unintelligible concept by capitalizing it."[87]

The significance of all this is that Hegel secularized the three-stage (or "dialectical") mystic-heretic creatology. The messianic Marx, looking for a theoretical engine to drive his revolutionary socialist agenda, hitched the communist wagon to the Hegelian dialectic.

Rothbard raises the Faust theme, in the air as Hegel propounded his philosophy, as emblematic of the Hegelian movement, a symbol that communicates the air of megalomania that pervaded the German intelligentsia at the time. Faust puts Hegel's system in its context as the philosophical expression of German Romanticism, of the idea of man as tragic being whose tragedy lay in his separation from God. If God will not reach out to reunite with Man, then Man must aspire to become God. In searching for God (or, in the Hegelian lingo, *Weltgeist,* or World-Spirit), a man (or, rather, Man) finds . . . *himself.* The Hegelian answer, then, to the classic question put by the creatologists, "Why did God create the world?" is, as Rothbard puts it, "out of a felt need to become conscious of itself as a world-self."[88]

History, to the Hegelian, is an "unfolding" of this drive toward self-consciousness and the knowledge that man is God. Starting out in total darkness as to his divine nature and origins, Man at the beginning of history embarks on a process of creative self-actualization that finally unfolds, at the end of history, in reunion with the *Weltgeist*.

Citing the work of M. H. Abrams on the Romantic writers of the nineteenth century, Rothbard traces the evolution of the dialectic through poets and novelists as well as philosophers and theologians, and makes the Abramsian argument that "the Romantic vision constituted the secularization of theology."[89] Not only Wordsworth but Keats and Coleridge basked in the Romantic imagery of the man-god, pantheism, and the three-stage dialectic of collective reunion with God. In Germany, where the obscurantist fog of mysticism was even thicker, the German Romantics, including Hegel, Schelling, Schiller, Holderlin, and Fichte—all of them theology students, with Hegel, at the University of Tubingen—were the ideological palace guard of the Prussian-German national state.

While generally ignoring individuals as unimportant cogs in the cosmic machinery, Hegel conceded that, on very rare (but vitally important) occasions, "great men" arise who embody the dialectical convulsions of the *Weltgeist*. Rothbard points out that "during a time when most patriotic Prussians were reacting violently against Napoleon's imperial conquests . . . Hegel reacted very differently," writing in an exultant letter to a friend that the sight of Napoleon, "this World-soul," riding down the main street of his city signaled the "end of history."[90]

Like his fellow Romantics, and like many intellectuals

throughout Europe, Hegel's initial embrace of the ideals of the French Revolution gave way to revulsion and retrenchment in the doctrines of state absolutism. For the reformed revolutionary (or "neoconservative") Hegel, the state, specifically the German state, was an expression of the *Weltgeist*, or God. Disobedience ensured alienation from one's "true" self; true freedom is the "freedom" to submit to authority, specifically, the authority of King Friedrich Wilhelm III, the reigning Prussian monarch.

Hegel, it turns out, was among the first of a long line of repentant radicals who became court intellectuals, apologists for the establishment whose overthrow they had once anticipated with unalloyed glee. Hegel was duly rewarded with a powerful and prestigious position at the newly created University of Berlin. Hegel's "bombastic and hysterical Platonism," as Karl Popper characterized the Hegelian philosophy, was nothing but an updated version of countless apologias for absolutism spun out by court intellectuals since time immemorial. Backed by the power of the Prussian state, Hegelianism "was able to sweep German philosophy during the nineteenth century, dominating in all but the Catholic areas of southern Germany and Austria."[91]

The death of Hegel, however, and the formation of a "left-Hegelian" movement among the radical student movement at the turn of the century in Germany, led to a reevaluation of the Hegelian "correct line." Disillusioned with the regime of King Friedrich Wilhelm III, the Left-Hegelians were getting ready for another lurch in the direction of the World-Spirit, another great revolution that would spell the end of the present state, and, this time, give birth to world communism. For a while, two strands of this messianic communism competed for hegemony in the world communist movement: the explicitly Christian and mystical writers, represented by such writers as the Polish Count August Cieskowski, and the secularized version represented by Marx. In the end, the atheists won out, and the stage was set for Marxism. The point is that this amounted to the secularization of an essentially religious concept. This secularization of mystic-heretical creatology, carried out by the nineteenth-century Romantics, and the Hegelians, gave full scope for the "scientific" socialist, Marx, to build his own system of materialist communism, in which religious messianism was transmuted into the moody dialectical musings of the German Idealists. Energized by the proletariat, and the momentum of the dialectic, the engine of history would ride roughshod over the *bourgeoisie* and establish a world communist state. Putting a modern materialist gloss on the old mystical-Boehmian concept of *nisus*, Marx posited the theory of class struggle as the catalytic force driving mankind toward the inevitable communist revolution.

Rothbard writes that "there is no place in his system where Marx is fuzzier or shakier than at its base: the concept of historical materialism, the key to the inevitable dialectic of history." The concept of the material productive forces, which has talismanic status in Marxist "science," is supposed to determine everything; according to Marx, all human behavior is determined by various "modes of production" and the "economic structure of society." Everything else in human society—not only politics and law, but the arts—is relegated to the level of the "superstructure" which lies atop the "base," which is, at bottom, technology. Where did this technology come from? Marx does not bother to address this sensitive question—sensitive to Marx and the Marxists, that is, since to attribute it to individual human beings would reverse the desired cause-and-effect "materialist" argument that technology determines consciousness. Citing Mises to the effect that, for the Marxists, speculation as to the origin of tools and machines is *verboten*—"they are, that is all; we must assume that they are dropped from heaven"—Rothbard then goes on to make the further point that "any changes in technology must therefore be dropped from heaven as well."[92]

Rothbard's critique of the Marxian concept of "ideology"—as consciousness molded by the "class interests" of whatever class the speaker happens to belong to—mocks the idea as "self-refuting." For what of the Marxist system itself, created, as is well known, by bourgeois intellectuals such as Marx? Marxism is either disinterested "science," or hopelessly class-biased; it cannot be both.

Furthermore, the whole Marxist concept of "class" is illogical and inconsistent: for, in his discussion of "oriental despotism" and feudalism, the two historical stages previous to capitalism, Marx defines the class privileges of the rulers as state-derived; the despots and their favorites deriving their wealth and power from the state, and the feudal landlord deriving his wealth and privileges from similar state action. But suddenly, when he gets to capitalism, the relationship between class and power undergoes an unacknowledged shift, from the enjoyment of state-derived privileges to the fact of selling or buying labor in a voluntary agreement on the free market. In his theory of classes, as presented in the last chapter of the third volume of *Capital*, Marx promises but does not deliver an answer to the grave contradictions in his theory.

In a spellbinding narrative tracing the origins of the Marxist conception of class, Rothbard identifies the original libertarian class analysis of French economists J. B. Say, Charles Comte, and Charles Dunoyer, as distorted and transmuted by the confused Comte de Saint-Simon. While the Comte–Dunoyer class analysis defined the two eternal antagonists as the state versus the people, the socialist and egalitarian Saint-Simonians substituted the employer–employee model. Once a fellow-traveler of the libertarian laissez faire radicals grouped around the French periodical *Le Censeur*, who hailed the rise of laissez faire and industrialism as two aspects of the same historical impulse, Saint-Simon broke with them to form his own sect. The Saint-Simonians, the first group to use the word "socialist," advocated a totalitarian state run by an alliance of technocrats and central bankers. Whereas Comte and Dunoyer had envisioned the end result of the new industrialism to be a stateless future in which "the government of men would be replaced by the administration of things," the Saint-Simonians dreamed of the day when this industrialism would be administered by the new elite at the head of the state: investment bankers, intellectuals, and engineers. The Saint-Simonian movement enjoyed a tremendous vogue in Europe, and, in an interesting bit of intellectual detective work, Rothbard shows how Marx undoubtedly was influenced by Saint-Simon. Yet Marx shifts back and forth between the Comte–Dunoyer and Saint-Simonian versions, much to the confusion of future historians, not to mention his followers.

The idea that embodies the Marxist system, and that explains all its features, seems, says Rothbard, to be a trivial statement, and that is: "Karl Marx was a communist." Communism was the be-all and end-all of his system, the reason and the ultimate end, the culmination of history and the secularized Kingdom of God brought down to earth, and everything else in the mighty Marxian system was designed to support and uphold it. With the abolition of property, money, and the division of labor at the apex of the Marxian intellectual edifice, the rest was just scaffolding, often hastily assembled, and so shaky as to require any number of supports and makeshift braces to hold it in place.

MARXISM—A TISSUE OF FALLACIES

One such essential brace, as Rothbard points out, was the system of Ricardian economics. In contrast to the French theorists of laissez faire, who concentrated on the market as the transactions of individual entrepreneurs engaged in mutually beneficial exchanges, the British paradigm developed by David Ricardo and Adam Smith stressed "production" and "distribution" as if these concepts could exist unconnected to individual actors. In Ricardo, as Rothbard puts it, "the worst of Smith was magnified and intensified," with the worker put in conflict with the employer, and the landlord in conflict with consumers and manufacturers. Add to this a gloomy Malthusian view of ever-increasing population and consequent immiseration of the masses, and the basic elements of the Marxist theory of inherent class struggle were put in place. And "not only that," writes Rothbard, but "a delighted Marx found that Ricardian doctrine was, in effect, a quantity of labor theory of value." Jumping on the Ricardian-Smithian insistence that value was equal to labor hours, not even counting such real-world costs as rent, Marx constructed his theory of capitalist "exploitation" as a radical Ricardian seeking to return the "surplus value" of the workers' labor to its rightful owners.[93]

Another delight for Marx was Adam Smith's strange division of production into the material and the immaterial, with the latter not being recognized as legitimate "production"—an idea that blended well with Marxist materialism. Indeed, while Ricardo, as a follower of Adam Smith, was an advocate of laissez faire, and opposed most government intervention in the economy, the faultiness of his technical analysis—and the great Smithian diversion away from the sophisticated proto-Austrian insights of the Continental economists, who emphasized subjectivism and entrepreneurship—gave birth to a whole school of Ricardian socialists, which Rothbard describes in learned detail.[94]

Like Ricardo and Smith, Marx starts out, in the first volume of *Capital*, by defining production as the production of material goods: immaterial goods are deemed not to be of any value. It would *seem*, says Marx, that these commodities exchange for each other in certain proportions that are variable and subjective, but in fact this is not the case. And why not? Because the fact that these two commodities are exchangeable at all means that they must be equivalent, that is, *equal* in value. The focus here is all wrong, right from the start, for it should be not on the commodities being exchanged, but on "the individuals, the actors, *doing* the exchanging."[95]

Marx further refined the crude Ricardian version and qualified his labor value theory to mean "socially necessary labor" as representing the true cost of production; but this amounted, as Rothbard trenchantly points out, to circular reasoning, for it turns out that this "socially necessary labor" is the amount of labor *required by the market*, and not just the sheer number of labor hours embodied in a commodity produced by means of a time-consuming and obsolete process. "So market values, prices, and productivities are being used to try to explain the determinants of those same values and prices."[96]

Of the grave problems raised by Marx's labor theory of value, the gravest is that labor-intensive industries should yield the highest products. Contrary to the idea that profit is derived from exploiting the surplus value of the workers' labor, however, the hard fact is that profit rates of highly capitalized industries are *not* lower than in labor intensive industries; Marx himself recognized the problem, and promised a solution in a later volume of *Capital*. Like his promised explication of the theory of classes, the publication of this solution never came.

Marx was not really all that interested in analyzing the workings of the capitalist market, except to derive from this analysis his "laws of motion," which doom capitalism to death by its own hand. In brief, these Marxist "laws" claim that, since profit is the appropriation of the "surplus value" of the workers' labor, and since profits are ever-diminishing, therefore the capitalists would be continually squeezing the workers and cutting into their "subsistence" wages: this is the famous "immiseration" of the masses that is supposed to ignite the inevitable communist revolution.

The roots of these "laws" are to be found, as Rothbard shows, in the works of such procapitalist economists as Smith and Ricardo, both of whom "discovered" that the rate of profit inevitably falls. Marx took this up, especially the idea that the accumulation of capital over time eventually lowers the profit rate to zero. But if profit rates eventually reach "equilibrium," and there is no profit in investment, then why do capitalists continue to invest and search after ever-declining profits? Marx posited a capitalist "instinct"—a weak fallback position indeed. Most Marxists, including Marx himself (in volume 3 of *Capital*) wound up abandoning the labor theory of value, the linchpin of the whole Marxian system.

Rothbard's survey of the Marxists' scrambling to explain how and why, instead of being progressively "immiserated" since the time of Marx, the workers' standard of living has risen at a fantastic rate, is instructive (and amusing), in light of his theme of the origins of messianic communism as an essentially religious impulse in secular disguise. Some Marxists have gone the route of denial, stoutly maintaining that the workers' standard of living has fallen and continues to fall. These theoreticians are a small minority, however, with the bulk of Marxists taking one or another fallback position: the rise of imperialism has made the Western workers into a "labor aristocracy" that oppresses the entire earth, with the Third World cast in the role of the proletarians. While other popular explanations for the delay in the immiseration process abound, another major tactic of the Marxist apologists has been, as Rothbard says, "to change the terms of the argument and the prediction." Instead of complete impoverishment, the neo-Marxists claim, Marx *really* meant "relative" impoverishment. But "will a worker with two color TV sets rise up in revolution because Rockefeller or Lee Iacocca or Hugh Hefner has a larger set in each room? We are a long, long way from immiseration. The coming inevitable wrath of the proletariat has turned, at last, to farce."[97]

The crowning absurdity at the heart of the Marxist "laws of motion" is that these "laws" fail to answer the key question: *qui bono*? For if profits are continuously falling, and the system is *also* continuously grinding down the workers, then "who," asks Rothbard, "is *benefitting* in the distribution of the economic pie?" The Ricardians (the most consistent being Henry George and his followers) had the landlords to blame for the growing impoverishment of all other classes. The Marxists, trapped by the mechanics of their own system, had no one.

Rothbard makes the telling point that Marx, in his assault on the capitalist system, often seems to be spinning out several often incompatible theories, "hoping that one of them, at least, might stick." Thus, his arguments in favor of a cyclical crisis of capitalism, based on three alleged flaws in the capitalist system:

1. *The theory of underconsumption.* This theory holds that the accumulation of capital and the resulting flood of production outstrips the ability of the workers to consume it. The Rothbardian reply is that such a theory "explains too much." A capitalist system that continually overproduces would be in a state of *permanent* crisis. How does this underconsumptionist theory account for the existence of booms? The problem with the Marxian (and Smith-Ricardian) theories of underconsumption is that the function of the price system is completely dropped out of the equation. The significance of the fact that businessmen make a series of errors, leading to a downturn, fails to impress itself on the Marxian-Smithian-Ricardian mind as a failure of the function of the price system.

2. *The theory of declining profits.* In this theory, the accumulation of capital and the resulting fall in prices leads to a recession in the market for capital goods, which then leads to a depression in the

economy at large. But this does not explain, as Rothbard points out, why, suddenly, entrepreneurs should stop investing, especially in light of the earlier Marxist contention that capitalists have what amounts to an instinctual urge to seek profitable opportunities. Marx also fails to account for the possibility that, even if the rate of profit may fall, extension of the market "might well increase the *absolute amount* of aggregate profits."[98]

3. *The view that boom and bust cycles are inherent in the market.* In the free market, the "anarchy of production" cannot coordinate the increasing number of variables in an ever-more-complex and gigantic economy; individual economic actors cannot possibly calculate or know as much as central planners. In criticizing the Ricardian concept of equilibrium, Marx was more Ricardian than Ricardo in insisting that *true* "equilibrium" is the stasis of a planned economy. Rothbard underscores his theme of "Smith-Ricardo, precursors of Marxism," by pointing out that "what Marx overlooked is precisely what the Ricardians overlooked: both failed to look at the *real* market economy, of entrepreneurs and a price system," and insisted on living in "the cloud-land of long-run equilibrium."[99]

Marx and his followers projected the brash self-confidence of ideologues who looked down on their enemies from the commanding heights of an impressive theoretical edifice. Marxism posed as a fully integrated system of thought that explained not only the workings of the economic system, but "even the workings of the universe." As Rothbard shows, Marx only created "a veritable tissue of fallacies." Furthermore, "the jerry-built structure" of this system "was constructed and shored up in desperate service to the fanatical and crazed messianic goal of destruction of the division of labor, and indeed of man's very individuality."[100]

MARX'S DEATH MARCH— SATANIC SOCIALISM

Rothbard's definitive treatment of Marx as "an atheized variant of a venerable Christian heresy" weaves together the various thematic strands that run through both volumes of the *History*. The Kuhnian theory of the paradigm shift, in Rothbard's creative hands, maps the straight line from Smith to Marx through Ricardo. The Kauder thesis is expanded to explain the rise of communism as a consequence of the Reformation, a theological phenomenon secularized by German Romantics and their British imitators.

As Rothbard points out in the concluding paragraph of the section on Marxism, there has been an attempt in recent years to separate a benign "young Marx" from the elder Stalinist Marx. Rothbard shows that "there is only one Marx, whether early or late." In a perceptive and original analysis of the young Marx's early poetry, often dismissed as adolescent musings of no consequence, Rothbard pinpoints the pure hatred of life, of humanity, and of the natural law at the core of young Marx's psychology, which gave birth, in the man, to a monstrous system of almost satanic evil. The satanic theme that runs through Marx's poetic utterances is clear from the very interesting selections quoted by Rothbard, such as this ode, dedicated to his father, entitled "The Fiddler":

> See this sword?
> The prince of darkness
> Sold it to me.

And what could be more explicit than:

> With Satan I have struck my deal,
> He chalks the signs, beats time for me
> I play the death march fast and free.[101]

This death march has been the *leitmotif* of the twentieth century, an era which Rothbard denounced in his famous inaugural speech as president of the John Randolph Club as the century of mass murder, totalitarianism, socialism, and devastation on a scale unmatched in all of human history. "Repeal the twentieth century!" he declared, retrace your steps to that fateful crossroads where a wrong turn was taken. What he wanted to regain, in that context, was the lost legacy of the Old Right. In the *History* he was seeking the recognition and restoration of what he called "paradigms lost." Against the idea of history as an automatic series of ascending steps toward the truth and the light, Rothbard held up the vision of knowledge lost and then rediscovered, and of history an uncertain and for that reason heroic struggle to maintain and improve the human condition.

The *History* unifies Rothbard's ideas and interests into one vast and mighty system: it provides the link to his other works, and gives us a bird's eye view of his thought: it is truly the apotheosis of his system. Unlike other system-builders, however, Rothbard did not seek to enclose or imprison his successors within another confining paradigm and does not describe a closed system. His aim was rather to open up vast and heretofore unexplored vistas in the realm of economic thought, and in this he was a great liberator. The *History* marks the beginning of the end of the scientistic theories of economics, whose failure he chronicles in its pages, and the beginning of a new humanism, not only in economics but in all the social sciences. It is the beginning of a revolution, the end result of which will be the rehumanization of the humanities.

NOTES

1. Mises to Rothbard, 29 May 1950.

2. Murray N. Rothbard, "New Light on the Prehistory of the Austrian School," in *The Economics of Mises*, ed. L. Mogs (Kansas City: Sheed and Ward, 1976), pp. 67–77.

3. Rothbard to Evers, 16 April 1983.

4. Rothbard, *Economic Thought Before Adam Smith*, volume 1 of *An Austrian Perspective on the History of Economic Thought* (Brookfield, Vt.: Edward Elgar Publishing Company, 1995), p. xv.

5. Ibid., p. vii.

6. Ibid., p. ix.

7. Ibid., p. x.

8. Ibid., pp. 13–15.

9. Ibid., p. 16.

10. Ibid.

11. Ibid., p. 17.

12. Ibid., p. 18.

13. Ibid.

14. Ibid., p. 21.

15. Ibid.

16. Ibid., p. 22.

17. Ibid., p. xvi.

18. Ibid., p. xii.

19. Ibid., p. 137.

20. Ibid.

21. Ibid., p. 169.

22. Ibid.

23. Ibid., pp. 141–42.

24. Ibid., pp. 191–92.

25. Ibid., p. 213.

26. Ibid., p. 247–48.

27. Ibid., p. 262.

28. Cited in ibid., p. 264.

29. Ibid.
30. Cited in ibid., p. 265.
31. Cited in ibid., p. 266
32. Ibid.
33. Ibid., pp. 266–67.
34. Ibid., p. 267.
35. Ibid.
36. Ibid., p. 272.
37. Interview with JoAnn Rothbard.
38. Rothbard to Justin Raimondo, 18 March 1990.
39. Rothbard, *Economic Thought Before Adam Smith*, p. 227.
40. Ibid., p. 282. Crudely put, Gresham's law is "bad money drives out the good." But this doesn't get to the crux of the matter. As Rothbard put it, Gresham's law is "the insight that if two or more moneys are legally fixed in a relative value by the government, then the money over-valued by the government will drive the undervalued money out of circulation."
41. Ibid.
42. Ibid., p. 292.
43. Ibid.
44. Ibid., pp. 292–93.
45. Ibid., p. 293.
46. Ibid., p. 294.
47. Ibid.
48. Ibid., p. 295.
49. Ibid., p. 299.
50. Ibid., p. 302. See also Pitirim Sorokin, *Fads and Foibles in Modern Sociology* (Chicago: Henry Regnery, 1956), pp. 103, 110, and passim.
51. Ibid., p. 304.
52. Ibid., p. 309–10.
53. Ibid., p. 310.
54. Ibid., p. xiii.
55. Ibid., p. 311. Rothbard examines the evidence, and comes to the conclusion that Davenant didn't have any statistics or "Baconian research

programs" to back up his assertions, and that Davenant and his arithmetical confreres "made it all up, as part of their 'new science.' "

56. Ibid., p. 315.
57. Ibid., p. xiii.
58. Ibid., p. 345.
59. Ibid., p. 348.
60. Written in the 1730s but not published until 1755.
61. Rothbard, *Economic Thought Before Adam Smith*, p. 352.
62. Ibid.
63. Ibid., p. 361.
64. Ibid.
65. Ibid., p. 371.
66. Ibid., p. 375.
67. Ibid., p. 366.
68. Ibid., p. 394.
69. Ibid., p. 444.
70. Ibid., pp. 444–45.
71. Ibid., p. 448.
72. Ibid.
73. Ibid., p. 466.
74. Ibid., p. 468.
75. Cited in Rothbard, *Classical Economics*, volume 2 of *An Austrian Perspective on the History of Economic Thought* (Brookfield, Vt.: Edward Elgar Publishing Company, 1995), p. 303.
76. Ibid., p. 305.
77. Ibid., p. 306.
78. Ibid., p. 310.
79. Ibid., p. 312.
80. Ibid., 318–19.
81. Ibid., p. 318.
82. Ibid.
83. Ibid., pp. 322–23.
84. Ibid., p. 349.
85. Ibid., p. 350.

86. Ibid.

87. Ibid., p. 351.

88. Ibid., p. 352.

89. Ibid., p. 358.

90. Ibid., p. 354. For more on Hegel, historical "endism," and the Hegelian infatuation with Napoleon, see Francis Fukuyama, "The End of History?" *The National Interest* (summer 1989). See also Alexander Kojeve, *Introduction to the Reading of Hegel* (New York: Basic Books, 1969).

91. Rothbard, *Classical Economics*, p. 356.

92. Ibid., p. 373.

93. Ibid., p. 392.

94. Ibid., pp. 394–403.

95. Ibid., p. 410.

96. Ibid., p. 411.

97. Ibid., p. 427.

98. Ibid., p. 431.

99. Ibid., p. 432.

100. Ibid., p. 433.

101. Ibid., p. 339.

8

THE LEGACY

In its scope, complexity, and daring originality, Rothbard's *History of Economic Thought* is evidence of the kind of expansive intelligence that can only be called genius. That is why, toward the end of the second volume, it is heart-rending to read, in an aside to his discussion of Pareto, that "we shall see in a later volume, how Pareto's thesis led him to . . ." etc.[1]

Tragically, there was to be no later volume. As the first and second volumes were being readied for publication, Rothbard was eager to get on with the third volume, and talked as if it were, in his mind at least, already written. This was his typical method: to mentally map out and completely compose a book or an article in his head, and then sit down and rapidly set the words to paper. The story of the history of economic thought in the twentieth century, the rise of the Austrians, the triumph of Keynes, the crisis of the Keynesian paradigm, and what was to be, in an important sense, the summation and cementing of the Rothbardian system—all this and much more was lost when one of the greatest minds of the twentieth century flickered out.

This tragedy was celebrated by the malevolent William F. Buckley Jr. in an obituary in which ignorance and malice combined to exude pure hatred.[2] Rothbard's death, he exulted, meant "the end of his influence on the conservative-libertarian movement." Besides being in questionable taste, Buckley's bizarre display of chest-beating on a dead man's grave was decidedly premature. Rothbard's monumental achievement will endure long after the collected works of the sailboating publicist molder into a well-deserved oblivion. Buckley despised Rothbard for not signing on to the Cold War crusade, and illustrates his contempt with a well-turned lie about how "Rothbard physically applauded Khrushchev in his limousine as it passed by on the street."[3] This claim leaps out at those who knew Rothbard personally as a blatant falsehood: the notion of this notoriously sedentary man, who rarely left the confines of his own home and neighborhood, rushing down the steps of his apartment house and dashing downtown to applaud *anyone*, never mind a Russian dictator, is absurd on its face. "Murray couldn't handle moral priorities," says Buckley—*this* from a man who once declared his fulsome support for "Big Government for the duration [of the Cold War]," because only "a totalitarian bureaucracy within our shores" could defeat the Red Menace.[4]

Buckley writes that "Murray Rothbard had defective judgment," but, in retrospect, it is Buckley whose judgment is defective at best. As it turned out, the Soviets were overthrown—by an internal upheaval, not U.S. military forces—and yet the totalitarian bureaucracy hailed by Buckley back in 1952 ("even with Truman at the reins of it all"[5]) shows no signs of withering away. Far from it, its tentacles are everywhere, stronger and more intrusive than at any time in our history—and we have Buckley, as much as anyone, to thank for that.

Buckley is appalled by a speech delivered before the John Randolph Club, in which Rothbard detailed the series of purges on the

Right conducted by the editors of *National Review*. But nowhere does he dispute the facts. He quotes Rothbard's speech: "And so the purges began. One after another, Buckley and *National Review* purged and excommunicated all the radicals, all the nonrespectables. Consider the roll call: isolationists (such as John T. Flynn), anti-Zionists, libertarians, Ayn Randians, the John Birch Society," and Southern regionalists less than enamored by the cult of Martin Luther King. Buckley airily dismisses this version of history by berating Rothbard for supposedly believing "that Khrushhchev was morally preferable to Eisenhower." But what *about* John T. Flynn, to take just one particularly egregious and well-documented example? Flynn was a great investigative journalist and vocal opponent of the New Deal. His leadership of the New York branch of the America First Committee placed him in the front ranks of the Old Right leadership. In the 1950s, when Buckley started *National Review*, Buckley asked Flynn to contribute a piece. The old America Firster submitted an article that denounced the Cold War and the military-industrial complex as "a job-making boondoggle." Rejecting the article, Buckley sent along a check for $100 and a letter scolding Flynn for failing to appreciate the "objective threat of the Soviet Union," which, the young master sternly explained to the grizzled veteran of the Right, "is a threat to the freedom of each and every one of us." Flynn promptly returned the check, noting that he was "greatly obligated" for "the little lecture."[6] John T. Flynn, the premier publicist and journalist of the Old Right, never did appear in the pages of Buckley's journal.

Buckley excoriates Rothbard for what he terms his "deranging scrupulosity" which led him to disbelieve in such conservative icons as Herbert Hoover, Ronald Reagan, Milton Friedman, "and Newt Gingrich." While Rothbard was the first on the Right to blaspheme these elder gods, he was not the last, but was merely ahead of his time. As Rothbard pointed out in his John Randolph Club speech and elsewhere, it was Buckley's own scrupulosity on the issue of the Cold War that deranged the conservative movement.

Buckley's invincible ignorance, combined with his own personal and political agenda, prevents him from seeing the larger significance of Rothbard's thought and its impact on the ideological landscape. "In the end," he opines, Rothbard was left "with about as many disciples as David Koresh had on his little redoubt in Waco. Yes, Murray Rothbard believed in freedom, and yes, David Koresh believed in God."

Buckley's obvious animus blinded him to the growth of libertarianism as a political and intellectual force, a phenomenon for which Rothbard deserves no small part of the credit. Ironically, E. J. Dionne, a liberal commentator, is far more understanding of Rothbard's true significance as the catalyst of a movement on the cutting edge of American politics. In his book, *Why Americans Hate Politics*, Dionne traces the development of conservative thought in the sixties, and tells the history of the libertarian-conservative split in somewhat more objective terms. "As a formal movement," he concludes, "Libertarianism would make only limited progress. As an attitude, libertarianism, without the capital letter, would grow much more."[7]

Dionne traces the development of the libertarian movement, from the historic convention of Young Americans for Freedom to the birth, rise, and decline of the Libertarian Party. He accurately recounts the Hamowy-Buckley confrontation in the pages of the *New Individualist Review*, and gives a capsule history of the Koch-Crane years, while playing down the split with Rothbard. Dionne seems to appreciate Rothbard's significance as a libertarian thinker and strategist, but he gets it wrong when he confuses the tactical maneuverings of Ed Crane with Rothbard's own views. "Although Rothbard, ever the individualist, suspected Koch and Crane of dangerous tendencies toward 'pragmatism,' " he writes, "the Koch-Crane strategy reflected Rothbard's central political insight:

that libertarianism's political base was to be found outside the realm of the conservative movement."[8]

He then goes on to cite the record of *Inquiry* magazine, which "seemed more interested in social issues and foreign affairs—the issues on which libertarians were on 'the left' of the conventional political spectrum. . . . The magazine sought to stay true to the libertarian faith on all issues, but in a way that made it a kindred spirit to the adversary culture of the left."[9]

Rothbard's "central political insight" was *not* that the future belonged to the yuppies and liberal media constituency that Ed Crane imagined would rally around the Libertarian Party and its 1980 presidential candidate. He *always* believed that libertarians ought to orient toward the great American middle class, that is, the overwhelming majority of Americans. Dionne mentions the fact that LP candidate Ed Clark described himself as a "low-tax liberal" but fails to mention Rothbard's furious response. He writes of the "Rothbard-Koch-Crane strategy of an 'opening to the left,' " but, as we have seen, Rothbard rejected this strategy after 1978. Dionne takes at face value the description of libertarianism penned by Ernest van den Haag: "Libertarianism is opposed to all conservative traditions, to tradition itself."[10]

Dionne's misunderstanding of libertarianism as antipathetic to tradition not only confuses a political philosophy with a cultural stance, but also ignores the long and illustrious *libertarian* tradition, which, according to his lights, is a contradiction in terms. Dionne counterposes traditionalism and libertarianism, falsely proclaiming that adherents of the latter are "fully prepared to overthrow tradition—and religion—in the name of Enlightenment rationalism."[11]

Libertarianism, based on the supremacy of natural law over man-made "law," is the quintessence of tradition and internally consistent with the concept of religion. Indeed, Rothbard wrote two large volumes on the role of religion as the preserver and defender of individual liberty through the ages. Dionne's view of libertarianism is facile and derivative, a projection of his own liberal-rationalist inclinations.

That neither Buckley nor Dionne appreciate the true significance of Rothbard and his impact on the history of social thought is understandable. Although Buckley had the colossal nerve to call one of his books *Confessions of a Libertarian Journalist*, and Dionne writes about the movement in a sympathetic tone, neither could be considered libertarians, even in the loosest construction of an increasingly elastic term.

That this misunderstanding of Rothbard and his thought should extend to many of the man's own followers, and former followers, requires some more complex explanation. Leaving aside the bitterness of old factional disputes, the entire constellation of libertarian organizations and thinktanks can be said to be fixated—or, in some cases, *stuck*—in one particular chapter of Rothbard's intellectual odyssey.

In a very broad sense, the increasingly influential Cato Institute has carried out the old Rothbardian strategy outlined in *Toward a Theory of Libertarian Strategy*. They have stuck to the emphasis on building cadre that was so much a part of Rothbard's strategic vision. They have also hewed to the Rothbardian dictum, during the Cold War years, on the necessity of building an independent libertarian movement ostensibly beyond left and right. Most importantly, they continue to consistently uphold the Rothbardian dedication to a peaceful noninterventionist foreign policy. During the first Gulf war, Cato bravely stood up to the war hysteria, an act for which they were roundly denounced. In their own way, and without fully acknowledging the enormous contribution of Cato's intellectual father and founder, they have stayed true to their Rothbardian roots.

The Libertarian Party, living in considerably reduced circumstances, seems to have reverted to an earlier incarnation. Today, it resembles nothing so much as the libertarian movement of the sixties, when Rothbard and Karl Hess were leading their student followers out of the conservative movement—free-market economics with a countercultural flourish. The visions of electoral success that intoxicated party activists back in the late seventies and early eighties have largely dissipated, but the faithful remnant seems not to have noticed that time has passed them by. Like the permanently moribund Socialist Labor Party, which fielded candidates from the 1860s up until very recently, the LP will no doubt persist unto perdition. While longevity is not success, it is the best the party faithful can hope for.

Rothbard invested a lot of time and attention in Cato and the LP, but in the end he rejected them both—without, however, rejecting the idea of an organized libertarian movement. In the last decade of his life Rothbard's institutional loyalties were invested in the Ludwig von Mises Institute, which embodies the "paleolibertarian" phase in his development. Less dramatically, the Mises Institute refocused Rothbard's energies away from politics and back onto a scholarly track, giving him the moral and organizational support he needed to carry on his work. After his death, the Mises Institute remains the center of Rothbardian "orthodoxy," which celebrates him not only as the architect of a systematic theory of liberty based on private property rights, and the greatest figure of the Austrian School, but also as the quintessential man of the Old Right.

These three major branches of the libertarian movement—whatever their differences and their relations with Rothbard the man—are all Rothbardian in that they owe their basic orientation to one or another phase of his intellectual evolution. They are all, for better or for worse, his children, whether they acknowledge it or not.

"It is typical of American *Kultur* that it was incapable of understanding H. L. Mencken," wrote Rothbard in an essay celebrating

the art and ideology of the man he called "The Joyous Libertarian."
It is not surprising that the same incapacity impedes any real
understanding of Rothbard by such typical pundits as Buckley and
Dionne, nor even that the misunderstanding extends to many libertarians, including some who knew him.

In his appreciation of Mencken, Rothbard wrote: "It is difficult
for Americans to understand a *merger* of high-spirited wit and devotion to principle; one is either a humorist, gently or acidly spoofing
the fables of one's age, or else one is a serious and solemn thinker.
That a man of ebullient wit can be, in a sense, all the more devoted
to positive ideas and principles is understood by very few."[12]

A more succinct and accurate portrait of Rothbard, the man
and the thinker, would be hard to imagine. In a sense, "The Joyous
Libertarian," written in 1962, is the most autobiographical of all his
works, for clearly he saw much of himself in Mencken. As a young
Old Rightist in his mid-twenties, a member of the tiny and largely
ineffectual community of libertarian scholars and activists, Rothbard's discovery of the Sage of Baltimore was something of a revelation: it was like looking in a mirror. In describing Mencken's
dilemma as "an individualist and a libertarian in this day and
age." he was also describing his own:

> He finds himself in a world marked, if not dominated, by folly,
> fraud, and tyranny. He has, if he is a reflecting man, three pos-
> sible courses of action open to him: (1) he may retire from the
> social and political world into his private occupation . . . (2) he
> can set about to try to change the world for the better, or at least
> to formulate and propagate his views with such an ultimate hope
> in mind; or, (3) he can stay in the world, enjoying himself
> immensely in this spectacle of folly.[13]

These were the choices faced by young Rothbard in the late

1940s, and his discovery of Mencken as a role model was an important impetus in the direction he would eventually take. For those who took the third route were required to have "a special type of personality with a special type of judgment about the world," a personality that resembles nothing so much as the adult and fully matured Rothbard to an astonishing degree. Required above all is the kind of self-confidence that is "supremely 'inner-directed' with no inner shame or quaking at going against the judgment of the herd," and this quality, as we have seen, Rothbard had in abundance.[14]

"He must, secondly," he continued, "have a supreme zest for enjoying life and the spectacle it affords; he must be an individualist who cares deeply about liberty and individual excellence, but who can—from that same dedication to truth and liberty—enjoy and lampoon a society that has turned its back on the best that it can achieve." Certainly this describes and explains much of Rothbard's political and social commentary in the *Libertarian Forum* and its successors, the polemics, the analyses of New York mayoral races, and his political activities. Rothbard's political interests and activities "should be understood in the context of what a political maven he was," says Ralph Raico. "He always loved conventions and elections and would pick some side to fervently root for. On election nights, he'd be busy following the returns, trying to figure out some last ditch way for his guy to win in the electoral college."[15]

Like Mencken, Rothbard loved the spectacle of political conventions, the human drama and especially the humor, nearly all of it unintentional. Unlike Mencken, however, he was *not* "deeply pessimistic about any possibility of changing and reforming the ideas and actions of the vast majority of his fellow-men," as Rothbard described Mencken's outlook, nor did he "believe that *boobus Americanus* is doomed to be *boobus Americanus* forevermore." His faith in the average American complemented his disdain for the elites. Rothbard, the persistent populist, consistently rooted for charismatic challengers of the status quo, from his ringing defense of Joe McCarthy to his enthusiasm for Ross Perot. He knew that the battle against the state was necessarily a protracted conflict. Without disputing the Hayekian view that it is necessary to educate a generation of intellectuals, however, he also believed in the necessity—and possibility—of bypassing and short-circuiting the elites, and appealing directly to the overwhelming majority of people, who are the exploited victims of state power.

"Of course," writes Rothbard, "Mencken had other qualities, too," and here is as good a mini-portrait of the author himself as anyone is likely to sketch: "enormous gusto, a sparkling wit, a keen and erudite appreciation of many fields of knowledge, [and] a zest for the dramatic events of the everyday world." This zest for drama is what made Mencken "a born journalist." Yet, Rothbard writes, "despite his omnivorous passion for intellectual fields and disciplines, he had no temperament for fashioning rigorous systems of thought—but then, how many people have?"

The answer is: not many. And not many of these combine the Menckenian style with that kind of intellectual rigor, a sense of fun *and* of high seriousness. Rothbard managed to do it, and in this merger of qualities not often found in the same person is the key to understanding the man and his life.

The magnitude of his achievement was such that his legacy—not only as an economist but as a system-builder and ideological entrepreneur—is assured. First, as an economist, he succeeded in firmly establishing the Austrian School of economics in America, expanding and refining the legacy of his great mentor, Ludwig von Mises, and separating out the pure Misesian perspective from all others. As a system-builder, the intellectual edifice that was the work of a lifetime is complete in its general outlines and solid at its base. Keeping in mind the limitations of scientific analogies, the totality of his writings presents the equivalent of a unified field theory of the social sciences.

As an intellectual entrepreneur, it is useful to contemplate his career in this area on a number of levels. First, as Mises's most accomplished and ambitious pupil, he enjoyed an amazing success. Single-handedly reviving and championing the "lost" (or overlooked) knowledge of the Austrian School, he not only rediscovered their insights but also introduced them to a new generation of teachers and students.

As the builder of an ideological movement, however—a role to which he devoted an enormous amount of time and energy—his success is more problematic. The Libertarian Party, which he eventually abandoned, is reduced to an insignificant sect. The wave of right-wing populism hailed by Rothbard in the last years of his life as the agency of libertarian social change has yet to fulfill its bright promise. Yet it is far too early to judge his success as a movement-builder. The effect of Rothbard's work in this area is such that it will not be felt for a long time.

While Rothbard was in many ways the antipode of Marx, not only ideologically but temperamentally, the similarities are just as striking: both were unapologetic partisans in the battle of ideas who insisted on personally jumping into the fray. One whose life-long ambition was to create a system that would destroy all possibility of human freedom, and the other whose career was devoted to the preservation and triumph of liberty—can it be that the haphazardly constructed and often refuted system of the former will have inspired millions, while the much more systematic and closely argued Rothbardian paradigm will sink, without a trace, into historical obscurity?

Without falling into the Adventist trap of forecasting the exact day and hour of the coming libertarian revolution—without looking for any mechanism of history to ensure that ultimately a statue of

Rothbard will be erected where the Washington headquarters of the
IRS used to stand—it is safe to say that the legacy of Murray Rothbard, far from going unrecognized, will only grow with the passing
of time. Even politically, the area where his legacy is yet uncertain,
the Rothbardian paradigm has the potential to become a living
force. As the Marxists used to say, the point is not just to understand
the world, but to change it. This is the passion that drove Rothbard
through all his days—a passion for justice that could not be contained, not by the ivy-covered walls of academia, the ivory tower
world of "thinktanks," or the organizational constraints and strictures of a political sect. The idea of being the object of a cult was, for
him, a laughable proposition; he rebelled too readily against the
groupthink mentality and narrow complacency of the sectarian personality. Certainly he would never have collaborated in or approved
of a sect devoted to the endless reiteration of his own doctrines.

Yet there is no doubt that he intended his writings to be read as
a series of letters to the future: not as a dogma, but as a guide to
action. The libertarian torch—held aloft, single-handed, for so
long—is now being picked up by a new generation of scholars,
journalists, and activists. Rothbard's legacy is their chief asset, and
by this I mean not only his ideas but also his indomitable spirit,
which is preserved in his published works. Rothbard was one of
the greatest social theorists of modern times, but that is not the
whole of his legacy: there is also the wit, the humor, and the irre-
pressibility of the man. A unique combination of high seriousness
and intellectual playfulness permeates his work and his life. This
is what gave him the inner strength to persist—the ability to laugh,
to use humor to light up the darkest hour, to find joy and even
hope in spite of everything. In every word he ever wrote, Rothbard, the eternal optimist, transmits that spirit down through the
years. This is the essence of his legacy, and his gift to the world.
This is the secret weapon in the arsenal of liberty: what Randolph

Bourne called "the secret of life," "this fine youthful spirit," that "keeps one's reactions warm and true"—if only we have the wisdom and the courage to use it.

In describing Mencken's unique role in American culture in the twenties, Rothbard might have been describing his own career:

> He sailed joyously into the fray, slashing and cutting happily into the buncombe and folly he saw all around him, puncturing the balloons of pomposity, gaily cleansing the Augean stables of cant, hypocrisy, absurdity, and cliché, "heaving," as he once put it, "the dead cat into the temple" to show bemused worshippers of the inane that he would not be struck dead on the spot. And in the course of this task, rarely undertaken in any age, a task performed purely for his own enjoyment, he exercised an enormous liberating force upon the best minds of a whole generation.[16]

Whether it is exercised upon the minds of this generation, or the next, the liberating force of Rothbard's ideas is gathering momentum. He built a monument to liberty, a mighty edifice that towers over the horizon and cannot be ignored—a challenge and a reproach to the guardians of the status quo, and an inspiration to the revolutionaries of tomorrow.

NOTES

1. Murray N. Rothbard, *Classical Economics*, volume 2 of *An Austrian Perspective on the History of Economic Thought* (Brookfield Vt.: Edward Elgar Publishing Company, 1995), p. 456.

2. William F. Buckley Jr., "Murray Rothbard, RIP," *National Review*, 6 February 1995.

3. Ibid.

4. William F. Buckley Jr., "A Young Republican's View," *Commonweal*, 25 January 1952.

5. Ibid.

6. See Justin Raimondo, *Reclaiming the American Right* (Burlingame, Calif.: Center for Libertarian Studies, 1993), p. 112.

7. E. J. Dionne, *Why Americans Hate Politics* (New York: Simon & Schuster, 1991), p. 270.

8. Ibid., p. 273.

9. Ibid.

10. Ibid., p. 274.

11. Ibid., p. 282.

12. Murray N. Rothbard, "H. L. Mencken: The Joyous Libertarian," *New Individualist Review* 2, no. 2 (summer 1962): 15. Emphasis in original.

13. Ibid.

14. Ibid., pp. 15–16.

15. Ralph Raico to the author, 12 March 1999.

16. Rothbard, "H. L. Mencken: The Joyous Libertarian," p. 16.

SELECTED BOOKS BY MURRAY N. ROTHBARD

A complete bibliography of Murray N. Rothbard's published works would be too long to include in this volume. Articles cited in the text are referenced in the notes at the end of each chapter; in any case, a complete online bibliography is available at http:// www.mises.org/mnrbib.asp.

Man, Economy, and State: A Treatise on Economic Principles. 2 vols. Princeton, N.J.: D. Van Nostrand Co., 1962.

The Panic of 1819: Reactions and Policies. New York: Columbia University Press, 1962.

America's Great Depression. Princeton, N.J.: D. Van Nostrand Co., 1963. Reprint, Los Angeles: Nash Publishing Co., 1972.

What Has Government Done to Our Money? Colorado Springs, Colo.: Pine Tree Press, 1963.

Economic Depressions: Causes and Cures. Lansing, Mich.: Constitutional Alliance, Inc., 1969.

Power and Market: Government and the Economy. Menlo Park, Calif.: Institute for Humane Studies, 1970.

Education, Free and Compulsory: The Individual's Education. Wichita, Kans.: Center for Independent Education, 1972.

The Essential von Mises. Lansing, Mich.: Bramble Minibooks: 1973.

For a New Liberty, the Libertarian Manifesto. New York: Macmillan,1973. Revised edition, New York: Collier Books, 1978.

Egalitarianism As a Revolt Against Nature and Other Essays. Washington, D.C.: Libertarian Review Press, 1974.

A New Land, a New People: The American Colonies in the Seventeenth Century. With L. P. Liggio. Vol. 1 of *Conceived in Liberty*. New Rochelle, N.Y.: Arlington House Publishers, 1975.

"Salutary Neglect": The American Colonies in the First Half of the Eighteenth Century. Vol. 2 of *Conceived in Liberty*. New Rochelle, N.Y.: Arlington House Publishers, 1975.

Advance to Revolution 1760–1784. Vol. 3 of *Conceived in Liberty*. New Rochelle, N.Y.: Arlington House Publishers, 1976.

The Revolutionary War 1775–1784. Vol. 4 of *Conceived in Liberty*. New Rochelle, N.Y.: Arlington House Publishers, 1979.

The Ethics of Liberty. Atlantic Highlands, N.J.: Humanities Press International, 1982.

The Case for a 100 Percent Gold Dollar. Auburn, Ala.: Ludwig von Mises Institute,1991.

Freedom, Inequality, Primitivism, and the Division of Labor. Auburn, Ala.: Ludwig von Mises Institute, 1991.

The Case Against the Fed. Auburn, Ala.: The Ludwig von Mises Institute, 1994.

Economic Thought Before Adam Smith. Vol. 1 of *An Austrian Perspective on the History of Economic Thought*. Brookfield, Vt.: Edward Elgar Publishing Company, 1995.

Classical Economics. Vol. 2 of *An Austrian Perspective on the History of Economic Thought*. Brookfield, Vt.: Edward Elgar Publishing Company, 1995.

Wall Street, Banks, and American Foreign Policy. Burlingame, Calif.: Center for Libertarian Studies, 1995.

Making Economic Sense. Auburn, Ala.: The Ludwig von Mises Institute, 1995.

The Logic of Action One: Method, Money, and the Austrian School. Glos, UK: Edward Elgar Publishing Ltd., 1997.

The Logic of Action Two: Applications and Criticism from the Austrian School. Glos, UK: Edward Elgar Publishing Ltd., 1997.

INDEX

Radical Libertarian Alliance, 179, 228

Radosh, Ronald, 162, 163

Raico, Ralph, 82, 83–84, 92, 110, 135, 230, 232, 241, 141, 194, 379

Raimondo, Justin, 18–19, 230–32, 236–37, 245–46, 295

Ramparts, 173, 175, 176

Rand, Ayn, 109–34, 138, 155, 181

  appeal of, 129–30

  as cult leader, 122–23, 128–29, 131–32

  on eminent domain, 133

  on foreign policy, 134

  and free will, 114–17

  grandiosity of, 121

  and Greenspan, 275

  and individualism, 113–14

  on Mises, 132

  and *National Review*, 373

  as philosopher, 111–12, 132

  and Physiocrats, 340–41

Randolph, John, 278

Ravenal, Earl, 245, 246, 247, 248

Ray, Clarence, 284

Read, Leonard E., 41–42, 241

Reagan, Ronald, 155, 195, 373

Reason, 200, 231, 235

Red Channels, 64

Reed, James A., 287

Reformation, 307

Regnery, Henry, 79, 161

Reisman, George, 82, 85–86, 92, 110, 128

Republican Party, 33, 39, 40–41, 62, 80, 82, 161, 281, 286, 293

Resch, George, 156

Review of Austrian Economics, 260, 261, 263

Rhee, Synghman, 103, 143

Ricardo, David, 345, 359–60, 362

Rich, Andrea, 279, 280

Rich, Howie, 279, 280

Rickenbacker, William F., 107

Riverside School, 31–32

Rizzo, Mario J., 184

Rockefeller, David, 271

Rockefeller Foundation, 63

Rockford Institute, 276–78, 280

Rockwell, Llewellyn H., Jr., 259–63, 264, 266–68, 283

Roosevelt, Archibald, 85

Roosevelt, Franklin Delano, 14, 33, 37, 92, 96, 137–38, 168, 287

Rosen, Jake, 172

Rosicrucians, 329, 337

Rote Fahne, 77

Rothbard, David, 24–28, 31, 33, 34, 35, 37, 59–61, 118

Rothbard, JoAnn (Schumacher), 42–43, 54, 62, 82–83, 139, 227, 282, 296, 304, 325

  and A. Rand, 119, 124–25

Rothbard, Murray Newton

Personal

  birth, 23

  character of, 12, 16–18, 241–43, 345